STUDIES IN EVANGELICAL HISTORY AND THOUGHT

Evangelicals and Aesthetics from the 1750's to the 1930's

STUDIES IN EVANGELICAL HISTORY AND THOUGHT

Evangelicals and Aesthetics from the 1750's to the 1930's

Chad P. Stutz

Copyright © Chad P. Stutz 2016

First Published 2016 by Paternoster

Paternoster is an imprint of Authentic Media
PO Box 6326, Bletchley, Milton Keynes MK1 9GG

authenticmedia.co.uk

The right of Chad P. Stutz to be identified as the author of this Work has been asserted by him in accordance with the Copyright, Designs and Patents Act 1988.

All rights reserved. No part of this publication man be reproduced, stored in a retrieval system, or transmitted, in any form or by any means, electronic, mechanical, photocopying, recording, or otherwise, without the prior permission of the publisher of a license permitting restricted copying. In the UK such licenses are issued by the Copyright Licensing Agency, Barnard's Inn, 86 Fetter Lane, London EC4A 1EN.

British Library Cataloguing in Publication Data

A catalogue record for this book is available from the British Library

ISBN 978-1-84227-852-9
978-1-78078-333-8 (e-book)

Printed and bound by Lightning Source

STUDIES IN EVANGELICAL HISTORY AND THOUGHT

Series Preface

The Evangelical movement has been marked by its union of four emphases: on the Bible, on the cross of Christ, on conversion as the entry to the Christian life and on the responsibility of the believer to be active. The present series is designed to publish scholarly studies of any aspect of this movement in Britain or overseas. Its volumes include social analysis as well as exploration of Evangelical ideas. The books in the series consider aspects of the movement shaped by the Evangelical Revival of the eighteenth century, when the impetus to mission began to turn the popular Protestantism of the British Isles and North America into a global phenomenon. The series aims to reap some of the rich harvest of academic research about those who, over the centuries, have believed that they had a gospel to tell to the nations.

Series Editors

David Bebbington, Professor of History, University of Stirling, Stirling, Scotland, UK

John H.Y. Briggs, Senior Research Fellow in Ecclesiastical History and Director of the Centre for Baptist History and Heritage, Regent's Park College, Oxford, UK

Timothy Larsen, McManis Professor Christian Thought, Wheaton College, Illinois, USA

Mark A. Noll, McAnaney Professor of History, University of Notre Dame, Notre Dame, Indiana, USA

Ian M. Randall, Director of Research, Spurgeon's College, London, UK, and Senior Research Fellow, International Baptist Theological Seminary, Prague, Czech Republic

To my family, near and far

Contents

Acknowledgments x

Bibliographic Note xii

Abbreviations xiii

INTRODUCTION
Evangelicals, Aesthetics, and History 1
    The Evangelical Aesthetic Tradition: Some Major Themes 5
    The Evangelical Critical Establishment 11
    The Structure of This Book 16

CHAPTER 1
The Emergence of an Evangelical Philosophical Aesthetics 19
    The "Asymmetry" of the Puritan Aesthetic Tradition 19
    The Enlightenment and Evangelical Aesthetic Discourse 33
        Jonathan Edwards and the Nature of True Beauty 38
        John Wesley's "Thoughts upon Taste" 46
        Mental Philosophy and Aesthetic Conservatism: Hannah
        More's "Preface to the Tragedies" 49
    Towards the Evangelical Romanticism of the Nineteenth Century 53

CHAPTER 2
Expressing the Ideal: Changing Conceptions of Art and Imagination 58
    Art as a Function of Mind: Evangelical Expressivism 60
    The Growth of Aesthetic Idealism 66
    From Devilish to "the vision and the faculty divine": The Imagination
    Reconsidered 78
    Anti-Romantic Reactions: Evangelical Classicism and the "*Terra
    Firma* of Common Sense" 84
    Aesthetic Apologias: Art's Purpose and Uniqueness 89

CHAPTER 3
What Has the Gospel of Christ to Do with the Gospel of Art?   99
   Aesthetic Skeletons in the Protestant Closet   104
   Reconciliation, Subordination, and the Ideal of Productive Tension   112
   The Religio-Aesthetic Balance I: Christianity as Aesthetic Horizon   115
     Art and Religion as Distinct Categories   115
     Art and Salvation   120
     Art and Idolatry   126
   The Religio-Aesthetic Balance II: Christianity as Aesthetic Condition   130
   Some Signs of Fatigue   135

CHAPTER 4
Aesthetic Ministrations: Art, Morality, and the Christian Nation   138
   "Occult Pathos": Art and the Tradition of Anti-Didactic Moralism   141
   "Occult Pathos" Gone Wrong: Negative Influence, Sentimentality, and the Novel   157
   "A mighty engine ... for the elevation of the nation": Art's Service to Christian Society   162
   Defending the Moral Influence Theory amid Growing Doubts   170

CHAPTER 5
Art, Aesthetics, and the Fundamentalist-Modernist Controversy   179
   Liberals, Evangelical Romanticism, and the Protestant Ideology   182
   Conservatives and the Return of Ambivalence   188

CONCLUSION
Theology, Aesthetics, and Liberalization   207

Bibliography   211

Index   234

Acknowledgments

This project began as a dissertation at Boston College under the direction of Judith Wilt, Dennis Taylor, and Cynthia Lynn Lyerly, and although it has since evolved in myriad ways, it remains profoundly indebted to their wisdom and guidance. With characteristic insight, Judith not only helped me repeatedly to clarify my ideas but also to consider new possibilities and perspectives. Her ongoing support has been indispensable in bringing this book to fruition, and I am grateful for her continued willingness to serve as a mentor, offering sage advice and much-needed encouragement at critical junctures. Dennis likewise provided me with extensive feedback along the way, supplying several crucial insights at what I now realize were key moments in the development of my thinking. Lynn not only brought to bear her historian's eye for detail but also showed me the meaning of collegiality and selflessness during a time of great personal adversity. I also want to express my gratitude to Roger Lundin, whose unexpected passing in November 2015 has left an incomparable void in the world of Christian academia. His willingness to respond in detail to a rather lengthy query "out of the blue" gave me the necessary confidence to embark on this project in earnest, while his later advice and thoughtful questions likewise proved invaluable. Whatever this book's strengths, they are very much the result of these influences, while its weaknesses remain very much my own.

In addition, I have been blessed by the intellectual and spiritual camaraderie of friends and colleagues, which has enabled me to persevere through the inevitable "lean" periods of research and writing. Jeramie Rinne, Mark Jennings, Bob Olsen, Mike Jacobs, and Andrew Stuart have been continual sources of great wisdom and good humor. I am also thankful for the enthusiasm and encouragement of Jim Zingarelli ("Z") and my colleagues in the English Department at Gordon College: Andrew Logemann, Andrea Frankwitz, Mark Stevick, and Lynn Marcotte. Graeme Bird, moreover, graciously answered an eleventh-hour question regarding a linguistic technicality. At Paternoster, Mike Parsons has provided a wealth of support, both technical and moral, and I am grateful for his knowledge and expertise.

Finally, words cannot express the debt I owe to my family. Without the encouragement and financial support of my in-laws, William and Janice Rinne, this book would have been impossible. Sadly, my father-in-law passed away not long after I had signed the publication contract, but his legacy continues to be felt in countless ways, and he is sorely missed. My parents, Philip and Valerie, in addition to providing financial assistance, have honored me with the sort of love and reassurance, but also honesty, which only parents can give. I am grateful, too, for the patience and affection of my children Jason, Susana, and Eliza, who continue to bless (and impress) me in unforeseen ways. My greatest debt, however, is to my wife Jillayne, whose love, longsuffering, and sacrifice are unsurpassed. On too many occasions to count, she has listened with something like supernatural fortitude as I struggled to articulate an idea. Were it not for her wisdom, support, and understanding, I could never have completed this project.

Bibliographic Note

The rapid digitization of eighteenth and nineteenth-century periodicals has greatly increased the accessibility of many of the source materials used for this study. I have benefited immensely from two such databases, the American Periodicals Series (published by ProQuest) and the British Periodicals Online (Collections I and II, published by ProQuest Chadwyck-Healey), through the O'Neill Library, Boston College, Chestnut Hill, MA. Given the number of periodical articles cited, however, identifying the requisite database information for individual citations would have proven too cumbersome and distracting. For this reason, I have cited all periodical material in the notes and bibliography in a conventional format without reference to its digital or non-digital origins. (For further information on digitized titles, see the "Abbreviations".) In addition, I have opted in most instances to cite reviews using the short titles often found at the tops of consecutive pages of periodicals. In many cases, these short titles (or some variation thereof) are also those listed in major periodical indexes, whether traditional or electronic. I have therefore avoided using "Rev. of ..." except in instances when no short titles exist. Finally, I have adopted a uniform system of citation for all periodical material: Author Name [where available], Title, Periodical Name Vol. # (Date), Pg. #s.

Abbreviations

ABM	*American Baptist Magazine*†
ABRCR	*American Biblical Repository and Classical Review*
AM	*Arminian Magazine*‡
APTR	*American Presbyterian and Theological Review*†
AR	*The Andover Review; a Religious and Theological Monthly*†
BM	*Baptist Magazine*
BMM	*Baptist Missionary Magazine*†
BQ	*Baptist Quarterly*†
BQR	*Baptist Quarterly Review*†
BR	*Baptist Review*†
BST	*Bible Student and Teacher*
BRPR	*Biblical Repertory and Princeton Review*†
BW	*Biblical World*†
BrQR	*British Quarterly Review*‡
CA	*Christian Advocate* [Methodist]†
CAJ	*Christian Advocate and Journal*†
CAJZH	*Christian Advocate and Journal and Zion's Herald*†
CAmb	*Christian Ambassador*
CA[P]	*Christian Advocate* [Presbyterian]†
CI	*Christian Index*†
CO	*Christian Observer*†
Cong	*Congregationalist*
CR	*Christian Review*
CS	*Christian Spectator*
ECI	*Edinburgh Christian Instructor*
ER	*Eclectic Review*‡
FBQ	*Freewill Baptist Quarterly*
HMM	*Harper's Monthly Magazine*
LQR	*London Quarterly Review*‡

Abbreviations

MerR	*Mercersburg Review*†
MMQR	*Methodist Magazine and Quarterly Review*†
MQR	*Methodist Quarterly Review*†
MR	*Methodist Review*†
MR[S]	*Methodist Review* [South]
NYE	*New York Evangelist*†
O	*Outlook*†
PM	*Presbyterian Magazine*
PMQR	*Primitive Methodist Quarterly Review*
PMQRCAmb	*Primitive Methodist Quarterly Review and Christian Ambassador*
PQR	*Presbyterian Quarterly Review*
PR	*Princeton Review*†
QCS	*Quarterly Christian Spectator*†
Rec	*The Record*
RQR	*Reformed Quarterly Review*†
S	*The Searchlight*
SPR	*Southern Presbyterian Review*
ST	*The Sword and the Trowel; A Record of Combat with Sin and of Labour for the Lord*
W	*The Watchman*†
WMM	*Wesleyan-Methodist Magazine*‡
ZH	*Zion's Herald*†

† Available in whole or in part in the American Periodicals Series database.
‡ Available in whole or in part in the British Periodicals Online database.

INTRODUCTION

Evangelicals, Aesthetics, and History

In April 1863, the *Southern Presbyterian Review* published consecutive articles, the juxtaposition of which may strike modern readers as peculiar and even shocking. The first of these, "The War of the South Vindicated," concluded with a rousing summons couched in the rhetoric of biblical prophecy charging all Southerners to rally in defense of the Confederate cause: "let the trumpet blow in Zion, and let all her watchmen lift up their voice;—let all the people, everywhere, old and young, bond and free, take up the warcry, and say, each to his neighbor, 'Gather ye together, and come against them, and rise up to the battle.'"[1] If this article's unabashed promotion of a war effort that, if successful, would have preserved intact the institution of slavery seems distasteful and offensive, it is rendered even more surprising by that which followed. Immediately after this vindication of the Southern cause appeared the conclusion of a two-part article begun in the January issue, "On the Nature and Uses of Art."[2] Published at the height of the Civil War between the Emancipation Proclamation and the Battle of Gettysburg, this article examined at length and at times with admirable depth many of the issues central to modern aesthetics. Here in the pages of an evangelical periodical not even the bloodiest conflict in American history could suppress what appears to have been an abiding interest in the minds of its contributors, editors, and readers in art, beauty, and the imagination.

This book examines the discourse of philosophical aesthetics among a subset of British and American evangelicals before the mid-twentieth century. It attempts to describe how evangelicals have historically addressed a handful of key theoretical questions related to the fine arts and to uncover some important connections between aesthetics and other theological and philosophical developments within the transatlantic world. It is not a history of evangelical art or artists, nor is it a work of art criticism; thus, references to specific art objects occur sparingly. Rather, it is an intellectual history of critical discourse relating to the arts. Furthermore, while it does claim to offer a broad account of the evangelical

---

[1] Thomas Smyth, "The War of the South Vindicated," *SPR* 15 (Apr. 1863), 514.
[2] Joseph LeConte, "On the Nature and Uses of Art," *SPR* 15 (Jan. 1863): 311-48; "On the Nature and Uses of Art," *SPR* 15 (Apr. 1863): 515-48. On LeConte, see Lester D. Stephens, *Joseph LeConte: Gentle Prophet of Evolution* (Baton Rouge: Louisiana State University Press, 1982).

aesthetic tradition from its emergence in the eighteenth century to the fundamentalist-modernist controversy of the early twentieth century, it focuses mainly on the aesthetic discourse of the nineteenth century—primarily, though not exclusively, as it was articulated in the pages of denominational periodicals.

The subset of evangelicals treated here consists mostly of Baptists, Congregationalists, Evangelical Anglicans, Methodists, and Presbyterians. These denominations and their institutions arguably constitute the historical and geographical center of evangelicalism. Historically, they either served as the doctrinal and pietistic soil out of which evangelicalism grew or were virtually coeval with its earliest manifestations. Geographically, they maintained a significant transatlantic presence from at least the eighteenth century (in some cases earlier), thus distinguishing themselves from emergent sects whose influence remained comparatively restricted to either Britain or the United States. Consequently, although the term "evangelical" has traditionally encompassed a much wider range of like-minded Protestants,[3] these groups provide a duly representative cross-section of historic evangelicalism. The establishment of these denominations within Anglo-American culture also meant that they had greater social and intellectual resources at their disposal to nourish a reflective approach to the arts—resources that younger, upstart denominations frequently lacked. In addition to these groups, one other denomination also features prominently in the following pages—the German Reformed Church, particularly as represented by the Mercersburg theology.[4] While the Mercersburg theology was an American phenomenon and its leading figures, John Williamson Nevin and the German immigrant Philip Schaff, often bore a critical relationship to the evangelical center, their principal mouthpiece the *Mercersburg Review* (later the *Reformed Quarterly Review*) regularly allotted space to aesthetic topics over the course of the nineteenth century, making Mercersburg of special interest to a study of this kind. At the same time, the aesthetic discourse of German Reformed writers was remarkably consistent with that of other evangelicals and thus serves to highlight both the breadth and uniformity of the evangelical aesthetics of the period.

---

[3] For various attempts to define evangelicalism, see David Bebbington, *Evangelicalism in Modern Britain: A History from the 1730s to the 1980s* (Grand Rapids: Baker, 1992), 2-17; Mark A. Noll, *Between Faith and Criticism: Evangelicals, Scholarship, and the Bible in America* (San Francisco: Harper and Row, 1986), 3; Timothy Larsen, Introduction, *Biographical Dictionary of Evangelicals*, ed. Timothy Larsen, David Bebbington, and Mark A. Noll (Downers Grove: Intervarsity Press, 2003), 1; Donald W. Dayton and Robert K. Johnston, eds., *The Variety of American Evangelicalism* (Downers Grove: Intervarsity Press, 1991); Donald M. Lewis, *Dictionary of Evangelical Biography, 1730-1860* (Peabody: Hendrickson, 2004); and George Marsden, *Fundamentalism and American Culture* (Oxford: Oxford University Press, 2006), 229-57.

[4] On Mercersburg, see Mark A. Noll and Cassandra Niemczyk, "Evangelicals and the Self-Consciously Reformed," *The Variety of American Evangelicalism*, 204-21; James Hastings Nichols, *Romanticism in American Theology: Nevin and Schaff at Mercersburg* (Chicago: University of Chicago Press, 1961); Mark A. Noll, *A History of Christianity in the United States and Canada* (Grand Rapids: Eerdmans, 1992), 239.

The decision to focus on the nineteenth century, moreover, is not an arbitrary one, for the decades coinciding with Victoria's reign marked an unusually fertile period in the history of evangelical thinking about the arts. To a far greater extent than has often been realized, nineteenth-century evangelicals contributed to the development of western culture's "institution of high art."[5] Amid the many evangelistic efforts, moral crusades, and programs of social reform for which they are justly famous, evangelicals found time to engage not only in the production and appreciation of art in a variety of mediums but also in energetic and sustained reflection on the theoretical foundations of such practices. Far from simply indulging in reactionary polemics against the dangers of fiction or the supposed visual excesses of Catholicism (although such polemics remained common enough), critics from across the evangelical spectrum generated a sophisticated body of "philosophical criticism" on a variety of aesthetic questions. They eagerly debated such topics as the nature of art, the relationship between art and Christianity, the role of art in society, the essence of beauty, and the function of the imagination. Both the extent to which these critics carried their speculations and the ardor with which they pursued them were largely unprecedented. Art and aesthetics were accorded an intellectual and even spiritual value which they had rarely, if ever, enjoyed among the self-professed theological descendants of the Protestant Reformation, and evangelicals attempted to think deeply about them.

A major purpose of this study, therefore, is to put to rest the still prevalent notion that evangelicalism has been plagued for much of its history by a chronic case of aesthetic myopia. Although a handful of scholars, most notably Doreen Rosman in her pioneering *Evangelicals and Culture* (1984), have gone some way in exposing the limitations of this view, it has proven exceptionally resilient.[6] Indeed, it remains something of an understatement to say that the evangelical tradition is not exactly known for its refined taste, fervid sponsorship of the fine arts, or the quality and quantity of its aesthetic theorizing. The Roman Catholic, High Anglican, and Unitarian traditions, although not immune to periodic outbursts of aesthetic anxiety (one recalls Gerard Manley Hopkins's act of poetic immolation as a poignant Victorian example), have generally valued the fine arts. By contrast, evangelicalism's relationship to art and aesthetics has often been read as an extension of Reformation iconoclasm and/or Puritan austerity. At best, evangelicals have tolerated art as a useful didactic instrument for inculcating moral or doctrinal truths while at worst they have shunned it as a worldly distraction or idolatrous snare. Evangelical philosophical reflection on art, moreover, when not hampered by the anti-intellectualism from which many evangelicals have purportedly suffered, has been severely limited or altogether mundane.

---

[5] See Nicholas Wolterstorff, *Art in Action: Toward a Christian Aesthetic* (Grand Rapids: Eerdmans, 1980), 19-63.

[6] See Doreen M. Rosman, *Evangelicals and Culture* (London: Croom Helm, 1984) and the excellent work of David Morgan, especially *Protestants and Pictures: Religion, Visual Culture, and the Age of American Mass Production* (New York: Oxford University Press, 1999).

Writing in the *Christian Herald* in 1969, Clyde S. Kilby, an evangelical Professor of English at Wheaton College, provided what has become a standard diagnosis when he pointed to "The Aesthetic Poverty of Evangelicalism": "Now when we look ... to contemporary evangelical Christianity, we find a great oddity. The people who spend the most time with the Bible are in large numbers the foes of art and the sworn foes of the imagination.... Evangelicals hear the great 'I am' of God, but they are far less aware of the 'I am' of his handiwork."[7] Kilby's criticism, of course, was directed specifically at the evangelicalism of the mid-twentieth century in which the influence of fundamentalism was still palpable. One hears in his lament and subsequent plea for greater aesthetic sensitivity clear strains of that neo-evangelicalism which, in the years following World War II, set about the task of awakening a new generation of evangelicals to a cultural sensitivity and rapprochement largely absent among its fundamentalist forbears. The decades since Kilby's aesthetic *cri du coeur* suggest that his call has not fallen upon deaf ears, as evangelicals popular and academic have turned with increasing zeal to both aesthetic theory and praxis.[8] Notwithstanding this recent flood-tide of interest in the arts, however, observers have often echoed Kilby's diagnosis of "aesthetic impoverishment" when it comes to the evangelical tradition as a whole. That is, the evangelicalism of the eighteenth and nineteenth centuries is thought to have been as aesthetically impoverished as the evangelicalism of the mid-twentieth. The popular narrative of evangelicalism's relationship to the arts has long been one of distaste, distrust, and disinclination.[9]

This narrative, however, fails to take into account much of what evangelicals have actually said about art at different periods in their history. Alongside tales of the supposed incongruity of art and evangelical religion, one must place numerous statements by evangelicals themselves testifying to the positive value of art and aesthetic experience. "We are of the opinion that the evangelical canon admits of the appropriation of all belonging to taste and imagination ...," argued

---

[7] Clyde S. Kilby, "The Aesthetic Poverty of Evangelicalism," *The Christian Imagination*, ed. Leland Ryken (Colorado Springs: Shaw Books-WaterBrook, 2002), 277.

[8] For a tiny cross-section of this activity, see Francis Schaeffer, *Art and the Bible: Two Essays* (Downers Grove: Intervarsity Press, 1974); Wolterstorff, *Art in Action*; Franky Schaeffer, *Addicted to Mediocrity: Contemporary Christians and the Arts* (Wheaton: Crossway, 1981); Philip Graham Ryken, *Art for God's Sake: A Call to Recover the Arts* (Phillipsburg: P&R, 2006); and Daniel J. Trier, Mark Husbands, and Roger Lundin, eds., *The Beauty of God: Theology and the Arts* (Downers Grove: IVP Academic, 2007).

[9] See Horton Davies, *Worship and Theology in England: From Watts and Wesley to Maurice, 1690-1850* (Princeton: Princeton University Press, 1961), 236; L.E. Elliott-Binns, *The Early Evangelicals: A Religious and Social Study* (London: Lutterworth, 1953), 435; Introduction, *The Longman Anthology of British Literature, Volume 2B, The Victorian Age*, ed. Heather Henderson and William Sharpe (Boston: Longman, 2010), 1072; Walter E. Houghton, *The Victorian Frame of Mind 1830-1870* (New Haven: Yale University Press for Wellesley College, 1957), 127; and Richard D. Altick, *Victorian People and Ideas: A Companion for the Modern Reader of Victorian Literature* (New York: Norton, 1973), 271; Rosman, *Evangelicals and Culture*, 1-9 passim.

the *London Quarterly Review* in 1854,[10] and for much of the nineteenth century such an attitude was very much a part of Anglo-American evangelical thought. Although undeniably funny or repulsive by turn, the crazy Miss Clacks and the brooding Mr. Brocklehursts of Victorian fiction with their obsessive anxieties about the "world" reveal little about the realities and inner complexities of nineteenth-century evangelicalism and its attitudes towards cultural pursuits such as art. Like all good caricatures, such depictions suggest a portion of the truth, but they do so at the expense of nuance and a clear sense of the historical development specific to the evangelical community. This study therefore seeks a more refined understanding of evangelicalism's historical engagement with the fine arts. It aims not only to recover a largely forgotten tradition of evangelical discourse about aesthetics but also to restore some idea of the peculiar complexities of this history.

Given its focus on a particular religious community (or set of related communities), this book is also concerned with the historical interconnectedness of aesthetics and theology. On one level, it attempts to understand shifts in philosophical aesthetics as enabled in some measure by contemporaneous shifts in theological convictions. This is not to suggest that changes in evangelical thinking about art between the eighteenth and twentieth centuries were motivated exclusively by theological developments, only that theological developments played a significant role. On another level, however, this book also attempts to understand how shifts in theology were aided and abetted by aesthetics. As M.H. Abrams argued long ago, many of the key concepts in modern aesthetics are themselves migrants from the field of theology.[11] During the mid-to-late nineteenth century, certain concepts in the field of aesthetics (e.g., the idea of the "aesthetic" itself) were reabsorbed by theology with sometimes dramatic results. Aesthetics and theology thus interacted in complex ways, and this study makes an effort to elucidate at least some of these important dynamics. While it is first and foremost an examination of the evangelical aesthetic tradition, it is secondarily an exploration of the theological consequences of this tradition.

The Evangelical Aesthetic Tradition: Some Major Themes

The following narrative traces the gradual movement of Anglo-American evangelicals away from the complicated and often ambiguous aesthetic legacy of their Puritan predecessors towards a more extensive and urbane conception of art's possibilities, as well as towards a greater appreciation of aesthetics as an im-

---

[10] "The Works of the Rev. Richard Watson: with Memoirs of His Life and Writings," *LQR* 2 (Mar. 1854), 222. See also "The Evils of an Unsanctified Literature," *BRPR* 15 (Jan. 1843), 65.
[11] See M.H. Abrams, Preface, *The Mirror and the Lamp: Romantic Theory and Critical Tradition* (London: Oxford University Press, 1953), viii.

portant field of study. Initially, this process was slow-going. Despite what appears to have been a broadening of taste among some eighteenth-century evangelicals, early efforts at aesthetic theorizing were confined to a small company of innovators such as Jonathan Edwards and John Wesley. The writings of Edwards and Wesley offer important evidence of an evolving aesthetic consciousness, but in general philosophical reflection on the arts by eighteenth-century evangelicals remained limited. This lack of reflection resulted from a number of factors, including both the residual presence of Puritan anxieties about certain kinds of art and the scorching fires of revivalist fervor, which in the early and heady days of a movement could often prove all-consuming. It is worth remembering, too, that both our contemporary conception of the "fine arts" and what would eventually become the discipline of modern philosophical aesthetics were themselves only just beginning to emerge in the eighteenth century.[12] Over time, however, evangelicals learned to speak in the fledgling vocabulary of modern aesthetics. This evolution of evangelical interest in aesthetics was largely a consequence of evangelicalism's contact with various facets of Enlightenment thought—most significantly the writings of the Scottish common sense philosophers. Through exposure to Enlightenment philosophies often encountered in college classrooms, educated evangelicals came to share their age's interest in the many problems of "mental philosophy." Typically marking the culmination of the college curriculum, the study of mental philosophy sought to catalogue and analyze the powers and faculties of the human mind, among which were such aesthetically-oriented faculties as the imagination and taste. Through the many courses and textbooks devoted to the examination of the human mind, evangelicals learned to see the fast-expanding field of aesthetics as a legitimate form of scientific inquiry, and they increasingly viewed the appreciation of art and beauty as an indispensable part of human experience.

While the mental philosophy of the Scottish Enlightenment, among other factors, helped to acclimate evangelicals to the emerging discipline of aesthetics, it was the critical tenets of romanticism—many of which were themselves outgrowths of Enlightenment theories of mind[13]—that did most to shape the theoretical doctrines of evangelical writers throughout the nineteenth century. By the

---

[12] See Paul Oskar Kristeller, "The Modern System of the Arts: A Study in the History of Aesthetics (I)" and "The Modern System of the Arts: A Study in the History of Aesthetics (II)," *Essays on the History of Aesthetics*, ed. Peter Kivy (Rochester: University of Rochester Press, 1992): 3-34, 35-64; and Paul Guyer, "The Origin of Modern Aesthetics: 1711-35," *The Blackwell Guide to Aesthetics*, ed. Peter Kivy (Malden: Blackwell, 2004): 15-44.

[13] See James Engell, *The Creative Imagination: Enlightenment to Romanticism* (San Jose: toExcel, 1999), ix; Walter Jackson Bate, *From Classic to Romantic: Premises of Taste in Eighteenth Century England* (New York: Harper Torchbooks, 1946); William Charvat, *The Origins of American Critical Thought 1810-1835* (Philadelphia: University of Pennsylvania Press, 1936); and Gavin Budge, ed., *Romantic Empiricism: Poetics and the Philosophy of Common Sense, 1780-1830* (Lewisburg: Bucknell University Press, 2007).

1830s, romanticism had begun to exert a profound influence on diverse segments of Anglo-American evangelicalism, affecting everything from homiletics to eschatology.[14] In the ensuing decades, evangelical conceptions of art were also effectively romanticized, and it is no exaggeration to say that the criticism published in evangelical venues throughout much of the nineteenth century was in large part either an extension of romantic theory or a reaction to the perceived excesses of such theory. As one might expect, the degree of such romantic leanings varied from author to author and periodical to periodical. Some, guided by Samuel Taylor Coleridge and the spread of German idealist thought at mid-century, published full-scale idealist manifestos touting art as a vehicle of divinity and the artist as deep-seeing sage. Others were content simply to laud the healing powers of beauty, to insist on the distinction between poetry and science, to look to the imagination as the apex of human powers, or to praise art's potential as an agent for shaping individual and social virtue. And nearly ubiquitous was that most prized of romantic aesthetic principles—the belief that, whatever else art is, it is essentially the *expression of human emotion*. Just as importantly, however, romanticism determined the style and rhetoric of the theory and criticism that appeared in the pages of evangelical periodicals. Art, as well as the burgeoning industry of philosophical criticism, were treated with a "high seriousness" that would have amazed an earlier generation of evangelicals.

From one perspective, it is not especially surprising that nineteenth-century evangelicals, when they began turning in earnest to theoretical considerations of art, embraced the principles of romantic criticism. As David E. Latané, Jr. has observed, early-nineteenth-century criticism often amounted to little more than an "attempt to consolidate the innovations of the Romantics."[15] It may seem something of a foregone conclusion, therefore, that those evangelicals who donned the mantle of critic and took up their pens would have harbored romantic inclinations. They were in fact participating in the cultural enterprises of their age. From another perspective, however, the willingness of evangelical critics to embrace romantic theories of art was indicative of important theological and philosophical shifts within evangelicalism, for romantic aesthetic theory was it-

---

[14] See David W. Bebbington, "Evangelicalism in Modern Britain and America: A Comparison," *Amazing Grace: Evangelicalism in Australia, Britain, Canada, and the United States*, ed. George A. Rawlyk and Mark A. Noll (Montreal: McGill-Queen's University Press, 1994), 189-91. For discussions of romanticism's influence on nineteenth-century Protestant aesthetics, see Diane Apostolos-Cappadona, *The Spirit and the Vision: The Influence of Christian Romanticism on the Development of 19th-Century American Art* (Atlanta: Scholars, 1995); Morgan, *Protestants and Pictures*; and Ryan K. Smith, *Gothic Arches, Latin Crosses: Anti-Catholicism and American Church Designs in the Nineteenth Century* (Chapel Hill: University of North Carolina Press, 2006). Scholars have tended largely to focus on liberal Protestants and aesthetics.
[15] David E. Latané, Jr., "Literary Criticism," *A Companion to Victorian Literature & Culture*, ed. Herbert F. Tucker (Malden: Blackwell, 1999), 395.

self implicated in assumptions concerning the nature of God, human beings, language, and the world that were potentially at odds with orthodox Protestant doctrine. In contrast to traditional Protestant conceptions of the transcendence of God, the depravity of human beings, the necessity of supernatural regeneration, and the dangers of approaching God through humanly devised means, romanticism stressed the immanence of the "divine" in all things, the innate goodness of humankind, the power of natural "influence," and the value of human autonomy and creativity. Viewed in the context of evangelical history, therefore, aesthetic discourse proved to be yet another arena in which the liberalizing trends of the nineteenth century could be played out.

The full implications of these trends took time to develop, however, and the aesthetic theories formulated in nineteenth-century evangelical periodicals were not always mere codifications of romanticism. Sometimes of course they were. But in other instances evangelical writers, especially the more theologically conservative ones, refused to swallow romanticism whole. On occasion, this opposition to aspects of romanticism took part in a larger Victorian critical reaction to romantic theory, as when the editor of the *London Quarterly Review* explicitly sided with Matthew Arnold's Preface of 1853 against what he saw as the excesses of romantic expressivism.[16] At other times, evangelical writers attempted to qualify some of the more minatory claims of romantic aesthetics by bringing to bear traditional and decidedly unromantic doctrines like the Fall, total depravity, and salvation through Christ alone. Such critics found themselves engaged in a complex process of appropriation and resistance, and indeed Victorian evangelical critics are arguably at their most interesting in those moments when they endeavored, with varying degrees of success, to balance orthodox theology with romantic notions of art. It was in these moments that a unique effort at synthesis emerged, if only briefly.

Yet it was not the theoretical tenets of "mainstream" romantic critics and artists alone that shaped nineteenth-century evangelical aesthetics. Other factors also impacted evangelical thinking about the arts. One of the most important of these was evangelicalism's continuing negotiations with its own Puritan past. Over the course of the late eighteenth and early nineteenth centuries, many evangelicals steadily drifted away from the theological moorings of their Puritan ancestors. In one sense, this process was merely the undercurrent of the romanticizing trend noted above. As evangelicals departed from their earlier theological roots, they increasingly welcomed romantic understandings of God and human nature. This theological trend, moreover, coincided with and even enabled a similar movement away from the perceived restraints of the Puritan aesthetic tradition. What is particularly significant about this process in its relation to aesthetics was its growing self-consciousness, not only among liberals but also among some conservative and moderate evangelicals. Over the course of the nineteenth

---

[16] See chapter 2.

century, evangelicals came more and more to see the aesthetic legacy of Puritanism as the entity against which their own aesthetic thought was to be defined. At times, this anti-Puritanism necessitated some careful rhetorical maneuvering, especially among those conservatives who sought to retain some identification with Puritan theology and piety while distancing themselves aesthetically. But however this process took place, it was rarely neat and tidy, and even as many writers struggled to repudiate what they construed as the negative aesthetic legacy of their Puritan past, Puritan attitudes continued to inform the ways in which other evangelicals thought about art and beauty.

A second factor was the traditional evangelical disdain for all things Catholic, which continued to affect evangelical conceptions of art throughout the nineteenth century, sometimes in surprising ways. Evangelicals, of course, were well aware of Catholicism's claim to aesthetic supremacy—a claim that prior to the Victorian period many more or less happily conceded, wearing their taste for simplicity and their aversion to certain kinds of visual imagery as spiritual badges of honor. Throughout the nineteenth century, assaults on the alleged decadence and visual splendor of Catholicism were not unusual, and some theorists persisted in distancing themselves from Roman Catholic practice in explicit ways. Studies by David Morgan and Ryan K. Smith, however, have described shifting Protestant attitudes during the nineteenth century towards the visual and towards art in general in terms of a process of Protestant "Catholicization."[17] Intriguingly, Smith attributes this process of Catholicization not to a decline in anti-Catholic sentiments but rather to anti-Catholicism itself. Acutely aware of what many American Protestants perceived as a growing "Catholic 'threat,' Protestant denominations adopted one of its most potent, yet seemingly most superficial, components—its imposing physical presence."[18] Thus, to attract converts in an increasingly hostile religious free market, Protestants assumed an attitude of "If you can't beat 'em, join 'em." As we will see, both British and American evangelical critics were occasionally quite forthright in their aesthetic challenges to Catholicism, engaging in self-conscious attempts to assert the superiority of Protestant aesthetics and even to claim in good Protestant (and whiggish) fashion that all that is good and true in modern aesthetics could be traced to the liberating effects of the Reformation. Yet whether the process was implicit or explicit, nineteenth-century evangelical Protestants were increasingly emboldened to challenge Catholicism's claims to aesthetic dominance.

A third important factor was what may be called the "Protestant ideology" of the nineteenth century. With roots in Puritanism, the Protestant ideology saw Protestant Christianity, morality, the nation (or more broadly "civilization"), and cultural progress as bound together in intricate and mutually supportive ways. For Victorian evangelicals (and even for some non-evangelicals), this ideology served as a basic framework for understanding the world. Over the course of the

---

[17] Morgan, *Protestants and Pictures*; Smith, *Gothic Arches*.
[18] Smith, *Gothic Arches*, 10.

late eighteenth and nineteenth centuries, however, art and aesthetics were gradually grafted into this ideology. Once again, ideas drawn from the Enlightenment and from romanticism served as important catalysts. In this case, it was the theory of art's power to influence morality through the conduit of the feelings that paved the way for art's eventual inclusion in the Protestant ideology. Great art, critics asserted, has the capacity to refine the moral constitution of both individuals and society as a whole. In an era when many believed that Christian nations were accountable to God for their collective actions and subject to God's judgment for national sins, evangelicals welcomed art as an ally in the ongoing struggle to preserve Christian society. For some, art's subtle magic in the service of morality seemed increasingly to offer a non-sectarian means of stabilizing society that avoided the divisive intricacies of intellectualized dogma. Once art had been successfully legitimized in terms of this ideology, it was all but certain that evangelical interest in art and aesthetics would continue to grow.

The romantically-inclined theory and criticism found in many denominational periodicals was thus refined in various ways by traditionally evangelical concerns. It was this "evangelical romanticism"[19] that dominated the fruitful period of aesthetic theorizing during the Victorian era and shaped both liberal and conservative notions of art long afterwards. Ultimately, however, the evangelical *pax aesthetica* of the Victorian period was not to last, for as the century drew to a close evangelicals were forced to confront the harsh realities of modernism. Under the weight of new scientific and philosophical developments, the social and theological framework that had long sustained evangelicalism faltered at last, and as a result the cultural sway that evangelicalism had enjoyed in both Britain and the United States began in the 1870s to enter a period of decline. By the turn of the century, the "evangelical united front"[20] that had prevailed for much of the nineteenth century was nearing collapse as the gathering forces of both fundamentalism and modernism began radically altering the evangelical landscape and with it evangelicalism's relationship to aesthetics. In general, formal aesthetic discourse shared the fate of so many other evangelical cultural pursuits in the early decades of the twentieth century, and for many of the same reasons. Art and aesthetics became predominantly the property of a liberal and mostly urban elite, while fundamentalists largely ignored theoretical discourse about the arts in order to turn their attention to the menace of modern science and the hermeneutic complexities of premillennial catastrophe. As liberal Protestants continued to explore art's spiritual possibilities and praise its cultural virtues in ever more expansive ways, conservatives for the most part abandoned

---

[19] Cf. Diane Apostolos-Cappadona's use of "Christian Romanticism" in *Spirit*, 1-2. Although our concepts overlap somewhat, I prefer "evangelical romanticism" to the broader "Christian Romanticism." In her 1988 doctoral thesis (later published as *Spirit*), Apostolos-Cappadona employed the term "Romantic Evangelicalism." She does not, however, explain this change.

[20] See Charles I. Foster, *An Errand of Mercy: The Evangelical United Front, 1790-1837* (Chapel Hill: University of North Carolina Press, 1960).

aesthetics to a modernist intelligentsia. "Fundamentalists of the first half of [the twentieth century]," observes Roger Lundin, "wrote almost no essays of significance on the arts."[21]

This is not to suggest that fundamentalists failed to appreciate art or aligned themselves against aesthetic discourse per se. In some cases, the relative absence of such discourse among fundamentalists was more the result of a narrowing of interests triggered by a small conglomerate of perceived threats (evolutionary theory, biblical criticism) than of any prejudice against art or beauty. In other cases, a strong populist element within fundamentalism was quick to see the excesses and pretensions of some fin-de-siècle and modernist aesthetics as a source of mockery and scorn. Still others rejected on doctrinal grounds the tendency of some liberal Protestants to conflate the aesthetic with the religious—a trend that had been gaining ground throughout the nineteenth century. Even so, the evidence suggests that when fundamentalists did think about art, they retained many of the commonplace assumptions that had defined the evangelical romanticism of the mid-nineteenth century. Consequently, although early-twentieth-century conservatives repudiated the more grandiose claims of liberals concerning art and largely discontinued the formal investigation of aesthetics cultivated by their predecessors, both liberals and conservatives remained the joint heirs of evangelical romanticism.

The Evangelical Critical Establishment

The evangelical aesthetic discourse of the nineteenth century was sustained by a growing critical establishment that consisted of clergymen and academics but also poets, artists, and, as the century progressed, an expanding class of "professional" critics and editors.[22] This critical establishment served alongside institutions of higher learning as the main custodian and arbiter of aesthetics within the evangelical community. The primary vehicle through which this establishment operated was the vast array of religious weeklies, monthlies, and quarterlies typically sponsored and funded by individual denominations and their affiliated institutions. Evangelical critics did occasionally publish books and other independent treatises on aesthetics, but they reserved the lion's share of their activity for the many periodicals of the era. The characters of these periodicals, moreover, spanned the gamut from academic to popular. Periodicals like the Old School

---

[21] Roger Lundin, "Offspring of an Odd Union: Evangelical Attitudes toward the Arts," *Evangelicalism and Modern America*, ed. George Marsden (Grand Rapids: Eerdmans, 1984), 144.

[22] Nineteenth-century critics increasingly reflected on their methodologies, which contributed to the professionalization of criticism: As Laurel Brake observes, "The self-consciousness of the Victorian critics and their preoccupation with their own critical practices and discourse indicate the perceived importance ... of this mode of literary production" ("Literary Criticism and the Victorian Periodicals," *Yearbook of English Studies* 16 [1986], 97).

Presbyterian *Biblical Repertory and Princeton Review* or the German Reformed *Mercersburg Review*—publications connected with specific universities and confessional traditions—were edited by and aimed at professional theologians and clergy. These publications were the academic journals of their time, and they typically followed what has become the standard monthly or quarterly publication schedule. Others, like the Southern Baptist *Christian Index* or the Anglican *Record*, targeted a more diverse lay audience and tended to appear weekly. Still other periodicals situated themselves at the contact zone between the academic and popular. A number of religious periodicals in particular seem to have occupied this middle ground. As P. Mark Fackler and Charles H. Lippy have noted, it is not "always easy to classify [nineteenth-century] religious periodicals as being predominantly of academic or of general interest."[23] These publications often sought to mediate for non-academic or non-professional readers ideas emanating from intellectual circles.[24] In consequence, they attempted to balance intellectual rigor with widespread appeal.

Simply plotting periodicals on a continuum between academic and popular, however, threatens to obscure a defining feature of the nineteenth-century evangelical critical establishment—namely, its vanward position in the very process of social transformation that consolidated the bifurcation between a so-called high culture nurtured by an intellectual elite and a so-called low culture patronized by a populist majority. The evangelical critical establishment did not merely inherit a division between high and low culture, they helped produce it. Western society, of course, had long been divided in sundry ways along elite-populist lines, but as democratic sympathies swept across Europe and America in the eighteenth and early nineteenth centuries, mutual suspicions deepened and dividing lines became fixed.[25] With advances in science and technology, knowledge became ever more specialized and control over this knowledge increasingly belonged to a highly educated minority. By the early twentieth century, the modern division between high and low had become firmly entrenched. The evangelical critical establishment, like Victorian critics at large, played a vital role in fostering this division within Anglo-American culture and within evangelicalism itself. Evidence of this widening rift between an elite coterie and the populist masses may be glimpsed in the editorial agendas of several evangel-

---

[23] P. Mark Fackler and Charles H. Lippy, Preface, *Popular Religious Magazines of the United States*, vii. See also Lippy, Preface, *Religious Periodicals of the United States: Academic and Scholarly Journals*, ed. Lippy (New York: Greenwood, 1986), vii-ix. On British religious periodicals, see Josef L. Altholz, *The Religious Press in Britain, 1760-1900* (New York: Greenwood, 1993). A still useful general survey is *The Victorian Periodical Press: Samplings and Soundings*, ed. Joanne Shattock and Michael Wolff (Leicester: Leicester University Press, 1982).
[24] Lippy, Preface, *Religious Periodicals*, vii.
[25] See Nathan O. Hatch, *The Democratization of American Christianity* (New Haven: Yale University Press, 1989), esp. 5, 218-19 and Houghton, *Victorian Frame*, 96, 124ff.

ical periodicals. In the late eighteenth and early nineteenth century, denominational publications concentrated by and large on those theological and revivalistic concerns dear to evangelicals' hearts. There were occasional exceptions, but since most evangelicals saw the dissemination of Protestant Christianity not only as the lynchpin of Anglo-American civilization but also as tangible evidence of the coming millennium, missionary "intelligence," both foreign and domestic, made up a large percentage of these publications' content. Over the course of the nineteenth century, however, a growing number of these periodicals began aiming for a more cosmopolitan format that sought to take stock not only of theological debates and missionary triumphs but also cultural pursuits, including art and aesthetics. In some instances, editors and denominational leaders transformed existing publications, developing formats that engaged more highbrow interests. Before the 1870s, for example, the British *Baptist Magazine* had catered primarily to devotional and theological concerns, but in the December 1879 issue the editors announced an expanded agenda, which called for the publication of substantial articles related to matters "Devotional," "Literary," and "Scientific." In fact, this newly stated agenda only made explicit what had already begun to occur, for the format of the *Baptist Magazine* had been undergoing subtle changes since the beginning of the 1870s, if not earlier. From 1880 onward, the magazine interacted more extensively with intellectual culture—a trend that other evangelical periodicals of the era followed.[26] At other times, editors opted to create new periodicals from scratch, sometimes with the express intent of broadening the cultural horizons of readers. Both the American *Christian Advocate* and British *London Quarterly Review* were founded out of a similar conviction that too many Methodists were sorely lacking in intellectual sophistication.[27] The fascination of many evangelicals with the activities of high culture and the respectability these activities conferred was on the rise.

Perhaps more than any other institution of the eighteenth and nineteenth centuries, art and aesthetics represented and reinforced this emerging opposition between high and low culture. Indeed, art itself came to be seen as a crucial index of cultural refinement. Those who could produce and appreciate art possessed special genius and sensitivity. As members of an elite class, they wielded immense cultural capital. In addition, art was increasingly subdivided into low and high varieties: "popular art" might provide escape or entertainment, but "serious art" *mattered*.[28] Significantly, nineteenth-century evangelicals were complicit in

---

[26] The American *Methodist Magazine* underwent a similar transformation in 1830, transitioning to an "intellectually oriented quarterly" (Fackler and Lippy, Introduction, *Popular Religious Magazines*, xii). See also Michael R. McCoy, "The Methodist Review," *Religious Periodicals*, 353-57.

[27] See Robert H. Krapohl, "Christian Advocate," *Popular Religious Magazines*, 101 and Barbara J. Dunlap, "The London Quarterly and Holborn Review," *British Literary Magazines: The Victorian and Edwardian Age, 1837-1913*, ed. Alvin Sullivan (Westport: Greenwood, 1984), 204.

[28] See Lawrence W. Levine, *Highbrow/Lowbrow: The Emergence of Cultural Hierarchy*

fostering this division through their own expanding institutions of education and criticism; as a result, the evangelical community as a whole came to model this split. Evangelicals, that is, both accepted and recapitulated the distinction between high and low art. The Methodist intellectual Nathan Bangs, founding editor of the *Christian Advocate*, revealed something of this growing high cultural sensibility when he criticized the popular tunes of camp meetings, referring to them contemptuously as "ditties" and claiming they "possessed little of the spirit of poetry and therefore added nothing to true intellectual taste."[29] This observation offers an important corrective to those who would associate the history of evangelical taste almost entirely with popular or folk culture. One cannot limit this history to the hymns and spirituals of the camp meeting, the cover art of religious weeklies, or the pious coming-of-age novels that remain popular among evangelical readers today, although obviously such artifacts form a part of this history. But to restrict one's attention to these aspects of evangelicalism's encounter with art and aesthetics is to miss the bigger picture. In reality, many Victorian evangelical critics were just as likely to affirm Matthew Arnold's view of "culture" as they were to denounce his view of religion. Over the course of the nineteenth century, there emerged among evangelicals an elite class of critics who acted as impassioned proponents of what came to be known as "high aesthetic culture."[30]

In addition to its elite status as the arbiter of high aesthetic culture, this evangelical critical establishment exhibited two other notable characteristics. First, it was transatlantic in scope. Evangelicalism, long held together by an international network of revenue streams, voluntary societies, itinerant evangelists, pietistic practices, and shared doctrines, had from its inception been a transatlantic phenomenon par excellence.[31] From the late eighteenth century, a mounting army of denominational periodicals, many of which circulated in whole or in part between Britain and America, provided a vital means of sustaining and renegotiating this network. The British *Christian Observer*, for instance, was republished in its entirety in America. Other periodicals such as the *British and Foreign Evangelical Review* intentionally cultivated a global perspective, issuing original articles by British authors alongside reprints drawn from American evangelical magazines. In other cases, articles or redacted excerpts found their way across the Atlantic, appearing in sister publications run by congenial editors with comparable agendas. Many such exchanges involved texts of a theological or missionary nature. As the nineteenth century advanced, however, articles devoted to

---

in America (Cambridge: Harvard University Press, 1988), who describes this process as the "sacralization of culture." See also Raymond Williams, *Culture and Society 1780-1950* (Harmondsworth: Penguin, 1971).

[29] Qtd. in Hatch, *Democratization*, 202. Cf. a similar remark by Philip Schaff qtd. on p. 147.

[30] See "Esthetic Culture," *CAJ* 40 (7 Dec. 1865), 386.

[31] See Richard Carwardine, *Transatlantic Revivalism: Popular Evangelicalism in Britain and America, 1790-1865* (Westport: Greenwood, 1978).

art and aesthetics also began crisscrossing the Atlantic, giving rise to a critical institution truly international in reach.

One of the more interesting examples of this transatlantic exchange was a piece entitled "Fine Art: Its Nature, Necessity, and Offices," which originally appeared in the American *Methodist Quarterly Review* in April 1874. Prior to its publication, the text was delivered by the Rev. George Lansing Taylor, a minister in the Methodist Episcopal Church and a poet of local renown in eastern New York, at the opening of Syracuse University's College of Fine Arts on September 18, 1873.[32] This opening was itself historically significant, for it marked the creation of the first degree-granting program in the fine arts in the United States. That Methodist Syracuse (a young and struggling institution) rather than Unitarian Harvard or Catholic Notre Dame effectively institutionalized the academic study of fine art in America suggests the high premium that educated evangelicals placed on the arts by the latter half of the nineteenth century, as well as the corresponding drive to legitimize their own status as proponents of high aesthetic culture. Just as importantly, however, the rapid migration of Taylor's text from the *Methodist Quarterly Review* to the British *Wesleyan-Methodist Magazine* (with some emendations) highlights the transnational character of the evangelical critical establishment. Although Taylor's lecture originated in a uniquely American moment, its aesthetic doctrines resonated with fellow evangelicals across the sea.[33]

Second, the nineteenth-century evangelical critical establishment was also interdenominational in scope and ecumenical in spirit. At first glance, it is tempting to read the titles of evangelical periodicals (e.g., the *Primitive Methodist Quarterly Review* or the *Baptist Review*) as evidence of ongoing sectarian strife, but the trend among nineteenth-century evangelicals was overwhelmingly in the direction of *non*-sectarianism. This spirit of cooperation within the evangelical critical establishment facilitated the spread of aesthetic thought across the Anglo-American evangelical world. Not only did British Methodists borrow from their American counterparts, as in Taylor's case, but Methodists in general also borrowed from Congregationalists and Presbyterians. Tellingly, the establishment's non-sectarian makeup was embodied in the Syracuse University ceremony of 1873. In addition to remarks by Taylor and various university officials, prayers and/or further remarks were offered by a Baptist, a Congregationalist, and even a Unitarian, who, according to a later account, bewailed the fact that Harvard

---

[32] For more on Taylor, see "Rev. George Lansing Taylor, D.D.," *Alumni Record of Wesleyan University, Middletown, Conn.* (Hartford: Case, Lockwood & Brainard, 1883), 642-44 and "Taylor, George Lansing," *Appleton's Cyclopedia of American Biography*, vol. 6, ed. James Grant Wilson and John Fiske (New York: D. Appleton, 1889), 44.

[33] George Lansing Taylor, "Fine Art: Its Nature, Necessity, and Offices," *MQR* 34 (Apr. 1874): 231-46 and "Fine Art a Record of Civilization," *WMM* 20 (Aug. 1874): 703-709.

was not doing more to "encourage art."[34] The presence of a Unitarian at the inauguration of the College of Fine Arts reveals how the ecumenical spirit of evangelical critics could, by the latter half of the century, extend even beyond the conventional boundaries of the evangelical fold. Evangelical periodicals of the era, including some conservative ones, were quite capable of eschewing rigidly authoritarian editorial policies in favor of those that prioritized the relatively free exchange of ideas, and they sometimes published critics whose evangelical credentials would have been in doubt according to a strict theological standard. This openness ensured the fluid movement of aesthetic ideas among a range of evangelicals and even between evangelicals and non-evangelicals.

The nineteenth-century evangelical critical establishment was thus an elite and increasingly professionalized body of writers, editors, and publishers that often operated across national and sectarian lines even as it drew much of its support from denominational organizations. One important consequence of this observation is that a study like this one will concern itself with the discourse of an educated middle class. Aesthetics in the nineteenth century was a deeply political affair and even the most recondite critic could not ignore the challenges presented by the working classes. Art, in fact, was often marketed as a solution to working-class woes. Yet such arguments reveal more about the middle class and its political anxieties than about working-class attitudes towards art. A second consequence is that it invites one to focus on what middle-class evangelicals held in common rather than their differences. One might possibly and even profitably speak of a Baptist or Methodist aesthetic, or a British Presbyterian versus an American Presbyterian aesthetic. Subtle variations no doubt existed among denominations and countries.[35] This book, however, is less concerned with differences than with similarities, whether denominational or geographical. In keeping with the spirit of cooperation that prevailed among many evangelicals in the mid-nineteenth century, it seeks the common ground.

The Structure of This Book

This book is both chronological and topical in approach. Chapter 1 provides some necessary historical background by charting the emergence of a modern aesthetic discourse among evangelicals. It begins with an examination of the aesthetic legacy of the Puritans and the problems and possibilities this legacy created for later evangelicals. It then describes through some close readings of key texts the evangelical encounter with Enlightenment aesthetics and the effects of this encounter on evangelical thinking about the arts. Chapters 2-4 transition to a topical format to explore how evangelicals addressed several fundamental aesthetic questions during the period of heightened critical activity in the nineteenth

---

[34] George Lansing Taylor, "Syracuse University—Inauguration of the College of the Fine Arts," *CA* 48 (2 Oct. 1873), 317.

[35] On some similarities and differences between British and American evangelicals, see Bebbington, "Evangelicalism in Modern Britain and America".

century. Collectively, these chapters document evangelicals' changing conceptions of art in relation to various facets of the Protestant ideology. Chapter 2 explores the influence of romanticism on evangelical attempts to articulate the nature of art and imagination. Chapter 3 investigates the way in which critics sought to formulate the relationship between art and Christianity. Chapter 4 examines how evangelicals theorized the moral power of art and the ways these ethico-aesthetic theories interacted with evangelical conceptions of the "Christian nation." Chapter 5 draws the main narrative to a close through its exploration of the fundamentalist-modernist controversy of the early twentieth century and its consequences for the evangelical aesthetic tradition.

Although each of these chapters has a unique aim, readers will discover some overlap as ideas appear and reappear in different contexts. Such overlap is inescapable given the entangled nature of ideas. Readers will also find that I have tried to strike a balance between extended analyses of representative texts and broad syntheses based on multiple sources. My hope is that I have managed to capture something of the richness and texture of evangelical aesthetic discourse without also taxing the patience of readers. At the same time, this book makes no effort to supply an exhaustive account of the evangelical aesthetic thought of the eighteenth through the early twentieth centuries. For the sake of manageability, I have had to treat in cursory fashion many of the aesthetic questions with which evangelicals have historically wrestled. I have touched only briefly, for example, on evangelical conceptions of creativity, although many interesting connections exist between these conceptions and various theological concerns. The same holds true for evangelical understandings of both "taste" and "nature," issues fraught with lingering ambiguities inherited from the Puritans. I have, I trust, said enough to provide a general sense of evangelical thinking on these subjects, but much (happily) remains to be said.

Finally, in the interests of scholarly disclosure it is worth mentioning that I write as an evangelical in the Reformed Baptist tradition. This project is in many ways a deeply autobiographical one, and it began as an attempt both to come to terms with what appeared to be evangelicalism's conventional discomfort with art, and to place the recent explosion of evangelical interest in aesthetics in historical perspective. While I am encouraged by this fresh interest in the arts, what has at times seemed absent from the conversation is a clear sense of tradition—of building on past gains or learning from past mistakes. Despite this personal investment, however, my objective throughout has been descriptive and historical rather than partisan, and I have done my best to steer clear of polemics. Especially where art and aesthetics are concerned, it is all too easy to adopt silently and uncritically an aesthetic standard of judgment (often something approximating a modernist one) in order to champion or disparage a given group. I am not, I hope, uncritical of either the western aesthetic tradition or the ways in which evangelicals have at various times engaged this tradition. My argument, therefore, is not an attempt to promote nineteenth-century evangelicals by proving that they were as aesthetically savvy as the romantics. Frankly, I remain ambivalent about evangelicals' adoption of many of the tenets of romantic aesthetics. Rather, my desire is that this study will serve not only to enrich our understanding of a hitherto understudied aspect of evangelicalism but also, more broadly, to illuminate the problems and pitfalls, the discoveries and rewards, inherent in any attempt to contemplate the beauty of holiness and the holiness of beauty.

CHAPTER 1

The Emergence of an Evangelical Philosophical Aesthetics

To appreciate the character of evangelical aesthetics in the nineteenth century, one must begin with the aesthetic tradition of the Puritans. Evangelicalism, which traces its modern origins to the transatlantic revivals that shook the Anglo-American world in the 1730s and 1740s, was in many ways the direct recipient of Puritan theology and piety. While Puritanism obviously had the most enduring impact on evangelicals in the Reformed tradition, it shaped the Wesleyan-Arminian heritage as well.[1] Early evangelicals shared with their Puritan predecessors a number of important doctrinal and devotional emphases, including the necessity of conversion, the Reformation dictum of *sola Scriptura*, the substitutionary work of Christ on the cross, and a heartfelt religious devotion.[2] When it came to art, however, the Puritans bequeathed to evangelicals a more ambiguous legacy of problems, limitations, and latent possibilities. This tradition would continue to exert its influence, both positively and negatively, on evangelical theorizing about art well into the nineteenth century. In the latter half of the eighteenth century, however, evangelicals interacting with developments in Enlightenment mental philosophy began to depart from some aspects of this Puritan tradition even as they continued to be molded by others. By the early nineteenth century, many educated evangelicals had become interested in the new "science" of aesthetics and were coming to see art as an invaluable component of human experience.

The "Asymmetry" of the Puritan Aesthetic Tradition

The Puritans are notorious for their supposed hostility towards art, beauty, and imagination. Over the last few decades, however, a number of studies have demonstrated that the Puritans entertained far more nuanced conceptions of art and the aesthetic than traditional stereotypes would allow. Still, if the Puritan tradition fails as an exemplar of unmitigated anti-aesthetic sentiment, as unsympathetic critics might have us believe, neither are Puritan attitudes towards art

---

[1] See, for example, John Wesley's "Preface to Extracts from the Works of the Puritans," *The Works of John Wesley* (Grand Rapids: Baker, 2007), 14:228.
[2] David Bebbington, *Evangelicalism in Modern Britain: A History from the 1730s to the 1980s* (Grand Rapids: Baker, 1992), 34-35.

likely to appear perfectly congenial to modern observers. Perhaps the most felicitous description of the Puritan aesthetic legacy is that it was mixed or, to borrow a term from aesthetics, "asymmetrical." Puritanism helped forge an imagination which, even as it foreclosed on some aesthetic possibilities, gave birth to others.

One manifestation of the Puritan tradition's asymmetry was its complex stance towards visual representation. The alleged visual sparseness of Puritan culture, like much about the Puritans, has often been misrepresented. The Puritans were by no means the iconophobes they are sometimes made out to be. It is difficult, in fact, to find among Puritan writers a blanket condemnation of visual representation, and many willingly followed John Calvin in affirming that "sculpture and painting are gifts of God."[3] To a limited extent, such views even found concrete expression in a small number of sanctioned forms. In the early years of the Reformation, books and Bibles typically featured illustrations, and woodcuts and drawings were common among Puritan communities in the sixteenth and seventeenth centuries. Portrait painting was also widely accepted. Two of the most successful English portrait painters of the sixteenth century, Hans Holbein and Nicholas Hilliard, were strongly influenced by the Reformation and developed aesthetics that reflected this vision. The Puritan imagination also found visual expression in both gardens and new styles of architecture.[4] Such examples aside, however, the visual arts fared comparatively poorly, and despite Calvin's positive declaration on behalf of painting and sculpture, anything approaching a sophisticated art culture was relatively absent from the lives of ordinary Puritans.

There were several reasons for Puritanism's lack of emphasis on the visual. Most importantly, Puritan attitudes towards visual representation were shaped by ongoing theological debates over the proper use of religious imagery. These debates, of course, were nothing new. They had occupied Western Christendom intermittently since the patristic period and had been rekindled by the Lollards in the late Middle Ages.[5] The Reformation, however, brought fresh intensity to these debates. What the Reformers (with the notable exception of Luther) and Puritan divines agreed on, contrary to Rome, was that images had no place in the context of worship. In *A Reformed Catholic* (1597), an exploration of the similarities and differences between Protestants and Catholics, William Perkins stated clearly the Puritan position on images in the church: "We hold it unlawful for us to make any image, any way to represent the true God: or, to make any image of any thing in way of religion, to worship God much the less the creature thereby."[6] The Protestant case against images in the sanctuary rested on scriptural

---

[3] John Calvin, *Institutes of the Christian Religion* (Peabody: Hendrickson, 2008), 1.11.12. Subsequent references appear parenthetically in the text.

[4] See William A. Dyrness, *Reformed Theology and Visual Culture: The Protestant Imagination from Calvin to Edwards* (Cambridge: Cambridge University Press, 2004), 90-141.

[5] See W.R. Jones, "Lollards and Images: The Defense of Religious Art in Later Medieval England," *Journal of the History of Ideas* 34 (1973): 27-50.

[6] William Perkins, *A Reformed Catholic* (London: Printed by John Legatt, Printer to the

and patristic precedents (both of which Protestant polemicists were quick to cite), but as Perkins's treatise reveals, it crystallized in the heat of Reformation controversies with Rome. One important byproduct of this anti-Catholic polemical context was the enduring notion that visual art was properly the province of Catholicism, or rather, that certain kinds of visual art were somehow *not* Protestant.

At the heart of the Reformation-Puritan case against images in the worship space was an abiding concern to avoid idolatry. The scriptural *locus classicus* for this argument was the Second Commandment, and Protestant writers invariably cited this passage, along with 1 John 5:21, as the first and last word on the subject. Most Reformers and Puritans considered this biblical prohibition authoritative, but many were also keenly aware that there remained a certain hermeneutic flexibility in this passage that Catholics were wont to exploit. One may, for instance, distinguish between idolatrous and non-idolatrous uses of images (e.g., between icons and idols). The Reformation position, however, was rooted in an adamant refusal to allow distinctions of this sort. According to many Protestant writers, *any* image used in worship was by definition an idol. As Calvin bluntly put it: "God makes no comparisons between images, as if one were more, and another less befitting; he rejects, without exception, all shapes and pictures, and other symbols by which the superstitious imagine they can bring him near to them" (1.11.1). Not all idols were images—numerous forms of idolatry had nothing to do with visual representation—but all images in the context of worship were idols.

This identification of religious images with idolatry sprang from a robust conception of God's radical transcendence, which rendered any attempt at representation incomplete and therefore idolatrous. Because God is infinite spirit, it is impossible to contain him in the finite, material form of an image. "So soon as the mind frames unto itself any form of God," argued Perkins in his *A Warning Against Idolatry* (1616), "(as when he is popishly conceived to be like an old man, sitting in heaven in a throne with a scepter in his hand) an idol is set up in the mind."[7] Richard Baxter similarly raised the problem of representing the divine in *The Catechising of Families* (1682). "Is it lawful to make any picture of God?" he inquired, to which the appropriate answer was "No: For pictures are the Signs of Corporeal things, and it is Blasphemy to think God like a Bodily Substance...."[8] To attempt to give form to that which transcends all form was sacrilege, for according to Perkins images "do as little beseem [God's] endless glory, as a picture of an Ape, or of a fool doth the excellency of an Emperor" (*Warning* 676).

Universitie of Cambridge, 1616), 587-88. Subsequent references appear parenthetically in the text.
[7] William Perkins, *A Warning Against Idolatry* (London: Printed by John Legatt, Printer to the Universitie of Cambridge, 1616), 686. Subsequent references appear parenthetically in the text.
[8] Richard Baxter, *The Catechising of Families* (London: Thomas Parkhurst, Jonathan Robinson, and John Lawrence, 1707), 106.

In addition, the Puritan case against images rested on what has come to be called the Regulative Principle. First articulated by English Puritans, the Regulative Principle consisted of two complementary injunctions. Positively, the Regulative Principle held that God requires his people to abide by all of the regulations for worship explicitly ordered by Scripture. Negatively, God's people must also avoid anything not explicitly enjoined by Scripture.[9] Thus, God had prescribed once and for all in his revealed Word the acceptable forms of worship. To depart from these was not only to stand in violation of God's express commands but also to engage in idolatry. One "way of erecting an idol," wrote Perkins, "is, when God is worshipped otherwise, and by other means, then [sic] he hath revealed in his word. For when men set up a devised worship, they set up also a devised God" (*Warning* 674). Since Puritan writers could find no biblical precedent for the use of images in worship, introducing them amounted to idolatry. Even when artificers had good intentions, their efforts yielded nothing more than a false and therefore idolatrous image of God:

> Again, an image of a feigned god, is a flat idol in the common judgement of all. Now the image, that is erected to the honour of the true God, is [also] an image of a feigned God. For God will not be honoured by any image of man's appointing, though the honour be never so much directed to him in the mind and intention of man: and therefore the thing that is honour is indeed a god of a man's devising, who will hear, be present, and give his blessing in, at, and before images. Hence it follows, that the image which is supposed to be the image of God, is indeed the image, not of God, but of an idol: and every image of an idol is an idol. (*Warning* 687)

Clearly, God does not particularly value human creativity in worship. To imagine a God that does is itself to misrepresent God and in effect to create an idol. Accordingly, any representation of this image-welcoming deity would be nothing but an "image of an idol." Moreover, as this passage suggests, the term "invention" took on a negative connotation in Puritan discussions of worship. "Our principal care and desire," wrote John Cotton, "is to administer ... the ordinances of Christ himself ... in their native purity and simplicity, without any dressing or painting of human inventions."[10] Visual religious imagery was one such invention, and it would thus be a grave error to welcome it into the sanctuary. Doing so would signal a depraved desire to flaunt imagination at the expense of God's perfect ordinances.

The rejection of religious images as idolatrous also entailed a staunch denial of the visual, or at least the visual as fashioned by human beings, as a special conduit of the divine. God, the Puritans believed, is not "present" in any unique

---

[9] See Mark A. Noll, *America's God: From Jonathan Edwards to Abraham Lincoln* (Oxford: Oxford University Press, 2002), 377.

[10] Qtd. in Leland Ryken, *Worldly Saints: The Puritans as They Really Were* (Grand Rapids: Academie, 1986), 123.

way in visual representations.[11] To some extent this denial of divine presence in the visual was an effect of the oft-noted Protestant campaign against the superstitious medieval appropriation of relics and other "charged" objects, including images—itself an extension of the Reformed emphasis on God's transcendence.[12] At the same time, as Perkins made clear, God's absence from the religious image was also a function of God's sovereign, mysterious will. In his rebuttal of the Catholic claim that honoring religious images is analogous to honoring the seal of an earthly magistrate, Perkins highlighted a fundamental difference between the two cases—namely, that whereas an earthly prince wills the use of certain images as signs of his presence, God does not, "and so are not images signs and monuments, either of God's presence, or pleasure: because God will not be worshipped in them, by them, or at them; neither doth he bind his presence or his hearing of us to them" (*Warning* 684). Quite simply, God has freely opted out of the visual. In emptying the visual of God's special presence, however, the Puritans effectively relocated this presence elsewhere. As William A. Dyrness has observed, in the Reformed tradition God's presence was to be sought not in the visual but in the preached word and in the active lives of the faithful.[13] "If any man be yet desirous of images," wrote Perkins in *A Golden Chain* (1590), "he may have at hand the preaching of the Gospel, a lively image of Christ crucified."[14]

But what of the use in church settings of images which in no way purport to be representations of the Godhead? Would paintings that depict key events in the biblical narrative not constitute an appropriate application of Gregory's influential thesis that images serve as an educational tool for the unlearned? A number early Protestants answered negatively. Calvin, though he granted that "historical" images may have didactic value, insisted that this didactic function must be exercised outside of the worship space. The problem for Calvin was the troubling pull of depravity, for even if historical images present no theological difficulties, the human propensity for idolatry is such that what begins as proper use will unavoidably degenerate into abuse. "[W]e know too well from experience," Calvin explained, "that the moment images appear in churches, idolatry has as it were raised its banner; because the folly of manhood cannot moderate itself, but forthwith falls away to superstitious worship" (1.11.13). Even if all other scriptural and theoretical difficulties could be laid to rest, Protestants still had the seemingly irrefutable facts of human psychology on their side.

Nevertheless, despite their stand against the use of images inside the church, the Reformers and Puritans in no way disavowed visual representation in general.

---

[11] See Dyrness, *Reformed Theology*, 72-84.
[12] See Charles Taylor, *A Secular Age* (Cambridge: Belknap, 2007), 72. "Charged" is Taylor's term.
[13] Dyrness, *Reformed Theology*, 83-84.
[14] William Perkins, *A Golden Chain* (London: Printed by John Legatt, Printer to the Universitie of Cambridge, 1616), 37.

On the contrary, many writers discriminated between the "lawful" and "unlawful" use of images. As Calvin argued, "I am not, however, so superstitious as to think that all visible representations of every kind are unlawful. But as sculpture and painting are gifts of God, what I insist for is, that both shall be used purely and lawfully—that gifts which the Lord as bestowed upon us, for his glory and our good, shall not be preposterously abused, no, shall not be perverted to our destruction." Calvin drew a further distinction between "historical" representations, "which give a representation of events," and "pictorial" representations, "which merely exhibit bodily shapes and figures." The first type may be useful for teaching; the second, however, was "only fitted for amusement." Calvin did not denounce amusement per se, though from the context it appears that he valued the utility associated with didactic images more highly than those designed for mere pleasure. It was, moreover, the latter sort of image that Calvin believed had primarily, and scandalously, adorned the walls of churches (1.11.12). He therefore discriminated not only between kinds of imagery but, as Dyrness points out, "between pleasure and worship."[15] For Calvin, whatever purely aesthetic pleasure one might derive from visual images had to be experienced outside the sanctuary.

Perkins, however, articulated in plain terms what was perhaps the central Puritan distinction regarding images—that between images used for religious and "civil" purposes. In *A Reformed Catholic*, Perkins found that Protestants could agree with Catholics that visual representation has a proper role to play in the civil sphere: "We acknowledge the civil use of images as freely and truly as the Church of Rome doth. By *civil use* I understand that use which is made of them in the common societies of men, out of the appointed places of the solemne worship of God. And this to be lawful, it appeareth; because the arts of painting & graving are the ordinance of God: and to be skilful in them is the gift of God...." Images may be used to beautify homes; they may be stamped on coins; they may be employed as a means of remembering deceased friends; and, following Calvin, they may serve to depict historical events, including those recounted in the Bible. Perkins even allowed that biblical histories "may be painted in private places" (587). In a sense, then, what the Puritans advocated was a firm separation of church and state in the domain of aesthetics.

This severing of visual art and human invention from the spiritual center of communal life would have lasting implications for the ways in which evangelicals approached art. Since the religious value and status of art in the context of worship was suspect, aesthetic theory and praxis would have to take place outside the holy of holies in the "secular" domain. Initially, the divide between sacred and secular so commonplace today barely existed in the minds of Puritans. For the Puritans, all of life was sacred, from participation in the Lord's Supper to the

---

[15] Dyrness, *Reformed Theology*, 79.

plowing of fields.¹⁶ Consequently, to expel art from the sanctuary was not necessarily to desacralize it. In fact, in distinguishing between the civil and religious uses of visual representation, Puritan writers had constructed a space in which art could theoretically flourish. This expulsion did ensure, however, that for many years to come art would have a certain *kind* of religious significance. If the spiritual descendants of the Puritans wished to cultivate art to a greater extent than the Puritans themselves (which they did), then they would have to do so for the most part outside of the formal structures of the church. And whatever role they ultimately assigned to art would have to be something other than ecclesiastical. The Puritan "problem of presence" also introduced difficulties for later evangelical theorists. In the debate over religious imagery, the Puritans had denied that such images bear any special capacity to mediate the presence of God. Similarly, all "lawful" uses of the visual—civil, historical, and ornamental— were by definition also devoid of God's distinct presence. Visual representation might be religious in the sense that it could be done to the glory of God, as with all morally upright activities, but it could not be religious in the sense of maintaining any singular contact with the divine. Whatever spiritual value art possessed was a function of the artist's motivation rather than of art's intrinsic status as a unique object, discourse, or mode of perception and production.

The strong moralistic tendencies of Puritanism may also have contributed to the lack of a vibrant visual arts culture. Concerns over the relation of art to social justice, for example, reflected this moralism. If society is full of impoverished people, some reasoned, then how can one justify spending time and money on lavish paintings and ornamentation? In his *A Treatise Declaring and Showing ... that Pictures and other Images are not to be Suffered in the Temples and Churches of Christian Men*, a work widely disseminated in England (it was translated into English in 1535), the German Reformer Martin Bucer chastised those who would overlook the poor in favor of extravagant church décor: "For suche expenses which ought to have been made upo [*sic*] poore nedy folke (whom as beynge the very lyve image of God it was convenyent to have socoured and made our frendes with our lyberalyte) we have wastefully bestowed upon styckes and stones."¹⁷ To allocate resources to painting and sculpture rather than the alleviation of suffering among fellow human beings seemed folly of the worst sort. Although Bucer's claims focused yet again on the specifically religious use of images within the sanctuary, one can see how this kind of argument could be potentially more sweeping than even the theological censure of images, which had managed amid the heat of sectarian controversy to leave room for the civil use of imagery. When presented in such stark moral-economic terms, it was unlikely that painting of any sort could survive a head-to-head confrontation with human indigence. (Which of you fathers, if your son asks for bread, will give him a

---

¹⁶ See Taylor, *Secular Age*, 61ff. and *Sources of the Self: The Making of the Modern Identity* (Cambridge: Harvard University Press, 1989), esp. Part III.
¹⁷ Qtd. in Dyrness, *Reformed Theology*, 92.

portrait instead?) As with theological concerns over the place of visual art in the church, Bucer's socio-moral anxieties would continue to haunt subsequent Puritan and evangelical thinking about the arts. Should the committed evangelical spend limited resources in support of missionaries in Africa or cultural development at home? To be sure, this question may pose something of a false dilemma; many nineteenth-century evangelicals seem to have discovered a way to do both. But they were never quite able to put the question to rest.[18]

The Puritan emphasis on the moral potential inherent in all aspects of ordinary existence also translated into a decided preference for the humble, simple, useful, and unadorned. Extravagant embellishment was partly an ethical problem since it betrayed an unhealthy desire for ostentatious self-display and a preoccupation with this-worldly details.[19] This Reformation-Puritan propensity to see visual stylistic qualities as expressive of moral qualities helped to shape Protestant attitudes towards the visual arts. Calvin insisted that even if one conceded that art may serve to instruct the illiterate, one would still be faced with the seeming prodigality and indecency of many Catholic images: "For what are the pictures or statues to which they append the names of saints, but exhibitions of the most shameless luxury or obscenity? Were any one to dress himself after their model, he would deserve the pillory" (1.11.7). For many Protestants, the (Catholic) visual art of the sixteenth century was an offense to their moral sensibilities and continued exposure posed a danger that was simply not worth the risk.

There were, moreover, socio-political factors that contributed to Puritanism's limited attention to the visual. As John Dillenberger has argued, exposure to the visual arts in England and America before the eighteenth century was curiously lacking compared to the rest of continental Europe. Most visual art in England had been the property of monasteries, many of which suffered destruction at the hands of both Henry VIII and Oliver Cromwell. "The result," Dillenberger observes, "was that most individuals never encountered the visual arts...." By contrast, although continental Reformers likewise sought to exclude visual images from church settings, many continued to interact with visual art in other facets of life—a phenomenon which grew less common in England after 1580. In England, what little visual art existed remained in the hands of the wealthy aristocracy until the late eighteenth and early nineteenth centuries. Yet even the British gentry's interest in painting and sculpture developed at a pace remarkably slower than their continental counterparts. For much of the nineteenth century, in fact, it was not uncommon for critics to observe that while the English-speaking world had the upper hand in poetry and literature, it had only recently begun to make

---

[18] See, for example, James Smetham, "Modern Sacred Art in England," *LQR* 18 (Apr. 1862), 70-71 and Josiah Strong, *Our Country: Its Possible Future and Its Present Crisis*, rev. ed. (New York: Baker & Taylor, for the American Home Missionary Society, 1891), 233-36.

[19] John Dillenberger, *The Visual Arts and Christianity in America: From the Colonial Period to the Present* (New York: Crossroad, 1988), 10-11.

progress in painting and sculpture.[20] In addition, some Puritans had good reason to associate the arts with the social power structures from which they, as conscientious objectors, had been largely excluded prior to the English Civil War. Not only would the Puritans' marginal political status have reinforced their opposition to the art culture of the Catholic-leaning Carolingian court but the need to deal with the pressing difficulties of their own persecutions would have left little time for pursuing the arts.[21]

If the visual arts presented special problems for the Puritans and their descendants, the activity of the imagination posed similar difficulties. In the sixteenth and seventeenth centuries, many Puritans believed that the imagination was particularly prone to deception. This capacity for deception threatened to interfere with the mind's ability to apprehend truth, both natural and spiritual, and thus it was imperative that this faculty be handled with care.[22] The root of the imagination's corruption was the ever-present problem of depravity. As Perkins wrote in *A Treatise of Man's Imaginations* (1607), "so soone as [a person] beginneth to thinke, to reason or conceive of anything, so soone doth he imagine and conceive that which is evil ... *The minde and understanding part of man is naturally so corrupt, that so soone as he can use reason, he doth nothing but imagine that which is wicked, and against the Law of God*."[23] Of course, as Perry Miller has noted, for the Puritans no human faculty was beyond the reach of depravity; consequently, all aspects of the human personality were subject to the ebbs and flows of negative criticism based on the needs of the moment.[24] But whereas caveats about the misuse of the reason, for example, were balanced by the high esteem in which the Puritans generally held this faculty, the imagination less often benefited from such positive regard. Indeed, the imagination frequently elicited the cautionary admonitions of Puritan preachers.

Despite the Puritans' profound awareness of the far-reaching effects of depravity, many writers placed a high premium on the mind's capacity to perceive the cosmos accurately. The Puritans typically subscribed to a form of epistemological realism in which the mind was believed to have direct access to the thing-in-itself. Truth was a matter of the mind's right correspondence to an object.[25] This confidence was underwritten by the longstanding conviction that God was creator of both the universe and the mind, and thus there exists a fundamental accord between subject and object. Admittedly, sin could interfere with this natural harmony, but once an individual had experienced saving grace, the mind was

---

[20] See "English Schools of Art," *ER* 23 (Jan. 1848), 81-82 and "Comparative Literary Rank of Nations," *LQR* 11 (Jan. 1859): 377-95.
[21] Dillenberger, *Visual Arts*, 10-13.
[22] On Puritan psychological theories, see Perry Miller, *The New England Mind: The Seventeenth Century* (Cambridge: Belknap, 1982), 239-79.
[23] William Perkins, *A Treatise of Man's Imaginations* (London: Printed by John Legatt, 1617), 458.
[24] Miller, *New England Mind*, 257.
[25] Miller, *New England Mind*, 149.

capable of functioning properly once again. Right perception, furthermore, was an obligation, for misperception amounted to a distortion of God's creation and thus, in a sense, of God himself. Honoring God aright demanded that one correctly perceive his works as they are, not as one subjectively colors them.

Puritan concerns about the imagination were therefore founded upon a desire to maintain this epistemological ideal. The imagination was potentially dangerous because, given its special place in the human psychological apparatus, it could disrupt the normal dynamics of natural perception. When appropriately bound to sensory data, it served its assigned purpose; when left to its own devices, the unbridled imagination had the power to lead reason astray, incite the will and affections directly, and conjure misshapen images lacking any correspondence with reality. Such imaginary constructs were nothing less than an affront to God since they betrayed discontent with his sovereign design. As Richard Sibbes complained, "The life of many men ... is almost nothing else but a fancy; that which chiefly sets their wits awork and takes up most of their time is how to please their own imagination, which setteth up an excellency, within itself, in comparison of which it despiseth all true excellency and those things that are of most necessary consequence indeed."[26] For Puritans like Sibbes, any departure from the reality God had willed was indicative of a fevered brain.

It is not difficult to grasp the constraints that such a view can place on one's conception of art. It would seem, for one, to lead naturally to an aesthetic that foregrounds art as mimesis. What better way to honor the God of Creation than to attend to the divine artistry in detail? At its most extreme, such an approach might yield some form of realism, even hyper-realism. It is no coincidence perhaps that realist painting thrived in seventeenth-century Holland, a country heavily influenced by Calvinism.[27] Nor is it surprising that when England eventually did turn its attention to visual art, it excelled at portrait and landscape painting. At the same time, this deference to God's created order tends to militate against "fiction," or the imaginative in our contemporary sense, whether visual or literary. There exists, then, a latent and possibly irreconcilable tension between divine and human creativity. In the traditional debate over the precedence of nature or art, most Puritans would have sided with nature as the marvelous handiwork of God.

Cautionary statements about the risks of a wayward imagination were not unique to Puritans. Cartesian philosophers, for instance, had similarly granted the imagination a low place in the scale of intellectual value.[28] Yet the Puritans sometimes added a further, religious rationale for distrusting the imagination. According to some writers, the imagination was vulnerable to the immediate

---

[26] Miller, *New England Mind*, 257; Richard Sibbes, *The Soul's Conflict*, qtd. in Miller, *New England Mind*, 258.

[27] On Calvinism's influence on Dutch realism, see Dyrness, *Reformed Theology*, 189-212.

[28] See Monroe Beardsley, *Aesthetics from Classical Greece to the Present: A Short History* (Tuscaloosa: University of Alabama Press, 1975), 169.

agency of the devil. Satan does not need to talk in "an audible voice" or to exhibit "things to our bodily eyes," for he "hath a closer and more secret way of access to our Imaginations, in which he can represent the Images of things, and hold them before us."[29] Yet whether Satan infiltrated the imagination directly or an individual's innate sinfulness led to disorder and distortion, the imagination was prone to trickery. Careless exercise of the imagination not only falsified natural perceptions but also produced ideas liable to be mistaken by the deceived or ignorant for genuine spiritual perceptions. It was this problem of authentic spiritual experience that occupied Jonathan Edwards in his famous *Treatise Concerning Religious Affections* (1746).[30]

As in the case of visual art, however, the Puritan tradition manifested a certain asymmetry regarding the imagination. Despite the often caustic criticisms that Puritans leveled against the imagination, they did not understand it solely as a liability. Although given to deception, the imagination was a God-given faculty with an important (if somewhat prosaic) role to play in normal human psychology. A few writers went further still, granting the imagination a special place in human experience. Edwards, whose view of the imagination in *Religious Affections* represented the negative side of the Puritan tradition, elsewhere allowed the imagination a more positive function in the contemplation of spiritual things: "Such is our nature that we cannot think about invisible things without a degree of imagination."[31] Another such writer was Richard Sibbes.[32] Although he cautioned readers in *A Soul's Conflict with Itself* against the dangers of living a life of pure fancy that ignored the realities of God's creation, Sibbes also believed it possible for human beings to "make ... fancy serviceable ... in spiritual things." For Sibbes, the imagination possessed the power to adorn truth in ways that not only made it more agreeable but also enabled it to move the affections. A verbal image, for instance, as found in poetry and oratory, complements and even surpasses a propositional statement in its ability to engage the heart. Puritan preachers frequently put this theory to good practical use, for despite the pains taken to let the text interpret itself, Puritan sermons were often saturated with rich verbal imagery designed to enliven the imaginations of listeners.[33] Thus, although many writers stressed the dangers of the imagination over its possibilities, the Puritan tradition was by no means uniform in its cautions or univocal in its criticisms.

---

[29] Qtd. in Miller, *New England Mind*, 257.
[30] See Jonathan Edwards, *A Treatise Concerning Religious Affections*, ed. John E. Smith (New Haven: Yale University Press, 1959), esp. 212-214.
[31] Jonathan Edwards, "Experiencing God," *Theological Aesthetics: A Reader*, ed. Gesa Elsbeth Thiessen (Grand Rapids: Eerdmans, 2004), 173. See also Terrence Erdt, *Jonathan Edwards: Art and the Sense of the Heart* (Amherst: University of Massachusetts Press, 1980).
[32] This reading of Sibbes relies on Dyrness, *Reformed Theology*, 168-71.
[33] See Ryken, *Worldly Saints*, 125 and Erdt, *Sense of the Heart*, 70-77. On Puritan homiletic theory, see Lisa M. Gordis, *Opening Scripture: Bible Reading and Interpretive Authority in Puritan New England* (Chicago: University of Chicago Press, 2003).

The asymmetry of this tradition is perhaps most evident, however, in the generally favorable attitude of many Puritans towards art forms other than the visual. If visual art remained, in Dillenberger's words, little more than "an appendage, not really expressive of humanity's spirituality,"[34] other arts fared better. The predominantly auditory bearing of Puritan culture, together with Puritanism's strong emphasis on cultivating the intellect, provided a context in which nonvisual arts such as music and especially poetry could develop. Of course, Puritan resistance to the theater is legendary, and many Puritans viewed fictional narrative with great suspicion. Generally, however, the Puritans "held to a belief in the poet's high calling."[35] In addition to Milton, Puritan culture could claim the likes of Anne Bradstreet, Michael Wigglesworth, and Edward Taylor, as well as a host of lesser known poets.[36] A taste for poetry was not only common but considered a proper part of a liberal education. In his popular manual for aspiring ministers, *Manuductio ad Ministerium*, Cotton Mather included a section on "Poetry and Style" where he acknowledged that "Poetry ... has from the very beginning been in such request, that I must needs recommend unto you some acquaintance with it." Nor could Mather "wish" upon his divinity-student-readers "a soul that shall be wholly unpoetical."[37]

Contrary to stereotypes of Puritan austerity, many also displayed a keen sensitivity to the beautiful. For instance, the plain white meetinghouses of New England, long taken as symbols of the drabness of Puritan culture, were at times painted in vibrant hues, including red, yellow, and green.[38] It was nature, however, that supplied most Puritans with an immediate source of beauty. Calvin had referred to creation as "this most beautiful theater," comparing it also to "a large and splendid mansion gorgeously constructed and exquisitely furnished" (1.14.20). Many who followed in the Reformed tradition agreed. Thomas Shepard took up Calvin's metaphor of creation-as-theater, insisting that the only possible response to this "stately theater of heaven and earth" is to "conclude ... that the finger, arms, and wisdom of God hath been here."[39] The poet Anne Bradstreet confessed that when she beheld the "Trees all richly clad," "Rapt were my senses at this delectable view."[40] The Puritans showed a deep appreciation for the splendors of nature, reveling in the universe as a spectacle of God's glory.

---

[34] Dillenberger, *Visual Arts*, 15.
[35] Perry Miller, "Literary Theory," *The Puritans: A Sourcebook of Their Writings*, vol. 2, (New York: Harper Torchbooks, 1963), 667.
[36] Timothy Edwards, Jonathan's father, was himself a versifier of some merit. See Wallace E. Anderson, "Editor's Introduction," *Scientific and Philosophical Writings*, by Jonathan Edwards, ed. Anderson (New Haven: Yale University Press, 1980), 4.
[37] Cotton Mather, "Of Poetry and Style," Miller, *The Puritans*, 684, 685.
[38] Dyrness, *Reformed Theology*, 220.
[39] Qtd. in Ann Stanford, *Anne Bradstreet: The Worldly Puritan: An Introduction to Her Poetry* (New York: Burt Franklin, 1974), 95.
[40] Anne Bradstreet, "Contemplations," *The Works of Anne Bradstreet*, ed. Jeannine Hensley (Cambridge: Belknap, 1967), ll. 4, 8.

Yet even as they marveled at the beauty of God's handiwork, many writers perpetuated the Christian-Platonic belief that material beauty is but a faint shadow of a greater Beauty beyond. Ultimately, "the Puritan notion of beauty was firmly eschatological."[41] Only in heaven will humans possess the capacity to perceive genuine Beauty. Earthly beauty thus bespeaks an absence, a falling short, which in turn engenders a longing for something greater. In this world, wrote John Owen, "the view of [Christ's] beauty and glory does not last." In a post-resurrection state, however, when all impediments have been removed, the redeemed will be granted "one pure act of spiritual sight in looking on the glory of Christ."[42] Many Puritan meditations on nature exhibit a similar tripartite structure: the writer passes from a pleasurable experience of worldly beauty through a recognition of its insufficiency to a final expression of longing for the religio-aesthetic completeness of the Beatific Vision. At times, Puritan writers chose to sacrifice earthly beauty on the altar of heavenly glory, denigrating material beauty for its fleeting charms. At other times, they affirmed the legitimacy of material beauty even as they sought to imagine something greater. According to Bradstreet, heavenly beauty was not an overturning of earthly beauty but its consummation: "I wist not what to wish, yet sure thought I, / If so much excellence abide below, / How excellent is He that dwells on high, / Whose power and beauty by His works we know?"[43] An eschatological-aesthetic gaze, an apprehension of authentic Beauty, marked the end for which many Puritans strived. Edwards would develop this notion more fully in the 1750s in dialogue with Enlightenment aesthetics.

Just as important for the later history of evangelical aesthetics, however, was Puritanism's proactive stance towards "culture." In H. Richard Niebuhr's famous terms, Puritanism sought to "transform" culture.[44] God ruled over all dimensions of existence, not simply the formally or institutionally religious. The Puritans, therefore, as noted earlier, admitted no real distinction between the sacred and secular. Reformed thinkers stressed the spiritual potential inherent in ordinary life and across society, and they encouraged all people, not just the spiritual "elite," to think theologically about their endeavors. This Puritan emphasis on cultural transformation was part of a comprehensive socio-religious vision linking God, the individual, the church, and the nation in a relationship of mutual obligation held together by the concept of the covenant—an concept which hearkened back to God's covenant with ancient Israel.[45] This nascent religious

---

[41] Dyrness, *Reformed Theology*, 248.
[42] John Owen, "The Glory of Christ," *Theological Aesthetics*, 167, 168.
[43] Bradstreet, "Contemplations," *The Works of Anne Bradstreet*, vol. 2, ed. Jeannine Hensely (Cambridge: Belknap, 1967), ll. 9-12.
[44] See H. Richard Niebuhr, *Christ and Culture* (San Francisco: Harper SanFrancisco, 2001), esp. 190-229.
[45] See Noll, *America's God*, 35-39; Miller, *The New England Mind*, 476-77; Stephen Foster, *The Long Argument: English Puritanism and the Shaping of New England Culture, 1570-1700* (Chapel Hill: University of North Carolina Press, 1991), 213 and n. 60; and

nationalism would provide an important context for subsequent evangelical theorizing about art. If art could find no legitimate place in the church proper, it could nevertheless aid in the development of Christian society.

Yet if the Puritan willingness to see all of culture as a potential space for Christian thought and service theoretically opened the door to serious reflection on art, this reflection remained throughout the seventeenth and early eighteenth centuries more of a possibility than an actuality. Although the Puritans wrote poetry, played music, cultivated gardens, and occasionally fashioned visual images, they rarely approached these activities with formal aesthetic concerns in mind. Beyond their theological proscription of images in the church or their musings on the imagination, the Puritans demonstrated little conscious interest in art as a source of special philosophical problems.[46] As a result, Puritan culture lacked anything approximating a critical establishment. In one sense, this lack of a developed aesthetic discourse is not surprising given that such a discourse was hardly widespread in the seventeenth century. Hence it would be anachronistic to fault them for failing to participate in a mode of investigation only beginning to take shape in Anglo-American culture at large. Something approaching a belletristic form of criticism did not appear in America, for example, until the middle of the eighteenth century.[47] But the absence of such a discourse is nevertheless significant, for it is the emergence of such a self-conscious discourse among later evangelicals that distinguished them from their Puritan predecessors.

Puritan culture was not of course bereft of assumptions concerning the nature and purpose of art, and such assumptions did occasionally find expression. But in fact the very nature of these assumptions may have made the notion of aesthetics as a unique field of study, had the Puritans been able to conceive of such a thing, seem superfluous, for art as a mode of human activity was easily subsumed under one of two headings. Either it was valued as a species of innocent "amusement" or for its "utility." Both poetry and painting, for instance, were useful for conveying truth in a pleasing manner. Art, therefore, tended to be understood in the former case as a mode of recreation akin to other leisure activities or in the latter case as a secondary means of transmitting or making palatable knowledge also disseminated elsewhere through different methods (e.g., sermons and treatises).[48] To be sure, a recreational and/or utilitarian view of art and a

---

Michael McGiffert, "God's Controversy with Jacobean England," *American Historical Review* 88 (1983): 1151-74.

[46] See Miller, "Poetry," *The Puritans*, 547. Even Norman S. Grabo, who argues for the existence of "literary criticism" in seventeenth-century America, describes it as "largely unconscious, accidental, and unsystematic" ("Running the Gauntlet: Seventeenth-Century Literary Criticism," *ELH* 67 [2000], 708).

[47] Miller, "Literary Theory," *The Puritans*, 669.

[48] Cf. Neil Harris's argument that in late-eighteenth and early-nineteenth-century America, "enlightened rationalists" saw art as a form of "luxury" and potential corruption (*The Artist in American Society: The Formative Years 1790-1860* [New York: George Braziller, 1966], 28-53).

mature philosophical aesthetic discourse are not necessarily mutually exclusive, and in fact the utilitarian emphasis of Puritanism would continue to exert an influence on evangelical aesthetics even as Victorian evangelicals helped to foster a theoretical establishment that even the most artistically-inclined Puritan could never have imagined. What separated the scattered and diffuse statements of the Puritans from the careful aesthetic formulations of nineteenth-century evangelicals, however, was evangelicalism's early affinity for certain aspects of Enlightenment thought.

The Enlightenment and Evangelical Aesthetic Discourse

Until the early nineteenth century, appreciation and consumption of the arts among evangelicals largely followed the generic asymmetry of the Puritan tradition. Poetry and music remained popular forms of recreation, providing a source of innocent amusement and intellectual stimulation during leisure hours. Specific tastes tended to reflect the neoclassicism of the age. In keeping with the fashionable sensibilities of the time, evangelicals relished the poetry of Alexander Pope, Jonathan Swift, Edward Young, and James Beattie.[49] By contrast, the appreciation of arts such as painting and sculpture developed only slowly. Evangelicals, motivated like the Puritans by strong theological convictions and a staunch anti-Catholicism, continued to criticize the use of images in the sanctuary.[50] A relative indifference to the visual seems to have persisted as well. In contrast to the multitude of critical pronouncements on poetry throughout John Wesley's journals and letters, for example, his reflections on painting and sculpture are but few. "Of pictures I do not pretend to be a judge," he conceded after a visit to Hampton Court in 1772.[51] When, at roughly the same period, President Witherspoon of Princeton purchased out of his own pocket a collection of prints for the university, the Board of Trustees (which included a number of clergymen) denied him any compensation for his troubles.[52] The theater, too, provided a persistent source

---

[49] See Bebbington, *Evangelicalism*, 67-68; Doreen M. Rosman, *Evangelicals and Culture* (London: Croom Helm, 1984), 134; Jonathan Edwards, Entry 188, *The "Miscellanies" (Entry nos. a-z, aa-zz, 1-500)*, ed. Thomas A. Schafer (New Haven: Yale University Press, 1994), 33; John Wesley, Journal entry for Friday, Jan. 15, 1776, *Works* 4:64; "Thoughts on the Character and Writings of Mr. Prior," *Works* 13:418-25; "Thoughts on the Power of Music," *Works* 13:470-73. On Wesley's tastes, see Frederick C. Gill, *The Romantic Movement and Methodism: A Study of English Romanticism and the Evangelical Revival* (London: Epworth, 1954), 55-59.

[50] Wesley, for instance, rehashes traditional Puritan arguments on this point in *A Roman Catechism, Faithfully Drawn Out of the Allowed Writings of the Church of Rome, with a Reply Thereto*, *Works* 10:107-12. See also Horton Davies, *Worship and Theology in England: From Watts and Wesley to Maurice, 1690-1850* (Princeton: Princeton University Press, 1961), 236-38.

[51] John Wesley, Journal entry for Friday, 7 Feb. 1772, *Works* 3:452.

[52] Frederick Rudolph, *Curriculum: A History of the American Undergraduate Course of Study since 1636* (San Francisco: Jossey-Bass, 1977), 140.

of vexation for many evangelicals, just as it had for the Puritans, while the century's newest genre, the novel, was also greeted with alarm.

Yet if eighteenth-century evangelicals continued to be guided by Puritan attitudes in their patronage of specific arts, how they thought about art was beginning to change. One important indicator of this change was the growing concern among some with "correct taste." Unlike the Puritans, who, according to Dyrness, cultivated an aesthetic in which "beauty of the whole design would not have been either intended or excluded,"[53] evangelicals began both to intend beauty and to lament its exclusion. The Baptist minister Robert Hall, for instance, worried that "neglecting the unrivalled productions of genius left us by the ancients" would result only in "a deterioration of taste."[54] Wesley, moreover, justified the omission of some previously well-received hymns from an updated edition of his *Pocket Hymn Book* on the basis of aesthetic considerations alone: "These I did not dare to palm upon the world, because fourteen of them appeared to me very flat and dull; fourteen more, mere prose, tagged with rhyme; and nine more to be grievous doggerel." Although a friend had informed him that some of these thirty-seven pieces continued to be "hugely admired," Wesley assured him that he was "sorry for it." These hymns "will bring a deep reproach upon the judgment of the Methodists," and he would "not increase that reproach by countenancing, in any degree, such an insult both on religion and common sense."[55] Occasionally, evangelicals even attributed their new attention to matters of taste to Christianity itself. As British missionary Henry Martyn observed, "Since I have known God in a saving manner, painting, poetry, and music have had charms unknown to me before. I have received what I suppose is a taste for them; for religion has refined my mind, and made it susceptible of impressions from the sublime and beautiful."[56] Each of these statements reflects in its own way the conventional neoclassical concern with "decorum," while Hall's and Martyn's remarks show a familiarity with specific issues at the heart of Enlightenment aesthetics (i.e., the debate over the respective merits of the ancients and moderns; discussions of the beautiful and sublime). More importantly, though, the concern over correct taste points to an emerging awareness of beauty and art not only as conscious desiderata but also as unique categories of experience.

The birth of evangelical aesthetics, as with much of modern aesthetics generally, was largely a result of the eighteenth century's interest in mental philosophy and its systematic attempts to map the individual powers of the human mind. Initially, aesthetics was not even primarily concerned with the so-called fine arts, an idea only just beginning to take shape. What would become the discipline of

---

[53] Dyrness, *Reformed Theology*, 219.
[54] Qtd. in Bebbington, *Evangelicalism*, 67.
[55] John Wesley, Preface to *A Pocket Hymn Book, for the Use of Christians of All Denominations*, *Works* 14:343, 344. Elsewhere, Wesley concedes that "The Methodists in general have very little taste for any poems but those of a religious or a moral kind" (Letter CCCCXCVII, 6 Dec. 1788, *Works* 12:437).
[56] Qtd. in Davies, *Worship*, 237.

philosophical aesthetics grew out of an interest on the part of Enlightenment philosophers in questions about the structure of the mind and its ability to perceive the world around it. When in 1735 the German philosopher Alexander Baumgarten coined the term "aesthetic," he did so to describe a peculiar category of "confused perception," which he believed formed an important dimension of knowledge overlooked by earlier rationalist thinkers.[57] Those in the wake of Baumgarten gradually came to see the perception of beauty and the production of art as comprising a unique set of problems, and by the turn of the nineteenth century eminent philosophers were delivering regular courses of lectures on the fine arts in German universities. In Britain, too, empiricist philosophers had been asking similar questions about the mind. John Locke's desire to explore "the discerning faculties of a man, as they are employed about the objects which they have to do with" helped to lay the groundwork for a renewed consideration of such aesthetically significant powers as the imagination and taste and ensured human psychology would provide the intellectual context within which the problems of modern aesthetics would be thought for decades to come.[58]

Ultimately, however, it was not the mental philosophy of Locke (who had little to say about aesthetics) but that of a series of Scottish philosophers after him that was responsible for the advancement of aesthetic thought in Britain and America during the eighteenth century. Frances Hutcheson, Archibald Alison, Alexander Gerard, Edmund Burke, David Hume, Hugh Blair, Lord Kames, Thomas Reid, and Dugald Stewart were all Scotsmen who, despite their differing views, made significant contributions to aesthetic theory and criticism. As numerous historians have argued, moreover, evangelicalism was profoundly shaped by the philosophy of the Scottish Enlightenment during the latter half of the eighteenth century, particularly the common sense realism of Reid and Stewart.[59] Although evangelicals initially embraced common sense philosophy primarily as an antidote to Humean skepticism and a source of moral stability in

---

[57] On Baumgarten, see Kai Hammermeister, *The German Aesthetic Tradition* (Cambridge: Cambridge University Press, 2002), 3-13.

[58] John Locke, *An Essay Concerning Human Understanding*, ed. John W. Yolton (London: J.M. Dent, 2001), 1.1.2. Subsequent references appear parenthetically in the text. See also Walter John Hipple, Jr., *The Beautiful, The Sublime, & The Picturesque in Eighteenth-Century British Aesthetic Theory* (Carbondale: Southern Illinois University Press, 1957), 305.

[59] See Sydney E. Ahlstrom, "The Scottish Philosophy and American Theology," *Church History* 24 (Sep. 1955): 257-72; Theodore Dwight Bozeman, *Protestants in an Age of Science* (Chapel Hill: University of North Carolina Press, 1977); Robert E. Chiles, *Theological Transition in American Methodism, 1790-1935* (Lanham: University Press of America, 1983); Mark A. Noll, "Common Sense Traditions and American Evangelical Thought," *American Quarterly* 37 (Summer 1985): 216-38 and *America's God*, esp. chap. 6; Bruce Kuklick, *Churchmen and Philosophers: From Jonathan Edwards to John Dewey* (New Haven: Yale University Press, 1985); Michael Gauvreau, "The Empire of Evangelicalism: Varieties of Common Sense in Scotland, Canada, and the United States," *Evangelicalism: Comparative Studies of Popular Protestantism in North America, the British*

politically uncertain times, Scottish philosophy was also a rich repository of aesthetic ideas. Investment in Scottish mental philosophy thus placed evangelicals at the cutting edge of Enlightenment aesthetics.

By the end of the eighteenth century, interest in the problems of mind had assumed institutional form in college and university courses on "mental and moral philosophy." In the United States, these courses, typically taught by college presidents during one's senior year, represented the pinnacle of a student's academic career. The content of these courses, most of which derived from Scottish philosophers well into the nineteenth century, addressed aesthetic problems such as beauty or imagination in terms of psychological dynamics.[60] Textbooks customarily included sections on "taste" and "imagination," which in turn led to discussions of beauty, sublimity, creativity, and various artistic genres. Although it would still be some time before American instructors began delivering lectures devoted to the fine arts as had been done in Scotland and Germany since the late eighteenth century,[61] these courses offered educated evangelicals their first encounter with the philosophical study of aesthetics. British evangelicals likewise confronted aesthetic problems through courses in mental philosophy. Because of the religious tests in place at Oxford and Cambridge that prevented dissenters from taking degrees, many evangelicals attended Scottish universities,[62] placing them at the very hub of aesthetic activity in the eighteenth century and exposing them to the latest theories of art.

The Enlightenment's programmatic exploration of human mental faculties may have been decisive in legitimating art and aesthetics in the minds of those

---

Isles, and Beyond, 1700-1990 (New York: Oxford University Press, 1994): 219-252; George Marsden, *Fundamentalism and American Culture* (Oxford: Oxford University Press, 2006); William Charvat, *The Origins of American Critical Thought 1810-1835* (Philadelphia: University of Pennsylvania Press, 1936); Anand C. Chitnis, *The Scottish Enlightenment and Early Victorian Society* (London: Croom Helm, 1986); Bebbington, *Evangelicalism*, esp. 59-60, 143; and David Allan, *Virtue, Learning and the Scottish Enlightenment: Ideas of Scholarship in Early Modern History* (Edinburgh: Edinburgh University Press, 1993), esp. 235-37. On common sense philosophy in general, see S.A. Grave, *The Scottish Philosophy of Common Sense* (Oxford: Clarendon Press, 1960).

[60] See Terence Martin, *The Instructed Vision: Scottish Common Sense Philosophy and the Origins of American Fiction* (New York: Krause, 1969), 13-32.

[61] Thomas Reid composed his *Lectures on the Fine Arts* in 1774, while Friedrich Wilhelm von Schelling delivered lectures on *The Philosophy of Art* at Jena in 1802-03 and Hegel at the University of Berlin in 1820. Similar lectures were being given in some American institutions by the early 1840s. See "Notes of Lectures on Æsthetics by Dr. F.A. Rauch, President of Marshall College. Delivered to the Junior Class in 1841" (T.A., "What Is Poetry?" *MerR* 11 [July 1859], 382).

[62] See Chitnis, *Scottish Enlightenment*, 40-44. On religious tests in the nineteenth century, see Charles Edward Mallet, *Modern Oxford* (New York: Barnes & Noble, 1968), 196-98, 256, 292-93, 325ff., 330-33, 433-36 and Martha McMackin Garland, *Cambridge Before Darwin: The Ideal of a Liberal Education, 1800-1860* (Cambridge: Cambridge University Press, 1980), 70-71.

evangelicals whose sensibilities had been shaped by the ambiguities of Puritanism, for this approach ultimately lent a kind of "scientific" sanction to the study of beauty and art. "Manifold are *the advantages of criticism*," noted Lord Kames in his influential *Elements of Criticism* (1762), "when ... studied as a rational science."[63] The idea that art designated a fit object of philosophical inquiry may have offered just the sort of rationale some evangelicals needed to leave the difficulties of Puritanism behind. The rational investigation of the aesthetic faculties of the human mind did not of course dispense with all Puritan anxieties surrounding art and imagination. Many of the concepts advanced by Enlightenment aestheticians were themselves given to ambiguity and were therefore as capable of confirming Puritan prejudices as displacing them. What the new methodology allowed for, however, was a modicum of critical distance, which, in light of the tenets of the new psychology itself, required that faculties such as the imagination and taste, as well as the objects of these faculties, receive fresh consideration.

The study of mental philosophy also supplied evangelicals with another important idea that helped to place art and aesthetics in a new perspective: psychological "balance." The faculty psychology of the day held that one ought to cultivate each human power to its fullest extent. Within this scheme, some powers might be rightfully subordinated to others in accordance with the natural constitution and appropriate regulation of the human mind, but no power or faculty ought in principle to be ignored.[64] In America, this criterion of mental balance was articulated in the Yale Report of 1828. According to the Report, "as the bodily frame is brought to its highest perfection, not by one simple and uniform motion, but by a variety of exercises, so the mental faculties are expanded, and invigorated, and adapted to each other, by familiarity with different departments of science." A true education, noted the Report, sought "a proper *balance* of character."[65] Given Yale's position in the early nineteenth century as one of America's foremost institutions (with close evangelical affiliations), the logic of the Report would have been familiar to a broad base of evangelical students and educators. While the Yale Report's main objective was to vindicate liberal arts education and study of the classics,[66] it also delivered a broad justification for the investigation and appreciation of art. Failure to cultivate the aesthetic dimension of one's personality threatened the ideal of psychological balance. This ideal, as later chapters will show, enabled nineteenth-century evangelicals not only to defend the claims of art but also to confront the shortcomings of the Puritan aesthetic tradition.

---

[63] Henry Home, Lord Kames, *Elements of Criticism*, ed. Peter Jones (Indianapolis: Liberty Fund, 2005), 1:14.
[64] Daniel Walker Howe, *The Political Culture of the American Whigs* (Chicago: University of Chicago Press, 1984), 29.
[65] Qtd. in George M. Marsden, *The Soul of the American University: From Protestant Establishment to Established Nonbelief* (New York: Oxford University Press, 1994), 82.
[66] See Marsden, *American University*, 81-82.

The second half of the eighteenth century therefore marks the dawn of a formal aesthetic discourse among evangelicals. In contrast to the steady growth of aesthetics among non-evangelical writers, however, critical reflection on art and beauty among evangelicals advanced slowly. Not until the nineteenth century would a sustained evangelical aesthetic discourse flourish. One reason for the slow progress during this period may have been the lingering influence of Puritan austerity. "[I]t is not surprising," wrote one early student of the Evangelical Movement in Britain, "to find Evangelicals deficient in any appreciation of art and the aesthetic side of life. Some went further, and, with the Puritans, looked upon beauty as the snare of the evil one, a siren voice luring them from the strait path of righteousness."[67] This austerity manifested itself not only in evangelical attitudes towards specific art forms such as the visual but also in convictions about the proper use of time and resources. Art may have been innocuous enough, but many still identified it primarily with leisure and it therefore ranked low on the list of evangelical priorities. This observation suggests a second reason for the comparatively slow development of evangelical aesthetics. As a child of the Great Awakening, evangelicalism was still a young movement that for much of the eighteenth century remained focused on spreading revival and fighting important theological battles—occupations that left few opportunities for cultivating the arts. Various socio-political hardships also took their toll. In the United States, evangelicals during the early nationalist period faced the enormous task of negotiating the aftermath of the Revolution. In addition, denominations such as Baptists and Methodists, which stood outside of the Congregationalist-Presbyterian establishment in New England or which seemed to threaten the social stability of the dominant culture, were engaged in battles of their own that likely helped to curtail widespread interest in cultural pursuits easily associated with hegemonic control.[68] The same applied to dissenters and Methodists in Britain, whose uncertain relationship to the power structures of the Established Church also rendered them socially suspect. Such hardships left many evangelicals with little time to enjoy the arts let alone reflect deeply on them. These challenges, however, did not prevent a handful of thinkers from grappling with the ideas of their time. At least some evangelicals were beginning to develop a modern understanding of aesthetics.

Jonathan Edwards and the Nature of True Beauty

One early specimen of philosophical aesthetic discourse among evangelicals was Jonathan Edwards's *A Dissertation on the Nature of True Virtue*, composed in

---

[67] L.E. Elliott-Binns, *The Early Evangelicals: A Religious and Social Study* (London: Lutterworth Press, 1953), 435.
[68] See, for example, Nathan O. Hatch, *The Democratization of American Christianity* (New Haven: Yale University Press, 1989) on the widespread populism of some denominations in the early republic and Cynthia Lynn Lyerly, *Methodism and the Southern Mind, 1770-1810* (New York: Oxford University Press, 1998) for an account of Methodism's subversive relation to "gentleman culture" in the South.

1755 and published posthumously ten years later. Edwards was an innovative thinker who was both shaped by and critical of Enlightenment thought. He was familiar with, among others, the writings of Locke, Shaftesbury, Hutcheson, and Hume, and he often engaged them in creative ways. Typically, his objectives were traditional and Puritan (e.g., defending the doctrine of original sin), but the methodology and content of his arguments were also grounded in the philosophy of his day. By far the aesthetic concept that garnered Edwards's greatest attention was beauty, and throughout his many writings he meditated on its nature, its place in human experience, and its purpose in the divine plan. Although Edwards had occasionally discussed beauty in his earlier writings, *The Nature of True Virtue* represents his most extended treatment of the subject. This treatment, however, for all its richness, was hardly for its own sake. As his title suggests, Edwards's main concern was moral-theological, and he intended the essay as a rejoinder to recent developments in moral philosophy, especially the "moral sense" school of Shaftesbury and Hutcheson.[69] The teachings of the moral sense philosophers, which held that human beings possess a natural inclination towards the good, stood in stark contrast to the traditional Augustinian understanding of human beings' innate depravity. In this latter view, individuals are incapable of any action that could be considered meritorious in God's sight; consequently, "true virtue," in Edwards's typical eighteenth-century terminology, is possible only for those redeemed by grace. Although Edwards found some aspects of the Hutchesonian ethical tradition compelling, he had no intention of abandoning his Augustinian roots, and thus the primary task Edwards set for himself was to show his readers in what true virtue consists and to demonstrate that the capacity for such virtue belongs solely to the regenerate.

From the outset it is clear than any discussion of ethics must also involve aesthetics, at least by analogy: "Therefore, I suppose, I shall not depart from the common opinion," Edwards writes, "when I say, that virtue is the beauty of the qualities and exercises of the heart, or those actions which proceed from them." To ask in what true virtue consists is to ask what "renders any habit, disposition, or exercise of the heart truly *beautiful*."[70] That a discussion of ethics necessarily implicates aesthetics was a reflection of the moral tradition, or "common opinion," to which Edwards was responding. Central to Hutcheson's ethical theory was the notion that humans possess both moral and aesthetic senses which function in parallel fashion. "What is approved by this [moral] sense," wrote Hutcheson in his *Short Introduction to Moral Philosophy*, "we count as *right* and *beautiful*, and call it *virtue*; what is condemned, we count as *base* and *deformed* and

---

[69] See Third Early of Shaftesbury (Anthony Ashley Cooper), *Characteristics of Men, Manners, Opinions, Times, Etc.*, ed. John M. Robertson (Gloucester: Peter Smith, 1963) and Frances Hutcheson, *An Inquiry into the Original of Our Ideas of Beauty and Virtue*, ed. Wolfgang Leidhold (Indianapolis: Liberty Fund, 2008).

[70] Jonathan Edwards, *The Nature of True Virtue, Ethical Writings*, ed. Paul Ramsay (New Haven: Yale University Press, 1989), 539. Subsequent references appear parenthetically in the text.

vicious."[71] Just as the aesthetic sense spontaneously and pleasurably perceives the beauty of a material object, so the moral sense perceives and approves benevolent behavior. Yet not only are the operations of the two senses analogous but so are their respective objects of perception, for what beauty and virtuous action have in common are the principles of symmetry and harmony. When, for example, a criminal receives a punishment that accords with the crime or a victim is awarded proper compensation for wrongs endured, the moral sense takes pleasure in the perception of balanced and proportionate action. On this account, morality is largely a function of rudimentary aesthetic principles.[72]

Edwards does not discount this approach entirely. He allows that human beings possess a kind of moral sense that takes pleasure in orderly conduct. This "natural" moral sense (which, in keeping with eighteenth-century moral philosophy, Edwards equates with "conscience") is in fact indispensable to the smooth functioning of society.[73] What Edwards is unwilling to concede is that natural conscience has anything to do with the exercise of *true* virtue. True virtue, he insists, must always have reference to God, and although he couches his thesis in metaphysical rather than theological terms, Edwards's notion of virtue is finally theocentric: "True virtue most essentially consists in benevolence to Being in general. Or perhaps, to speak more accurately, it is that consent, propensity, and union of heart to being in general, which is immediately exercised in a general good will" (540). All will admit upon reflection that on some level the object of one's virtuous benevolence is the *being* of another. But if such is the case, then it follows that "that Being who has *most* of being, or has the greatest share of existence ... will have the *greatest* share of the propensity and benevolent affections of the heart" (545-46). This object is of course God himself, the "Being of beings, infinitely the greatest and best" (550). To be sure, benevolence to being in general may lead to virtuous action towards "any one particular being" (541), but true virtue cannot begin at the level of the particular. To begin thus would be to accept mistakenly a part for the whole—to sacrifice the *"highest good"* to a merely local good (545). This was the fundamental error of Hutcheson and his followers. "[I]t may be asserted in general," declares Edwards, "that nothing is of the nature of true virtue, in which God is not the *first* and the *last*" (560).

Yet as his opening paragraphs make clear, Edwards also agrees with Hutcheson and other eighteenth-century moralists that there is such a thing as the "beauty of virtue." "That which is called 'virtue,'" he writes, "is a certain kind of beautiful nature, form or quality" (619). However, as Norman Fiering observes, Edwards concludes that Hutcheson had erred by inverting the proper order of things and predicating moral judgments on a kind of aesthetic judgment:

---

[71] Qtd. in George Marsden, *Jonathan Edwards: A Life* (New Haven: Yale University Press, 2003), 465.

[72] Norman Fiering, *Jonathan Edwards's Moral Thought in Its British Context* (Chapel Hill: University of North Carolina Press, 1981), 112, 108.

[73] Marsden, *Edwards*, 469.

"Hutcheson's close comparison of the aesthetic sense and the moral sense ... reversed the order of the Creation and erroneously made the perception of material relations, such as regularity, equality, proportion, and symmetry, the prototype for the perception of intelligent ethical relationships."[74] Insofar as the natural conscience is concerned, Edwards concurs with Hutcheson's analysis of the aesthetic grounds of ethics. But such an analysis failed to get at the heart of true virtue. Instead, Edwards argues that aesthetic relationships are an embodiment or extension of ethical relationships, or that the formal beauty of material objects—what Edwards calls "secondary beauty"—is but a dim reflection of a "primary" or "spiritual beauty," which consists in the willing "consent" of one being to another. In positing what Fiering calls an "aesthetics of consent," Edwards essentially relegates Hutcheson's aesthetics to the level of "secondary beauty," just as he had demoted Hutcheson's moral sense to the level of natural conscience.[75]

Edwards introduces the notion of spiritual beauty vis-à-vis a discussion of the proper "object[s] of a virtuous benevolence." The first of these, noted earlier, is "being in general" (545). In addition to being itself, however, there is a *"second object of a virtuous propensity of heart,"* namely, *"benevolent* being." When one not only values the being of another but also recognizes in this being the existence of a like benevolence to being in general, this recognition "draws forth greater love to him" (546). It is this benevolent disposition to being in general which one perceives in the other that constitutes the beauty of this being: "all spiritual beauty lies in these virtuous principles and acts [i.e., those which proceed from a love to being in general], so 'tis primarily *on this account* they are beautiful, *viz.* that they imply *consent* and *union* with Being *in general*" (548). Beauty, then, is ultimately a moral and spiritual category. On Edwards's account, a person is most "beautiful" when most devoted to God, that is, when the individual "does above all things seek the *glory of* God, and makes *this* [the] supreme, governing, and ultimate end" (559). In fact, the epithet beautiful is applicable in its highest sense only to those who demonstrate love to being in general, for "This is the primary and most essential beauty of everything that can justly be called by the name of virtue" (548).

No one, however, can match the expanse of God's own love towards being in general (as Edwards concludes, *"divine virtue ...* must consist primarily in [God's] *love to himself"* [557]). Thus if true beauty consists in benevolence to being in general, God himself must be truly beautiful above all things: "For as God is infinitely the greatest being, so he is allowed to be infinitely the most beautiful and excellent.... God's beauty is infinitely more valuable than that of all other beings..." (550-51). Key to Edwards's moral-aesthetic system, then, is the disinterested apprehension of divine beauty. Disinterestedness was to become

---

[74] Fiering, *Edwards's Moral Thought*, 108.
[75] Fiering, *Edwards's Moral Thought*, 80, 112, 114. The phrase "aesthetics of consent" appears on p. 114.

a staple ingredient in theories of aesthetic contemplation after Kant. As David Morgan notes, however, Edwards's disinterestedness "was not a state of dispassionate observation in the manner that Kant and others described ... but an abandonment, founded on a self-denying impulse, of the soul into divine grace." In Edwards's view, one contemplates the beauty of God for His own sake, but this is not an affectively neutral act by the percipient; to the contrary, one's contemplation of God brims with desire and passion. This disinterested perception of God's beauty, however, has no visual or formal component since to perceive the primary beauty of God is to perceive His infinite moral benevolence.[76]

In addition to primary beauty, Edwards acknowledges the existence of a "secondary and inferior kind of beauty" (561). This second category relates to the beauty of material forms and is "not peculiar to spiritual beings, but is found even in inanimate things; which consists of a mutual consent and agreement of different things, in form, manner, quantity, and visible end or design; called by the various names of regularity, order, uniformity, symmetry, proportion, harmony, etc." (561-62). Edwards spends an entire chapter exploring different kinds of secondary beauty, and not surprisingly his ideas are indebted to Enlightenment theories on the subject. As he admits, secondary beauty is "the same that Mr. Hutcheson, in his treatise on beauty, expresses by uniformity in the midst of variety" (562). In the usual eighteenth-century fashion, Edwards's notion of secondary beauty encompasses not only what we would think of as the formal qualities of an art object but also such "immaterial" things as the "order of society" (568). Edwards clearly appreciates this secondary beauty, despite its "inferiority" to spiritual beauty, and the chapter in which he treats at length the nature of secondary beauty offers solid evidence of some evangelicals' early engagement with Enlightenment aesthetics. The specific details of Edwards's analysis, however, improve little upon Hutcheson and so need not concern us here.

Far more important is his conception of the *relationship* between primary and secondary beauty. According to Edwards, "all the beauty to be found throughout the whole creation"—viz., all secondary beauty—"is but the reflection of the diffused beams of that Being who hath an infinite fulness of brightness and glory" (550-51). All natural beauty is therefore a material embodiment of divine benevolence, of the Beauty of God. Specifically, the symmetry of an object is a genuine (though distant) reflection of the "consent," or harmonious love, between spiritual beings. The relationship of sides and angles in an equilateral triangle, for example, furnishes an image of a person's virtuous love to God and of God's supremely virtuous love to people. "The reason," writes Edwards, "or at least one reason, why God has made this kind of mutual agreement of things beautiful and grateful to those intelligent beings that perceive it probably is that there is in it some image of the true, spiritual original beauty, which has been spoken of: consisting in being's consent to being, or the union of minds or spiritual beings in a

---

[76] David Morgan, *Visual Piety: A History and Theory of Popular Religious Images* (Berkeley: University of California Press, 1998), 29, 77.

mutual propensity and affection of heart" (564). Edwards thus held to an idealist conception of the relationship between material and spiritual beauty, and indeed his hierarchy of beauty reflects a longstanding Christian-Platonic tradition. His conception owed much to both the Cambridge Platonists, with whose work Edwards was familiar, and the views of Shaftesbury; nor was it inconsistent with Puritan understandings of the beauty of heaven. Consequently, as Fiering points out, Edwards denied Hutcheson's view that "the beauty of true virtue" is "reducible somehow to ... ordinary aesthetic criteria or explicable by them."[77] Instead, aesthetic criteria are but earthly emblems of heavenly love.

One other conclusion that Edwards draws, if only in passing, from his idealist hierarchy of beauty hints at an idea that would later become widespread among nineteenth-century evangelicals, although in a significantly altered form. Edwards hypothesizes that one reason God has established a hierarchy of beauty intelligible to human beings is the sheer pleasure it brings God "to observe analogy in his works" (564). This hypothesis led Edwards to develop elsewhere elaborate typological readings of natural objects as "images of divine things."[78] But there is another reason that may help to explain God's purpose in establishing such a hierarchy:

> And here by the way, I would further observe, probably 'tis with regard to this image or resemblance which secondary beauty has of true spiritual beauty that God has so constituted nature that the presenting of this inferior beauty, especially in those kinds of it which have the greatest resemblance of the primary beauty, as the harmony of sounds, and the beauties of nature, have a tendency to assist those whose hearts are under the influence of a truly virtuous temper, to dispose them to the exercises of divine love, and enliven in them a sense of spiritual beauty. (565)

The perception of secondary beauty, it seems, potentially increases one's desire for the performance of true virtue. Natural beauty not only enlivens one's apprehension of divine beauty but also helps to move one morally. Although Edwards does mention the "harmony of sounds", his primary reference, following the well-established Puritan tradition, is to the beauties of nature. He does not, in short, develop a comprehensive theory of the moral potential of human art. In fact, aside from some illustrations drawn from music and architecture, the arts do not figure prominently in the treatise at all. But neither does Edwards exclude them, and in principle at least he gestures towards a conception of art as a vehicle of moral and social influence.[79]

---

[77] Fiering, *Edwards's Moral Thought*, 113; see also pp. 108-109.
[78] See Jonathan Edwards, *Typological Writings*, ed. Wallace E. Anderson and Mason I. Lowance, Jr. with David H. Watters (New Haven: Yale University Press, 1993).
[79] Alan Heimert argues that Edwards's conception of beauty was central to Calvinist visions of society in eighteenth-century America (*Religion and the American Mind: From the Great Awakening to the Revolution* [Cambridge: Harvard University Press, 1966], 95-158, esp. 102-03). However, cf. Erdt's criticism of Heimert's thesis (*Sense of the Heart*, 83-84).

Yet Edwards's version of this theory could apply only to "those whose hearts are under the influence of a truly virtuous temper." To glimpse secondary beauty as a reflection of primary beauty requires that one be capable of first perceiving primary beauty itself. "It is impossible," however, "that any one should truly *relish* this beauty, consisting in general benevolence, who has not that temper himself" (549). The perception of primary beauty, just like the exercise of true virtue, is available only to those who have been regenerated by divine grace. Human beings in their natural state can appreciate secondary beauty when they see it, but as Sang Hyun Lee observes, "even when man is experiencing the 'inferior' forms of resemblance, he is not grasping their true meaning, since he has no knowledge of the true ground of their beauty."[80] The mere appreciation of secondary beauty, moreover, has nothing to do with true virtue, or "truly virtuous taste." "Who will affirm that a disposition to approve of the harmony of good music, or the beauty of a square, or equilateral triangle is the same with true holiness, or a truly virtuous disposition of mind?" (573). If there existed any necessary correlation between virtue and the perception of secondary beauty, then one's "delight in the beauty of squares, and cubes, and regular polygons in the regularity of buildings, and the beautiful figures in a piece of embroidery, would increase in proportion to [one's] virtue; and would be raised to a great height in some eminently virtuous or holy men; but would be almost wholly lost in some others that are very vicious and lewd" (573). Secondary beauty is available to all, though only the regenerate can appreciate it fully. True beauty, however, is the sole province of the redeemed.

One can imagine how an Edwardsean philosopher might have developed aspects of Edwards's theory of beauty in the context of human art. It seems consistent with his premises, for example, to suggest that in relation to taste, one ought to think in terms of a two-tiered aesthetic. Both the regenerate and unregenerate percipient can grasp the formal beauty of art objects, but only the regenerate percipient possesses the capacity to "appreciate" this beauty as a reflection of God. The precise significance of art objects would therefore differ according to one's redemptive status. In addition, at least for the regenerate something like a theory of art's salutary moral influence seems warranted. In fact, the status of art might actually rise on this account since it would be seen as a means of disposing one "to the exercises of divine love." Whatever the possibilities of Edwards's reflections for a full-fledged theory of art, however, his influence on the later history of evangelical aesthetics proved minimal. One element of Edwards's aesthetics that did survive into the nineteenth century, at least in a limited way, was his emphasis on spiritual regeneration as a prerequisite for both full aesthetic contemplation and the moral benefits of aesthetic experience. One does occasionally meet with Victorian evangelicals who, in the spirit of Edwards and Henry Martyn, posited some connection between regeneration and taste. For the

---

[80] Sang Hyun Lee, "Mental Activity and the Perception of Beauty in Jonathan Edwards," *Harvard Theological Review* 69 (1976), 384.

most part, however, eighteenth and early-nineteenth-century evangelicals failed to develop Edwards's theological reflections on aesthetics in any systematic fashion.

Why evangelicals, particularly in America, failed to capitalize on Edwards's aesthetic insights is difficult to say. One reason may have been that the immediate stewards of the Edwardsean tradition (e.g., Samuel Hopkins and Joseph Bellamy) opted to stress the *ethical* dimensions of Edwards's thought over the metaphysical and aesthetic. This decision resulted partly from a felt need to moderate the "harsh" tenets of traditional Calvinism in response to the moral polemics of a growing legion of anti-Calvinist critics.[81] Nothing like Edwards's form of idealism would reappear in aesthetic contexts among evangelicals until the mid-nineteenth century, and then the direct source of such ideas was not the (theistic) idealism of Edwards but that of German philosophers, which, if it could sometimes be pressed into the service of Christianity, lacked the theological precision of Edwards's system. On occasion, later critics proposed something close to Edwards's idealism, but Edwards himself was rarely, if ever, cited as a precedent. This disproportionate attention to the moral aspect of the Edwardsean heritage even found expression in the decisions of Edwards's later editors. When the American Tract Society republished Edwards's *Religious Affections* in the nineteenth century, it eliminated those passages pertaining to "the disinterested contemplation of divine beauty."[82]

Ironically, this focus on the ethical aspects of Edwards's writings contributed to the eventual deconstruction of Edwards's entire system of morality. Whereas Edwards had attempted to co-opt Hutcheson's ethico-aesthetic scheme on behalf of Calvinist orthodoxy, this very scheme gradually came to displace for many evangelicals Edwards's theory of "true virtue." As Calvinist orthodoxy gave way, so too did Edwards's particular aesthetic insights, for Edwards's aesthetic thought was finally inseparable from his theology. As evangelicals embraced Scottish philosophy, the peculiar religio-aesthetic theorizing of Edwards no doubt came to seem like an exercise in obscurantism. Nevertheless, Edwards's methodical explorations of beauty are an important record of evangelicalism's growing attention to philosophical aesthetics. Although his specific contributions to the later history of evangelical aesthetics were scant, his receptivity to numerous developments in modern aesthetics helped establish a pattern of engagement for subsequent evangelical critics. Aesthetics was becoming a serious philosophical issue, and evangelicals would increasingly learn to value this mode of thinking.

---

[81] See Marsden, *Edwards*, 500 and *The Evangelical Mind and the New School Presbyterian Experience: A Case Study of Thought and Theology in Nineteenth-Century America* (New Haven: Yale University Press, 1970); Noll, *America's God*; Kuklick, *Churchmen*; and Conrad Cherry, *Nature and Religious Imagination: From Edwards to Bushnell* (Philadelphia: Fortress, 1980).
[82] Morgan, *Visual Piety*, 80-81, citing Joseph A. Conforti, *Jonathan Edwards, Religious Tradition, and American Culture* (Chapel Hill: University of North Carolina Press, 1995).

John Wesley's "Thoughts upon Taste"

Whereas Edwards addressed the age-old problem of beauty, the second great figurehead of Anglo-American evangelicalism, John Wesley, turned his attention to another pressing issue in Enlightenment aesthetics—taste. Wesley's "Thoughts upon Taste" first appeared in the December 1780 issue of the *Arminian Magazine*, and like Edwards's *True Virtue* it responded directly to recent developments in Scottish aesthetics. In contrast to Edwards's weighty treatise, the essay is relatively brief, and its periodical origins suggest it was intended for a wide audience. Unlike the creative speculations of Edwards, moreover, Wesley's treatment of taste is more derivative. Even so, "Thoughts upon Taste" demonstrates a broad awareness of contemporary theories, and it serves not only as further evidence of an emerging aesthetic discourse but also as an early example of the periodical criticism that would become a hallmark of the evangelical critical establishment of the nineteenth century.

Wesley's essay was occasioned by a reading of Alexander Gerard's famous *Essay on Taste*, which Wesley "entered upon ... with great expectation" in light of Gerard's established expertise on the subject.[83] Gerard's essay had originally appeared in 1759 after receiving a prize from the Edinburgh Society for the Encouragement of Arts, Sciences, Manufactures, and Agriculture. A second edition was published in 1764 and a third edition in 1780, which included a new section on "the standard of taste." Wesley's opinion of Gerard is mixed. On the one hand, he concedes that Gerard's treatise remains the best available on the subject. On the other hand, he expresses disappointment that Gerard's reflections are neither well organized nor "well digested," and "there are assertions almost in every chapter, which are exceedingly disputable" (465). Gerard's essay has been called "the most elaborate investigation of the faculty of taste during the eighteenth century,"[84] and it may have been this very elaborateness which frustrated Wesley. His biggest complaint, in fact, is that Gerard has failed to offer any "just definition of the subject" (465). It is possible for a reader to walk away from the text, Wesley claims, without having any clear answer to the question, "What is taste?" (466). Wesley's critique, while debatable, is characteristic of his usual Lockean attitude toward linguistic precision.

The bulk of the essay consists of Wesley's attempt to clarify the nature of taste, catalogue its various manifestations, and offer suggestions for its improvement. In doing so, he retraces ground covered by other eighteenth-century philosophers of taste, albeit in a highly simplified form. He does not, for example, explore the nature of beauty, as Hutcheson and Gerard had done, and although he briefly distinguishes taste from both "imagination" and "judgment," he does not attempt a detailed examination of the relationship between taste and other faculties. In general, his essay takes its bearings from the Hutchesonian tradition,

---

[83] John Wesley, "Thoughts upon Taste," *Works* 13:465. Subsequent references appear parenthetically in the text.
[84] Hipple, *Beautiful*, 67.

though Addison turns out to be his most frequent reference point. Following Hutcheson, who had expanded Locke's sensory apparatus beyond the merely physical to include the internal moral and aesthetic "senses," Wesley defines taste as "a faculty of the mind, analogous to the [physical] sense of taste." It is "that internal sense which relishes and distinguishes its proper object." In keeping with other eighteenth-century analyses, Wesley actually posits the existence of several tastes, or rather "species of taste." If taste is directed to a "proper object" of pleasure and there are a variety of pleasing objects in the world, then there must be different types of taste corresponding to these objects: "And as various as those objects are, so various are the species of taste" (466). In practice, Wesley plays somewhat freely with the term "object". At times, he uses "object" to refer to *specific* objects ("metaphysics" or "flowers, meadows, fields, or woods"). Throughout much of the essay, however, he writes not about particular objects but about classes of objects. Thus he observes (as both Hutcheson and Edwards had done) that some people have a taste for "objects of the understanding," such as mathematical formulae: "when we say, a man has a taste for the mathematics, we mean by that expression, not only that he is capable of understanding them, but that he takes pleasure therein" (467). Here, though, "object" refers not to a particular mathematical formula like the Pythagorean Theorem but to a certain *type* of object.

Wesley continues this classification by types. In addition to objects of the understanding, Wesley isolates two other classes of objects, each of which has its corresponding species of taste or "internal sense." The second species of taste is an aesthetic one, or "that which relates to the objects that gratify the imagination" (467). At this point, he relies heavily on the "ingenious thoughts of Mr. Addison," particularly his "Essay on the Pleasures of the Imagination" (466). Addison had suggested that the imagination takes pleasure in three sorts of objects—the grand, the novel, and the beautiful—and Wesley follows this scheme precisely: "Thus we are accustomed to say, a man has a taste for grandeur, for novelty, or for beauty; meaning thereby, that he takes pleasure in grand, in new, or in beautiful objects, whether they are such by nature or by art." In the context of Wesley's reading of Gerard, however, his reliance on Addison represents a reversion of sorts, for Gerard had posited a total of seven internal "senses." The first three corresponded to the classes of objects suggested by Addison, but Gerard had also assigned senses to imitation, harmony, ridicule, and virtue.[85] Wesley, therefore, prefers Addison's simpler taxonomy to Gerard's expanded one. Even so, within Wesley's Addisonian system it turns out "there is an unbounded variety ... some having a taste for grandeur, some for beauty. Some again, have a taste for one kind of beauty; and others for another. Some have a taste for the beauties of nature; others for those of art. The former for flowers, meadows, fields, or woods; the latter for painting or poetry" (467). Wesley's approach suggests that "taste"

---

[85] However, Addison's categorization persisted throughout the eighteenth century (Hipple, *Beautiful*, 16).

is a collective term comprising multiple sub-tastes, each with its own proper object. In thus describing taste, however, he was once again following the lead of his contemporaries. Reid, for example, had spoken of "a prodigious variety of different tastes," both external and internal, in his 1774 *Lectures on the Fine Arts*.[86] Gerard had also employed the word "taste" rather flexibly, using it to refer to both the internal senses individually, as well as to their coordinate action: "Any *one* of the internal senses, existing in vigour and perfection, forms a particular species of taste ... but *all* of them must at once be vigorous, in order to constitute taste in its just extent."[87] Wesley's many "species of taste" are therefore theoretically resolvable into the single "faculty" of taste, although he does nothing to clarify the details of this resolution.

Like Edwards and the Hutchesonians, Wesley also accepts the existence of a moral sense, or a taste "whereby we relish the happiness of our fellow-creatures, even without any reflection on our own interest, without any reference to ourselves." Interestingly, however, he makes little effort to qualify this benevolism in light of the doctrines of grace or original sin. Unlike Edwards, who took great pains to subordinate Hutcheson's theory of the moral and aesthetic senses to his own system of divine grace, the most Wesley will venture on this score is that "there is something still in the human mind, in many, if not in all, (whether by nature, or from a higher principle,) which interests us in the welfare" of others (467). One should not, perhaps, make too much of this. For one thing, Wesleyan Arminianism, as Calvinist critics frequently pointed out, left greater room for natural human ability; hence Wesley's reluctance to situate the moral sense definitively in the realm of grace or nature is not unexpected. Wesley had, moreover, earlier criticized Hutcheson along more Edwardsean lines.[88] Viewed in the context of an emerging evangelical aesthetic discourse, Wesley's most important declaration regarding the moral sense may have been his proclamation of its superiority to the aesthetic sense: "Is not this taste of infinitely more value, than a taste for any or all the pleasures of the imagination?" (467). As for Edwards and many others in the eighteenth century, morality still trumped the aesthetic: art "for its own sake" would never have crossed the minds of Enlightenment philosophers, evangelical or otherwise.

---

[86] Thomas Reid, *Thomas Reid's Lectures on the Fine Arts* (The Hague: Martinus Nijhoff, 1973), 36. Reid's lectures remained in manuscript form until 1973. Wesley, therefore, would not have known Reid's lectures directly, but they represent a common eighteenth-century view of taste.

[87] Alexander Gerard, *An Essay on Taste. To Which Is Now Added Part Fourth, of the Standard of Taste; with Observations Concerning the Imitative Nature of Poetry* (Edinburgh, 1780), 73 (2.1). On Gerard, see Hipple, *Beautiful*, 67-82 and George Dickie, *The Century of Taste: The Philosophical Odyssey of Taste in the Eighteenth Century* (New York: Oxford University Press, 1996), 29-54.

[88] See Wesley, Journal entry for Thursday, 17 Dec. 1772, *Works* 3:485-86; Sermon CV, "On Conscience," *Works* 7:186-94, esp. 188-89.

Finally, Wesley's conception of taste, despite its inherent multiplicity, was ultimately, like Gerard's, an objective one.[89] He was apparently untroubled by the problem of discrepant tastes which so exercised Hume. Each species of taste relishes what is "truly excellent in its kind" (468), and for this reason tastes can be improved. The remainder of the essay is thus taken up with Wesley's advice for the rectification of taste, and indeed the last portion shifts to an almost exclusive focus on aesthetic taste. Much of this advice is typical eighteenth-century fare and is of little consequence here. One passage, however, deserves comment. In discussing what he terms a "correct" or "fine taste"—one in which an individual "relishes whatever, either in the works of nature or of art, is truly excellent in its kind" (468)—Wesley asserts that Addison's definition requires revision. Addison had restricted the faculty of fine taste to the beauties of writing, but Wesley argues that this concept should be expanded to include anything beautiful in either nature or art. He concludes: "Such a taste as this is much to be desired, and that on many accounts. It greatly increases those pleasures of life, which are not only innocent, but useful. It qualifies us to be of far greater service to our fellow-creatures" (468-69). For Wesley, aesthetic pleasure has become a force for good; it now has an important socio-moral dimension. Unlike many Puritans, who tended to view aesthetic pleasure as an ancillary concern or as a kind of bonus above and beyond whatever the intellectual and rational benefits derivable from art, Wesley attributes social significance to pleasure itself. This idea was not, of course, unique to Wesley, and it was by 1780 fairly widespread. Kames, for example, had suggested as much in his *Elements of Criticism*. Edwards, as noted above, had also proposed something along these lines, although he carefully restricted its application to those who, through enabling grace, are capable of grasping primary beauty. Wesley, however, makes little attempt to limit this idea to the regenerate. Art's socio-moral powers are potentially available to all, regardless of one's state of grace. Although Wesley's lack of qualification may have been a casual omission, the idea of aesthetic pleasure as a means of cultivating morality apart from grace would eventually play a major part in nineteenth-century evangelical aesthetic thought.

Mental Philosophy and Aesthetic Conservatism: Hannah More's "Preface to the Tragedies"

The writings of Edwards and Wesley point to the gradual formation of an evangelical philosophical aesthetics. At times, however, the mental philosophy of the Enlightenment could also reinforce timeworn Puritan suspicions. As Terence Martin has argued, Scottish common sense philosophy initially served to aggravate historic anxieties concerning the imagination—a phenomenon that contributed to the early-nineteenth-century distrust of fiction.[90] In a similar vein, Hannah More's "Preface to the Tragedies" (1801) draws upon empiricist theories of

---

[89] See Hipple, *Beautiful*, 69 and Dickie, *Century of Taste*, 47.
[90] See Martin, *Instructed Vision*, 57-103.

mind to shore up traditional Puritan arguments against the theater, revealing how ideas that were elsewhere promoting evangelical engagement with aesthetics could likewise lend new weight to old antipathies.

The occasion of More's Preface was her controversial decision to include in an edition of her collected works some tragic dramas composed in the late 1770s, prior to her conversion to Christianity. On the one hand, More wishes to explain to readers familiar with her later censures of the stage why she has chosen to reprint such pieces. To suppress them, she argues, would have been perceived as "disingenuous."[91] On the other hand, More also seizes the opportunity to express the principled disapproval that represents her mature position. She is not, however, simply interested in highlighting the dangers inherent in "bad" plays, which she believes are already obvious to virtuous persons; instead, she undertakes "the unpopular task of animadverting on the dangerous effects of those which come under the description of good plays; for from those chiefly arises the danger (if danger there be), to good people" (504). More, in short, wants to demonstrate why even the good plays are bad. To support this unenviable thesis, she draws on a range of arguments, some of which reiterate well-established critiques of the theater any Puritan would have recognized. What may seem good to the non-Christian, for example, may betray its true darkness to the redeemed (506). Christian viewers who insist on their exemption from the negative effects of the stage, or who argue that to the pure all things are pure, must also recall their obligation to weaker brothers and sisters not to be a "stumbling-block" (510)—an argument made all the more poignant by More's suggestion that one's observation of audience response (laughter, applause, etc.) impacts how one processes action onstage (506). Tragedy, moreover, is a dubious genre in that it takes as its central principle the pagan ethic of "honour" rather than Christian virtues (504).

Yet the weight of More's case rests on her psycho-aesthetic argument for the nefarious effects of witnessing a dramatic performance. Despite her passing assertion that tragedy is predicated on pagan morality, the danger of the stage lies for More almost wholly in its status as sensory spectacle. In fact, she allows that the private reading of plays can be beneficial for readers; *watching* a play, however, involves serious risks: "I think, then, that there is a substantial difference between seeing and reading a dramatic composition; and that the objections which lie so strongly against the one, are not, at least in the same degree, applicable to the other." But why does material otherwise deemed safe when consumed in private present a danger when viewed on stage? More's reply concerns the immediacy of the sensations (especially visual ones) experienced during a performance. Dramatic poetry "may be read with safety, because it can there be read with soberness. The most animated speeches subside into comparative tameness, and ... produce no ruffle of the passions, no agitation of the senses, but

---

[91] Hannah More, "Preface to the Tragedies," *The Works of Hannah More* (New York: Harper, 1852), 1:502. Subsequent references appear parenthetically in the text.

merely afford a pleasant, and, it may be, a not unsalutary exercise to the imagination" (508). Whereas reading necessitates reflection and thus employs the reason, dramatic performances circumvent the reason and affect the senses directly, dazzling and overwhelming them. The difficulty with dramatic spectacles is their non-rational appeal to the passions, for they threaten to efface the clear ideas expressed in propositional form that served as the gold standard for many eighteenth-century thinkers.[92] Contrasting one's experience of listening to a sermon with viewing a play, More notes the differences in their presentations. Whereas the Sunday sermon offers "humbling propositions," it is theater's purpose "not only to preach, but to personify doctrines":

> Doctrines, not simply expressed, as those of the Sunday are, in the naked form of axioms, principles, and precepts, but realized, embodied, made alive, furnished with organs, clothed, decorated, brought into lively discourse, into interesting action; enforced with all the energy of passion, adorned with all the graces of language, and exhibited with every aid of emphatical delivery, every attraction of appropriate gesture.... Is not the competition too unequal? (508)

Such criticisms, of course, are consistent with earlier Puritan attacks on the stage. The Christian-Platonic tradition, moreover, had always viewed sensory indulgence with marked suspicion. It is interesting in this light to note the decision by the editor of the first American edition of More's collected works to append to her Preface the conclusion of Jeremy Collier's "Short View of the Immorality and Profaneness of the English Stage" (1699). In the editor's opinion, it seems, More's critique carries on a noble tradition of anti-theatrical sentiments, and in fact nothing in Collier's conclusion is at odds with the thrust of More's argument. On one level, then, More's disapprobation is hardly shocking, and there is nothing particularly novel in her intentions.

Yet More's case is not merely a rehashing of shopworn arguments; rather, it is deeply informed by its Enlightenment context. Her contradistinction, for example, between the sermon, which consists of "axioms, principles, and precepts," and the "semblance of real action" encountered in a stage production leading to "a kind of enchantment" (508), draws upon the sort of science-art/intellect-emotion dichotomy popularized by Bacon and Locke, among others. The effects of dramatic performances, according to More, are akin to Locke's conception of the effects of wit, in which "beauty appears at first sight, and there is required no labour of thought to examine what truth or reason there is in it" (2.11.2). As did Locke, More isolates the aesthetic, implicitly acknowledging its singular affec-

---

[92] See also More's *Strictures on the Modern System of Female Education*, in which More singles out the "want of precise signification of ... words" as "the cause of very obscure and uncertain notions" when reasoning about moral matters (*Works* 1:349). Tellingly, More quotes Locke to support her argument.

tive power, only to locate its moral threat precisely in this power. This paradoxical dynamic can be traced as far back as Plato, but its appearance in the Preface is the result of eighteenth-century developments.

In the same way, More's concern for the sensational dimension of dramatic productions acquires much of its urgency from its subscription to an empiricist philosophy of mind. Locke, as is well known, had argued in the *Essay* that all knowledge is originally a product of experience. Simple ideas, which serve as the basis for all our more complex ideas, are those that the mind arrives at involuntarily via sensation, reflection, or both. Once received, moreover, simple ideas cannot be purged: "These *simple ideas*, when offered to the mind, *the understanding* can no more refuse to have, nor alter when they are imprinted, nor blot them out and make new ones itself, than a mirror can refuse, alter, or obliterate the images or *ideas* which the objects set before it do therein produce" (2.1.25). This empiricist model, in which the mind passively acquires impressions, led in turn to the striking conclusion that "the personality is formed by its sensations,"[93] and although Locke's theory of the mind's composition of complex ideas may have preserved some room for agency, identity was essentially a product of sensory experience. This notion was reinforced by another of Locke's famous postulates, the "association of ideas." Some ideas, Locke believed, "have a natural correspondence and connexion with one another"; others, however, owe their connections to chance or custom. One purpose of education is to sever these habitual associations, for they have "such an influence and [are] of so great force to set us awry in our actions as well moral as natural, passions, reasonings, and notions themselves, that perhaps there is not any one thing that deserves more to be looked after" (2.33.5, 9).

It is not difficult to see how such a theory could exacerbate traditional Christian misgivings about the senses. One could, in effect, be carried off to hell by one's perceptions and associations. Since the mind receives sensory impressions that, once there, cannot be eliminated by any natural act, the only solution is to avoid such impressions altogether. More's allegiance to this empiricist model and her fears regarding its negative consequences for those who frequent the playhouse are clear:

> We cannot be too often reminded, that we are, to an inconceivable degree, the creatures of habit. Our tempers are not principally governed, nor our characters formed, by single marked actions; nor is the colour of our lives principally determined by prominent, detached circumstances; but the character is gradually molded by a series of seemingly insignificant but constantly recurring practices, which, incorporated into our habits, become part of ourselves.

---

[93] Ernest Lee Tuveson, *Imagination as a Means of Grace: Locke and the Aesthetics of Romanticism* (Berkeley: University of California Press, 1960), 76.

Such habits can "silently eat out the very heart and life of vigorous virtue" (505). More thus expresses a traditional Christian concern in the framework of Enlightenment empiricism. Even as her "animadversions" perpetuate a legacy of Puritan castigation and critique, they partake in many of the debates surrounding Enlightenment epistemology and aesthetics. More's Preface demonstrates how the effects of evangelicalism's contact with the Enlightenment were not always immediate, nor especially revolutionary. Even aesthetic "developments" could be put to conservative uses.

Towards the Evangelical Romanticism of the Nineteenth Century

As More's Preface confirms, evangelical aesthetic discourse developed slowly throughout the eighteenth century. Essays like Wesley's "Thoughts upon Taste" were relatively scarce, as were statements like Henry Martyn's about the psycho-aesthetic effects of conversion. Rarer still were explicitly theological reflections on aesthetics of the Edwardsean kind. Nevertheless, Enlightenment mental philosophy, while occasionally bolstering old prejudices, was instrumental in dislodging evangelicals from the strictures of the Puritan tradition and leading them toward the mature aesthetic discourse of the mid-to-late nineteenth century. The *Arminian Magazine*'s decision, for example, to publish a poem by Phillis Wheatley in 1784 (the year of Wheatley's death) reflected not only the social conscience of Wesley but also the evangelical interest in Enlightenment aesthetics. Entitled "On Imagination," this paean to the creative faculty, which participated in a popular tradition of poetic reflections on the imagination dating back to Mark Akenside, would have been unthinkable to a Puritan writer only a century before:

> Thy various works, imperial Queen, we see,
> How bright their forms! how deckèd with pomp by thee!
> Thy wondèrous acts in beautèous order stand,
> And all attest how potent is thy hand.
>
> Imagination! who can sing thy force?
> Or who describe the swiftness of thy course?
> Soaring through the air to find the bright abode,
> Thè empyrèal palace of the thundèring God.
> ....
> Such is thy powèr, nor are thine orders vain,
> O thou leader of the mental train:
> In full perfection all thy works are wrought,
> And thine the sceptre o'er the realms of thought.[94]

---

[94] [Phillis Wheatley], "On Imagination," *AM* 7 (Dec. 1784): 672-73.

"Leader of the mental train" typifies the empiricist psychology of the Enlightenment, but such a poem, with its exuberant praise of the imagination as an "imperial Queen" winging her way to "Thè empyrèal palace of the thundèring God," also offers a foretaste of the romantic bent of later evangelical criticism. The *Arminian Magazine*'s backing of Wheatley's lofty view of the imagination marks the early stages of a transition in evangelical thinking about the arts.

This transition is further evident in a brief piece of criticism issued by a British Baptist minister and poet the following year. Daniel Turner's *Devotional Poetry Vindicated ... To Which Is Added a Short Essay On Genius* stands at the head of a long line of critical retorts to Samuel Johnson's infamous declaration concerning the impossibility of good devotional poetry, and it provides yet another example of evangelicals in dialogue with the leading ideas of the time. The *Short Essay on Genius*, like Wesley's "Thoughts upon Taste," takes up a favorite Enlightenment topic, and Turner displays a wide knowledge of seventeenth- and eighteenth-century French criticism and poetry, including Boileau and Racine. The essay's real significance, however, lies in its incipient romanticism and its high claims for poetry. Turner's proto-romanticism reveals itself most clearly in the conviction that true poetry is a matter of sincere feeling rather than simple ornament or fanciful fiction. In contrast to Johnson's assertion that "The Essence of Poetry is Invention," which in Johnson's view renders it unsuitable for revealed Truth, Turner contends that "the Essence of Poetry lies rather in the Grandeur and Sublimity of the Sentiment, the Boldness and Justness of the Metaphors and Figures, and the harmonious Turn of the Expression."[95] Christianity, he maintains, supplies human beings with the grandest conceivable ideas, making it the greatest possible subject for poetry. Turner, however, takes this insight one step further. In an argument that anticipates Wordsworth's Preface to *Lyrical Ballads*, he theorizes that poetic language is the spontaneous product of passion: "Besides, there is a certain kind of Enthusiasm, or extraordinary Elevation of Sentiment, that naturally fires the Mind, fills it with bold Metaphors, and lively Epithets, and leads it into a peculiarly harmonious Arrangement of the Forms of Expression...." (10). Turner here anticipates the expressivist theories that would predominate among evangelical critics beginning in the 1820s and 1830s.

His most vital point, however, is that the value of poetry extends beyond mere amusement. After establishing, contra Johnson, a theoretical basis for good devotional poetry, Turner highlights its usefulness in furthering piety. He offers the conventional qualification that poetry cannot be "the *Mother* of Devotion," but it can serve as "a very useful *Handmaid* to it" (28). Poetry "has ever been a principal instrument in the Hand of the divine Providence, of cherishing and supporting the Spirit of Piety and the Interest of Religion and Virtue among Mankind"

---

[95] Daniel Turner, *Devotional Poetry Vindicated, in Some Occasional Remarks on the Late Dr. Samuel Johnson's Animadversions Upon That Subject in His Life of Waller, To Which Is Added a Short Essay on Genius* (Oxford: Printed for the Author, 1785), 17. Subsequent references appear parenthetically in the text.

(29). If so, then poetry has a high calling that extends beyond its uses as a common leisure activity, and Turner draws precisely this conclusion: "Nor is it reasonable to suppose, that an Endowment of such high Original, and so capable of serving the Interest of Religion, and the immortal Happiness of Mankind, should be employed ONLY in the Business of even innocent Amusement." But Turner does not stop here. He advances the daring claim that poetry "affords its Possessor the most refreshing Prælibations of the Pleasures of the upper and better world" (32). Turner, like Edwards, restricts these adumbrations of heavenly pleasure to those who have received grace through Christ, but he nonetheless accords poetry a stature few activities could equal.

Turner's treatise offers another glimpse of the direction that evangelical aesthetics would take in the nineteenth century. On the one hand, *Devotional Poetry Vindicated* draws liberally on the aesthetics of the Scottish Enlightenment. Turner attributes his understanding of poetry to the writings of Hugh Blair, Chair of Rhetoric and Belles Lettres at the University of Edinburgh (vii). On the other hand, Turner's proto-romantic apology for devotional poetry, like Wheatley's praise of the imagination, highlights the transition from Enlightenment to romantic aesthetics. It would be some time before evangelical aesthetics was fully romanticized, but evangelicals nevertheless followed the lead of Anglo-American culture at large. Even more importantly, Turner's religious argument for the high status of poetry signaled the beginning of the end for the customary view of art as little more than amusement, thereby paving the way for evangelicals' acceptance of the more audacious (and much less orthodox) claims of romantic poets and critics.

By the turn of the century, as Doreen Rosman has argued, evangelicals had finally begun to shed the vestiges of Puritan austerity and adopt a favorable, albeit cautious, stance towards the arts. The first three decades of the nineteenth century still proved slow going for some evangelical critics. Although "the traditional charge of philistinism" is not quite applicable, notes Rosman, "even ... the most cultured evangelicals" found it difficult "to reconcile their enjoyment of the arts with their faith."[96] Still, William Wilberforce could confidently assert in 1797 that "The Christian relaxes in the temperate use of all the gifts of Providence. Imagination, and taste, and genius, and the beauties of creation, and the works of art, lie open to him."[97] That many evangelicals were beginning to agree with him may be seen in the growing number of essays and reviews devoted to philosophical criticism published in evangelical periodicals. The first decade of the nineteenth century saw the founding of the British *Eclectic Review*, one of the earliest evangelical periodicals to feature regular discussions of aesthetic topics. In the 1810s, articles treating aesthetics appeared with increasing frequency

---

[96] Rosman, *Evangelicals and Culture*, 246.
[97] William Wilberforce, *A Practical View of Christianity*, ed. Kevin Charles Belmonte (Peabody: Hendrickson Publishers, 1996), 237.

in other publications as well. In 1812, the *Christian Observer*, the famous mouthpiece of the Clapham Sect, reviewed two tomes of Scottish aesthetics, Archibald Alison's *Essays on the Nature and Principles of Taste* (reissued in 1811) and Dugald Stewart's *Philosophical Essays*, which included lengthy sections on beauty and sublimity. The same decade also witnessed the publication of a protracted debate on the merits of fiction and an inquiry into "Sacred Poetry."[98] By the 1820s, it was not uncommon to meet with articles on art and aesthetics in both British and American evangelical periodicals.

After the 1830s, the aesthetic sparks generated by evangelicalism's engagement with the Enlightenment finally burst into flame. To some extent, the flourishing of evangelical aesthetics after the 1830s was part of a broader cultural shift as evangelicals transitioned from a focus on theology and evangelism to a more comprehensive vision of society. As Mark A. Noll observes of American evangelicals, "by the 1830s ... a new era had begun. While the single-minded pietism that fueled early evangelical mobilization never passed away, it was increasingly joined by other concerns. The business of organizing Christian civilization took its place alongside the business of saving souls."[99] British evangelicals, meanwhile, shared this investment in the business of organizing Christian civilization, a main facet of which was the propagation of an aesthetic culture underwritten by the theoretical exploration of art.[100] Here, at least, one element of the Puritan tradition survived intact: the desire to construct a nation that was thoroughly Protestant. For the Puritans, art had occupied no significant place in this vision, although its inclusion had always been a hypothetical possibility. Now, art and aesthetics were increasingly seen as crucial elements in this vision. In addition, this interest in Christian civilization coincided with a growing desire for "respectability" among denominations such as the Baptists and Methodists, which had traditionally occupied positions of "dissent."[101] An increased interest in high aesthetic culture was one manifestation of this newfound longing for respectability.

Most importantly, though, it was during the 1830s that evangelicalism felt at last the full effects of the romantic movement.[102] Romanticism injected a new

---

[98] "Alison's Theory of Taste," *CO* 11 (Feb. 1812): 91-105; Review of *Philosophical Essays*, by Dugald Stewart, *CO* 11 (Oct. 1812): 654-75; "On the Influence of the Literature of Fiction," *CO* 16 (June 1817): 370-74; Excubitor, "On the Influence of the Literature of Fiction," *CO* 16 (July 1817): 425-29; Cereticus, "On Sacred Poetry," *CO* 16 (Oct. 1817): 644-50.

[99] Noll, *America's God*, 183.

[100] See Ian Bradley, *The Call to Seriousness: The Evangelical Impact on the Victorians* (London: Jonathan Cape, 1976). Bradley's account of evangelicalism's influence on art culture tends to overemphasize evangelicalism's role as an agent of censure (see pp. 37 and 98).

[101] See Hatch, *Democratization*, 91.

[102] See Bebbington, *Evangelicalism*, 103 and "Evangelicalism in Modern Britain and America: A Comparison," *Amazing Grace: Evangelicalism in Australia, Britain, Canada, and the United States*, ed. George A. Rawlyk and Mark A. Noll (Montreal: McGill-

energy and confidence into the mature aesthetic discourse of evangelical writers and editors. Guided by the romantics, evangelical critics also turned with new self-awareness against their Puritan forefathers, and if they did not always denounce the Puritans en masse, they were quite content to throw the Puritan aesthetic tradition—or their projections of it—under the bus in order to buttress their views of art. It is to some of the main features of this anti-Puritan evangelical romanticism that we now turn.

Queen's University Press, 1994), 189-91. The dating of my account parallels Harris and Charvat's discussions of wider American culture.

CHAPTER 2

Expressing the Ideal: Changing Conceptions of Art and Imagination

Near the conclusion of an 1867 review of E.S. Dallas's *The Gay Science*, J.H. Rigg, a British Methodist who would later edit the *London Quarterly Review*,[1] finally lost patience with what he regarded as Dallas's predilection for the vague and mystical. According to Dallas, the glory of art is its "Secrecy" since, as he had contended, the "field of art is the unknown and unknowable." In Rigg's view, however, Dallas's acquiescence to the impenetrable mystery of art left much to be desired:

> Why has not Mr. Dallas long before this stage of his book come away from the haze of generalities, and defined with something like precision what the sphere of art includes? To say that it is the sphere of pleasure is but flourishing an unknown quantity before our eyes. What have poetry and the arts in common? Why may they be classed together? What are their common objects? What is the region which they occupy in common?[2]

Although Rigg's frustration sprang from the peculiar vagaries of Dallas, his questions represent a perennial difficulty in modern aesthetics, for any attempt to articulate a coherent philosophy of art must confront a basic problem: how to define *Art*. Or, as James Rogers bluntly framed it in the opening line of another article in the *London Quarterly Review*: "What is Art?"[3]

Grand inquiries like these may sound suspiciously essentialist to contemporary ears,[4] but countless nineteenth-century writers, both evangelical and non-evangelical, assumed that questions regarding the foundational nature of art

---

[1] Rigg helped found the *Review* as well, which commenced publication in 1853 (though he would not edit it until the 1880s). See Barbara J. Dunlap, "The London Quarterly and Holborn Review," *British Literary Magazines: The Victorian and Edwardian Age, 1837-1913*, ed. Alvin Sullivan (Westport: Greenwood, 1984), 203-209.
[2] J.H. Rigg, Review of *Gay Science*, by E.S. Dallas, *LQR* 28 (Apr. 1867), 163.
[3] James Rogers, "The Science and Poetry of Art," *LQR* 4 (July 1855), 403. The article was in fact published anonymously. In attributing it to Rogers, I am following *The Wellesley Index to Victorian Periodicals, 1824-1900*, vol. 4, ed. Walter E. Houghton et al. (Toronto: University of Toronto Press, 1987), 383, 699.
[4] On the difficulty of defining art, see Dabney Townsend, *An Introduction to Aesthetics* (Malden: Blackwell, 1997), 39-52.

might reasonably admit of an answer. Victorian writers were not ignorant of the difficulties associated with defining "Art," nor did they approach the matter blithely. Sidney Dyer, writing in the *Baptist Quarterly* in 1867, characterized the efforts of critics to pinpoint the quiddity of poetry as Babel redivivus: "That there is such a thing as poetry, no one will for a moment question. We see it, we hear it, we feel it ... but when we ask the critic what it is, a new confusion of tongues takes place, as the various schools give their conflicting responses."[5] Almost without exception, however, these same writers did not hesitate to venture their own definitions of art or poetry or painting, and even those authors who gingerly avoided raising the issue in explicit terms routinely formulated more or less distinct conceptions of art amid other speculations or amid the demands of practical criticism. Articles and reviews abounded with such phrases as "Art is ...," "Poetry is ...," or "Music is...."

For evangelicals after the 1830s, art was increasingly serious business. Although writers like Daniel Turner had advanced high claims for the value of art in the 1780s, the dominant position for many evangelicals remained one of casual acceptance. As Rosman explains, "Art might be a desirable embellishment of society but it was no more than an embellishment ... a toy to be contrasted with true religious treasure."[6] Art could serve as a comparatively innocent source of relaxation or amusement, but aside from its diversionary and ornamental uses, it had little to do with the urgencies of life or pressing matters of eternal concern. This view contrasts sharply with the view later advocated by many evangelical writers at mid-century. Consider, for example, the rhapsodic conclusion to Rogers's "The Science and Poetry of Art," published in 1855:

> for Art is not, nor ought to be regarded as, the frivolous embellishment of an idle and voluptuous existence, but the fine inspiration of a thoroughly accomplished understanding,—an understanding not severed from the heart, and commencing only with the rigid formalities and iron mechanisms of worldly science, "purchasing knowledge by the loss of power;" but fed, and warmed, and brightened, and endued with genial sagacity by the living soul that flows through and impregnates its whole substance and activity. As long as there are faculties in man which find their aliment and satisfaction in nothing else than ideal semblances of the good, the true, and the beautiful, so long will Art remain a profound necessity of human nature....[7]

There is an unmistakable gravitas in this passage that would likely have surprised an earlier generation of evangelicals conditioned to view art with either levity or indifference, if not downright hostility. No longer is art a "frivolous embellishment"; it has become, as Rogers solemnly declares, "a profound necessity of human nature." Playful adornment has given way to "fine inspiration" and a "living soul," and art seems somehow to have descended from on high. Of course, such

---

[5] Sidney Dyer, "Literary Criticism," *BQ* (1 July 1867), 318.
[6] Doreen M. Rosman, *Evangelicals and Culture* (London: Croom Helm, 1984), 161-62.
[7] Rogers, "Science and Poetry," 424-25.

passages represent one end of the evangelical spectrum of opinion concerning art. Not all evangelicals abandoned older views of art, nor were all suspicions that art was but fleeting and temporal allayed. Yet the fact that this kind of passage existed at all in the pages of a periodical like the *London Quarterly Review* points to a critical shift in evangelical conceptions of art: they were beginning to reflect the romantic suppositions of the age. By the 1850s, a number of evangelical critics were avowed Coleridgeans (in aesthetics if not necessarily theology) who asked and answered questions about the essence of art within a conceptual framework inherited from Anglo-American romantics and from moderate forms of German idealism. Even those evangelicals who proved unwilling to follow Coleridge into the ethereal regions of Teutonic speculation accepted as normative other aesthetic doctrines derived from romantic critics—most prominently, the notion of art as self-expression. By mid-century, evangelicals had discovered in the question What is art? both new significance and new answers.

Art as a Function of Mind: Evangelical Expressivism

M.H. Abrams has summed up the aesthetic orientation of romanticism as one in which theorists "pose and answer aesthetic questions in terms of the relation of art to the artist, rather than to external nature, or to the audience, or to the internal requirements of the work itself."[8] Within this genetic paradigm, art is a function of the unique consciousness of the artist; whatever else it might be, it is invariably subjective. "Poetry is the spontaneous overflow of powerful feelings," wrote Wordsworth in his oft-quoted statement from the Preface to *Lyrical Ballads*.[9] By the middle-third of the nineteenth century, many evangelical critics were operating squarely within this framework. In 1845, for example, an author reviewing Leigh Hunt's *Imagination and Fancy* for the *British Quarterly Review* approved of Hunt's "calling poetry 'the utterance of a passion'" since "it refers us back at once to the poet's mind."[10] Rogers argued in a similar vein concerning art in general: "Thus we are thrown back upon the human mind, its powers and laws, both of perception and activity, for the origin of Art."[11] The *Biblical Repertory and Princeton Review* also acknowledged the subjective nature of art. Although beauty is "an objective quality in nature," it is subject to alteration by the mind, a process that reaches its culmination in art: "We have already stated how the apprehension of the objective beauty of nature is modified, when it comes to be blended with the thoughts and feelings of the mind itself. Now it is obvious that this subjective element must be more predominant in that class of beauties which

---

[8] M.H. Abrams, *The Mirror and the Lamp: Romantic Theory and Critical Tradition* (London: Oxford University Press, 1953), 3.
[9] William Wordsworth, "Preface to *Lyrical Ballads*," *Wordsworth's Literary Criticism*, ed. Nowell C. Smith (Bristol: Bristol Classical, 1980), 15.
[10] "Leigh Hunt's *Imagination and Fancy*," *BrQR* 1 (May 1845), 571, 572.
[11] Rogers, "Science and Poetry," 404.

it is the object of poetry, and of art generally, to reproduce."[12] This acceptance of the premise that aesthetic problems are best handled in the context of mental powers and laws affected evangelical understandings of the nature of art in significant ways.

To begin with, evangelicals gradually came to embrace the romantic doctrine of art, and especially poetry, as self-expression. (Preliminary steps in this direction, one may recall, had been taken by Turner in 1785). "In treating of the imitative arts," noted the Presbyterian *Christian Advocate* in 1823, "poetry lays claim to a high place. It may be called the melody of the mind."[13] This particular writer attempted to navigate between a neoclassical conception of art as imitation and a contemporary romantic view of art as an outgrowth of the poet's psyche. Poetry could still be classified primarily as imitation, but imitation had itself commenced an inward turn. By the 1830s, the notion of art and poetry as self-expression was appearing with greater frequency in evangelical treatises and reviews. In his *Lectures on General Literature, Poetry &c.* delivered in 1830 and 1831, James Montgomery defined poetry as "the shorthand of thought," arguing that "Language ... is a dead letter till the spirit within the poet himself breathes through it, gives it voice, and makes it audible to the very mind." Language, Montgomery continued, must spring "from a full mind."[14] For a writer in the *Eclectic Review*, the best poetry arises "when hand, and head, and heart are all free to exercise spontaneous thought, and give utterance to unfettered feeling."[15] Evangelicals were proving quite receptive to the introspective focus of romantic aesthetics—a point that did not escape the notice of one contemporary observer. A "great change" has "taken place in modern poetry," wrote an author in the *Quarterly Christian Spectator*, a change "which [has] turned the eye of the poet from external objects to the world of passions within." Poetry, the author averred, arises "in the deep and mystic recesses of the human soul," and in a move that was as yet rare among evangelicals in 1833, he bowed to German aesthetics by citing Friedrich von Schlegel's view of poetry as "invention, expression and inspiration."[16]

These statements from the 1830s serve as a valuable index to evangelicalism's relationship to "mainstream" developments in transatlantic aesthetics. When one M.C.H., writing in the *Wesleyan-Methodist Magazine* in 1831, assured his audience that "It would be idle to *argue* that all poetry, of whatever class, must emanate from the original and inward *music of the mind*" because "On this point there

---

[12] Review of *Robert Burns; as a Poet, and as Man*, by Samuel Tyler, *BRPR* 21 (Apr. 1849), 252, 257.
[13] B., "Influence of the Fine Arts," *CA*[P] 1 (Mar. 1823), 115.
[14] James Montgomery, *Lectures on General Literature, Poetry, &c.* (New York: Harper, 1844), 171, 138, 140.
[15] "Sacred Poetry," *ER* 1 (May 1837), 462.
[16] "Influence of the Christian Religion on Poetry," *QCS* 5 (June 1833), 199, 198, 200. For a similar late-Victorian statement, see L. Oscar Kuhns, "The Ancient and Modern Feeling for Nature," *MR* 13 (Nov. 1897), 924.

can be no dispute," he not only sounded remarkably like William Hazlitt but also anticipated John Stuart Mill's description of poetry as "the expression or uttering forth of feeling" two years later.[17] By the time Mill published his thoughts on the nature of poetry, such thoughts had already become axiomatic, as M.C.H.'s refusal to enter into first principles makes clear. By the 1830s, then, many evangelicals had moved well beyond the point of expressing hostility or apathy towards art. Furthermore, if Mill's essay is evidence of the broad dissemination of romantic expressivism, then evangelicals, at least in the case of poetic theory, appear to have caught up with their non-evangelical contemporaries.[18]

As the century progressed, the view that poetry and art are essentially an outpouring of the artist's mind became standard fare among evangelical critics, the effusiveness with which it was sometimes posited growing in proportion to its status as aesthetic truism. In 1866, the *Christian Observer* waxed Shelleyan in its description of the poet who "first sings to relieve himself, like the nightingale, having no other end than the pleasure of his own outpouring."[19] Upon his appointment to the Professorship of Rhetoric and English Language and Literature at Princeton College, James C. Welling delivered an inaugural address on "The True Sources of Literary Inspiration" in which he plainly aspired to that same eloquence which he maintained could only come from within: "The well-head of eloquence, if it is to flow in copious and limpid streams, must gush up from the depths of the soul; the spray of the fountain that is fed by a force-pump glitters for a moment in the sun, and then runs dry. We can express only the Beauty and the Force that are in us—which we have made an integral part of our nature."[20] This fountain metaphor, so typical of romantic descriptions of the creative process (its industrial reference to force-pumps notwithstanding), underscores another key element of the aesthetic theory adopted by evangelical critics, namely, that art and poetry are the expression of *emotion*. Poetry is not the enunciation of propositions, doctrines, or abstract truths but the outpouring of an artist's feelings, heart, imagination, or soul. "It has been well remarked that 'sentimental feeling is the first requisite in lyric poetry,'" observed the *Christian Spectator*.[21] The *Christian Advocate and Journal and Zion's Herald* agreed: "Poetry is the

---

[17] M.C.H., "On Sacred Poetry," *WMM* 10 (Sep. 1831), 609; J.S. Mill, "What Is Poetry?" *Mill's Essays on Literature & Society*, ed. J.B. Schneewind (New York: Collier, 1965), 109. See William Hazlitt, "Introductory—On Poetry in General," vol. 2 of *The Selected Writings of William Hazlitt*, ed. Duncan Wu (London: Pickering & Chatto, 1998), 174-75. M.C.H.'s articles were also published in the American *MMQR*.

[18] For additional statements from the period that include expressivist elements, see "Occasional Pieces of Poetry," *CS* 7 (1 June 1825): 324-27; M.C.H., "On Sacred Poetry," *WMM* 10 (Oct. 1831): 676-83; "Montgomery's *Lectures on Poetry*," *ER* 10 (July 1833): 1-22; and Edward Otheman, "The Moral Influence of the Fine Arts," *MMQR* 17 (July 1835): 318-32.

[19] "Poetry and Its Uses," *CO* 66 (1866), 116.

[20] James C. Welling, "The True Sources of Literary Inspiration," *BRPR* 43 (Jan. 1871), 112.

[21] "Lyric Poetry," *CS* 7 (1 Aug. 1825), 408.

offspring of a mind heated to an uncommon degree; it is a kind of spirit thrown off in the effervescence of agitated feeling."[22] Yet it was an author in the *British Quarterly Review* who perhaps best demonstrated the identification of poetry with emotion:

> We feel convinced that, so long as the human heart exults with rapture, or droops with sorrow—palpitates with hope, or is overwhelmed with despair—melts with love, or rages with jealousy—glows with anger, or is maddened with revenge—is, in short, the subject of those innumerable feelings to which it can find utterance only in the language of the bard—so long will there be materials for poetry of the highest class.[23]

By the 1840s, the pregnant musings of Turner had matured into a full-grown expressivism.

It is important to recall that the expressivist theories advocated by prominent romantic poets and critics rarely evinced a thoroughgoing subjectivism. Poetry was not a matter of simple effusion, an unmodified eruption of the heart; rather, art and poetry were viewed as the special products of an interchange between the artist's imagination and the world of sense perceptions.[24] William Blake, it is true, deplored the mind's subservience to nature, and he undoubtedly came closest to conceiving of the relationship between the imagination and nature in unilateral terms.[25] However, Blake, ever the radical, was unusual in this regard, and it was left to Wordsworth to state the more moderate and typical position of the British romantics. For Wordsworth, the mind-nature relationship was one of cooperation and "alliance": empirical reality is never completely effaced but is instead "acted on and transformed by the feelings of the poet."[26] In this respect, evangelical theorists were by and large Wordsworthian (and Coleridgean) rather than Blakean. That many mid-nineteenth-century evangelicals nonetheless accepted the idea that art and poetry are the products of the mind's unique interaction with the objects of perception is abundantly clear. "The poet aims not merely to paint the scenes of nature, but to invest them with the thoughts and feelings

---

[22] Robert Hall, "Poetry and Philosophy," *CAJZH* 6 (22 June 1832), 169. Hall originally wrote this text in the 1780s. Since the *Advocate* apparently found it appealing enough to reprint in the 1830s, I have treated it as an 1830s piece throughout.
[23] "Poetry and Civilization," *BrQR* 4 (Aug. 1846), 378. See also "National Literature, the Exponent of National Character," *BRPR* 24 (Apr. 1852), 221-22; Dyer, "Literary Criticism," 321; William A. Knight, "A Contribution towards a Theory of Poetry," *BrQR* 57 (Jan. 1873), 180; Edwin Mims, "Poetry and the Spiritual Life," *MR*[S] 44 (1896-7), 396; and "The Preacher and the Poet," *MR* 19 (Mar. 1903), 216-17.
[24] On the many permutations of this principle, see Abrams, *Mirror*, 62-64.
[25] See William Blake's letter "To the Reverend John Trusler, August 23, 1799," *Blake's Poetry and Designs*, ed. Mary Lynn Johnson and John E. Grant (New York: Norton, 1979), 449.
[26] Abrams, *Mirror*, 53. See also Wordsworth's passage on the "infant Babe" in Book 2 of the 1850 *Prelude*, ll. 255-60 (*The Prelude: 1799, 1805, 1850*, ed. Jonathan Wordsworth, M.H. Abrams, and Stephen Gill [New York: Norton, 1979], 79-80).

which they excite in his own mind; and to clothe them with the power of awakening sympathetic emotions in the bosom of others," explained the *Biblical Repertory and Princeton Review* in 1849.[27] In a similar vein, "Personification is the life of poetry," argued the *Christian Advocate and Journal*: "The poet looks upon nature, not with the philosopher, as composed of certain abstractions ... but he breathes upon them, and they quicken into personal life, and become objects, as it were, of personal attachment."[28] At times, critics came close to defining poetry not as a particular genre, a peculiar use of language, or even the specific artifact generated by an artist's emotional encounter with objective reality but as the interaction between mind and object itself. "The fact is," argued Dyer, "the poetic principle does not so much exist in a given object, as in the point and light in which we view it, and our capacity to draw on the powers of imagination to array the imperfect and real with the semblance and perfections of an ideal existence."[29] Poetry had, in Dyer's case, become a special sort of hermeneutic, and although he was yet far from Blake's absolutism of the imagination, the balance between mind and nature has tipped decisively in favor of mind.

In granting preeminence to the transformative powers of the artist's mind and emotions, evangelical critics were altering and even rescinding ideas that had long characterized the Puritan aesthetic tradition. For the Puritans, what had counted most was an accurate apprehension of the natural world. A subjective interpretation of reality signaled not genius but disordered fancy.[30] This principle served as a crucial guide in matters of theology and philosophy, but many Puritans had also been reluctant to abrogate this standard when it came to art. Although Puritan poetry incorporated a variety of conceits, such figurative devices were often seen as an adornment of reality rather than a reinterpretation of it. In other cases, Puritan writers had granted that the imaginative modification of reality was essential to poetry; however, they had simply treated it (not unlike Locke) as a species of harmless play acceptable in its place but not to be taken too seriously. Edward Leigh, for one, had defined poetry in 1656 as "an art of deceit, which measureth expressions, not by the truth of the subject, but by the strength of the imagination working upon it." He had even suggested that it "principally serves for venting extraordinary affections." Yet for this reason it was best categorized as "the luxury of Learning."[31] By the 1830s, however, evangelical writers had united with the romantics in celebrating poetry and art for their ability to refashion the created order via the metamorphic power of the individual imagination. This re-creation, moreover, was no playful "luxury"; instead, it was

---

[27] Review of *Robert Burns*, 257.
[28] "What Is Poetry?," *CAJ* 26 (30 Oct. 1851), 173.
[29] Dyer, "Literary Criticism," 319. Cf. Mill, "What Is Poetry?," 107.
[30] On Puritan approaches to the world in relation to the claims of later romantic poets, see Perry Miller, *The New England Mind: The Seventeenth Century* (Cambridge: Belknap, 1982), 258.
[31] Edward Leigh, *A Treatise of Religion & Learning* (London: Charles Adams, 1656), 48.

a profoundly serious activity. The Puritan emphasis on the objective apprehension of the natural world lived on until at least the 1860s in evangelicalism's commitment to common sense realism and Baconian science;[32] art, however, had become by definition that which existed in opposition to such "scientific" perception.

One corollary of this view was the tendency to disparage, displace, or redefine a central concept in the western aesthetic tradition: imitation, or mimesis. While the concept of imitation had never been particularly stable—one need only recall how quickly Aristotle recast Plato's usage—it had endured as a powerful presence in western thought.[33] Romantic expressivist theories, however, did much to challenge the traditional view of art as imitation. At times, theorists opposed imitation and expression absolutely, as when John Keble criticized Aristotle's conception of poetry: "Aristotle ... considered the essence of poetry to be *Imitation*.... *Expression* we say, rather than *imitation*."[34] Others retained the term but revised it to fit more comfortably within a theory that prioritized the artist's mental contribution to the art object, as when Hazlitt suggested in Plotinian fashion that the poet mirrors the inner self.[35] In the main, though, it became a negative term signifying what true art is *not*. Although imitation had rarely been synonymous with a meticulous duplication of external reality, in its juxtaposition to the forming powers of the active mind, it now came to represent passivity and mechanism.

It is thus further evidence of the romantic influence on evangelical conceptions of art that many writers reiterated this negative idea of imitation. "The extensive province of Imitation is very sterile;—it produces nothing," noted an allegorical foray into "The Empire of Poetry" by Fontenelle, reprinted in the *Christian Index* in 1831.[36] Genuine art is not a faithful reproduction in which the artist reflects nature with mimetic precision. Rather, the reverse is true. Nature reflects the mind and emotions of the artist: "the highest poetry is not that which most closely imitates nature in its descriptions; but which suggests the highest thoughts and the purest emotions by its pictures of nature."[37] Joseph LeConte illustrated the extent to which evangelicals had come to embrace the view of art as an expression of mind and emotion, and the corresponding distaste for any

---

[32] On "Baconianism" as an empirical approach rooted in Scottish common sense realism, see Theodore Dwight Bozeman, *Protestants in an Age of Science* (Chapel Hill: University of North Carolina Press, 1977).

[33] One of the most influential statements of this view in the English critical tradition was of course Sir Philip Sidney's *Apology for Poetry*, *The Longman Anthology of British Literature, Volume 1B, The Early Modern Period*, ed. Clare Carroll and Andrew Hadfield [New York: Longman, 2010], esp. 1003-1005). Even for Sidney, however, "imitation" did not mean a facsimile but a beautification of nature.

[34] Qtd. in Abrams, *Mirror*, 48.

[35] See Hazlitt, "On Poetry in General," 167.

[36] "The Empire of Poetry, by Fontenelle," *CI* 5 (22 Oct. 1831), 265.

[37] Review of *Robert Burns*, 306.

theory that smacked of mechanical passivity. As a whole, LeConte's aesthetic was no uncritical regurgitation of romantic expressivism. Regarding imitation, however, his disdain was as pronounced as any:

> Pure imitative art is mechanic art, and that, too, of the lowest kind. It requires neither sense of beauty nor imagination, but only accurate measurement. It exercises neither imagination nor feeling, but only the understanding. The copyist of nature bears the same relation to the true artist, which the ordinary manufacturer of the steam engine does to its great inventor and creator, James Watt.[38]

LeConte's attack on imitation, replete with the binaries central to romantic aesthetics (imagination-understanding, mechanic-organic, feeling-intellect, imitation-creation), exemplifies the tendency of one strand of romanticism to conceptualize imitation in terms that served as a useful foil for expressivist theories.

Yet not all critics maligned imitation as vociferously as LeConte; some opted instead to follow an alternative line of romantic thought which retained the notion of art as imitation by redefining it. For LeConte, imitation and copy were synonymous: both signified the sort of facsimile generated by a passive reception of sensory data. For those evangelicals who knew their Coleridge, however, the matter was not so simple. Coleridge had attempted to preserve imitation by linking it to the active powers of the imagination. Imitation, in Coleridge's sense, involved the conscious shaping power of the artist, whereas copy was equivalent to mechanical reproduction. In addition, artists should not imitate objects in their sensuous minutiae but must grasp their ideal essence or spirit. Following Coleridge, some evangelicals were beginning to entertain the notion that perhaps art has transcendental significance.

The Growth of Aesthetic Idealism

Whatever their idiosyncrasies, nearly all nineteenth-century evangelical critics were convinced that art is "ideal." For most, in fact, this was the sine qua non of any definition of art. "If there is one word by which we would test an artist or a critic, a single term in which we could sum up the essence of a mind, or the end and purpose of a life, it should be the word *ideal*.... And shall art alone be destitute of this vision and faculty divine?"[39] At other times, reflecting the romantic preoccupation with the grounds of art in the mind of the artist, critics shifted their attention to the psychological *process* of idealization: "Although real life is the source of inspiration, every true artist throws a certain degree of idealization into his work. Without this, it cannot be a work of art."[40] Yet whether they emphasized the ideal as an object of perception or the process of idealization, evangelicals were united in the belief that art is essentially ideal.

---

[38] Joseph LeConte, "On the Nature and Uses of Art," *SPR* 15 (Jan. 1863), 317-18.
[39] "Art: Its Aspirations and Prospects," *ER* 9 (Feb. 1855), 130-31.
[40] Robert Waters, "Genius in Action: The Realists," *CA* (18 Oct. 1888), 688.

In insisting on art's ideality, evangelicals were perpetuating a well-established tradition. Like imitation, the concept of the ideal has a long history in the West. It has been associated with the beauty of classical Greek sculpture; it guided the approach of early-sixteenth-century painters like Raphael; and it played a prominent role in seventeenth and eighteenth-century neoclassicism. As Abrams explains, writers before the nineteenth century often employed the term to account for the departure of art objects from the observable forms of nature. In particular, the western tradition had emphasized what Abrams calls the "empirical ideal." While there are distinct variations of this idea, it refers generally to the representation of an object, the details of which have been "reassembled to make a composite beauty, or filtered to reveal a central form or the common denominator of a type, or in some fashion culled or ornamented for the greater delight of the reader."[41] An artist may render a rose, for example, either by combining the best attributes of several roses or by accentuating the beauties of a single model. This conception of the ideal stresses what is universal and common to all members of a species.[42]

Rosman has noted a similar fascination with the ideal among evangelicals before 1830. Late-eighteenth and early-nineteenth-century evangelicals, she argues, harbored a deep "sympathy for classicism," an observation which suggests that these writers understood the ideal in a basically neoclassical or empirical sense.[43] Yet even as these critics were busy sympathizing with the canons of neoclassical taste, other theorists, especially in Germany, had begun using the term ideal differently. For post-Kantian German philosophers (including Schelling, Hegel, and others), the ideal came to denote something more extensive than it had for British neoclassicists. Broadly conceived, German idealist philosophies understood history as a teleological process in which the "Absolute" gradually aspired to greater self-consciousness. To achieve self-awareness, the Absolute proceeded through a series of stages in which it objectified itself in nature and in the creative activity of humankind. In the widest sense, "ideal" referred to subjective consciousness, mind, or spirit over and against objective nature, unconscious process, or the "real," and only through the evolution of human consciousness could the Absolute come to know itself. In some cases, however, as in the aesthetics of Hegel, the ideal acquired a more specialized meaning. For Hegel,

---

[41] Abrams, *Mirror*, 53.

[42] See Abrams, *Mirror*, 35-42 on the varieties of this idea. Abrams also identifies in the classical tradition something he calls the "transcendental ideal" (see pp. 45-6). See also Walter Jackson Bate, *From Classic to Romantic: Premises of Taste in Eighteenth Century England* (New York: Harper Torchbooks, 1946), 7-14.

[43] Rosman, *Evangelicals and Culture*, 178-79. Rosman does not extensively examine evangelical understandings of the "ideal," though she repeatedly links this notion to (neo)classicism. She also contends that "Far less attention was paid by the evangelical press to poets more centrally within the romantic tradition, Coleridge, Shelley, and Keats" (180).

the "Ideal" signified the material embodiment of the Idea, or the Absolute apprehended as beauty in art.[44] When it came to practical techniques for the creation of art, idealist philosophies did not always exclude the sorts of approaches implied by the empirical ideal, but the ideal itself became a far weightier metaphysical concept. Careful attention to the manner in which some evangelicals appropriated the term "ideal" makes it clear that their understandings of this concept underwent an important transition in the mid-nineteenth century. While some writers continued to utilize "ideal" in a roughly neoclassical sense, others began to associate this concept with the transcendental or "spiritual". The ideal, in short, became part and parcel of an aesthetic ideal*ism*.

The growth of aesthetic idealism among evangelicals coincided with the diffusion of German thought during the middle of the nineteenth century. Before the 1830s, most evangelicals, as described earlier, were committed to Scottish common sense realism. Evangelicals had found in this philosophy an especially effective apologetic tool, for in its affirmation of a mind-independent reality, it enabled, according to Sydney Ahlstrom, "an all-out attack on both materialism and idealism, as well as the pantheism that either type of monistic analysis could lead to." Furthermore, according to the principles of common sense, the universe not only exists independently of the consciousness of human beings but is also distinct from (though not independent of) God himself, a point that reinforced traditional understandings "of God's transcendence, and made revelation necessary."[45] Common sense philosophy would continue to play an important role among conservatives well into the twentieth century. Gradually, however, German idealism began to impact evangelical thought. Idealism had already gained some traction in Britain through the writings of Coleridge, while Emerson and the Transcendentalists began advocating similar doctrines in America during the 1830s.[46] In addition, German ideas were carried to America by a growing number of prominent scholars who undertook advanced study in German universities. By the 1840s, references to Kant and other German philosophers were appearing in evangelical publications, and by the 1850s German philosophy had made significant headway in the halls of Anglo-American academia and in many artistic circles.[47] Writing in the *Southern Presbyterian Review* in 1851, one observer hailed

---

[44] On Hegel's Ideal, see *The Philosophy of Fine Art*, vol. 1 (London: G. Bell, 1920), 100; cf. 209-14.

[45] Sydney E. Ahlstrom, "The Scottish Philosophy and American Theology," *Church History* 24 (Sep. 1955), 268.

[46] See Ralph Waldo Emerson, "Nature," *Nature, Addresses and Lectures* (Boston: Houghton, Mifflin, 1904), 47-60.

[47] See, for example, "Kant, and Kantism," *MQR* 5 (Jan. 1845): 43-54 and Review of *The Historical Development of Speculative Philosophy, from Kant to Hegel*, from the German of Dr. H.M. Chalybäus, by Rev. Alfred Edersheim, *LQR* 2 (Mar. 1854): 285-87. See also Bruce Kuklick, *Churchmen and Philosophers: From Jonathan Edwards to John Dewey* (New Haven: Yale University Press, 1985), esp. 120-23, 132-41; George M. Marsden, *The Evangelical Mind and the New School Presbyterian Experience: A Case Study of Thought and Theology in Nineteenth-Century America* (New Haven: Yale University

Boston as the literary epicenter of America but added: "in no spot on our continent is there so strong a German influence as at and around Boston."[48]

In some instances, therefore, evangelical exposure to German thought was direct. It was not uncommon, especially during the latter half of the century, for evangelical periodicals to review German publications. In the case of the German Reformed Church, close ethnic ties ensured open channels to developments in Germany. When it came to aesthetics, however, it was German thought as transmitted by Coleridge that proved especially influential. Coleridge had been widely read in both his native Britain and America—thanks in part to Congregationalist James Marsh's 1829 American edition of Coleridge's *Aids to Reflection* and to the publication in 1854 of *The Complete Works of Samuel Taylor Coleridge*, edited by W.G.T. Shedd, a Presbyterian professor of church history at Andover Theological Seminary. In the United States, Coleridge's influence remained primarily confined to the Northeast until after the 1830s,[49] but even the conservative *Biblical Repertory and Princeton Review* was by the mid-nineteenth century conceding the far-reaching effects of Coleridge and idealist philosophy, and advocating its cautious investigation by students. "If any one author," wrote a Princeton contributor in 1855, "has exercised a stronger moulding influence on a certain class of minds in our country, that have grown up within the last twenty years, than Coleridge, we have yet to learn who he is."[50] Not all denominations welcomed idealist philosophies to the same extent,[51] but by the 1850s Coleridge had

---

Press, 1970), esp. chap. 7; Robert E. Chiles, *Theological Transition in American Methodism, 1790-1935* (Lanham: University Press of America, 1983); and David Bebbington, *Evangelicalism in Modern Britain: A History from the 1730s to the 1980s* (Grand Rapids: Baker, 1992), esp. chaps. 3-5.

[48] "Domestic Literature," *SPR* 1 (July 1851), 4.

[49] On Coleridge's reception in America, see Graham Neville, *Coleridge and Liberal Religious Thought: Romanticism, Science and Theological Tradition* (London: I.B. Tauris, 2010), 37-55; Mark A. Noll, *America's God: From Jonathan Edwards to Abraham Lincoln* (Oxford: Oxford University Press, 2002), 320; Conrad Cherry, *Nature and Religious Imagination: From Edwards to Bushnell* (Philadelphia: Fortress, 1980), 7; and William Charvat, *The Origins of American Critical Thought 1810-1835* (Philadelphia: University of Pennsylvania Press, 1936), 76-80.

[50] Review of *The Elements of Intellectual Philosophy*, by Francis Wayland; *A System of Intellectual Philosophy*, by Asa Mahan; and *Empirical Psychology; or, the Human Mind as Given in Consciousness*, by Laurens P. Hickok, *BRPR* 27 (Jan. 1855), 75. See also "Coleridge and Southey," *CR* 15 (July 1850): 321-53 and "Samuel Taylor Coleridge," *FBQ* 3 (Oct. 1855): 361-89. An earlier eight-volume edition of Coleridge's works had been published in Philadelphia in 1840.

[51] Noll suggests, for example, that New School Presbyterians were "more open to influences from nineteenth-century Romantic or idealist thought" than Old School ("Common Sense Traditions and American Evangelical Thought," *American Quarterly* 37 [Summer 1985], 219 n. 10). Likewise, Bebbington contends that Anglican Evangelicals tended to resist romantic ideas longer than Nonconformist denominations (*Evangelicalism*, 143-44).

become the closest thing some evangelical critics had to a patron saint of aesthetics.

One of Coleridge's more consequential attempts to formulate the nature of art was his 1818 lecture "On Poesy or Art." Grounded in the aesthetics of Schelling, this lecture marked a key moment in the Coleridgean mediation of German thought. Its brevity also made the lecture accessible, and critics seem in some cases to have borrowed directly from the terminology and concepts utilized therein. Coleridge begins his address by advancing what was to become a fairly conventional definition of art, emphasizing art's intermediate position between the ideal world of spirit and the material world of sense. "Now Art ... is the mediatress between, and the reconciler of nature and man. It is, therefore, the power of humanizing nature, of infusing the thoughts and passions of man into everything which is the object of his contemplation...."[52] The idea that art possesses both rational and material elements was a common feature of eighteenth-century British criticism—one can trace it back at least as far as Addison[53]—but Coleridge's understanding of this idea moves beyond that of eighteenth-century empiricists. For Coleridge, the essence of art lies in a subjective appropriation of objective reality, a passionate modification of the objects of perception. Art begins when the mind confronts images in nature; however, the artist possesses the power to mold and recombine these images according to a unifying idea that originates within. Art thus represents "the union and reconciliation of that which is nature with that which is exclusively human" (330).

Yet as Coleridge makes clear, the artist's "humanizing" of nature is neither a purely mechanical manipulation of sense data nor a unidirectional application of mind to matter. Although the ideas the artist impresses upon nature originate within, they are also paradoxically a consequence of the artist's perception of the essence of nature itself. Art, therefore, is both imitation and expression. "We all know that art is the imitatress of nature," writes Coleridge (330). However, neither "imitate" nor "nature" should be taken in its colloquial sense. To begin with, there is a difference, argues Coleridge, between "imitation" and "copy." A copy is akin to the imprint of a seal upon hot wax; an imitation (and all genuine art is imitation) involves a productive tension between likeness and unlikeness. Too much likeness, as in the case of wax models of the human figure, results in disgust since we find ourselves both jolted by the absence of life in a form wherein

---

[52] Samuel Taylor Coleridge, "On Poesy or Art," *Notes and Lectures upon Shakespeare and Some of the Old Poets and Dramatists with Other Literary Remains*, ed. H.N. Coleridge (New York: Harper, 1854), 328. I here follow the 1854 edition since it was the version evangelicals would have known. However, cf. *Lectures 1808-1819 On Literature II*, ed. R.A. Foakes (Princeton: Princeton University Press, 1987): 213-25 for a revised scholarly edition. Subsequent references appear parenthetically in the text.

[53] See Walter John Hipple, Jr., *The Beautiful, The Sublime, & The Picturesque in Eighteenth-Century British Aesthetic Theory* (Carbondale: Southern Illinois University Press, 1957), 15; cf. Henry Home, Lord Kames, *Elements of Criticism*, ed. Peter Jones (Indianapolis: Liberty Fund, 2005), 1:12.

we would normally expect to find it and frustrated by the realization that we have been deceived. Proper imitation, by contrast, "begin[s] with an acknowledged total difference, and then every touch of nature gives you the pleasure of an approximation to truth" (331). Secondly, Coleridge questions whether the artist must imitate everything in nature. He replies that the artist must imitate only the beautiful. According to Coleridge, beauty, at least in the case of living entities, "is not mere regularity of form" (331)—that is, it exists independently of any single material embodiment. Art, then, does not imitate the forms of nature (*natura naturata*) but rather the idea or essence (*natura naturans*) behind it: "The artist must imitate that which is within the thing, that which is active through form and figure, and discourses to us by symbols—the *Natur-geist*, or spirit of nature ... for so only can he hope to produce any work truly natural in the object and truly human in the effect" (333). Art is ideal, Coleridge contends, in that it embodies in an individual object a universal idea—an idea which, moreover, finds its incarnation via a process at the same time analogous to the grand forward motion of the *Natur-geist* operating in and through the dynamic development of nature. Indeed, "nature itself would give us the impression of a work of art, if we could see the thought which is present at once in the whole and in every part" (330).

How is it possible, though, for human beings to perceive the ideal, to grasp the inward essence of nature? Human beings, Coleridge suggests, can apprehend the inner spirit of nature because of the fundamental bond, or consubstantiality, that exists "between nature in the higher sense and the soul of man" (332)—a theory Abrams refers to as "psycho-natural parallelism."[54] For Coleridge, "to know is to resemble" (333) and hence human souls must bear an ontological affinity to the spirit of nature and to God; to grasp the essence of nature is in part to recognize the spiritual kinship of all things. Such rhetoric, of course, can tend towards the monistic or pantheistic—criticisms frequently leveled against idealist philosophies in the nineteenth century, not least by evangelicals themselves. Coleridge, however, was well aware of the dangers inherent in an unqualified idealism. Following Schelling, he aimed to "reconcile" the objective and subjec-

---

[54] Abrams, *Mirror*, 52. It is a matter of some debate whether one ought to read Coleridge in a Platonic sense. Abrams resists this interpretation: "Coleridge ... says that art imitates the *natura naturans*, the 'spirit of nature'; but in context, this turns out to be a way of saying that the 'idea,' or generative element in poetic composition, accords with that in external nature, in such a way as to insure a likeness between the evolving principle of a poem and what is vital and organic in nature" (314). In contrast, my reading is closer to J. Robert Barth's. Coleridge, I believe, was more genuinely Platonic than Abrams allows. See J. Robert Barth, S.J., *The Symbolic Imagination: Coleridge and the Romantic Tradition* (New York: Fordham University Press, 2001) and *Romanticism and Transcendence: Wordsworth, Coleridge, and the Religious Imagination* (Columbia: University of Missouri Press, 2003), esp. 119-36. Either way, the influence of Coleridge and idealism on evangelical aesthetics is clear.

tive, a goal which ipso facto assumes that nature exists independently of the individual ego. "For of all we see, hear, feel, and touch the substance is and must be in ourselves," writes Coleridge. And yet, "there is no alternative in reason between the dreary (and thank heaven! almost impossible) belief that everything around us is but a phantom, or that the life which is in us is in them likewise...." (333). Too much likeness, after all, ends in shock and disgust; for Coleridge, it was about "likeness in the difference, difference in the likeness, and a reconcilement of both in one" (331). Nor, it is worth adding, was Coleridge a pantheist. It is true, as J. Robert Barth observes, that Coleridge experienced an ongoing "conflict between his 'dynamic philosophy' and his Christian faith," but pantheism was a system that Coleridge "shunned all his life."[55]

One is now in a better position to catch the Coleridgean echoes, not to mention the wholesale borrowings, in the aesthetic theories of Victorian evangelicals. Two articles published in England in 1855 illustrate the extent to which some evangelical periodicals had become a forum for idealist philosophies in the Coleridgean vein. The first, Rogers's "The Science and Poetry of Art," does not mention Coleridge specifically, though the article is aglow with Coleridgean concepts and turns of phrase, many of them seemingly lifted from "On Poesy or Art." Consider, for instance, the article's opening paragraph: "What is Art? It is the ideal reflection of Nature. Not the mere literal imitation of its actual presentment; nor the production, by mechanical means, of effects supposed to be equivalent to those of Nature.... No: Art is the reflection or mimetic exhibition, of the appearances or sensible impressions of Nature, according to the *ideas*, *spirit*, and *design* of Nature."[56] Juxtaposed to the "ideal," to the "ideas" and "spirit" of nature, mimesis has undergone a process of spiritualization. Rogers contrasts the spiritual imitation proper to genuine art with a "mere literal imitation" carried out by "mechanical means," and he even cites as his example "the coloured wax casts of Madame Tussaud" (403), an illustration that bears a marked resemblance to Coleridge's reference to "waxen figures" as an instance of what he means by "copy."

Following this prologue, Rogers develops a theory of aesthetic idealism similar to Coleridge's. Art, he notes, is a product of the imaginative activity of the human mind. We are daily surrounded by aesthetic building blocks (sounds, lines, colors, etc.), but it requires the structuring powers of the mind to transform these into art: "[S]ome intelligent act, as of selection, arrangement, and subordination, must be required to bring these scattered materials within the scope and dominion of Art" (404). Hence art is the embodiment of an idea that takes its rise in the imagination. It stands, as Coleridge had put it, "between a thought and a thing" (330). "Be the material what it may," Rogers explains, "the subject first

---

[55] J. Robert Barth, S.J., *Coleridge and Christian Doctrine* (New York: Fordham University Press, 1987), 13, 19-20.

[56] Rogers, "Science and Poetry," 403. Subsequent references appear parenthetically in the text.

has a place in the mind of the artist, whence it springs into outward existence, clothing itself with a sensuous form, which is but a transcript ... of the form in which it arose in the imagination" (406). Once again, art is an expression of an artist's consciousness. As with Coleridge, however, beneath this actualization of the ideal through form rests a larger metaphysics of nature. If we could but discern it (a qualification also stipulated in "On Poesy or Art"[57]), we would be able to see nature as the manifestation of *"one cosmical idea"*—that is, as a revelation of the mind of God. In one of his most obviously Coleridgean (and Schellingean) passages, Rogers lays the metaphysical groundwork for his theory:

> It would be an easy task to multiply examples of the manner in which every divine idea reveals itself in Nature. Every thought of God, in the mystic language of Philosophy, is a *word*, a self-substantiating *fiat*; at once purpose, and execution according to the purpose. Nature itself, in the highest sense, namely, that of a spiritual power, or *Natur-geist, (natura naturus,)* is but a phrase significant of that general idea or design of which the entire frame-work of phenomena *(naturæ naturata)* is the form, the organism, and result.

This concept serves in turn as a model for those human imaginative endeavors that give birth to art. The term "Art," Rogers observes, applies to works that "are developed by a process analogous to that of Nature,—works wherein a central and sovereign idea is projected in a form which it prescribes and assumes for itself as its own proper heritage and nature...." (405). While the language here is clearly Coleridgean, Rogers's precise position concerning the metaphysical relationship between the *Natur-geist* he sees operating in nature and the *geist* he posits in the act of human creation remains murky. The difficulty turns on the word "analogous." Unlike Coleridge, Rogers makes no explicit reference to any intrinsic affinity between the human spirit and the divine spirit at work in the world. Consequently, it is possible to read this article as a diluted form of Coleridgean idealism, one in which the author's metaphysics of nature does not extend ontologically to human artistry but serves merely as a mirror-image of this process.[58] Yet whether or not one understands Rogers's metaphysics in a fully Coleridgean sense, his theory draws deeply from the wells of Coleridgean aesthetics.

What Rogers left his readers to infer, however, was made clear in an essay published in the *Eclectic Review* entitled "Art: Its Prospects and Aspirations," which opens by declaring the centrality of the ideal to a sound conception of art. Art is not mere imitation (the author initially associates imitation with the Dutch realists) but concerns itself with depicting what Sir Joshua Reynolds called "ideal beauty." Yet although he quotes Reynold's Third Discourse at some length, what

---

[57] "Hence nature itself would give us the impression of a work of art, if we could see the thought which is present at once in the whole and in every part" (330). This line was apparently added by H.N. Coleridge (see *Lectures*, 224 n. 26). Rogers, however, makes a stipulation akin to H.N.'s.

[58] Alternatively, one might say that Rogers interprets Coleridge as Abrams does.

interests this critic is the "transcendental tendency" of Reynold's view (131). Reynolds, in fact, is really more of a prefiguration of the author's conception of ideal art than the reality. For the reality, one must look to Coleridge:

> Coleridge had a true and profound insight into the character of art when he defined a picture as an intermediate something between a thought and a thing. The thing and thought stand respectively for the outer world of matter and the inner world of mind. The thing or object is received and taken from visible nature into the inner mind of the artist, and there being elaborated and combined with his individual idiosyncrasy of thought and feeling, comes forth a second time into actual existence under the new and created form of art. The primary element, the raw material, is nature, the forming power is mind, and the ultimate product art. Nature enters the mind a fact, a reality, issues forth a fiction, a poem, an ideality. (132)

Crucial here is not only the author's understanding of art as a union of spirit and matter—he refers directly to Coleridge's statement in "On Poesy or Art" that "art itself might be defined as of a middle quality between a thought and a thing"—but also his articulation of a psychodynamic model comparable to Coleridge's "secondary Imagination" in chapter 13 of *Biographia Literaria*. Art is fundamentally creative, fresh, original; artists are no slaves to sense but possess an "originating power" (133) that allows them to introduce something truly new into existence. Indeed, what gives art special value is that it embodies the human mind. "Art is not mere copyism of nature ..." the writer contends, following the contours of Coleridge's "On Poesy or Art," "but it is a new and creative principle in the world, operating on old materials, and out of existing elements fashioning a beauty and an excellence which nature strives after but never attains" (132).

Yet if art is essentially creative and expressive, in typical idealist fashion it is also a kind of heightened perception, or "imitation" in the Coleridgean sense. The artist does not simply conjure the ideal, nor does he cobble it together by way of mere association or abstraction; rather, it exists as a mind-independent entity awaiting apprehension by the artist: "The latent ideal is lying in partial concealment beneath each form and function; ... the poet and artist ... out of scattered fragments must complete the perfect whole ... through imagination, calling into new birth the type which nature had all but lost" (138-39). The artist, then, sees *through* nature to its ideal form. Unlike Rogers, however, this critic follows Coleridge exactly in positing a psycho-natural parallelism or consubstantiality to underwrite the high epistemological claims of his theory: "The mind reads nature, as we have said, through kindred sympathy of spirit; and it is thus, through intimate communion with her essence, that man, by force of his creative power working in the spirit of nature and his own spirit, gives birth to beauteous forms which nature has not yet realized. If it be said that this is a departure from nature, we deny it; but rather its consummation and fulfillment" (133). The writer, like Coleridge, carefully avoids the trap of subjectivism, but the metaphysical supposition of a common spirit within both objective nature and subjective consciousness—and thus of the union of the ideal and real, mind and nature, in and through the activity of the artist—is nevertheless clear.

The romantic idealism exemplified by these articles continued to shape evangelical definitions of art for the remainder of the century. The view of art as a mediator between the spiritual and material, for example, appeared with increasing regularity after the 1850s. "[I]t is the mission of the artist," declared the *Mercersburg Review* in 1859, "guided by a genial imagination and the laws of taste, to shape and transform ... rude material until it is best adapted to represent the particular thought or idea, which has been fermenting in his mind."[59] Reviewing recent editions of Hegel's and Friedrich von Schlegel's aesthetic works, the *Christian Review* borrowed Coleridge's terminology, stating that "Art is the mediatress between nature and mankind. It is the power of humanizing the external creation, by infusing thought and emotion into everything which is the object of contemplation."[60] Art is unique, suggested the *Presbyterian Quarterly Review* in 1862, precisely because of its hybrid nature: "[Art] lies between the rational and the sensible, dealing with both, but giving a result that differs from both."[61] Even an article on "Practical Aesthetics" published in 1880 abandoned the pragmatism of its title in favor of a romantic idealist perspective: "In all ideal creations it is the interfusion of ... spiritual qualities in their due order of rank and superiority with the sensuous feelings, controlling and controlled, which infused the unity of conception into the dead materials, until the whole glows with the Promethean spark of creation."[62] Not unlike Shelley's efforts in his *Defense* to convert the Platonic into the practical, "Practical Aesthetics" had become the Promethean and vice versa.

Like Coleridge and the critic in the *Eclectic Review*, evangelical thinkers typically avoided the pitfalls of a thoroughly subjectivist idealism, taking pains to affirm the objectivity of the ideal. "[N]ature ... does not create the poetic fire," insisted William A. Knight. "It only evokes it from the depths of the human spirit to which it has made appeal. Nor, on the other hand, does the poet project his own subjectivity upon nature, covering it with an ideal robe of glory that has been altogether wrought within himself. He is, before all things else, a *seer*."[63] Knight's statement demonstrates how a concern to preserve objectivity, with a little help from romantic conceptions of genius, could generate rather exorbitant claims for the importance of art and the epistemological reaches of the artist.

---

[59] T.A., "What Is Poetry?" *MerR* 11 (July 1859), 385.
[60] "Æsthetics," *CR* 26 (Oct. 1861), 590.
[61] "Symbols of Thought," *PQR* 10 (Apr. 1862), 632.
[62] "Practical Aesthetics," *BrQR* 71 (Jan. 1880), 54. For similar statements, see "Aesthetics," *PQR* 10 (July 1861), 27-29 (though see the discussion of this article below); Knight, "A Contribution," 185, 187; and W.M. Reily, "The Artist; The Seer and Minister of Beauty," *RQR* (1881), 388.
[63] Knight, "A Contribution," 186.

Still, although a concern for objectivity may have helped to assuage the epistemological anxieties of some, other evangelicals could prove as ambiguous as their non-evangelical counterparts when it came to specifying the nature of the ideal itself. While most were convinced the ideal was objective, some were apparently unsure exactly what the object was. This was especially true from the 1870s onward as the rhetoric of romantic idealism was naturalized and art and religion were increasingly seen as twin manifestations of humanity's higher consciousness. Writers not uncommonly slipped into a vague Platonic vocabulary when discussing the ideal nature of art:

> Poetry is the language of mental or spiritual exaltation. The poet is lifted above the common level of human experience. He dwells amid permanent realities. He has the power of penetrating beneath the momentarily changing phenomenal form to apprehend the real and unchanging substance; of rising above the realm of the transient and the mutable into the changeless and the eternal.... [H]e who makes a loophole through which to look into the invisible world of truth, beauty, and spiritual forces is a poet. Poetry, then, is invisible and spiritual beauty shining in upon us through appropriate material forms.[64]

Such was the opening salvo of an 1879 article on "Christian Lyric Poetry," an article as thinly Platonic as it was explicitly Christian. W.M. Reily, writing in 1881, displayed his Platonic credentials openly when he asserted that "the artist regards his object, not as a material thing, but as the reflection of an idea, and ... this latter is of significance to him only in so far as it brings him nearer to the Idea of ideas, which Plato designates as Eternal and Divine."[65] T.W. Hunt, drawing on Plato and Victor Cousin, glided almost imperceptibly from the language of "God" to that of "the infinite": "Beauty centres in God and is worshipped in him. Art is the representation of the infinite, and must therefore be religious in character and aim."[66] In 1893, the *Methodist Review* employed another term characteristic of German idealism: "The absolute reveals itself to human intelligence by an appeal to our sense of the beautiful, while in art the mind seeks to imitate the beautiful in nature, and thus gropes after thoughts of the absolute. Thus do we find a basis for the metaphysical in aesthetics."[67] Some evangelicals had, oddly enough, managed to find in art a basis for the metaphysical, though not always for the distinctively Christian.

Yet not all evangelicals who accepted the basic parameters of an idealist aesthetics were satisfied by the vague talk of the "absolute" epitomized by the *Methodist Review*. While some were content to speak ambiguously of the ideal embodied in art, others took pains to adjust the principles of aesthetic idealism to

---

[64] "Christian Lyric Poetry," *PMQRCAmb*, n.s. 1 (Jan. 1879), 129. See also "The Poems of Lewis Morris," *BM* 82 (Sep. 1890), 411.
[65] W.M. Reily, "The Artist," 394.
[66] Theodore W. Hunt, "Modern Aestheticism," *PR* 9 (1882), 150.
[67] J.W. Wright, "The Aesthetic in Religion," *MR* 9 (Jan. 1893), 90.

the requirements of evangelical orthodoxy. "Man would be ... in error were he to worship the ideal," asserted the *Presbyterian Quarterly Review*. "It is not the 'good,' the 'beautiful' and the 'true' that should bound the thoughts and measure the devotion of the soul." The writer, however, did not dismiss these ideals outright. What he objected to was idealism's tendency to treat these ideals as self-existent, impersonal abstractions. Christians, by contrast, grasp these ideals in and through a *personal* God: "Worshipping him we apprehend and love these ideals; not as qualities which float in our own fancy, or seem to exist in some unseen altitude 'very far away,' but in conscious Deity—the creating, governing, loving God." He likewise rejected extreme forms of idealism (e.g., Berkeley's) which saw the material world as mind-dependent. Once these qualifications had been made clear, however, the author was free to advance a basically idealist conception of art. "If we love art, it is because within it is a beam from the source of beauty. If we love song, it is a symbol to the ear of utterance unheard—of life, love, care and Fatherhood in heaven." In fact, by transferring "the doctrine of idealism to the Will of the Creator" (all reality is essentially a projection of God's mind), he secured for the material world a symbolic, even sacramental, status. Both nature and art had become expressions of the personal God of the Bible. While not identical, the theistic—indeed, the explicitly Christian—idealism of this writer in some ways paralleled Edwards.[68]

This critic's effort to graft orthodox principles onto a broadly idealist system of aesthetics (or vice versa) suggests one way in which some evangelicals sought to be philosophically progressive and theologically conservative at the same time. Idealism was tenable insofar as one could ground it in the personality of the biblical God. For other writers, however, idealism could be substantiated on the basis of another theological category: eschatology. The ideal does not merely exist as a super-sensuous entity, a Platonic form, or a timeless idea in the divine consciousness but rather affords a shadowy vision of the heavenly existence that awaits believers. Located within a concrete history of redemption, art provides a glimpse of future perfection. "The last and highest use of poetry," concluded the *Christian Observer* in 1866, "is to breathe energy, by breathing inspiration into our languid and labouring existence, and to serve as a bright and blissful substitute for a lost Paradise. It brings back the glory that has departed, and calls in, before its time, the glory that is to come."[69] At times, theorists characterized the creative process and activity of the imagination themselves in redemptive terms,

---

[68] "Symbols of Thought," 625-29. The author uses the romantic term "symbol," but his thinking is not unlike Edwards's notion of typology. See also Julian Ramsay's later criticism of Shelley: "the lesson which, above all others, [Shelley's poems] are calculated to teach is one which their author never consciously endeavored to inculcate—that man can only find the true end of his being in God, understanding that term not as it is understood by the Pantheist, but as representing a living, loving, personal Father" ("Percy Bysshe Shelley," *PMQR* [1889], 593-94). Ramsay's statement reflects the continuing desire to reject romantic poets' vague (pantheistic) interpretations of God.

[69] "Poetry and Its Uses," 119.

as did the 1855 *Eclectic Review* piece examined above. In his discussion of landscape painting, the writer considered the example of a tree. No perfect tree exists in nature, though "At its birth there was a certain ideal stamped on its nature, towards which ... it has every moment of its life been tending." It is the province of art and the artist to grasp this ideal where nature has failed: "By that insight which alone constitutes the artist [*sic*] mind, he must seize on the ideal, the essential and saving beauty, and working in the creative spirit of nature, remove the curse under which she labours, restoring a pristine excellence, or at least anticipating a future perfection" (138). Idealization therefore doubles as a mode of eschatological perception and a means of restoring in percipients a sense of prelapsarian perfection. "The artist's business is the idealisation of the actual, to show us nature as God made it, not as it is perverted by sin."[70] Ironically, it was the doctrine of the Fall that for these writers assigned to art deep significance and value. It was, one might say, an aesthetic version of the *felix culpa*.[71]

From Devilish to "the vision and the faculty divine": The Imagination Reconsidered

These discussions of idealization in terms of redemption and eschatology underscore the transformation that had taken place in evangelical conceptions of the imagination since the Puritans. For many Puritans, the imagination needed to be held at arm's length, for it was liable to skew one's natural and spiritual perceptions. The Puritan tradition did include more positive conceptions of the imagination's relationship to spiritual realities, but such statements were often overshadowed by warnings against overindulgence. By the mid-nineteenth century, however, many evangelicals had joined the romantic chorus in praise of the imagination not only as a faculty of artistic creation but also as an organ of transcendental perception. "[W]e dare to claim for the true, childlike, humble imagination," argued George MacDonald in the *British Quarterly Review* in 1867, "such an inward oneness with the laws of the universe that it possesses in itself an insight into the very nature of things." MacDonald's theory was no anomaly.

---

[70] Spes, "Art and Morals," *WMM* 119 (May 1896), 339.

[71] The idea that art overcomes the chaos engendered by the Fall has roots in the Renaissance. John Dennis also articulated a version of it in 1704: "The great design of Arts is to restore the decays that happen'd to Humane Nature by the Fall, by restoring Order" (*The Grounds of Criticism in Poetry, Contain'd in Some New Discoveries Never Made Before, Requisite for the Writing and Judging of Poems Surely* [London, 1704], 6). Dennis conceives of this project as the recovery of a lost cosmic order, but he does not suggest this order has pressing eschatological significance. Cf. James Smetham's alternative view: "[Art] may not, after all, be so much a lever to raise men from the fall, as one of his enjoyments when he *has* risen" ("Modern Sacred Art in England," *LQR* 18 [Apr. 1862], 79).

Evangelical readers, it seems, found it attractive enough for the *Christian Ambassador* to reprint a portion of the essay two years later.[72] In fact, nothing illustrates the evangelical affinity for romantic aesthetics as clearly as the transition of the imagination from devilish to, as Wordsworth put it, "the vision and the faculty divine."[73]

The shift from Puritan distrust to the romantic exaltation of the imagination as a sort of über-faculty capable of penetrating the spirit of the cosmos was on one level yet another consequence of evangelicals' investment in the mental philosophy of the Scottish Enlightenment. Beginning in the latter half of the eighteenth century, the imagination metamorphosed from a chiefly associative and aggregative faculty operating on stored sensory data in accordance with fixed mental laws to a creative and visionary faculty with the ability to conjure genuinely new ideas and grasp intuitively the metaphysical unity of all things.[74] Although romantic theories of the imagination like Coleridge's owed much to German thought as well, Scottish philosophers like Dugald Stewart, with whose writings educated evangelicals were familiar, played a vital role in this evolution. Given the pervasiveness of Scottish philosophy among evangelicals at the turn of the nineteenth century, it is little wonder that evangelical thinking about the imagination mirrored this same pattern of development.

Something of this transition may be glimpsed in a review of Stewart's *Philosophical Essays* published in the *Christian Observer* in 1812. Stewart, for his part, was alert to the common prejudices against the imagination as a faculty prone to evil, especially during the formative years of childhood. In reply, he suggested that the way to avoid a misguided imagination is not to stamp out a child's imaginative experiences but to train the imagination early through proper exercise. Stewart, in short, counseled more imagination, not less.[75] The reviewer found this position appealing: "It deserves ... to be seriously considered, whether the ordinary practice [of suppressing the imagination] has not been established upon contracted and erroneous views of human nature; and whether it does not, in effect, augment the evil which it proposes to correct."[76] Although he was not prepared to issue a final verdict on Stewart's views—something he hoped to do

---

[72] George MacDonald, "The Imagination: Its Function and Its Culture," *BrQR* 46 (July 1867), 52; "Imagination," *CAmb* 7 (Feb. 1869): 77-87. The evangelical fascination with this essay has continued. See *The Christian Imagination*, ed. Leland Ryken (Colorado Springs: Shaw Books-WaterBrook, 2002), 101-103.

[73] William Wordsworth, *The Excursion*, ed. Sally Bushell, James A. Butler, Michael C. Jaye, with David Garcia (Ithaca: Cornell University Press, 2007), 1.79.

[74] On this transition, see Abrams, *Mirror*; Bate, *Classic to Romantic*; James Engell, *The Creative Imagination: Enlightenment to Romanticism* (1981; San Jose: toExcel, 1999); and Ernest Lee Tuveson, *Imagination as a Means of Grace: Locke and the Aesthetics of Romanticism* (Berkeley: University of California Press, 1960).

[75] Similarly, Edmund Gosse would later speculate that if his intransigent parents had indulged his early desire for fiction, his own faith crisis may have been less severe (*Father and Son: A Study of Two Temperaments*, ed. Peter Abbs [London: Penguin, 1989], 50).

[76] Review of *Philosophical Essays*, by Dugald Stewart, *CO* 11 (Oct. 1812), 673.

later—his provisional support points to evangelicals' growing appreciation of the positive benefits of the imagination.

By mid-century, this tentative openness had been transformed among many critics into full-fledged support, and it was in some measure the Scottish philosophy that continued to drive this metamorphosis. As late as 1861, the *Presbyterian Quarterly Review* could describe the imagination in terms that closely resembled Stewart's discussion in *Elements of the Philosophy of the Human Mind*—so closely in fact that the writer even pirated Stewart's example of Milton's garden of Eden to illustrate the combining power of the imagination. The imagination, he asserted, is that "great faculty" involved in "the construction of new wholes.... She endows inanimate nature with life. She causes the motionless to move, the mute to speak, the passionless to beam with intelligence." The imagination is also the idealizing faculty: "She makes the idea more than it is in art and nature, and then goes on to ideal beauty, which no art can compass, and no object in nature can fully realize. Thus the imagination gives more than is returned to her, and then goes on to the creation of ideal beauty which she does not expect to be fully realized."[77] While this writer initially couched his discussion of the imagination in the conventional terms of eighteenth-century empiricist philosophy, the imagination ultimately found itself knocking on heaven's door. It is capable of conceiving (although art is not necessarily capable of embodying) a beauty that rises above the imperfect beauty of earth. Thus the imagination is a faculty of transcendent vision, of supra-worldly perception; or rather, it is almost such a faculty. In this case, the writer's theological convictions prompted him to stop short of granting the imagination full access to heaven; the imagination must rest content for now merely to listen at the door: "The conception of the artist is imperfect. Measured according to certain imperfect standards, it may be considered perfect; but can it be that a being so depraved as man, living in an atmosphere so impure, and surrounded with objects so deformed, can have the highest ideas of beauty? It is not possible. The standard on earth and in heaven are different." There remains, therefore, a fundamental gap between divine and earthly beauty that cannot be bridged even by the redeemed. Earthly perfection is the culmination of earthly existence, not the beginning of heavenly perfection: "But who does not believe that in a redeemed state, with the spirit regenerated, and the physical world purified by fire, there will be visions of beauty, such as yet never have tenanted the human mind, and objects of beauty, such as yet have never greeted the human eye?" Even so, one must not ignore earthly beauty since it is God's gift for humankind. In seeking the beautiful, one learns of the "benevolence" of God even as one's nature is "refine[d] and elevate[d]."[78]

---

[77] "Aesthetics," *PQR*, 30, 31. Cf. Dugald Stewart, *Elements of the Philosophy of the Human Mind, Vol. 1, to Which Is Prefixed, Introduction and Part First of the Outlines of Moral Philosophy. With Many New and Important Additions*, ed. Sir William Hamilton (Westmead: Gregg, 1971), 436.
[78] "Aesthetics," *PQR*, 32, 36, 37.

This writer was in many ways poised between an eighteenth and nineteenth-century conception of the imagination.[79] Yet even as he formulated the workings of the imagination according to the empirical terminology of the Scottish Enlightenment, he was gesturing towards a Coleridgean understanding of the imagination as an organ of quasi-divine creation and spiritual insight. In fact, some critics had described the imagination in such terms even earlier. In 1849, the *Eclectic Review* had invoked the increasingly popular distinction between fancy and imagination to argue that "the essential imaginings of poetry" are not "contradistinguished from 'God's truth'" but rather "*are* God's truths: just as much as the law of gravitation". James Fergusson, the author under review, had missed this point, partly because he had confused the workings of the imagination with "*fancy*". True imagination perceives divine truth whereas fancy gives birth to nothing but verbal window-dressing. The reviewer's reference point for this distinction was Ruskin's chapter on the "Penetrative Imagination" in volume 2 of *Modern Painters*[80] (published three years earlier), but the distinction had originated in the late eighteenth century (Stewart, for instance, had posited a similar scheme in 1792) and had received its most famous romantic exposition in Coleridge's *Biographia Literaria*. As noted earlier, the *Eclectic Review* drew upon Coleridge's theory of the imagination in 1855, and other direct references to Coleridge's imagination began appearing in evangelical periodicals in the 1860s. In 1867, J.H. Rigg explored both Coleridge's and Wordsworth's views of the imagination in his review of Dallas. Coleridge, Rigg conceded, was hampered by "his obscurity," as well as "the almost insane jargon of mysticism which mars his writings," but if one could translate his insights "with a reference to the Platonic idealism with which Coleridge was so deeply imbued," then "their meaning is worthy of respect." Although Rigg was not uncritical of either, he concluded that where the imagination was concerned, "we shall perhaps find that Coleridge and Wordsworth have come nearer to the true idea appertaining to the word than any other authorities." Significantly, however, the problem of depravity that had so exercised the writer in the *Presbyterian Quarterly Review* was muted or else dropped altogether. Moving fairly seamlessly (too seamlessly one might argue) from Platonic idealism to Christianity, Rigg cast Coleridge as a broadly Christian philosopher, who "according to his wont, appropriates Scriptural language to describe" earthly things "as 'the example and shadow of heavenly things.'" Such language is not inconsistent with Edwardsean typology and Rigg allowed that such things may be "discerned by the illuminated soul," but he held the Coleridgean imagination rather than the Edwardsean "spiritual sense" to be the source of such illumination: "Imagination, according to Coleridge's philosophy, is the

---

[79] Cf. M.C.H., "On Sacred Poetry," esp. 610.
[80] "Fergusson on True Principles in Art," *ER* 25 (Apr. 1845), 434. Cf. John Ruskin, *Modern Painters, Vol. 2*, ed. E.T. Cook and Alexander Wedderburn (London: George Allen, 1903), 249-88.

power of mind, the act, the quickening, the illumination, wherewith reason recognises in the outward and sensible the analogies of that which is spiritual, and thereby enables the understanding to gain a glimpse of their meaning."[81]

From the late 1860s, romantic statements regarding the powers of the imagination became common among evangelicals. In 1867, Henry N. Day contrasted his own romantic theory of the imagination, in which the artist bodies forth ideal conceptions that rise from within, to older mechanical theories: "No genuine work of art was ever a patch-work of combination. No poet, in his artistic processes, ever summoned before him, by an act of reproductive memory, the forms which had been previously given him in his observations and studies, and then set himself to selecting and combining." In truth, Day continued, "The artist shapes, he idealizes first; he first determines his artistic activity in a specific direction, and embodies it in a pure ideal, a proper spirit-form into which enters no matter...."[82] Such prioritizing of the conceptual over the material typified much romantic theory. Furthermore, as the imagination gradually became less mechanical and material, it became ever more "spiritual." Evangelical writers increasingly followed Coleridge, Ruskin, Emerson, and others in describing it in quasi-religious terms. Quoting Wordsworth, the *Congregationalist* noted the imagination's spiritual import in both this life and the next: "we may be sure that 'the vision and the faculty divine' will also have to do with our life in God hereafter.'"[83] Three years later, W.M. Reily described the imagination or "fancy" (he used the terms interchangeably) as follows: "one of the most legitimate and essential functions of the fancy is to see into the soul of nature, of which the universe is the full expression, but which is, in some sense, present and manifest in every part, that soul which must be regarded as the on-going and actualization of the divine creative word, and as such the revelation of the divine thought and will."[84] Not surprisingly, Reily's article was liberally seasoned with references to Plato, Carlyle, Coleridge, Cousin, and Emerson. A statement by James T. East in the *Wesleyan-Methodist Magazine* in 1900, however, offers perhaps the best measure of the vast ground the imagination had traversed even among conservative evangelicals throughout the nineteenth century. "Any starving of the imagination would be a calamity," East contended, "for 'the very design of imagination is to domesticate us in another, that is, in a celestial nature.'" East held a fundamentally orthodox understanding of Protestant doctrine. The God of which he spoke was clearly the personal God of the Bible, not the Absolute of Fichte, Schelling, or Hegel. In addition, he took care to highlight the place of the Atonement and regeneration in the lives of Christians. Yet in addressing imagination

---

[81] Rigg, Review, 160, 162, 161. See also "The Novel and Novel-Reading," *BRPR* 41 (Apr. 1869), 205 and Eugene Parsons, "Tennyson's Art and Genius," *BQR* 11 (Jan. 1889), 33-35. Parsons uses Ruskin's terminology (34) but also cites Coleridge on "esemplastic power" (35).
[82] Henry N. Day, "The Nature of Beauty," *APTR* 5 (July 1867), 410-11.
[83] T.C. Finlayson, "The Practical Uses of the Imagination," *Cong* 7 (1878), 400.
[84] Reily, "The Artist," 424.

and beauty, both earthly and heavenly, East turned not to Edwards but to Emerson, if only briefly. Even Emerson, it seems, had by the turn of the century been successfully baptized into the ranks of British Methodism.[85]

Not all evangelicals followed the general path charted here. Some conservative writers, like the author in the *Presbyterian Quarterly Review*, continued to express reservations about inflated views of the imagination that downplayed the need for grace as a prerequisite for spiritual perception. Such critics showed more wariness than East in making peace with the "spiritual" rhetoric of American Transcendentalism. Others warned of the psychological dangers of an overactive imagination—an argument that demonstrated extraordinary longevity, particularly in evangelical discussions of fiction.[86]

Nevertheless, the imagination's romantic evolution into a spiritual organ for perceiving ideal reality was significant both aesthetically and theologically. Aesthetically, romantic theories of the imagination helped to elevate evangelical conceptions of both art and the artist. If the imagination enabled one to "see into the life of things," then art was more than ornament or recreation; it was a new type of "truth" and thus worth taking seriously. Theologically, the imagination's conversion into a kind of spiritual instrument was indicative of the fact that traditional conceptions of grace and regeneration were growing obsolete. It is no coincidence that the rise of the evangelical romantic imagination paralleled the decline of Puritan understandings of the self as inherently depraved and subject to the sovereignty of God. Although often described in religious language, the romantic imagination did not rely on supernatural grace in order to function as an organ of amplified perception. True, not all people were equally endowed with imaginative power—not everyone could perform at the level of Coleridge's "Secondary Imagination" or Ruskin's "Penetrative Imagination"—but the imagination's power was natural rather than supernatural in its operations. For Coleridge, the Primary Imagination was so basic that simple perception was impossible without it. In some cases, the objects of the imagination's perception had themselves shifted into a natural register, resulting in something like Thomas Carlyle's "natural supernaturalism." In other cases, critics seemed to understand the imagination as a metaphysical faculty of which the objects of perception were the ideal forms of the divine. Now, however, rising above one's earthbound state

---

[85] James T. East, "The Ministry of Beauty," *WMM* 123 (July 1900), 502, 504. The quotation cited by East appears in Emerson's essay, "Poetry and Imagination," *Letters and Social Aims* (Boston: Houghton, Mifflin, 1904), 20.

[86] For some negative comments on the imagination, see R., "Popish Paintings," *ECI* 28 (July 1829): 492-98; "Religion of the Imagination," *CAJZH* 4 (16 Oct. 1829), 28; Francis Wayland, "The Abuse of the Imagination," *CAJ* 10 (13 Apr. 1836): 133-34 (an extract from Wayland's textbook); "Men of Taste," *CAJ* 29 (23 Mar. 1854), 48; and "The Imagination in Sin," *WMM* 123 (Dec. 1900): 901-905. On the psychological problems of fiction, see chapter 4.

did not require a prior act of condescension by God. The imagination had become, in the words of Ernest Lee Tuveson, "a means of grace."[87] As a creative faculty, moreover, the romantic imagination depended upon basic assumptions regarding the nature of human freedom, assumptions that would have seemed odd, if not scandalous, to the Puritans and Edwards. (Tellingly, Coleridge not only expended great energy defending the freedom of the will but he also developed an increasingly negative view of Edwards.[88]) The artist had become a symbol of autonomy, a being that possessed the ability to transcend the mechanical laws of nature and to "create" freely after the manner of God.[89] In disseminating romantic claims on behalf of the imagination, many evangelicals were moving swiftly away from the religio-aesthetic tradition of the Puritans. On the one hand, this meant an increased esteem for the fine arts; on the other hand, it signaled the further dissolution of Protestant orthodoxy.[90]

Anti-Romantic Reactions: Evangelical Classicism and the "*Terra Firma* of Common-Sense"

One measure of how influential romantic views of art and the imagination had become is the strength of the reaction to such views exhibited by another set of evangelical critics. Even as some writers were embracing idealism, others voiced doubts about key tenets of romantic theory. Some, for example, seem to have grown tired of what they perceived as the moral and aesthetic extremism to which expressivism had led. They were usually measured in their criticisms and rarely objected to expressivism in toto. Rather, their strategy was to propose that self-expression, while indispensable, was subordinate to other, more important concerns. Ironically, one of these concerns was the ideality of art. "[I]dealisation," argued H. Buxton Forman, "must always be regarded as a higher function of art than mere expression."[91] Whereas many critics had followed Coleridge in transcendentalizing the ideal, others (re)turned to a more classical conception of the ideal as a way to oppose the excesses of romantic expressivism. For these anti-

---

[87] I have borrowed this phrase from Tuveson's title.
[88] See "To John Ryland," 3 Nov. 1807, *Collected Letters of Samuel Taylor Coleridge*, vol. 3, ed. Early Leslie Griggs (Oxford: Clarendon, 1959), 35 and *Aids to Reflection*, ed. John Beer (Princeton: Princeton University Press, 1993), 158-60. See also Abrams, *Mirror*, 174.
[89] See Milton C. Nahm, "The Theological Background of the Theory of the Artist as Creator," *Essays on the History of Aesthetics*, ed. Peter Kivy (Rochester: University of Rochester Press, 1992): 75-84.
[90] For other romantic descriptions of the imagination, see J.C. Shairp, "The Aim of Poetry," *PR* (July-Dec. 1878), 451-54; "Practical Aesthetics," 52, 53; Allen Traver, "Thinking; Thought; Literature," *RQR* 28 (Jan. 1881), 122, 127; and Mims, "Poetry and the Spiritual Life," 394, 395.
[91] H. Buxton Forman, "Music and Poetry: Their Origin and Functions," *LQR* 39 (1872), 36.

romantics, the ideal was a means of protesting what they saw as the growing subjectivism of romantic art.

Joseph LeConte provides an example of this sort of approach. LeConte did not locate the ideal in simple opposition to self-expression but suggested that expression was subservient to the ideal. Expression is a necessary ingredient in art, but for an art object to qualify as "high art," it must also move beyond expression to something more essential: "Thus, we might briefly say that there are in all art, as well as in nature, two elements: the sensuous, or emotional, and the aesthetic. The first is some times called expression, life, power, passion, naturalness; the second, beauty, grace, unity, ideality. Now, in a high art the latter is always predominant; in a low art, the former is always predominant."[92] LeConte encapsulates the conventionally "romantic" (expression, life, power, passion, naturalness) and "classical" (beauty, grace, unity, ideality) aesthetic virtues, and although he ultimately grants priority to the latter, he nevertheless recognizes the importance of the former.

LeConte's aesthetic attempts to curb what he saw as the immoderate impulses within romantic aesthetics without entirely abandoning its central premises. An 1854 article in the *London Quarterly Review*, however, opted for a more aggressive line, arguing not only for the supremacy of the classical ideal over and against expressivism but also for the classical ideal over and against the historical determinism which the author associated with the idealist theories of art and history that exerted such a profound influence on nineteenth-century thought. Authored by Thomas M'Nicholl, the journal's editor, this piece undertook "to offer some brief remarks upon the leading characteristics of modern poetry." In general, M'Nicholl's view of modern poetry was not particularly favorable. He conceded that "there is so much to elicit admiration" but insisted that there is "still more that is fatal."[93] In its preference for aesthetic principles running contrary to many in the romantic tradition (despite M'Nicholl's assurances that he appreciates Shelley and Keats), the article offers an interesting point of contrast to the developments observed thus far.

M'Nicholl sets out to counteract an idea that had gained currency as a result of the developing historical consciousness of the late eighteenth and early nineteenth centuries—that poetry is a product of "the spirit of the age."[94] He admits that "true poetry may, in some faint degree, reflect the spirit of the age which gives it birth" (240), but he wishes to drive home that "the method of true art is not altered by the genius of an age" (241). The doctrine that the *zeitgeist* gives birth to poetry (another byproduct of German idealist theories of history) had

---

[92] LeConte, "On the Nature," 325, 331.
[93] Thomas M'Nicholl, "Modern Poetry: Its Genius and Tendencies," *LQR* 2 (1854), 238. Subsequent references appear parenthetically in the text.
[94] Writing in 1831, Mill suggested that "The 'SPIRIT OF THE AGE' is in some measure a novel expression. I do not believe that it is to be met with in any work exceeding fifty years in antiquity" ("The Spirit of the Age," *Mill's Essays on Literature & Society*, ed. J.B. Schneewind [New York: Collier Books-Macmillan, 1965], 28).

been for some romantics an enabling idea. It was preached at times in triumphalist tones, as when Shelley reveled with his usual rhetorical flamboyance in the thought that "Poets are the hierophants of an unapprehended inspiration" who "are themselves perhaps the most sincerely astonished at its manifestations, for it is less their spirit than the spirit of the age."[95] Shelley had found the idea an empowering one: poets are socially relevant because they are in tune with the pitch of time and poised at the edge of progress. Clearly, however, there is an implicit determinism in the notion that poets are the unconscious conductors of the intellectual currents of an age, and for M'Nicholl, writing in 1854, the idea had become more oppressive than empowering. In fact, two developments stemming from this notion had begun to trouble some Victorian critics. The first was the claim that only poetry which embodies an age's ethos counts as "true" poetry. Only "modern" subjects, that is, are fit subjects for verse. What had seemed to Shelley an aesthetically and politically liberating idea was hardened into a normative criterion. The second, darker development was the growing realization that to claim that poetry is a product of the spirit of the age was to accept the historicist consequence that poetry could be nothing *more* than a product of its age.

Against these perspectives, M'Nicholl turns to something like the classical ideal to reaffirm the universality and objectivity of art:

> The nature of art is essentially objective and constructive. A poem, like a painting, is strictly a composition, whose materials—selected almost in whatsoever place you will—are faithfully combined by the aesthetic faculty,—a faculty that is neither wholly intellectual nor wholly moral, that acts in great measure like instinct, but needs the co-operation of science and intelligence. (241)

There is little here that would have troubled the staunchest neoclassical critic. M'Nicholl's understanding of idealization is comparatively free of transcendental overtones: it is a matter of "composition" only, and although he leaves room in the artistic process for a certain amount of "instinct" (common enough in eighteenth-century theories of invention), his model has more in common with neoclassical theories of association than romantic conceptions of the imagination. (It is not insignificant that M'Nicholl summons in support of his argument the popular eighteenth-century dictum *ut pictura poesis*, which had given way among many romantic critics to a belief in the intrinsic kinship of poetry and music.[96]) "Poetry," he continues, "depends far more on the essential than the accidental; on the permanent than the temporary; on man himself than national costume or political conditions.... The best, and even the most popular, poems in the world, are those which are least shaped or coloured by the spirit of the au-

---

[95] Percy Bysshe Shelley, *A Defence of Poetry*, *Shelley's Prose and Poetry*, ed. Donald H. Reiman and Sharon B. Powers (New York: Norton, 1977), 508.
[96] See Abrams, *Mirror*, 50, 88-94.

thor's age" (241). There is, for M'Nicholl, little in art that is subjective or historically relative. Art is universal and objective in the neoclassical sense of these terms.

In fact, the article as a whole is something of an anti-romantic tour de force. Not only does M'Nicholl uphold the classical ideal, but he also ridicules the nimieties of the Byronic poet and calls attention to the hazards of expressivism:

> It is evident that the modern bard esteems no ordinary theme deserving of his song; and so he turns to glorify himself, and worship his own art by way of exercising it. His rhapsody is all about genius,—its sorrows, ecstasies, divinity, and might; what it can do if it only pleases, and what it scorns to do for so miserable an audience as humanity can furnish. No longer holding "the mirror up to Nature," he sits and turns it fairly on himself, and finds trace of thunder in every scar, and demon-beauty in every fantastic lock; the blue of his eye suggests (to him) the unutterable depths of heaven, and in the curl of his lip he reads and practises contempt for the paltry world of prose. (245)

So much for the extremes of romantic individualism. Near the end of his article, M'Nicholl issues a stern warning to young writers: "But let the new generation of poets beware ... how they permit the expressional parts of poetry to overlay its more substantial elements" (256). Poetry's "more substantial elements" refers, of course, to the general and universal.

Viewed from the broader perspective of Victorian criticism, however, M'Nicholl was no rogue classicist or avatar of aesthetic conservatism. In his concluding paragraph, he directs readers to the preface of a recently published volume by one Matthew Arnold (now commonly known as the Preface of 1853), as well as the preface to Henry Taylor's *Philip van Artevelde*. Both of these essays "will teach [young poets] ... how to avoid the false heroics of Byronic poetry," and in this he was surely correct. In his preface, Arnold insists on "the subordinate character of expression" in poetry and argues for the continuing validity of classical models. The ancients "knew what they wanted in Art, and we do not." Action and subject matter, not expression, are the necessary conditions for good poetry. As one scholar has put it, "Arnold's Preface to the 1853 edition of his poems was basically a rejection of romantic subjectivism,"[97] a rejection clearly affirmed by M'Nicholl. Arnold and M'Nicholl are also consonant in their rejection of any theory that restricts poetry to "modern subjects," for Arnold is anxious to assure readers that he has not eliminated *Empedocles* from the 1853 edition simply "in deference to the opinion which many critics of the present day appear to entertain against subjects chosen from distant times and countries: against the choice, in short, of any subjects but modern ones."[98] Taylor's preface mounts an

---

[97] J.D. Jump, "Matthew Arnold and the *Spectator*," *Review of English Studies* 25 (Jan. 1949), 64.
[98] Matthew Arnold, "Author's Preface, 1853," *The Works of Matthew Arnold* (Ware: Wordsworth, 1995), 13, 15, 3.

even fiercer attack on the excesses of romantic subjectivism. He denounces Byron and Shelley and laments that wisdom and intellect have been rejected in favor of intense feeling and vibrant imagery. According to the modern school, poetry "was to be, like music, a moving and enchanting art, acting upon the fancy, the affections, the passions, but scarcely connected with the intellectual faculties." Significantly, Taylor criticizes Byron for failing to represent humankind in terms of the ideal: "There is nothing in them [Byron's representations] of the mixture and modification,—nothing of the composite fabric which Nature has assigned to Man."[99]

The classicism of M'Nicholl was thus a decidedly Victorian classicism, a reaction to romantic extremism, which was gaining ground at mid-century. The formulation "Art is ideal," when understood in its classical sense, offered a means of evading both the Scylla of subjectivism and the Charybdis of determinism associated with some romantic theories of art. M'Nicholl's recuperation of the classical ideal was therefore both reactionary and progressive, a point which supplies another, perhaps unexpected piece of evidence that evangelicals were actively engaged in contemporary aesthetic debates. At the same time, this move demonstrates once again how pervasive romantic assumptions about art had become.

M'Nicholl had openly criticized romantic expressivism and at least indirectly furnished an alternative vision of the ideal stripped of the metaphysical drapery of German idealism. Some critics, however, opted for a more acerbic attack on the doctrines of idealism. Writing in the *Primitive Methodist Quarterly Review*, Henry J. Miller bewailed what he referred to as "The Teutonization of English Literature." Not published until 1885, the article provided a sardonic and somewhat belated response to the effects of German thought on English aesthetics, taking aim yet again at the presumed intemperance of romantic views.

Miller opposes idealism, which he racializes as German and repeatedly characterizes in terms of ephemeral substances like "gas" and "vapor," to common sense, which he identifies as English and depicts as solid and grounded. "How comes it to pass," he asks, "that we English, eminently a practical and hard-headed race, having once got our feet well planted on the good substantial *terra firma* of common-sense, have voluntarily stepped from our coign of vantage to trust ourselves to the unknown perils of the quaking bog of *a priori* mysticism?" Regrettably, the English "have allowed a huge sea of Teutonism to submerge [them], every wave of which is highly charged with Transcendental gas." Miller, in effect, reaches back to what he imagines as the good old days of pre-romantic philosophy when the realism of Reid and Stewart reigned. "[L]et us examine," Miller later suggests, "any poem, novel, or essay of (say) the year 1823, side by side with a like composition of the year 1883, and we shall soon see what a wide

---

[99] Henry Taylor, Preface, *Philip van Artevelde; A Dramatic Romance, in Two Parts* (Boston: James Munroe, 1835), ix, xiv.

gulf separates the two, both in conception and in execution." The reasons for this difference are obvious:

> In the days of our fathers it was the fashion for our literati to bring to bear upon the consideration of any given subject, not only the resources of a wide and varied culture, but an inexhaustible fund of shrewd common-sense, an unqualified hatred of epicene or sentimentality and affectation, a power of taking broad views, a terseness and vigour in giving them expression, and a consummate generalship in marshalling their thoughts. In these degenerate days, since we have become thoroughly Teutonised, we have altered all that. English habits of thought have sunk, drenched and overwhelmed under the successive deluges of Kantism, Fichteism, Hegelism, and Schopenhaverism which have poured down upon us. A perpetual drizzle from the land of Vapourdom has soddened us to the bone.

Thus he concludes, "No sublime, grandly imagined epic, no genuine drama, holding the mirror up to nature, not even a sweet, simple idyll, or the rudest of pulse-quickening lyrics, can exist in an atmosphere so rarefied." Interestingly, even the transgressions of Byron fare comparatively well amid this suffocating miasma of German philosophy. Whereas Byron had represented for M'Nicholl all that was wrong with English poetry, for Miller he has become a touchstone of sincerity. The self-expressions of Byron, at least, were genuine, but in German idealism "the magnified, attenuated, distorted 'I' is never in the ordinary moods of ordinary mortals. It is for ever high up in the clouds, or above them, amongst the Infinites. The only nouns it takes any cognizance of are the abstract ones. The vacant vision takes in the *ideal* afar off, but sees nothing of the *actual* close at hand."[100] Better the solid English ego of Byron than the diffuse transcendental ego of the Germans.

Despite Miller's passion (and humor), however, his argument was clearly too little too late, for his own editor appended a footnote which cast doubt on Miller's thesis: "While admitting there is more or less reason in Mr. Miller's drastic criticism, we cannot help thinking his views somewhat extreme and one-sided. It, indeed, surprises us no little that a writer of such perspicacity and vigour can see nothing but gross and unmitigated evil in the Teutonization of English Literature.—ED." Yet if the editor's footnote in one sense subverted Miller's position, it only confirmed it in another. English literature and aesthetics had in fact been "Teutonized," and many evangelicals, like Miller's editor, were far from seeing this development as a "gross and unmitigated evil."[101]

Aesthetic Apologias: Art's Purpose and Uniqueness

The question What is art? bears an intimate relationship to questions regarding art's purpose and value within human experience and culture. A theory that views

---

[100] Henry J. Miller, "The Teutonization of English Literature," *PMQR* n.s. 7 (Jan. 1885), 132, 133, 136, 137, 134.
[101] Miller, "Teutonization," 141.

art as embellishment or ornamentation will arrive at a far more restricted answer to the question What are the ends of art? than a theory which sees art as self-expression or the embodiment of ideal reality. As evangelical conceptions of art shifted after the 1830s, so also did their understandings of art's significance. Whereas earlier evangelicals had valued art largely for its diversionary and didactic qualities, many nineteenth-century evangelicals came to see art as a unique mode of discourse capable of making a distinctive and integral contribution to human existence.

During the Victorian period, both evangelicals and non-evangelicals agreed that what could not be justified with reference either to morality or eternity could hardly be justified at all. This already serious interest in the question of purpose grew more urgent, however, as a result of the claims issuing from some quarters that art lacked practical value. Utilitarians, whose aesthetic views have sometimes been compared to evangelicals', denounced poetry as falsehood and sought, like Plato, to exile it from the republic.[102] Rapid industrialization and advancements in technology, together with the spread of the scientific spirit into the deepest recesses of the Victorian psyche, encouraged many to see art as little more than a plaything in contrast to the mighty achievements of science. Charles Darwin is perhaps the best known example of a nineteenth-century intellectual whose devotion to science engendered a corresponding distaste for the Shakespeare he had enjoyed as a boy. Indeed, the social and intellectual progress so dear to Victorians seemed by its very nature to entail the inevitable abandonment of art, as Thomas Babington Macaulay famously argued.[103] In addition to these widespread cultural concerns regarding the purpose and value of art, evangelicals in particular faced other aggravating factors that made the consideration of art's ends all the more crucial. The most important of these was the continuing influence of Puritanism's asymmetrical aesthetic legacy, which left some evangelicals uncertain about art's ultimate status. Vestiges of this Puritan tradition received fresh emphasis within the context of nineteenth-century revivalism, merging with typically evangelical concerns to generate the potential for renewed doubts about the value of art. Was it possible to square a prolonged attention to aesthetics with an individual's obligation to evangelize, engage in social activism, and use one's time wisely in light of eternity? Such considerations raised difficult questions about whether pursuing the arts was consistent with conduct befitting a committed Christian. It is little wonder, then, that evangelical critics were forced to rethink the significance of art.

Evangelical defenders of art did not always agree on why art is valuable or on precisely how valuable it is. That they valued it, however, and believed it to have

---

[102] See Abrams, *Mirror*, 300-303. On evangelicals and utilitarians, see Richard D. Altick, *Victorian People and Ideas: A Companion for the Modern Reader of Victorian Literature* (New York: Norton, 1973), 165-202 and *The English Common Reader: A Social History of the Mass Reading Public, 1800-1900* (Columbus: Ohio State University Press, 1998), 99.

[103] On Macaulay, see Abrams, *Mirror*, 306.

a vital purpose is clear. Although many were careful to qualify the extent of art's influence,[104] none suggested that art is useless or that human existence would be equally satisfying without it. In fact, many writers advanced vigorous claims for the necessity of art. With regard to the question of art's fundamental purpose, the western aesthetic tradition had frequently relied on Horace's well-known maxim "to please and instruct." A number of evangelicals took this principle as their starting-point, though they sometimes leaned heavily towards either pleasure or instruction. Surprising, perhaps, given the puritanical attitude often attributed to evangelicals, is the extent to which some critics stressed the pleasure side of the Horatian equation. As early as 1814, John Foster betrayed some impatience with a text he was reviewing for having labored so tediously to defend the notion that the purpose of art is pleasure, something Foster took to be self-evident: "Perhaps the main purpose is still no more than to maintain and illustrate the principle or position, that the immediate object of poetry is to please; on which point, if any one has continued sceptical, in despite of the loads of paper that have been wasted on this frivolous topic, it would have been perfectly just to abandon him to the consequences of his obdurate perverseness."[105] This commitment to pleasure as the end of art also led some writers to reiterate the common distinction between the fine arts and so-called mechanic arts, or between beauty and utility.[106] The fine arts (music, painting, etc.) were devoted to beauty and pleasure; the mechanic arts (e.g., carpentry) served practical ends. This distinction, a product of eighteenth-century aesthetics, was foundational to the concept of "high art," and in affirming it evangelicals were in effect positioning themselves within the "elite" art world of the day. The conviction that certain activities existed mainly for the sake of pleasure also distinguished nineteenth-century evangelicals from their Puritan forbears. Although most were far from relinquishing a belief in art's "utility," the willingness of some to see art in terms of the enjoyment it afforded constituted a marked departure from those Puritans for whom pleasure remained an ancillary concern.

Still, few evangelicals endorsed art for purely hedonistic reasons. Many who deferred to the classical dictum understood that the best art maintained a productive balance between pleasure and instruction:

> The business of poetry, however, (and we affirm it unqualifiedly), being both to please and to profit, he who aims solely to please spends his strength upon fancy-articles, fit only for the bazaar-market: and he who aims solely to profit, at the peril of not pleasing, will lose his labour in proportion, because the reading public—"the

---

[104] See chapter 3.
[105] John Foster, "Dyer's Poetics," *ER* 11 (Apr. 1814), 371. For similar discussions, see Hall, "Poetry and Philosophy," 169; Otheman, "The Moral Influence," 318; M'Nicholl, "Modern Poetry," 243; and "The Minister and Fiction-Reading," *MR* (Sep. 1900), 718.
[106] See, for instance, Otheman, "The Moral Influence," 318 and John Ruskin, "The Useful and the Beautiful," *CAJ* 29 (22 June 1854), 97 (a reprinted excerpt).

few" as well as "the many"—will not please to be profited, unless they can profit by being pleased.[107]

If anything, critics tended to stress the instruction side of the equation by valuing art as a moral instrument. This was consistent with the trajectory of much Victorian theory and criticism in general,[108] although this emphasis should also be understood within the context of evangelicalism's engagement with romantic theory. It was partly the changed conception of art brought about by romanticism that enabled evangelicals to view art with a new degree of (moral) seriousness, which in turn laid the groundwork for expanded claims concerning its value. If art is nothing more than embellishment, then it is difficult to see it as anything more than amusement, something for which evangelicals had conventionally harbored ambivalence. Once they began to embrace the notion that art is something more than ornamentation or the playful use of language or color, however, evangelicals began to see it as central to human experience. "They undoubtedly entertain a very mean and degrading opinion of the polite arts," asserted one critic in 1831, "who consider them merely as subservient to amusement, or at most, to that cultivation of mind which *emollit mores, nec sinit esse feros*. The history of the world evinces that they have all a much higher and more beneficial influence upon the disposition and happiness of man."[109] In justifying art, the strategy of some writers was not so much to alter their view of amusement—Rigg insisted that "we have no right to indulge in mere amusement or pleasure, merely for the sake of amusement or pleasure"[110]—as to alter their view of art. Mere amusement was exactly that which true art is not. Day, for example, echoed Schelling's claim that aesthetics represents the apex of philosophy:

> The philosophy of Beauty, of the embodiment of idea in matter, is the true philosophy of life—a philosophy of higher significance, of higher interest, of higher importance, than the abstract science of the real, or of the good—just as the embodiment of the soul in the body is more to us than the nature of the soul or the nature of the body, in themselves.... The science of the Beautiful, not only has a just claim to rank coordinately, on scientific grounds, with that of the True and that of the Good, but it is the culminating science of this most generic class of sciences—last in its development in the growth of philosophy, but highest and most important every way to us.[111]

---

[107] "Sacred Poetry," 443. George Lansing Taylor even gave theological backing for the idea that beauty and utility exist in perfect harmony: "Beauty, not utility, is the immediate aim and end of fine art; but so has this universe been tempered together by Infinite Wisdom that, in their profoundest essence, these two are one and identical" ("Fine Art: Its Nature, Necessity, and Offices," *MQR* 34 [1874], 233).

[108] See Jerome Hamilton Buckley, *The Victorian Temper: A Study in Literary Culture* (New York: Vintage, 1951), esp. 124-84.

[109] "The Beauties of Music," *CAJZH* 5 (5 Aug. 1831), 197.

[110] Rigg, Review, 149.

[111] Day, "The Nature of Beauty," 417-18.

Turner had anticipated this move away from art-as-amusement in the 1780s, but by the mid-nineteenth century it had become the prevailing view among educated evangelicals.

Under romanticism's influence, evangelical conceptions of the *way* art serves as a moral instrument were subject to redefinition as well. "The true vocation of the poet," argued the *Eclectic Review* in 1845, "unquestionably is to animate the human race in its progress from barbarism towards virtue and greatness. He is appointed by Providence to arouse to generous exertion, and to console in distress."[112] The rhetoric and tone are as important here as the sentiments. Art and poetry are moral instruments, to be sure, but there is nothing in this view to suggest didacticism in the traditional sense; rather, the poet's job is to "animate" and "arouse." I will return to the relationship between art and morality in chapter 4; for now, it is sufficient to note that although most evangelicals stressed art's moral role, a new understanding of this idea had begun to emerge.

From a theoretical standpoint, however, the Horatian answer to the question of art's ends had always been vulnerable to the attacks of both positivists and puritans. A potential difficulty with the classical formula concerns the issue of art's uniqueness. Art is not the only discourse that can serve as a vehicle of morality; in fact, even if one grants that moral development is an objective of art, it is not obvious that art provides the most effective means of furthering this development. Would not sermons be a more efficient method of conveying moral truths? And if one takes Horace's "instruction" to refer to something like scientific knowledge, then would not a scientific paper be more appropriate than poetry? The criterion of pleasure, it turns out, raises similarly difficult questions. Art may well be pleasurable, but then so are games, conversation, eating, and even (at least for some) sermons. Detractors, therefore, whether utilitarians or puritans, needed only to suggest that art serves no *special* purpose to cast doubt on its value. A question facing critics, then, was whether art is unique, either in the ends to which it addresses itself, or, if it does share its aims with other discourses, then in the mode by which it achieves this end. W.M. Reily stated the problem succinctly: "Can necessity be predicated of art?... In other words, Is art an essential element in the divine order of the universe, or is it only by accident, it finds the place we see it assuming?"[113]

Many critics did in fact attempt to differentiate art from other discourses. The theory that art advances morality through special means was one such effort. In many cases, however, it was the romantic understanding of art as a product of the emotions that provided the grounds for such a distinction. During the eighteenth and early nineteenth centuries, a rather strict dichotomy between art and science had evolved in which art was viewed almost wholly in terms of feeling while science was viewed in terms of intellect or reason. As Wordsworth argued,

---

[112] "Recent Poetry," *ER* 18 (Dec. 1845), 665.
[113] Reily, "The Artist," 386.

the opposite of poetry is not prose but "Matter of Fact, or Science."[114] By mid-century, this distinction had become commonplace, and evangelical critics, like the rest of Victorian society, generally accepted it as normative. Henry Drummond, an associate of Edward Irving's, captured this opposition in his *Letter to Thomas Phillips* (1840): "The number of persons who really love and really estimate the highest productions in the fine arts must be very small, for they are matters of feeling, and not of logic."[115] This premise could be appropriated in various ways. It was, for example, often taken to mean that since art is a product of the artist's emotional interaction with the objects of perception, it proffers a singular vision of reality, a "truth" distinct from science. "The real mission of art," claimed the *Eclectic Review* in 1848, "is not that of a moralist or a metaphysician; but the interpretation of truth, more subtile, and less readily conveyable; the truth appreciable by *feeling*, not by simple intellect."[116] Certain kinds of truth are available only to the heart or imagination. Aesthetic perception, moreover, is not only emotional but also synthetic. Whereas science values an atomistic form of apprehension that breaks complex sense perceptions into elementary parts, aesthetic perception is holistic. "The artist has as keen an eye as the philosopher to penetrate the inner nature and truth of things," noted the *Mercersburg Review*, although he accomplishes this "by a species of inspiration or intuition, and not by the hard study, and tedious experiments of the man of science."[117] This idea had roots in the aesthetic speculations of British empiricists, a history evident in the terminology of an 1832 article in the *Christian Advocate and Journal and Zion's Herald*: "[I]t is the delight of poetry to combine and associate; of philosophy to separate and distinguish."[118] Art's holistic approach to the world grasps knowledge that is finally irreducible: "But ... how much is there in every susceptible heart, how much in every thoughtful mind, untranslatable into the technical idiom and common-place prose of every-day existence?"[119]

---

[114] Wordsworth, "Preface to *Lyrical Ballads*," 21n.

[115] Henry Drummond, *Letter to Thomas Phillips, Esq., R.A., on the Connexion between the Fine Arts and Religion, and the Means of Their Revival* (London: Fraser, 1840), 43. The pervasiveness of this dialectic can be seen in Edwards Amasa Park's 1850 address, "The Theology of the Intellect and That of the Feelings," *American Philosophical Addresses, 1700-1900*, ed. Joseph L. Blair (New York: Columbia University Press, 1946): 627-58. See, too, J.D.T.'s remarks in "Wordsworth's Conception of Nature," *PMQRCAmb* n.s. 6 (July 1884), 463; "Fergusson," 434; and T.A., "What Is Poetry?," 384. However, cf. Jonathan Smith's attempt to problematize this dichotomy in *Fact & Feeling: Baconian Science and the Nineteenth-Century Literary Imagination* (Madison: University of Wisconsin Press, 1994).

[116] "English Schools of Art," *ER* 23 (Jan. 1848), 76.

[117] T.A., "What Is Poetry?," 385.

[118] Hall, "Poetry and Philosophy," 169.

[119] Bernard Barton, "An Appeal for Poetry and Poets," *WMM* 15 (Aug. 1836), 589. This essay is an excerpt from Bernard and Lucy Barton, *The Reliquary: by Bernard and Lucy Barton. With a Prefatory Appeal for Poetry and Poets* (London: John W. Parker, 1836).

The art-science binary also served to underwrite another argument wielded in defense of art: the whole-person argument. This argument was a product of the eighteenth-century interest in mental philosophy, combining as it did faculty psychology with assumptions about God's creative purposes to arrive at the conclusion that art addresses a special, God-given need within human beings. In its basic form, the logic of the argument ran as follows: observation confirms that human beings possess some special faculty (taste, imagination, an aesthetic sense) that responds to beauty; one can assume that because it exists, God created it; because he created it, he must also have intended it to find at least partial fulfillment here on earth; art is the means of this fulfillment. Discussing the "Poetical Elements of the Bible," one critic suggested that God inspired the biblical authors to compose portions of Scripture in poetry because poetry addresses a specific dimension of humankind's psychological makeup: "There is no power or passion, no taste or sentiment, no instinct or aspiration of the soul of man, for which God has not made an adequate provision, to which he has not addressed an appropriate appeal."[120] In 1860, W.H. Bowen advanced a passionate plea on behalf of "Æsthetical Culture," beginning with an appeal to the whole person: "Man is made to love and appreciate the lovely, the attractive and the beautiful. Heart and mind demand them." Because of this, the pursuit of the aesthetic is a moral obligation: "We may not guiltlessly neglect to welcome any influence which can confer higher mental and moral efficiency, and promote a truer life.... It is the glory of the faith of the cross that it demands the development of the whole nature in compact unity."[121] Our love of the beautiful has been given to us by God, argued John M. Titzel in 1891, and "To gratify it properly can, therefore, never be wrong, but on the contrary, must always be commendable.... In the fact alone, therefore, that we have been endowed with the capacity for enjoying its productions, Art may be said to have its full justification."[122]

What made this the *whole-person* argument, however, was the added belief, rooted in the principle of psychological harmony sketched in the Yale Report of 1828, that to deny this aspect of human nature was to endanger one's psychic wholeness. "Undoubtedly, the best man, the most useful to his species," suggested a Methodist critic in 1881, "is he whose character is most equally balanced; and the most complete life is that which has been lived, so to speak, symmetrically."[123] In this context, art, many believed, plays a crucial role in maintaining balance. "[F]ine art is normal and necessary to man," argued George Lansing Taylor. "The æsthetic faculty is as actual and valid a part of man's nature as is his reason or his ethical faculty. Without this faculty man must be an alien and

---

[120] "The Poetical Element of the Bible," *SPR* 8 (July 1854), 94.
[121] W.H. Bowen, "Æsthetical Culture," *FBQ* 3 (Oct. 1860), 414.
[122] John M. Titzel, "Beauty and Art," *RQR* 3 (1891), 403. See also Thomas C. Upham's discussion of the imagination in his *Mental Philosophy; Embracing the Three Departments of the Intellect, Sensibilities, and Will* (New York: Harper, 1869), 1:432.
[123] "Unsymmetrical Lives," *PMQRCAmb* n.s. 3 (1881), 519.

stranger in the universe of beauty where he finds himself."[124] The *British Quarterly Review* asserted that "aesthetic culture becomes of great value in widening our intellectual sympathies, and supplying us with a corrective to those systems, whether of philosophy or religion, which, imparting an exaggerated development to certain elements of human nature, at the expense of other kindred elements, deprive each of that expansion essential to the symmetry of the whole."[125] Fulfillment requires equal development of the whole person, and since taste, imagination, and love of beauty are part of this person, art is necessary. One can easily appreciate the persuasive power of the whole-person argument. Not only does it posit that art appeals to a particular aspect of human character, thereby suggesting that it either does what nothing else can or does it better, but it also attributes this arrangement to the will of God. "The Sun of righteousness has risen with healing in His wings for our *whole* life," declared E.E. Higbee.[126] The argument thus gave divine sanction to art's unique contribution to human existence.

Since the standard dictated by the whole-person argument was mental balance, the argument could also be used to caution against the over-development of the aesthetic faculty. Too much of the aesthetic was just as bad as too little. Balance, moreover, should not be confused with equality. Genuine harmony may involve the proper subordination of some faculties to others. Thus Shedd warned in 1864 that "The aesthetic nature, unlike the rational or the moral, may be too much developed. The development of the taste and imagination must be a *symmetrical one*, in order to be a just and true one.... The true proportion, in this instance, is a subordination of the imagination and taste to the purposes and aims of the rational and moral faculties."[127] Shedd's statement was fairly typical, as the following chapter will show. Yet although the aesthetic faculty could, in the name of balance, be subordinated to the rational and moral, this same standard also required that the demands of the aesthetic faculty be fully satisfied.

To be sure, the belief that art is unique could often lead to far-flung claims regarding the value of art. It was but a short hop from the idea that art is *different from* science to the belief that art is *better than* science. Already in Drummond one catches a hint of aesthetic elitism. Only the few can genuinely appreciate art. If the positivists tended to elevate science above "mere" art, evangelical apologists for art sometimes followed Shelley down the path of zealous overcompensation. "Let it ever be borne in remembrance," proclaimed the *British Quarterly Review*, "that, to the dry utilitarian, who looks only to the profit of the passing hour,—paintings and statues, as well as palaces and temples, are things which we can do without; probably in a famine or a plague the artist might be deemed among the most valueless members of the community, yet all of this, not because

---

[124] Taylor, "Fine Art: Its Nature," 231.
[125] "Practical Aesthetics," 54. For other formulations of this argument, see Edward Otheman, [Untitled], *CAJ* 8 (22 Nov. 1833), 49; "Æsthetics," *CR*, 587-88; and "Music: Its Uses, Secular and Sacred," *CAmb* 4 (Feb. 1866), 26.
[126] E.E. Higbee, "The Relation of Christianity to Art," *MerR* 21 (July 1874), 342.
[127] William G.T. Shedd, "The Fundamental Properties of Style," *APTR* (Oct. 1864), 581.

his works are below, but above price."[128] Both science and art are necessary for human life, acknowledged the *Christian Review*, but "[Art] is more godlike than science; since, while the latter discovers, art creates."[129] "Feeling is the mighty fact of life," asserted another critic. "He who would have ingress and egress with lives must feel. And the poets have felt. They among them wear the world on their heart."[130] In general, the frequency and magnitude of such claims increased as the century progressed. Gradually, in fact, these earnest defenses of art began to carry some evangelicals, perhaps unwittingly, to the edge of doctrinal propriety and beyond, as when an author in the *Primitive Methodist Quarterly Review and Christian Ambassador* mused in 1879 that the hymns of the Church may express a religious truth that transcends the dry propositions of the historic creeds. "The heart is often more liberal and more orthodox than the head," the author opined. And in a gesture that no doubt would have seemed radical to many conservatives, he set aside dogma and sectarian differences in favor of an ecumenism of the heart mediated by "Christian Lyric Poetry." That even evangelicals had allowed non-evangelical hymns into their worship "must be accepted as indicating that there may be a faith of the heart deeper and more spiritual than that of the head. Our deepest convictions are not always expressed in the creeds which we honestly profess."[131] Such a claim, although still rare among conservatives, was little more than an extrapolation of the aesthetic principles embraced by evangelicals across the theological spectrum.

Whatever their differences, however, nearly all Victorian evangelical critics held fast to the conviction that art was worthy of defense. Surely art afforded more than simple amusement; it had a crucial role to play in life and society. This conviction was largely a result of the romantic influence on evangelical aesthetics, and it was reflected above all in the new *tone* adopted by evangelical apologists for art. Passion, urgency, conviction—these tonal qualities pervaded discussions of art in the denominational periodicals of the era.[132] This elevated sensibility may finally have been one of romanticism's most powerful legacies to nineteenth-century evangelical aesthetics. Unlike many critics, the Methodist painter James Smetham could not, in the end, admit that there was anything unusual about art in contrast to science; as such, his own defense of art was modest

---

[128] "Prospects of British Art," *BrQR* 2 (Nov. 1845), 481.
[129] "Æsthetics," *CR*, 588.
[130] "The Preacher and Poet," 217.
[131] "Christian Lyric Poetry," 136.
[132] The inflated rhetoric of some enthusiastic apologists for art did not escape the notice of more sober-minded critics. Reacting to Taylor's article in the *MQR*, a fellow Methodist quipped: "The article is evidently written *con amore*, and is itself a splendid specimen of one branch of art which [the author] has not delineated—the rhetorical art" ("The Methodist Quarterly," *ZH* 51 [30 Apr. 1874], 139A). For a particularly demonstrative defense of art, see "Art Education: The Place Art Should Take in a Christian Education," *CR* 25 (Oct. 1860): 618-31.

and restrained. Yet even Smetham could not resist a moment of descriptive fervor: "Knowledge and joy pour from [art] in a silent stream, wherever there are eyes to behold."[133]

---

[133] Smetham, "Modern Sacred Art," 72.

CHAPTER 3

What Has the Gospel of Christ to Do with the Gospel of Art?

Unlike the widening rift between science and religion which troubled many a late-Victorian intellectual, the ostensible tension between art and religion is an old one. Almost from the beginning, Christians struggled with the question of what role, if any, art and "culture" ought to play in the lives of believers. "What has Jerusalem to do with Athens?" Tertullian famously asked. As detractors throughout history have fondly pointed out, early Christians seemed to express little interest in art beyond a few rude, symbolic etchings on catacomb walls, a fact accepted by some as evidence of an intrinsic antipathy between the claims of worldly art and the claims of undefiled religion. Furthermore, the periodic eruption of iconoclastic movements—first in the eighth century and again during the Reformation—serve as reminders of Christianity's unresolved tensions between aesthetics and faith, between the alternating convictions that art is a sacrament and art is a snare. This ancient problem of art's relationship to religion resurfaced in the nineteenth century with new urgency. As Hilary Fraser has noted, the period "saw a proliferation of religio-aesthetic theories designed to reconcile the claims of Christianity and beauty, morality and art."[1] Evangelicals contributed their fair share to this proliferation. A brief survey of article titles in denominational periodicals between 1830 and 1900 suggests the extent of evangelical critics' preoccupation with the longstanding question of art's relationship to religion: "Influence of the Christian Religion on Poetry," "The Necessity of a Religious Literature," "Poetry: Its Social Uses and Religious Influences," "Art and Religion," "Esthetics in Religion," "Christianity and the Fine Arts," "Modern Literature and Christianity," "Christianity and Art," "The Relation of Art to Religion," "Relationship of Christianity to Art," "The Aesthetic in Religion," and "Reciprocity of Art and Religion."

Why did nineteenth-century thinkers, evangelical and non-evangelical, feel the need to theorize at such length the connections between religion and art? To some degree, such theorizing may have been a byproduct of increased exposure to art, and in particular visual art, especially after the 1850s. As methods of trans-

---

[1] Hilary Fraser, *Beauty and Belief: Aesthetics and Religion in Victorian England* (Cambridge: Cambridge University Press, 1986), 1.

portation became more reliable and affordable, the Anglo-American middle classes began traveling abroad to destinations in continental Europe and the Holy Lands. Ministers, in fact, made up a significant proportion of these travelers. Such trips raised the aesthetic awareness of sightseers by bringing them face to face with the great art of western culture. For those who could not afford to leave home in search of art, art could be brought home via new reproduction technologies that enabled the cheap dissemination of mass-produced prints. So-called high art could be found as never before on magazine covers and middle-class coffee tables. Many evangelicals, it seems, were at last taking full advantage of the allowance made by Puritanism for the "civil" use of visual art, increasingly importing such art into the home as a means of domestic beautification.[2] Such changes may have led some to question these developments in light of what most Victorians agreed were humankind's all-important religious duties. Key intellectual developments also fostered a renewed interest in the relationship between art and religion. Among these were dramatic claims on behalf of art by romantic theorists in England, Germany, and America, many of which adduced a close link between religious and aesthetic perception. Such claims tended to blur conventional distinctions between the religious and aesthetic, leading to fresh concerns about the relations between them. The emergence of what many perceived to be ritualist movements within Protestantism—Tractarianism in England and the Mercersburg theology in America—also prompted a reconsideration of the role of the aesthetic in church life. As Spurgeon complained in 1876, "the gentlemen of aesthetic taste are aping the ritualism against which it should have been their first business to protest."[3] Meanwhile, the ongoing consolidation of aesthetics as a discrete field of study led naturally to questions about art's relationship to other dimensions of human experience, especially religion.

One other factor, however, also encouraged a re-examination of the nexus of art and religion—the lingering influence of Puritanism. This influence was not strictly an evangelical problem, narrowly considered. It was, after all, Arnold, who, marshaling his own version of the whole-person argument singled out Hebraism-Puritanism-Nonconformism as the source of too many "incomplete and mutilated men." For Arnold, the persistence of a puritanical ethos was a problem

---

[2] See David Morgan, *Protestants and Pictures: Religion, Visual Culture, and the Age of American Mass Production* (New York: Oxford University Press, 1999); Neil Harris, *The Artist in American Society: The Formative Years 1790-1860* (New York: George Braziller, 1966), 28-53; Graham Howes, *The Art of the Sacred: An Introduction to the Aesthetics of Art and Belief* (London: I.B. Tauris, 2007), 29-44; and John Dillenberger, *The Visual Arts and Christianity in America: From the Colonial Period to the Present* (New York: Crossroad, 1988), 39-56. On Victorian travel and tourism, see Marjorie Morgan, *National Identities and Travel in Victorian Britain* (Houndsmills: Palgrave, 2001). On evangelical tourism, see Timothy Larsen, *Contested Christianity: The Political and Social Contexts of Victorian Theology* (Waco: Baylor University Press, 2004), 29-39.

[3] Charles Spurgeon, "The Power of Nonconformity," *ST* (July 1876), 306. See also Howes, *Art of the Sacred*, 33-34.

that threatened the best of national culture. Still, if the ghost of Puritanism also haunted many non-evangelical homes, evangelicals arguably bore a special relationship to this spirit, as Arnold himself testified. For whether or not his assessment of Puritanism was just (ironically, it may have been too one-sided), Arnold correctly perceived Nonconformists as the proper "successors and representatives of the Puritans."[4] As the rightful heirs of Puritanism, evangelicals felt uniquely the weight of this tradition and its ambivalent relationship to art.

As discussed earlier, Puritanism had created an atmosphere of uncertainty surrounding art that continued to affect eighteenth-century evangelicals even as a new aesthetic consciousness was beginning to dawn. Although by the mid-nineteenth century much of this ambivalence had been dispelled, some vestige of it may be seen underlying the Victorian proliferation of religio-aesthetic theories. What seems to have motivated evangelical critics' formal interest in the question of art's relationship to Christianity was, among other things, some residual anxiety within the evangelical community over the potential for a true rapprochement. The trepidatious preamble to an 1861 plea in the *Christian Advocate and Journal* for greater attention to the "esthetic element" betrayed just such an anxiety: "I am aware that there are some persons who may think it almost profaning a religious newspaper to occupy even a small portion of it with gossip about art and artists; but they must excuse your correspondent if he cannot sympathize with them."[5] Four years later, another author put the matter even more starkly: "Another cause of this neglect [of "esthetic culture"] is a misapprehension in regard to the relation between beauty and religion. In the minds of some, religion is dissociated from beauty, and high esthetic culture is regarded as wrong."[6] At stake here is the fundamental compatibility between art and evangelical Christianity. As we will see, evangelicals, at least the more conservative ones, discovered new reasons to resurrect certain "puritanical" arguments to fend off what they viewed as the more extreme implications of romanticism, but this is not the issue here. In these passages, the problem is not one of excess but of outright rejection.

For these critics and many others, however, the specter of Puritanism had for the most part been reduced to a vague force "out there" among the evangelical masses. Whatever the puritanical proclivities of ordinary evangelicals "on the street," these writers, like Arnold, "cannot sympathize with them." Clearly, an internal rift was emerging within evangelicalism between the educated proponents of "high" culture and the populist-minded many, who (if one accepts the preceding statements as accurate representations of popular evangelical sentiments) persisted in their puritanical sensibilities and skepticism regarding art. An article on "Poetry and the Spiritual Life" published in the mid-1890s offers a

---

[4] Matthew Arnold, *Culture and Anarchy*, ed. J. Dover Wilson (Cambridge: Cambridge University Press, 1963), 11.
[5] Dr. Leyburn, "Esthetics," *CAJ* 36 (25 Apr. 1861), 6.
[6] "Esthetic Culture," *CAJ* 40 (7 Dec. 1865), 386.

glimpse of just how deep this rift had become over the course of the century. Edwin Mims, an instructor at Cornell, recounted how, after a young speaker at "one of the leading churches of Southern Methodism" had "referred incidentally to Shakespeare" during his talk, a controversy ensued when a "prominent member" of the church delivered a diatribe on the injurious effects of Shakespeare to religion and morality. Unfortunately for the speaker, he discovered that "he was largely in the minority." Mims, however, lamented this form of anti-aesthetic religious populism, arguing "that the Church has not realized what a valuable ally is to be found in the great poetry of the world."[7] It appears, then, that evangelical attitudes towards the question of art's relationship to religion were also in part a function of this high-populist divide. Puritanical suspicions concerning art's contaminating influence on religion remained alive among some "average" evangelicals, while the harbingers of evangelical "high esthetic culture" increasingly argued that the claims of art and religion need not be at odds.

When it came to art's relationship to Christianity, this growing faction of evangelical cultural elites differed from their seventeenth and eighteenth-century predecessors in at least two ways. First, reconciliation (to use Fraser's term) became a conscious objective. For many Puritans and eighteenth-century evangelicals, the tendency had been to elevate pure religion at the expense of art. The question of art's relationship to religion, moreover, if and when it surfaced as a definitive dispute, had been approached largely in negative terms—that is, the emphasis was on determining the appropriate religious limits of art. Images must not be used in the sanctuary, for example, nor should preachers draw attention to their homiletic craft through excessive embellishments. Puritan writers, in short, eagerly defended religion, but they showed little interest in defending art. By contrast, many mid-nineteenth-century evangelical critics set out to demonstrate the way(s) in which art and religion might coexist. Even these high cultural critics agreed with the Puritans that Christianity does impose important strictures on art, but they also viewed the question of art's relationship to Christianity in the positive terms of reciprocity. In fact, the second difference between nineteenth-century evangelical critics and their predecessors was the newfound optimism with which many approached this task of reconciliation. Although Christians throughout the centuries had often found it difficult to maintain a healthy balance between the claims of art and religion, many Victorian critics held fast to the sanguine expectation that they could succeed where others had failed. Art and Christianity, they believed, might mutually enrich one another.

The "question of religion and art" is, in reality, an assortment of related but distinct problems. There are philosophical problems associated with aesthetic and religious perception, with the capacity of art to represent transcendent reality, or with the metaphysical status of Beauty. There are theological questions about God's role as creator, the position of art in the divine plan, or whether art can

---

[7] Edwin Mims, "Poetry and the Spiritual Life," *MR*[S] 44 (1896-7), 387, 388.

rightly qualify as a consecrated endeavor. As with debates regarding art's essential nature, however, nineteenth-century discussions of art's relationship to religion were often carried on in unapologetically abstract terms. If ART and RELIGION sometimes seem like personifications of two great social or ideological forces, it is because this is exactly how many critics viewed them. "It has for many years been a general observation among literary persons, that the flowers of Parnassus cannot thrive in the garden of Religion," noted the *Christian Observer* early in the century.[8] This rather ungainly attempt to formulate the matter in something like mythological terms captures the Victorian penchant for viewing the problem of art and religion as a recurring historical conflict between two ahistorical modes of human consciousness. "It now hardly needs to be said," remarked H.M. Du Bose in 1895, "that we hold it as an established fact that the two civilizations of the Jews and the Greeks represent specific tendencies—the one toward the ideals of faith, the other toward the ideals of art."[9] This dualistic scheme was not, of course, Du Bose's at all but rather Arnold's, a point which underscores how evangelicals had by century's end come to think about the problem of religion and art in distinctively Victorian terms.

This chapter examines evangelical attempts to theorize the relationship between art and Christianity. Sensitive to what they saw as the extremism of the Reformation tradition and Puritanism in particular, these critics increasingly sought to define their own aesthetic views over and against this tradition. As Neil Harris has noted, mid-nineteenth-century American clergymen "seemed particularly concerned with repudiating what they considered was an unfortunate though historically necessary Puritan inheritance,"[10] and many British clergymen followed suit. Indeed, Puritanism became an aesthetic straw man that could be attacked as needed. For some, these attacks were judiciously confined to aesthetics, and the trick was to defend the Puritans' theology and piety while denouncing their attitudes towards art. Other critics, meanwhile, showed less concern for Puritanism as a whole and attacked it indiscriminately. This anti-Puritanism, however, did not lead immediately to an unrestrained celebration of art. On the contrary, the nexus of religion and art remained a complicated one. In general, the religio-aesthetic ideal was for many critics conciliatory in nature: theoretically, art and religion exist in a kind of productive tension. Such critics looked to walk a fine line between what they characterized as Puritan extremism, in which art was portrayed as being in inherent conflict with Christianity, and the other extreme represented by more extravagant forms of romanticism, in which art was associated with an unorthodox and doctrinally vague "spirituality". Within this religio-aesthetic via media, many theorists argued that the proper relationship between art and Christianity was a *subordinate* one. In this view, art was seen as both limited by Christianity and uniquely empowered by it. Such a theory was

---

[8] Cereticus, "On Sacred Poetry," *CO* 16 (Oct. 1817), 644.
[9] H.M. Du Bose, "Authority in Art and Religion," *MR*[S] 42 (1895), 216.
[10] Harris, *Artist*, 301.

no simple didacticism (though moral concerns remained important); the currents passing between art and Christianity ran far deeper than the conventional belief that art could serve as a means of teaching the illiterate masses. Rather, Christianity provided both the psychological and social conditions for genuine art to flourish. It was the addition of this latter claim that most clearly separated nineteenth-century evangelical conceptions of art's relationship to Christianity from earlier conceptions. This religio-aesthetic harmony, however, was often difficult to maintain in practice, and it faced the constant danger of being pulled apart by both the strong tug of the romantic principles that many evangelicals had come to accept and the gnawing sense among some that the dream of a Protestant culture in which art could find its true fulfillment would finally prove illusory.

Aesthetic Skeletons in the Protestant Closet

Evangelical critics were keenly aware of the potentially embarrassing aesthetic skeletons in the Protestant closet. In particular, three periods in Christian history led to disquietude among those interested in defending the compatibility of art and religion: the early church, the Reformation, and Puritanism. For evangelicals, these were the theologically significant periods in which biblical Christianity existed in its purest form, free from the Romanist accretions and Scholastic subtleties of the Middle Ages. The difficulty was that there appeared to be in each of these periods an inverse relationship between doctrinal purity and aesthetic interest. Art seemed to shine most brightly when Christianity was most polluted by worldliness; or, the more aesthetically inclined Christianity became, the more religiously impure it became. "As Christianity became artistic," argued T. Harwood Pattison, "it became corrupt."[11] History thus offered prima facie evidence for the incongruity of art and Protestant religion. A number of critics, however, confident that art and Christianity are not natural antagonists, rose to the challenge, and they set about the task of accounting for what seemed a substantial deviation from their forbears.

Evangelical intellectuals developed a handful of key strategies for dealing with Protestantism's putative aversion to art. One strategy, applied to the early church, was simply to propose that the usual allegations regarding the anti-aesthetic prejudices of first-century Christians had been unduly exaggerated. "The new religion [i.e., Christianity]," claimed W.F. Taylor, "did not array itself against the love of art. There is much to disprove the sweeping assertion that Christianity in its effort to crush paganism became bitterly hostile to those forms of beauty by which the pagan religion was taught." One piece of evidence proffered by Taylor was the fact that the Apostle Paul nowhere condemns art, not even in those passages where one would most expect him to do so. He referenced Paul's injunction in 1 Corinthians 8 to avoid meat sacrificed to idols, noting that "while he commanded abstinence from this meat for the sake of others, not a word did he say against the idol itself." Taylor then shifted from a scriptural to

---

[11] T. Harwood Pattison, "The Relation of Art to Religion," *BQR* 8 (1886), 327.

an historical defense, asserting that "there are abundant facts to show the prevalence of art among the gentile Christians in the earliest years of the Church." Among these facts, he cited what naysayers had long seen as the proverbial exception that proved the rule—the "decorations" painted in the catacombs of Rome—as well as the apparent acceptance of art by some of the Church Fathers, "of whom not all feared its effect upon the purity of the faith."[12] Not surprisingly, this particular tack seems not to have been common during the period. Many readers would likely have found dubious a biblical interpretation that came dangerously close, however inadvertently, to a defense of idolatry; and although Taylor's basic method of arguing from Scripture carried great weight among evangelicals, it is probable that a majority of readers (especially those who continued to cherish some form of the Regulative Principle) would have found his argument from silence less than compelling. His historical case, moreover, while correct enough in its basic facts, strikes one as grasping at straws.

A more common version of this tactic was to argue that the early Christians and Reformers did not oppose art in principle but only its misuse. "The appropriation of [music] to the service of vice," asserted the Presbyterian *Christian Advocate* in 1823, "is a perfect perversion of its original purpose, for it was first used to express the devout feelings of the heart."[13] James Smetham posited that although "early Christians ... would not admit into their communion anyone who practised [art, and specifically painting]"—a stricture necessitated by art's prior association with paganism—these same Christians "with unconscious inconsistency ... carried in their hands lamps and vessels on which lyres, and palms, and lambs, and crowns were painted or embossed." The early church thus tacitly acknowledged art's "essential principle",[14] accepting in spirit what they could not accept in practice. In 1877, C.W. Bennett applied a similar logic to prominent Reformers. After surveying selected passages on art from the writings of such figures as Luther, Zwingli, and Calvin, Bennett concluded that "all go to show that with these earnest men there is a real appreciation of the beautiful—indeed, a true love of art. The whole force of their protest is directed against the shameful prostitution of sacred art to vulgar and unworthy ends...."[15] Critics made good use of this argument, not only as a means of explaining what seemed to be the less-than-stellar record of Protestantism concerning the arts but also as a starting-point for their own attempts at religio-aesthetic reconciliation. If, historically, Protestantism had never rejected art per se, then there were no authoritative grounds for doing so in the nineteenth century either.

---

[12] W.F. Taylor, "Christ in Art," *BQR* 8 (1886), 468.
[13] B., "Influence of the Fine Arts," *CA*[P] 1 (Mar. 1823), 115.
[14] James Smetham, "Modern Sacred Art in England," *LQR* 18 (Apr. 1862), 52. For another version of this argument, see E.E. Higbee, "The Relation of Christianity to Art," *MerR* 21 (July 1874), esp. 350-56.
[15] C.W. Bennett, "Catholicism and Protestantism as Patrons of Christian Art," *MQR* 29 (1877), 94.

The argument that Protestants had never in principle objected to the arts seemed plausible enough when brought to bear on the early church and the Reformation. At the very least, one could always point, as Taylor did, to the Roman catacombs or rehearse the humanist credentials of Reformers like Calvin. There was, too, one major exception among the Puritans that seemed to present the possibility of a similar kind of argument: John Milton. In 1841, the *Eclectic Review* tried to draw a distinction between *kinds* of Puritans. Questioning those who had uncritically cast aside Shakespeare simply because he had written for the stage, the article blamed such prejudices on the exaggerated views of "'precious Master [Philip] Stubbes,' whose vagaries have contributed more to cast unmerited obloquy on the early Puritans than any abuse of their enemies; and who, mistaking want of taste for Christian zeal ... recommends 'Fox's Book of Martyrs as the only legitimate 'recreation' for Christian men." In contrast, Milton, who had praised Shakespeare, was "a greater, a more consistent Puritan."[16] At stake, of course, was who constituted the true Puritan exception, Stubbes or Milton, and one can only speculate as to how convincing readers found this argument in 1841. Yet Milton notwithstanding, the Puritans presented a particularly challenging case. How was one to handle what appeared to be an open Puritan hostility to art?

Surely one of the stranger attempts to contend with the Puritan tradition was the effort made by some writers to aestheticize the Puritans themselves—to suggest, that is, that although the Puritans shunned aesthetic pursuits, they themselves constituted a form of "living art". One example of this aestheticization was Harriet Beecher Stowe's novel *The Minister's Wooing* (1859). Stowe casts as a central character in her novel the historical figure Dr. Samuel Hopkins, one-time student of Edwards and his theological heir apparent. Stowe's Hopkins is a stern figure, spending countless hours in his study wrestling with the nuances of Calvinist theology. Caring little for worldly preoccupations, he is heavenly-minded to the point of forgetfulness, and aside from the great theological questions of the moment, only his unrequited love for the young Mary Scudder moves him to action. He is almost, Stowe implies, as unapproachable as the radically transcendent God he serves. Stowe's aestheticization of the Puritans, however, extends beyond her choice of Hopkins as a main character. For while the novel is in many ways critical of Hopkinsianism and of Puritanism in general, Stowe sees in the Puritan tradition and in the figure of Hopkins a certain "romance": "you will find, if you will follow us, that there is as much romance burning under the snow-banks of cold Puritan preciseness as if Dr. Hopkins had been brought up to attend operas instead of metaphysical preaching, and Mary had been nourished on Byron's poetry instead of 'Edwards on the Affections.'"[17] The Puritans, Stowe suggests, harbored a "burning" poetical *spirit* even if this spirit did not

---

[16] "The Pictorial Edition of Shakespeare, Parts I to XXXI," *ER* 9 (May 1841), 542.

[17] Harriet Beecher Stowe, *The Minister's Wooing* (Hartford: Harriet Beecher Stowe Center-Rutgers University Press, 1998), 123.

manifest itself in the production of art objects. Underneath the dour Edwardsean exterior there lived an operatic and Byronic soul.

Nor was such a view confined to fiction. The tendency to aestheticize the Puritans appeared in critical contexts as well. The *British Quarterly Review*, while conceding that "Poetry declined" under Puritanism, undertook a defense of the Puritans that culminated in a kind of aesthetic appreciation of Puritan courage:

> If the theatre was shut, the place of religious assemblies was open; if the brilliant creations of Shakespeare and the elder dramatists were viewed with devout horror, the songs of Zion and the sublime strains of prophet-bards resounded night and day both in the council and the field.... Future generations will testify to their worth, and pronounce upon their virtues. Truly their lives were a great epic.[18]

The *Baptist Magazine* adopted a similar position in 1857: "Poetry in those old Puritans! Why not? They were men of like passions with ourselves. They loved, they married, they brought up children; they feared, they sinned, they sorrowed, they fought—they conquered. There was poetry enough in them, be sure, though they acted it like men, instead of singing it like birds."[19] The aesthetic concept most often applied to the Puritans was sublimity. Early British theorists of the sublime had often included great acts of moral courage and conquest in their lists of sublime objects,[20] and the sublime provided a useful means of bridging the gap between aesthetics (which the Puritans seemed to lack) and morality (at which the Puritans excelled). By "sublimating" the Puritans, evangelical critics could convert what appeared to be an aesthetic defeat into an aesthetic victory. The Puritans did not need to write poetry because they *lived* it. And while the Puritans may have opposed the arts, no one could justifiably claim that they opposed the aesthetic per se.

Critics sometimes deployed this argument in conjunction with another that proved popular among evangelicals seeking to overcome the difficulties of Protestant aesthetic history: the exigency argument. Promoters of the exigency argument claimed that during periods of fierce theological crisis, it was permissible, even requisite, to employ extreme measures that would otherwise be unacceptable in times of peace. These measures included the temporary suspension of aesthetic pursuits in the interests of an all-encompassing defense of biblical truth. J. Milner Macmaster, for example, applied this argument to the Puritans in 1879:

> It requires some charity, some historic imagination, to judge these men aright. They made their mistakes, and were punished for them; but let it be remembered that a course of action which would be fanatical now may have been prudent then. When the Puritans rejected music, painting, and architecture as aids to religion, they were

---

[18] "Poetry and Civilization," *BrQR* 4 (Aug. 1846), 362, 363.
[19] "The Poetry of Puritanism," *BM* 49 (Feb. 1857), 101.
[20] See Andrew Ashfield and Peter de Bolla, eds., *The Sublime: A Reader in Eighteenth-Century Aesthetic Theory* (Cambridge: Cambridge University Press, 1998).

engaged in a death-struggle with a giant superstition, which had made the means the end.[21]

The exigency argument contained a strong undercurrent of anti-Catholicism, as this passage attests. The "death-struggle" that critics like Macmaster nearly always had in mind was either the battle against paganism in the early church or, as here, Roman Catholicism (which for many evangelicals had a "pagan" quality of its own). Yet the beauty of this argument was that it allowed critics to read the religio-aesthetic dynamics of key moments in Protestant history as anomalies rather than as evidence of an intrinsic antinomy between art and evangelical Christianity. "Now the Puritan spirit was evidently a healthy, natural, and necessary reaction against the abuses of the times...," argued LeConte. "But, like all reactions, it has gone much beyond the line of truth and the limits of reason."[22] One could thus affirm the exemplary religious zeal of the Puritans while simultaneously dismissing their anti-aesthetic "extremism" as an aberration begotten by the historical context.

Occasionally, however, critics ignored the delicate balance of the exigency argument in favor of a more aggressive break with Puritanism. Samuel Harris, the Dwight Professor of Systematic Theology at Yale, delivered a series of lectures at Andover Seminary in 1870 in which he counterintuitively depicted the Puritan failure to pursue the aesthetic as a failure of morality. A Christian society, Harris argued, "does not exclude aesthetic culture. Its defectiveness in the Hebrew and the Puritan was the result of the incompleteness, rather than the completeness, of the moral life." Immediately, though, Harris tempered his bold accusation by retreating into the familiar territory of the exigency argument: "It was because morality came in the awfulness of law, rather than in the freedom of Christian faith and love, and even as love, in the Puritan, concentrating attention on the conflict with wrongs and oppressions immediately urgent, so as to leave no time for the completeness of human culture."[23] Ten years later, the *Baptist Magazine* made no such retreat but spoke plainly about the aesthetic errors of Puritanism:

> The Puritan party made a mistake in their treatment of poetry, akin to that into which they fell when dealing with music and painting. They attacked the arts themselves, instead of confining their strictures to the abuse of them. They overlooked the fact that a true poem or a great picture appeals to the Divinely implanted instincts of man's nature. So their efforts were unsuccessful.[24]

---

[21] J. Milner Macmaster, "Il Penseroso and L'Allegro," *BM* 71 (Apr. 1879), 171. See also "Church Architecture," *BRPR* 27 (Oct. 1855), 625-26.
[22] Joseph LeConte, "On the Nature and Uses of Art," *SPR* 15 (Jan. 1863), 312.
[23] Samuel Harris, *The Kingdom of Christ on Earth: Twelve Lectures Delivered before the Theological Seminary, Andover* (Andover: Warren F. Draper, 1874), 176.
[24] "Glimpses of Old English Life: Puritan and Actor," *BM* 72 (Aug. 1880), 342.

This writer was leveraging for the purpose of blame the central premise of an argument which, as noted above, had often been utilized by evangelicals in defense of both the early church and Reformation. Whereas other critics had suggested that the Reformers had not objected to art in principle but only to its misuse, this critic ventured the idea that this is precisely the distinction the Puritans had failed to make. In addition, the author seems to have had in mind something like the whole-person argument discussed in chapter 2. There dwell "Divinely implanted instincts" in the human mind that people ignore at their peril. The Puritans, however, did just this. Unlike Macmaster, who had argued the previous year that the Puritans were operating under a special dispensation with regard to art, the tenor of this passage suggests that there was, in truth, no good reason for the anti-aesthetic extremism of the Puritans. They had committed an error, plain and simple.

As this passage makes clear, there was by mid-century an intensifying current of anti-Puritanism within evangelical aesthetics, whether expressed in the comparatively guarded framework of the exigency argument or announced in transparently negative terms. Even the efforts of some critics to aestheticize the Puritans involved in the end a tacit admission that the Puritans had shunned both art and any kind of sympathetic critical discourse about the arts. Indeed, when it came to aesthetics, Puritanism served as *the* foil for evangelicals in a way that the early church and Reformation rarely did. By century's end, many evangelicals happily aligned themselves with Arnold in vilifying the aesthetic missteps of their Puritan forefathers. This anti-Puritanism manifested itself in both theory and praxis. Both the character (e.g., sentimental hymns and novels, Gothic architecture[25]) and the quantity of art objects produced by evangelicals throughout the nineteenth century provide tangible evidence of this fact. Even early-twentieth-century fundamentalists, who largely abandoned any serious interest in philosophical aesthetics and who sometimes viewed high aesthetic culture with an ambivalence of their own, would welcome the efforts of a Warner Sallman to an extent that Puritans and even eighteenth-century evangelicals could never have done. In fact, this anti-Puritanism in the realm of aesthetics can be seen in the context of a broader process of theological reconsideration. The Calvinism of the Puritans had been under scrutiny since the eighteenth century even among historically Reformed denominations. Wesleyan Methodism, of course, had embraced Arminianism from its inception, but by the early decades of the nineteenth

---

[25] See Sandra S. Sizer, *Gospel Hymns and Social Religion: The Rhetoric of Nineteenth-Century Revivalism* (Philadelphia: Temple University Press, 1978); Stephen Marini, "From Classical to Modern: Hymnody and the Development of American Evangelicalism, 1737-1970," *Singing the Lord's Song in a Strange Land: Hymnody in the History of North American Protestantism*, ed. Edith L. Blumhofer and Mark A. Noll (Tuscaloosa: University of Alabama Press, 2004): 1-38; Ryan K. Smith, *Gothic Arches, Latin Crosses: Anti-Catholicism and American Church Designs in the Nineteenth Century* (Chapel Hill: University of North Carolina Press, 2006); and Lynn S. Neal, *Romancing God: Evangelical Women and Inspirational Fiction* (Chapel Hill: University of North Carolina Press, 2006).

century even some staunchly Calvinist denominations had begun to alter their theological bearings in favor of a softened version of Reformed theology.[26] As evangelicals moved away from Puritanism theologically, they also moved away aesthetically and vice versa. This gradual erosion of Puritan theological authority contributed to a milieu in which those critics interested in new aesthetic ventures could distance themselves, albeit carefully in some cases, from the Puritan tradition without fear.

The extent to which Puritanism had become the bugbear of evangelical critics is evident when one contrasts these attitudes with those regarding the aesthetic legacy of the Reformation. Critics were frankly divided when it came to assessing the Reformation's effects on art. While some admitted its shortcomings, others took to the offensive and attempted to recast the Reformation as the driving force behind the positive developments of modern aesthetics. Some writers asserted that, far from having had an impoverishing effect on art, the Reformation had liberated it. Predictably, the target here was typically Catholicism and its claim to aesthetic superiority. "Roman Catholics," noted an author in the *Eclectic Review*, "have always boasted that their religion has been uniformly and exclusively favourable to the growth and development of the Fine Arts." This boast, however, was one which "Protestants have too easily received, and too quietly borne."[27] Bennett recited the standard charges. Catholicism had always insisted "that Protestantism was greatly wanting in aesthetic susceptibility—indeed, that it was essentially iconoclastic in spirit; that it caused a fearful destruction of works of art in the times immediately following the great schism, and that it ushered in a period of fearful art decadence."[28] Evangelicals countered that Catholicism, with its rigid authoritarianism, had oppressed creativity and retarded art's development. Freedom, these critics contended, is the necessary condition for good art, and it was not until the Reformation abolished medieval Catholic hierarchy that such freedom truly flourished. "It is capable of proof," wrote Pattison, "that only when the religion of the Caesar was in its decline, when the first stirrings of the Protestant Reformation were felt, did art learn the greatness of her might, and breathe the air of freedom."[29] Bennett agreed: "The Reformation, so far from being the *cause* of the decadence of sacred art, was a protest against the spirit which was destroying the very capacity for high art."[30] Contrary to Catholic allegations, the Reformation had redeemed art from the bondage of tyranny.

---

[26] See Sydney E. Ahlstrom, *A Religious History of the American People* (New Haven: Yale University Press, 1972), parts 4 and 5; Mark A. Noll, *America's God: From Jonathan Edwards to Abraham Lincoln* (Oxford: Oxford University Press, 2002), esp. chaps. 13-15; and David Bebbington, *Evangelicalism in Modern Britain: A History from the 1730s to the 1980s* (Grand Rapids: Baker, 1992), esp. chaps. 4 and 5.
[27] "The Relation of Roman Catholicism and Protestantism to the Fine Arts," *ER* 3 (Jan. 1858), 1.
[28] Bennett, "Catholicism and Protestantism," 79.
[29] Pattison, "The Relation of Art to Religion," 335.
[30] Bennett, "Catholicism and Protestantism," 94.

This argument is important for a number of reasons. First, it suggests that a negative factor motivating increased aesthetic interest among nineteenth-century evangelicals was, as Ryan K. Smith has argued, anti-Catholicism. This interest was not, as is sometimes thought, the result of a growing harmony between Catholics and Protestants but, paradoxically, an attempt by evangelicals (and Protestants generally) to prove their dominance.[31] Nineteenth-century evangelical aesthetics was therefore poised, somewhat precariously, between Puritanism and Roman Catholicism. Secondly, that aesthetics had now emerged as a site of religious contestation provides yet another measure of the significant transformation within evangelicalism. For many Puritans and eighteenth-century evangelicals, the proscription and/or strict regulation of art would have served as a marker of religious superiority. Certain arts were to be avoided not only as "worldly" but also as "idolatrous" and "Catholic." Although such caveats persisted, Victorian evangelicals were willing, even anxious, to meet Catholics head-to-head on the battleground of art. The objective was no longer to claim Protestantism's religious supremacy via the rejection of aesthetics but rather to claim it via the embrace of aesthetics. Protestantism could be said to trump Catholicism, inter alia, insofar as it supplied the necessary conditions for the creation of authentic art. Finally, it is crucial that those critics attempting to see something aesthetically positive in the Reformation tended to characterize this contribution in terms of individual freedom (as opposed to, say, a distinct theological insight). Describing what he viewed as post-Reformation advances "Both in sacred and secular music," Bennett attributed these to "that peculiar and darling principal of Protestantism—the unrestrained freedom of individual genius."[32] Evangelicals were effectively perpetuating in the domain of aesthetics a "whig" version of history,[33] thereby reinforcing an intricate ideological web linking Protestant Christianity, aesthetics, "progress", and even nationalism.[34] This propensity to celebrate individual freedom as a, or *the*, pivotal aesthetic legacy of the Reformation also bolstered the romantic conceptions of art and creativity evangelicals had come to embrace. By reading the Reformation as the origin of that individualism which may be said to underwrite the view of art as self-expression, such critics discovered implicit sanction for their (new) aesthetic views. Individual genius, it turns out, was a thoroughly Protestant notion.

Evangelicals had unmistakably taken to the offensive. In fact, when seen against the backdrop of Puritanism's lack of positive interest in exploring art, even evangelical "defenses" of the Protestant tradition amounted to a sort of offensive maneuver. From the 1830s onward, evangelicals had high hopes that Protestantism could provide the necessary framework within which high aesthetic culture could prosper.

---

[31] See Smith, *Gothic Arches*.
[32] Bennett, "Catholicism and Protestantism," 88.
[33] See Herbert Butterfield, *The Whig Interpretation of History* (New York: Norton, 1965).
[34] See chapter 4.

Reconciliation, Subordination, and the Ideal of Productive Tension

In rejecting the perceived severities of the Puritans, evangelicals were beginning to reimagine the relationship between religion and art. When it came to theorizing this relationship, many mid-nineteenth-century critics took a conciliatory view. This view, in theory, held that there is no intrinsic conflict between art and religion.[35] As the *Mercersburg Review* put it in 1859, "[T]rue Christianity is never hostile to the art of any nation or age, except as it is misapplied or untrue to itself."[36] At the same time, many evangelicals also held that art and religion exist in a hierarchical tension with one another: art is, in a sense, subordinate to Christianity. "We must insist, therefore, first of all, that art should always be subordinate to religion," Pattison declared.[37] This subservience did not imply any diminution of value; on the contrary, only when art was properly subject to the directives of religion could it find its genuine fulfillment. "All science, all politics, all art, all literature must lie low at the feet of religion, pure and undefiled, before they will find their true place and use," explained Smetham.[38] Echoes of the Augustinian *ordo amoris* are evident here, and it was precisely the logic of Christian-Platonic hierarchicalism that implicitly governed evangelical discussions of art and religion.[39]

According to this view, religion simultaneously bears a negative and positive relationship to art. On the one hand, religion acts as an aesthetic horizon, establishing boundaries for art (the most basic of which is the assertion that art and religion are categorically distinct) and policing these boundaries accordingly. Zealous champions of art have frequently associated this policing function with Puritanism (or with Plato), and to some extent this is true. An extreme Puritan or Platonic view polices art to the point of extinction. Yet the mere act of establishing religious limits to art's social or metaphysical scope does not itself constitute

---

[35] Cf. Neil Harris's discussion of clergymen's views of art and religion in nineteenth-century America: "Art and religion were not merely compatible, but interdependent. While religion needed art to grasp the worshiper's senses, to encourage his approach to the throne of God with the appropriate awful respect, artists required religion to reach their full potentialities; great art was impossible without a supporting consensus of belief" (149). Many conservatives would have frowned upon the notion that "religion needed art to grasp the worshiper's senses," although they would have affirmed the latter part of Harris's formulation. Harris comes closer to the kind of model many evangelicals had in mind when he writes: "When pressed, of course, some clergymen were careful to place limits around their enthusiasm [for art].... Poetry, music and art, as beautiful as they could be ... required the guidance of religion...." (*Artist*, 304-305).

[36] T.A., "What Is Poetry?" *MerR* 11 (July 1859), 387.

[37] Pattison, "The Relation of Art to Religion," 326. See also, for example, "Poetry and Its Uses," *CO* 66 (1866), 119 and "Esthetics in Religion," *CA* 42 (13 June 1867), 188.

[38] Smetham, "Modern Sacred Art," 77.

[39] This view, of course, was not unique to evangelicals. It was true of other Victorian Christians, including most notably the Tractarians. On Tractarian poetics, see G.B. Tennyson, *Victorian Devotional Poetry: The Tractarian Mode* (Cambridge: Harvard University Press, 1981).

the puritanical. This point is critical for understanding nineteenth-century evangelical aesthetics. Not only was evangelical aesthetic thought adopting an increasingly romantic outlook but there was also a marked anti-Puritanism among an expanding cadre of thinkers. Consequently, any view that takes evangelical strictures on art as evidence of an unmitigated Puritanism is ultimately amiss. The sheer quantity of ink spilled on the question of art's relationship to religion demonstrates that evangelicals were interested in more than a perfunctory recitation of art's dangers. To be sure, many critics agreed that if art could not be made subservient to religion, then it was art that would have to go. After assuring readers that "the beautiful in art is sister to the good and the true in religion," the *Presbyterian Magazine* issued a stern reminder that "poetry, music, and, in fact, all the ornamental arts, *apart* from religion, are useless for all good purposes, and when placed in opposition to it, are *worse* than useless...."[40] Here, at least, evangelicals showed solidarity with their Puritan predecessors. Such reminders, however, must also be read in historical context. What often necessitated statements regarding the possible abandonment of art (although the subordinationist model was designed to ensure that it was *only* a possibility) was the growing tendency on the part of some progressive intellectuals to see art, apart from doctrinally-specific forms of Christianity, as a point of contact with the "divine" or as a replacement for traditional belief.[41] Whether it was the German idealist contention that art was the key to repairing humanity's alienation from the natural world or Arnold's promise that poetry could serve as a substitute for lost faith, art assumed an unprecedented religious, or quasi-religious, significance. When seen in this light, statements that initially appear puritanical and passé turn out to be a plea for moderation. Evangelicals were in fact engaged in a tenuous effort to walk a razor-thin line between a de-aestheticized spirituality and a hyper-spiritualized aesthetic. If romanticism had offered evangelicals a newly elevated conception of art, it also threatened to destabilize the desired religio-aesthetic hierarchy by displacing orthodox Christianity altogether. Critics, therefore, were just as apt to protest the excesses of those who hailed art as a new kind of religion as they were to protest the excesses of Puritanism.

Ostensibly negative statements about art's limitations must also be read in the context of corresponding positive statements about its social, moral, religious, and aesthetic value. For if in the subordinationist view Christianity in one sense limits art, it also facilitates art and gives it meaning. "Let the scholar settle the just subordination of literature to Christianity," observed one critic in 1823, "then Christianity will approve and exalt his pursuits." (This article had earlier quoted

---

[40] "Thoughts on Church Music," *PM* 4 (July 1854), 306.
[41] Concerns over religious truth could also lead to religio-aesthetic ultimatums: "It must be quite certain, that if poetry cannot do without irreligion, mankind can do without poetry" (John Foster, "Dyer's Poetics," *ER* 11 [Apr. 1814], 373).

Henry Martyn's reflections on the impact of his conversion on his aesthetic appreciation).[42] Pattison expressed this seeming paradox explicitly: "Art, which must be subordinate to religion, and limited by it, must also receive from it its constant inspiration."[43] Critics formulated this relationship in myriad ways, but nearly all concurred that Christianity uniquely empowers art and enables it to flourish. "Such is the nature of the principles of the Gospel," noted the *American Baptist Magazine* in 1835, "that they readily interweave themselves into every serious subject of thought, imparting a peculiar modification to all. Their presence or absence will give a very different aspect to everything that has relation to the important interests of time, and to our condition in the life which is to come."[44] All cultural endeavors, argued E.E. Higbee in 1874, are subject to Christianity's influence: "In fine, the whole realm of practical, theoretical, and aesthetical activity has felt its presence and power."[45] Critics did far more than deny the existence of an intrinsic hostility between art and religion; they actively asserted the positive relationship between them.[46]

For many evangelicals, the relationship between art and religion was finally an uneven one: just as God can do without human beings but human beings cannot do without God, so Christianity can (if necessary) do without art but art cannot do without Christianity. When art accepts its place in the great chain of religio-aesthetic being, its value is extensive indeed; when it disrupts this hierarchy, chaos results. "The two must be woven in strictest harmony," urged W.H. Bowen. "[T]aste must never assume to dictate to religion, nor substitute for religion."[47] Such, at least, was the ideal conception of art's relationship to religion imagined by evangelical critics. In 1861, the *Presbyterian Quarterly Review* captured this ideal of productive tension perfectly. Faithful Christians ought to indulge neither a puritanical nor a vague transcendentalist view of art. The truth lies in a golden mean, a hierarchical tension:

> The example of our Puritan fathers should not be imitated.... [But also] We would not stimulate to the displacement of religion that we may enthrone art.... But there is a happy mean to be preserved, in which the spiritual shall not be overborne by

---

[42] B., "Influence of the Fine Arts," 116. The author quotes Martyn on p. 114.
[43] Pattison, "The Relation of Art to Religion," 334.
[44] "The Necessity of a Religious Literature," *ABM* 15 (Jan. 1835), 8.
[45] Higbee, "Relation of Christianity to Art," 341.
[46] One example of this trend was the continued protest of Samuel Johnson's view of devotional poetry. See Cereticus, "On Sacred Poetry"; Review of *The Widow of the City of Nain and Other Poems*, by an Undergraduate of the University of Cambridge, *CO* 18 (Feb. 1819): 114-20; James Montgomery, Introductory Essay, *The Christian Psalmist; or, Hymns, Selected and Original* (Glasgow: Chalmers and Collins, 1825): v-xxxiii; Montgomery, Introductory Essay, *The Christian Poet; or, Selections in Verse, on Sacred Subjects* (Glasgow: William Collins, 1828): v-xxxiii; Montgomery, *Lectures on General Literature, Poetry, &c.* (New York: Harper, 1844), 153; "Religious Poets and Poetry," *CR* 14 (May 1849): 271-85; and "English Sacred Song," *BM* 82 (Jan. 1890), 10.
[47] W.H. Bowen, "Æsthetical Culture," *FBQ* 3 (Oct. 1860), 424.

the purely aesthetic, and the aesthetic not wholly excluded from the higher spiritual. The predominant power is in religion. Aesthetics are subordinate.[48]

Of course, maintaining such a delicate balance in practice was often another matter. By the 1870s and 1880s, this balance was starting to break down as the divide between liberals, who were increasingly prepared to accept the romantic spiritualization of art, and conservatives widened. However, it is to an examination of some of the details of this ideal of productive tension to which we now turn.

The Religio-Aesthetic Balance I: Christianity as Aesthetic Horizon

Evangelical discussions of the ways in which Christianity limits art centered for the most part on three main issues: (1) art and religion as distinct categories of experience; (2) art's relationship to salvation; and (3) art's idolatrous potential. In the wake of romanticism and amid growing scientific and philosophical challenges to traditional Christianity, the nineteenth century engaged in widespread reconsideration of these topics, settling in many cases on less-than-orthodox solutions. Throughout the period, many evangelicals fought to maintain more traditional positions on these issues; yet even these defenses reveal that the ground was beginning to shift.

Art and Religion as Distinct Categories

The issue of art and religion as distinct categories of experience was at the core of some evangelicals' efforts to resist the more immoderate implications of romantic thought. The position of evangelical critics on this issue helps in turn to explain the positions they adopted on the questions of art and salvation, and art and idolatry. In contrast to the tendency of prominent nineteenth-century thinkers to blur the traditional distinctions between art and religion, evangelical critics struggled to preserve the uniqueness of each.

The nineteenth century witnessed a steady progression towards the conflation of art and religion, or a propensity to see aesthetic experience as fundamentally religious and religion as fundamentally aesthetic. This development has a complex history,[49] but briefly it manifested itself on at least three fronts. To begin

---

[48] "Aesthetics," *PQR* 10 (July 1861), 33. A portion of this article was reprinted as "Art and Religion," *CAJ* 37 (8 May 1862): 147. The cross-over from Presbyterian to Methodist periodicals demonstrates evangelical solidarity on this issue.

[49] See Charles LaPorte, *Victorian Poets and the Changing Bible* (Charlottesville: University of Virginia Press, 2011); Karl Beckson, *The Religion of Art: A Modernist Theme in British Literature 1885-1925* (New York: AMS, 2006); Nicholas Wolterstorff, "Art and the Aesthetic: The Religious Dimension," *The Blackwell Guide to Aesthetics*, ed. Peter Kivy (Malden: Blackwell, 2004): 325-39; James Turner, *Without God, Without Creed: The Origins of Unbelief in America* (Baltimore: Johns Hopkins University Press, 1985), 196-99, 252-54; Jacques Barzun, *The Use and Abuse of Art* (Princeton: Princeton University Press, 1974), 24-46; and Max Weber, *From Max Weber: Essays in Sociology*, ed. H.H. Gerth and C. Wright Mills (New York: Oxford University Press, 1946), 340-43.

with, there appeared a sophisticated body of post-Kantian aesthetic and philosophical thought which stressed the possibility of super-sensuous or transcendental perception. Schelling, to take a representative example, argued that the Absolute, which he increasingly identified with "God," could be apprehended through "intellectual intuition." These systems facilitated the gradual process of immanentization that scholars have noted in nineteenth-century thought. "Spirit" and "divinity" saturated the world, and what had traditionally been a matter of grace, revelation, or faith now entered the domain of metaphysics, intuition, and imagination. Moreover, these idealist systems frequently accorded art an important place in the progressive self-awareness of Absolute Spirit. Some evangelicals had already begun to move in this direction by the 1850s, but in the middle-third of the century many critics were still wary of what they saw as the theological dangers inherent in this view.

Secondly, the conflation of art and religion emerged as a defensive strategy for securing religion in the face of what seemed like indisputable scientific evidence that the factual claims of religion were false. If one could no longer accept religion as scientifically credible, then perhaps one could still appreciate it for what Arnold called its "unconscious poetry."[50] One might, in short, "save" Christianity by aestheticizing it. Some within the evangelical tradition had begun to adopt similar measures as a way of dealing with seemingly difficult or offensive doctrines. Although they did not carry their thinking as far as Arnold, both Horace Bushnell and Edwards Amasa Park turned to more "poetic" understandings of Christianity in what they believed was a noble effort to sustain it.[51] In doing so, they introduced what would become a defining characteristic of liberal Protestantism around the turn of the twentieth century.

Finally, the fusion of art and religion transpired on a social level. Over the course of the century, art and religion came to be seen as exercising analogous social functions. Already in 1833, the *Christian Quarterly Spectator* had conjectured that Christianity and poetry have similar ends: "The tendency and aim of Christianity is the same with the legitimate and highest efforts of poetry,—to interest man in man,—to lift him above the grossness of material things,—to spiritualize his nature, and fit him for a higher and nobler existence."[52] The idea became widespread that art and beauty offer powerful remedies for poverty and other social ills. For some non-evangelical thinkers, parks were as important as preaching. In 1882, the social activist H.O. Barnett asked how the poor could be raised up "to enjoy spiritual life." Rejecting the usual evangelical answer to this

---

[50] Matthew Arnold, "The Study of Poetry," *Essays English and American*, ed. Charles W. Eliot (New York: P.F. Collier, 1938), 65.

[51] On this trend, see Turner, *Without God*, 196-99. See also *Horace Bushnell: Selected Writings on Language, Religion, and American Culture*, ed. David L. Smith (Chico: Scholars, 1984) and Edwards Amasa Park, "The Theology of the Intellect and That of the Feelings," *American Philosophical Addresses, 1700-1900*, ed. Joseph L. Blair (New York: Columbia University Press, 1946): 627-58.

[52] "Influence of the Christian Religion on Poetry," *QCS* 5 (June 1833), 203.

question, Barnett argued that preaching had failed and new methods must be sought. Of the six new methods she offered, five had strong aesthetic components: the poor should be exposed to flowers, high-class music, afternoons in the country, the stories of great lives, and the Beauty of Art. "Picture galleries," she contended, "can become mission halls for the degraded." Elsewhere, Barnett did moderate her statement somewhat, admitting that "Pictures will not do everything. They will not save souls."[53] Nevertheless, she had raised the possibility that art may present a viable alternative to preaching the Gospel—a scandalous suggestion for most evangelicals. In fact, she had failed to mention the Gospel as conservative evangelicals would have understood it at all. If Barnett stopped short of equating aesthetic experience with salvation, she had issued a real challenge to traditional evangelical views. And although many evangelicals would have agreed with Barnett that art constitutes a meaningful source of moral and social refinement, they would have found spurious her strong faith in art at the expense of the Gospel.

The common denominator in all of these developments, however, was the tendency to define religion according to *feeling*.[54] It was Friedrich Schleiermacher, with his definition of religion as a "feeling of dependence," who pioneered the nineteenth century's formal philosophical reflection on this idea, although its roots may be traced to pietism and even to the Great Awakening and Evangelical Revival. Revivalism itself may have helped to reinforce this notion, despite the fact that evangelical revivalists rarely relinquished doctrinal concerns completely. This understanding of religion as fundamentally affective was crucial. As observed in the last chapter, there was an important axis of thought running through the nineteenth century which pitted art against science as unique discourses suited to the feelings and intellect respectively. Consequently, if religion, too, is more emotion than fact, then a natural alliance exists between art and religion over and against science. In some cases, however, this alliance morphed into oneness, as any attempt at a qualitative distinction between religious and aesthetic emotions faded into the background. Clive Bell's *Art* (1914) may be seen as an endpoint in this relentless march towards uniformity: art and religion alike "have the power of transporting men to superhuman ecstasies; both are means to unearthly states of mind. Art and religion belong to the same world.... The kingdom of neither is of this world."[55] Rudolf Otto's painstaking efforts in *The Idea of the Holy* (1919) to untangle this religio-aesthetic knot of affectivity offers one example of how widespread this merger had become throughout the Anglo-Saxon world by the early twentieth century.[56] Much of the nineteenth-

---

[53] H.O. Barnett, "Passionless Reformers," *Aesthetics and Religion in Nineteenth-Century Britain* ed. Gavin Budge (Bristol: Thoemmes, 2003): 6:226-33; "Pictures for the People," *Aesthetics and Religion*, 6:352.
[54] See Turner, *Without God*, 196-99.
[55] Qtd. in Wolterstorff, "Art and the Aesthetic," 328.
[56] See Rudolf Otto, *The Idea of the Holy: An Inquiry into the Non-Rational Factor in the Idea of the Divine and Its Relation to the Rational* (London: Oxford University Press,

century debate between theological liberals and conservatives amounted to a struggle over how one ought to locate religion on the art-science axis. Is religion closer to art/emotion or to science/intellect?

Evangelicals did not dispute the art-science dichotomy; it was so embedded in Victorian thought that it had largely passed beyond the limits of critical vision. Evangelicals, moreover, were far from denying that religion addresses the heart. Especially before the 1870s, however, many did insist on a qualitative distinction between religious and aesthetic emotion. Edward Irving, despite his otherwise romantic leanings, stressed that "poetry, and philosophy, and science, and sentiment, and every other more noble function of the soul, cannot, in their own strength, exalt themselves into religion."[57] "We are always grieved when we see these imaginative Christians," confessed the *Christian Advocate and Journal and Zion's Herald* in 1829. "They are certainly substituting the shadow for the substance. They feel a glow of imagination, and mistake it for the glow of devotion. They seem to love God just as they love the mountain, or the waterfall, or any sublime object."[58] A letter in the *Christian Index* complained of many people's penchant for mistaking aesthetic for religious feeling: "Many apparently do not distinguish between the pleasure arising from mere taste, and that satisfaction derived solely from humility.... Their worship is more poetical than godly." Indeed, "the pleasures of taste, are often mistaken for the spirit of devotion...."[59] Henry N. Day, whose aesthetics exhibit a familiarity with idealist thought, nevertheless decried in 1847 the "aesthetic mysticism" of the age: "Nor ... are we the dupes of that philosophical mysticism which would identify the true artistic spirit with the religious sentiment; which, in true pantheistic consistency, recognises in every creative genius a real incarnation of the Deity, and only there...."[60] It was not the intent of such statements to deny that aesthetic experience could initiate religious feelings of devotion. Evangelicals endorsed the idea that an appreciation of nature, for example, could lead to enhanced worship of the Creator.[61] The goal, rather, was to maintain a qualitative distinction: aesthetic feelings might lead to religious feelings, but the two are not identical.

Conservative writers, particularly those within strong confessional traditions, fought to preserve an essential distinction between religion and art by affirming

---

1950).
[57] Edward Irving, "Idolatry," *The Collected Writings of Edward Irving*, ed. G. Carlyle (London: Alexander Strahan, 1865), 4:15-16.
[58] "Religion of the Imagination," *CAJZH* 4 (16 Oct. 1829), 28.
[59] An Episcopalian, Letter to the Editor of the *Christian Index*, *CI* 6 (12 May 1832), 300.
[60] Henry N. Day, "Taste and Morals:—The Necessity of Aesthetic Culture to the Highest Moral Excellence," *ABRCR* (July 1847), 533.
[61] See "On the Moral and Religious Improvement that May Be Derived from Natural Beauty and Sublimity," *CS* 6 (1 Nov. 1824): 561-62; "Nature Guiding Up to God," *CI* 7 (29 Sep. 1832): 204-05; Dr. Percival, "The Advantages of a Taste for the Beauties of Nature," *CAJ* 8 (11 Oct. 1833): 28; "Moral Aesthetics; or, the Goodness of God in the Ornaments of the Universe," *BRPR* 24 (Jan. 1852): 38-52; and G. Rogers, "The Advantages of Cultivating the Love of Nature," *ST* (Sep. 1876): 391-402.

the cognitive content of religion. In his highly critical review of Bushnell's *God in Christ*, Charles Hodge rejected Bushnell's claim that "a great part of [Christianity's] dignity and efficacy consists in the artistic power of its form...." Bushnell had argued at length for a non-dogmatic view of the Atonement. Not only does the work of Christ exceed the capacities of human language but abstract doctrinal formulae fail to move the human spirit. According to Bushnell, the suffering of Christ acts as an aesthetic object, apprehended by the feelings and intended to produce a subjective impression of God's love and a hope for the future. The "matter" of Christ's work "does not lie in formulas of reason, and cannot be comprehended in them. It is more a poem than a treatise. It classes as a work of Art more than as a work of Science. It addresses the understanding, in great part, through the feeling or sensibility."[62] For Hodge, Christian doctrine was more rational than aesthetic, while religion's transformative power was an effect of the Holy Spirit and truth rather than aesthetic perception:

> It is among the first principles of the oracle of God, that regeneration and sanctification are not esthetic effects produced through the imagination. They are moral and spiritual changes, wrought by the Holy Ghost, with and by the truth as revealed to the reason. The whole healthful power of the things of God over the feelings, depends upon their being true to the intellect. If we are affected by the revelation of God as a father, it is because he is a father, and not the picture of one. If we have peace through faith in the blood of Christ, it is because he is a propitiation for our sins in reality, and not in an artistic form merely.[63]

Religion must be clearly distinguished from aesthetics. One cannot, as Hodge accused Bushnell of doing, reduce the supernatural power of religion to mere aesthetic effect.

The conservative insistence on a clear-cut distinction between religious and aesthetic experience could, if extrapolated to its furthest extent, end in the total dissociation of the two. It could, in short, fall back into a kind of puritanical attempt to quarantine art. An 1875 article on "Religious Art" came close to advocating just such an approach. The author's thesis, somewhat shocking for its time, was that "religious art" is an "expression ... entirely without meaning." The author admitted that art had a divine origin but scoffed at the notion that it could be, in any meaningful sense, religious: "Religion then, and art, though equally divine in origin and human in their sphere, are in their mode of influence and action totally distinct, and any purpose to combine the two must end in damage,

---

[62] Horace Bushnell, *God in Christ: Three Discourses, Delivered at New Haven, Cambridge, and Andover, with a Preliminary Dissertation on Language* (Hartford: Wm. James Hamersley, 1867), 204.

[63] Charles Hodge, Review of *God in Christ; Three Discourses delivered at New Haven, Cambridge, and Andover; with a Preliminary Dissertation on Language*, by Horace Bushnell, *BRPR* 21 (Apr. 1849), 268-69.

failure, and confusion."[64] This position, however, was rare. On the contrary, critics more often clung to the conviction that art could have a religious dimension without itself *becoming* religion and that religion could, in turn, work alongside, and in some cases through, the aesthetic without being reduced to the aesthetic. J.S. White noted in 1887, "it may be remarked that if religion has a sphere of its own, the converse must be equally true ... that is to say, there is a wide field in which art may be exercised without any direct bearing on religion." White's observation suggests how the same logic used to safeguard the singularity of religion could also supply a rationale for aestheticism. However, White himself had not yet forsaken the Victorian dream of wholeness. Analytical distinctions need not imply an actual separation: "But though distinct, they are not unrelated. There is no natural or necessary antagonism between them."[65] Bushnell had erred not in his suggestion that Christianity appealed to the feelings but that it appealed *predominantly* to the feelings. Thus, after Day had blasted the "aesthetic mysticism" of the age, he could nevertheless conclude that "it may be true for all this, that Christianity must work through the taste, as it must work through the intelligence."[66] Even Hodge, who inclined towards a "scientific" view of religion, acknowledged that "The revelations of God are addressed to the whole soul, to the reason, to the imagination, to the heart, and to the conscience."[67]

Art and Salvation

To some, the question of how art relates to salvation would seem a strange inquiry indeed—a weird consequence of evangelicalism's preoccupation with the Atonement or the obligation to evangelize. However, for conservative critics who sought to maintain a productive tension between Christianity and art, the question was not only natural but, given the propensity of some influential Victorians to find in art a substitute for what seemed a crumbling orthodoxy, necessary as well. Convinced that all are sinners in need of God's redemptive grace, conservatives were committed to the all-important task of spreading the Good News that Christ's death has atoned for sinners' rebellion against God. For Victorian evangelicals, conversion also had an important social dimension. Political legislation and education aided the quest for social amelioration, but no such efforts would succeed if people's hearts remained unregenerate. Given the centrality of evangelization and revivalism to evangelicalism, it seems inevitable that the question of art's relationship to the saving grace uniquely manifested in conversion would have arisen. This emphasis on conversion, furthermore, found itself increasingly in danger of being supplanted by secular forms of "salvation". Already in the late 1840s, liberal-minded writers like Bushnell had begun to reject the conversionist model of historic evangelicalism. In place of the traditional stress on a moment

---

[64] John T. Emmett, "Religious Art," *BrQR* 62 (Oct. 1875), 303, 334.
[65] J.S. White, "Religion and Art," *PMQRCAmb* n.s. 9 (Jan. 1887), 128, 129.
[66] Day, "Taste and Morals," 533.
[67] Hodge, Review of *God in Christ*, 269.

of decision, Bushnell substituted a theory of Christian nurture in which the ordinary influences of family and society unconsciously shaped the characters of children.[68] In addition, art was being peddled as a panacea for all sorts of spiritual and social problems. Not surprisingly, therefore, some evangelicals felt compelled to address art's connection to salvation.

Conservative critics generally adhered to the well-established view that art and aesthetic experience do not by themselves constitute forms of salvation.[69] Art and beauty serve a variety of noble ends, but they are incapable of accomplishing a work reserved for the Holy Spirit. To many evangelicals, the idea that art offers a form of salvation would have seemed downright naïve. The real problem was sin, and no art, however beautiful or arresting, could eliminate this blot or bring peace with God. Reacting in 1854 to the idea that "Only Art can elevate: the Gospel is Art," the *London Quarterly Review* forcefully declared that the only true Gospel is the Gospel of Christ:

> Nature does not save man from sin and misery; nor Art; nor Civilization; nor Commerce.... As servants to a community, purified by a spiritual power, they are of priceless value, and indescribable ornament; but as lords of man's heart, or the stay of his hope, they are usurpers, and their reign ends, as do usurpations.... Nothing is gospel for man that does not go into his nature, down to the root of his leaning to sin; and create within him a clean heart and a right spirit. Lover of Nature! lover of Art! lover of Civilization! lover of Commerce! we join you all. But if you would see the beauties you admire in the fairest posture, and wielding the utmost influence, join us in pointing all men, in great earnest, to Him who is "exalted a Prince and a Saviour, to give repentance and remission of sins,"—to make the individual "a new creature," and the whole earth a land of rest.[70]

Similarly, the *Wesleyan-Methodist Magazine* somewhat reluctantly acknowledged that Wordsworth, despite his incontrovertible genius, had strayed in attributing to Nature what can only be attributed to God, namely, the granting of grace unto salvation: "He erred ... in asserting for Nature a power which she does not possess; a power to lead back, by her mere teachings and influences, man's sinful, far-wandered spirit to truth, and God, and peace; a work this which only the good Spirit can do, and which He does by other and far different means."[71] Such statements register the unwillingness of some critics to capitulate fully to romanticism. Evangelicals may have been romantics when it came to aesthetics, but until the late nineteenth century (and for conservatives even longer) many held fast to traditional doctrines like the depravity of humankind and salvation through Christ alone.[72] Evangelicals were in fact avid readers of Wordsworth,

---

[68] See Morgan, *Protestants and Pictures*, 270-75 for a discussion of Bushnell and his contribution to Protestant notions of art's character-shaping capacity.
[69] See Doreen M. Rosman, *Evangelicals and Culture* (London: Croom Helm, 1984), 195.
[70] "Guide Books to the Crystal Palace," *LQR* 3 (Oct. 1854), 279.
[71] W.R.J., "Characteristics of Wordsworth's Poetry," *WMM* 15 (Apr. 1869), 323-24.
[72] The same approach governed evangelical attitudes towards Arnoldian "culture". See

but they could not condone his theological vagueness nor sanction his tacit claim that the beauty of Nature contains everything needful for salvation.[73]

Some critics seem to have stepped up their denial of art's salvific potential as the century drew to a close, perhaps in response to the claims of writers like Barnett. A number of articles published in the early 1880s reiterated that there can be no salvation in art. Discussing "Christianity and Art" in 1880, B. Hawley maintained that "The real wants of men on earth are to be met in Christ, who is the brightness of the Father's glory, and the express image of his person, and in the appointed and significant ordinances of Christianity."[74] W.J. Dawson, thought he saw in Tennyson's poem *The Palace of Art* a confirmation of this very idea. The poem, Dawson explained, testifies that "The need for some diviner salvation than art can offer, haunts with persistent bitterness the human spirit sheltered in its selfish splendour."[75] Even Henry J. Van Dyke, Jr., whose later liberalism led to trouble with the American Presbyterian hierarchy, still found it appropriate in 1883 to sound a similar refrain: "Nor can we hope to save this man, and such as he, by any moral ministry of art, however pure and strong. Poems and pictures will not deliver him from the kingdom of darkness into the kingdom of light.... There must be first a quickening, an awakening, a new birth in the inner nature of man, so that he shall know the good, desire it, seek it...."[76] Barnett and Arnold notwithstanding, the idea that art could redress the spiritual problems of humankind was not only misguided but dangerous.

Yet if conservatives rejected the idea that one could find an alternative form of salvation in art, they proved more ambivalent when it came to the related question of whether art might play a role in bringing sinners to Christ. Could the Holy Spirit work *through* art to convince a person of the need for salvation traditionally conceived? An article published in the *Eclectic Review* in 1841 answered this question with a resounding "Maybe." The article, a review of Drummond's *Letter to Thomas Phillips* and Edward Edwards's *The Administrative Economy of the Fine Arts in England*, tentatively allowed that art may serve as a locus of divine grace: "In the mere way of instrumentality, a glorious picture, a noble statue, a magnificent edifice, or a sublime piece of music, may on some rare occasions have even reached the soul of a sinner. The Almighty who would have all men to be saved, is not limited in His operations." The writer, however, knew his argument was potentially controversial: "We are fully aware that much difference of opinion may exist on this subject." Several pages later, he conceded that it is only "in very rare instances" that "the Holy Spirit of God has made use of certain exquisite productions to affect the understanding, or influence the

---

"Culture," *CAJ* 37 (30 Jan. 1862), 36.
[73] For an evangelical analysis of Wordsworth, see "Wordsworth Considered as a Religious Poet," *CR* 16 (July 1851): 434-60.
[74] B. Hawley, "Christianity and Art," *CA* 55 (1 July 1880), 419.
[75] W.J. Dawson, "Religious Doubt in Modern Poetry," *WMM* (Aug. 1883), 607.
[76] Henry J. Van Dyke, Jr., "Art and Ethics: In Some of Their Relations," *PR* (Jan.-Jun. 1883), 104.

heart."⁷⁷ Since God is sovereign in His choice of methods, art may sometimes provide an occasion for the intervention of divine grace. Generally, though, art bears no correlation to salvation. But why?

There were at least two reasons for this tendency to dissociate art and salvation. To begin with, the *Eclectic Review* writer criticized Edwards and Drummond for failing to keep in view "the usual means of promoting [true religion's] success according to the word of God." For evangelicals, this "usual means" referred to the preaching of the Word. Drummond, for instance, had made the standard claim that art serves as a missionary tool to instruct the "heathen," poor, and illiterate. To good Protestants, however, this sounded a lot like Catholicism or Tractarianism, and in fact the writer accused Drummond of being "a zealous Puseyite." Proclamation, not painting, was the means that God had ordained for the dissemination of the Gospel, and to introduce another was to substitute human methods for God-sanctioned ones. "Fancy him making all conceivable exertions for the benefit of the plastic arts at home, and the diffusion of christianity abroad ... in rendering the walls of the Islington seminary frescoed like catholic convents, or adding to the clergymen and schoolmasters in India, Jamaica, and New Zealand, a corps of artists from the Royal Academy!"⁷⁸ This perspective, of course, echoed Puritan anxieties about the dangers of "invention" and reflected the abiding influence of the Regulative Principle. Here, too, aspects of the Puritan tradition had survived intact. Indeed, many conservatives tended to see any means of evangelism other than the biblically mandated one of preaching the Gospel as representative of the extra-biblical accretions associated with Catholicism. "Religion is not taught by the painted semblances of Christ, but by the word and work of Christ Himself," argued the *British Quarterly Review*.⁷⁹ Consequently, although the Holy Spirit could work through means such as art, these means were undependable because not divinely appointed.

Equally important, however, was the reviewer's concern that even a theory which posits a wholly instrumental connection between art and salvation may slide imperceptibly into the belief that art communicates grace. Or perhaps more accurately, the author feared that the emotions deriving from an aesthetic encounter may too easily be confused with those attending a genuine experience of supernatural grace. Again, the problem was the potential conflation of art and religion. Noting the "enervating and ostentatious display of intellectual emotion" of which he believed art lovers were often guilty when viewing works of art, the reviewer cautioned readers against placing too much stock in such experience:

> Intellectualism is never to be despised, as we have repeatedly intimated; but neither must the fact be forgotten, that it may be, and generally *is* an entirely distinct affair, from the vitality of that knowledge which converts, and which alone saves a soul. We have seen the most secular and even sensual minds more deeply moved than

---

⁷⁷ "Administrative Economy of the Fine Arts," *ER* 10 (Sep. 1841), 240, 241, 249.
⁷⁸ "Administrative Economy," 249, 250, 251.
⁷⁹ Emmett, "Religious Art," 319.

we would venture to describe, before the Transfiguration of Raphael, in the Vatican ... and yet these very individuals, when the spectacle has terminated, have returned like the dog to their own licentiousness again, or like the sow that was washed to her wallowing in the mire! Such religious impressions, if deserving that name at all, are but the contortions of a corpse when in contact with the wires of a galvanic battery; the illusive and horrible imitations of a genuine quickening of the inner man![80]

It is perhaps no coincidence that "imitation" yet again connoted the absence of genuine spirit. The horror of the Coleridgean copy remained. But the missing element was not now spirit in any vague Emersonian sense but the Holy Spirit of orthodox Christianity. The aesthetic encounter that at first blush seemed the most vital of "spiritual" experiences could turn out to be a religious Frankenstein.

A number of evangelicals thus sought to distance art from the reception of "efficacious" or "saving" grace. Certainly aesthetic experience held no such power in itself, but neither was it a guaranteed site of such grace. Even art's vision of the ideal was not, as an 1891 article in the *Record* made clear, sufficient for salvation. Noting a recent sermon preached by the Bishop of Manchester, the *Record* pinpointed both the problem and the solution:

> In the course of his sermon his Lordship said there was a particular form of self-worship which was very popular in the city of Manchester. "We do not want religion," some people among us said; "we can ascend on the wing of art into the region of the beautiful and true." God forbid that he should deny that art had the power of raising men into the sphere of the ideal, or that he should deny that art, if it be true and great, had the power of enlarging and purifying the emotions. But it was one thing to get a fugitive glimpse of the ideal, and a very difficult thing to make that the permanent influence in the formation of human character.... [Humankind] needed nothing less than the continual inflowing of the light, grace, and power of the Divine Spirit of wisdom and love, which Jesus came to embody in His own Person and to naturalize in our race.[81]

This perspective helps to account for what may seem a curious omission in a number of mid-nineteenth-century evangelical discussions of art—the absence of a clear evangelistic emphasis (in the traditional sense). This absence stands in stark contrast to the rationale offered by some contemporary evangelical novelists, for example, who cite evangelism as a primary objective of their writing.[82] For many nineteenth-century critics, the correlation between art and salvation may have seemed a dubious one. Art could not accomplish what only the Holy Spirit can.

---

[80] "Administrative Economy," 249-50.
[81] "Art and Religion," *Rec* n.s. 10 (22 May 1891), 499.
[82] See Lynn S. Neal, *Romancing God: Evangelical Women and Inspirational Fiction* (Chapel Hill: University of North Carolina Press, 2006), 107-108 and Jan Blodgett, *Protestant Evangelical Culture and Contemporary Society* (Westport: Greenwood, 1997).

Even so, the strongly guarded contention of the *Eclectic Review* suggests that resistance to the idea of art's salvific potential was beginning to weaken. Why could art not, in rare instances, provide an occasion for efficacious grace? Further evidence of this weakening is apparent in an article that appeared in 1876 in *The Sword and the Trowel*, a publication founded by Charles Spurgeon. Contemplating in true romantic form "The Advantages of Cultivating the Love of Nature," G. Rogers concluded that "It is impossible to cherish the love of nature and of sin at the same time.... What man on his way to gratify worldly ambition or to revenge an insult, could see any beauty in a landscape, or any glory in a setting sun?" This statement has an Edwardsean ring to it insofar as it implies that sin may interfere with the perception of natural beauty. Yet Rogers also suggested that beauty could play some role in mitigating sin: "*The moral influence of the love of nature is not less in its favour than its conduciveness to health and to mental refinement.*" Interestingly, the *Sword*'s editor was conflicted on this point, and he inserted a footnote accordingly: "We are not *quite* sure of this [impossibility of loving sin and nature at the same time]: but our revered friend speaks for himself ... and the exceptions to this rule must be very few, if indeed there be any."[83] The editor may have been as uncertain about his uncertainty as he was about Rogers's thesis, but this very ambivalence indicates the ongoing tension between orthodoxy and romantic aesthetics. The *Record* article betrayed a similar ambivalence regarding the religious value of the ideal so central to nineteenth-century conceptions of art. On the one hand, the author seemed to allow that the ideal has real transcendent value. It is a true though "fugitive" glimpse into the Platonic realm of "the beautiful and true." On the other hand, this glimpse is not itself a source of saving grace. Such a view was not in fact inconsistent with evangelical taxonomies of grace, and indeed the author in the *Record* was careful to maintain an implicit distinction between the doctrines of efficacious and common grace. Not all critics, however, were so theologically cautious, and the belief that art is ideal may itself have been a factor in closing the gap between religion and art, thereby helping to undermine the ideal of productive tension.

Complicating the question of art's salvific potential was the fact that some critics had, since at least the 1840s, been chiseling away at the "problem of presence" inherited from the Puritans. Although evangelicals were disinclined to see art as an evangelistic tool, a growing number seemed willing to speak of art as a manifestation of God generally. Numerous writers followed Plato in positing a scale of beauties that culminated in Beauty Itself.[84] "All aesthetic beauty thus discovers a God—a being perfect in character, and worthy of universal homage and love ...," wrote Day in 1847. "It leads up in its own proper tendency, to the

---

[83] Rogers, "The Advantages," 393-94.
[84] See T.A., "What Is Poetry?," 403; "The Beautiful," *CAJ* 36 (12 Sep. 1861), 294; "Esthetic Culture," 386; "Practical Aesthetics," *BrQR* 71 (Jan. 1880), 55; Theodore W. Hunt, "Modern Aestheticism," *PR* 9 (1882), 150; and James T. East, "The Ministry of Beauty," *WMM* 123 (July 1900), 504.

perfect living Creator and governor of all. It displays him to the soul with a power peculiar to itself;—not in the inanimate form of abstract influence and deduction; not in the repelling, overwhelming terrors of mere rigorous sovereignty and dominion; but in the bright, attractive, wooing character of a God of perfect loveliness."[85] All Beauty, natural and artistic, reveals God. As the *Biblical Repertory and Princeton Review* observed: beauty "is the utterance of the divine, which gives its eloquence to the voice of nature. It is the expression of the divine, which lends its highest effulgence to the beautiful in poetry and art."[86] Critics conceded that earthly beauty but dimly reflects that of heaven, but they nevertheless insisted that beauty serves as an open channel to God. A proper taste, claimed Bowen, "beholds in finite objects a partial, incomplete revelation of supreme beauty. But this partial revelation has a reference to the complete, and so imparts completeness to the heart."[87] A few critics like Smetham continued to caution "that Divine power is no more inherent in [art] than in other modes of mere expression and communication,"[88] but many evangelicals were learning to see art, if not as a means of saving grace, as a contact point with God. "Why should not God reveal himself through inspired art as well as through inspired oratory and literature?" asked the *Methodist Review* in 1894.[89] By the 1890s, the question had become largely rhetorical.

Art and Idolatry

It is in evangelical discussions of art and idolatry that the long shadow of the Puritan tradition may be glimpsed most readily. Since the Reformation, the charge that the Church's patronage of the arts had plunged it into idolatry had been at the forefront of Protestant attacks on Catholicism. On the one hand, critics remained conscious of these dangers and reiterated some of the traditional Protestant warnings concerning art's idolatrous potential. The campaign against conflating art and religion was an attempt to avoid one kind of idolatry. On the other hand, these same critics frequently denied that art itself, even painting and sculpture, was intrinsically idolatrous. Idolatry remained an unfortunate theoretical possibility, but this should not deter one from enjoying the fine arts. By the century's close, both liberals and conservatives were even arguing for the introduction of art into their worship spaces.

The most typical caveat of evangelical critics concerned art's capacity to represent God. Any attempt to depict God in art was considered sheer folly since no human being can apprehend him fully. "The truth is," wrote Pattison, "that in religion, more than in any other study, science and art are alike powerless to

---

[85] Day, "Taste and Morals," 543.
[86] Review of *Robert Burns; as a Poet, and as Man*, by Samuel Tyler, *BRPR* 21 (Apr. 1849), 258.
[87] Bowen, "Æsthetical Culture," 419-20.
[88] Smetham, "Modern Sacred Art," 57.
[89] F.M. Bristol, "Reciprocity of Art and Religion," *MR* 54 (1894), 707-708.

fathom what is unfathomable, and to depict what will never submit to portraiture.... Religion, so far from being helped, may be, and in many cases is, harmed by representation."[90] The *Eclectic Review* thought "the unhappy idea of representing God in a work of Art ... a modern invention" since the early Christians had generally avoided images; when they did employ them, they did so only symbolically.[91] For many critics, this proscription applied to representations not only of God the Father but also Christ. As David Morgan has noted, "Many clergy in late-nineteenth-century America" expressed "disappointment ... in artistic depictions of Christ," even though such depictions were increasingly common.[92] "Christ is beyond the reach of art. The finite and restricted human mind and hand cannot efficiently describe Divinity in human form," declared the *British Quarterly Review*.[93] The *Christian Index* denounced all household paintings of Christ as being in bad taste, for "The infinite, divine perfections of Christ can not be represented upon canvas, nor sculptured in marble and it is impious to attempt it." For good measure, the periodical restated its opinion the following year: "No human artist can draw and paint the correct likeness of Christ as he was intended to be worshipped."[94] As Protestants had long been fond of arguing, to represent Christ "upon canvas" is idolatrous because it is impossible to represent Him completely. A partial representation is a false one, and false representation is idolatrous. "Let no Christian today fancy that the subtle powers of idolatry are obsolete," W.F. Taylor warned. "When once we imagine pictures of Christ in any way stir the heart to faith and love, when they become a means of devotion, then it is inevitable that our conception of him will be influenced by the picture—that is, by the attributes of him which it reveals." Human beings must reconcile themselves to the fact that "The painter's art cannot equal the Christian's spiritual vision."[95]

Some critics were also attuned to the deficiencies of language in capturing spiritual realities. The *Christian Index* acknowledged that the "spirit which pervades the heart when engaged in offices of humiliation and prayer, can never be well expressed, by the feeble power of verse."[96] The *Eclectic Review* likewise questioned the wisdom of rendering Scripture in verse: "It cannot be denied, and it need not be concealed, that all attempts to versify portions of Holy Writ, must fail in the main purpose of poetry, which is, *so* to adorn or dignify its themes, that by the new light thrown upon them, they may be exalted beyond any previous conception of their beauty or their grandeur, which obtained in ordinary minds." "[D]ivine themes," the author continued, "are necessarily degraded by

---

[90] Pattison, "The Relation of Art to Religion," 330-31.
[91] "The Relation of Roman Catholicism and Protestantism," 15.
[92] Morgan, *Protestants and Pictures*, 298. See pp. 292-304 on the history surrounding visual imagery appearing in late-nineteenth-century American "lives of Christ".
[93] Emmett, "Religious Art," 319.
[94] "Pictures," *CI* 60 (22 June 1882), 12; J.M.W., "Pictures," *CI* (26 Apr. 1883), 6.
[95] Taylor, "Christ in Art," 475, 476.
[96] An Episcopalian, Letter to the Editor, 300. See also Emmett, "Religious Art," 308.

human interpolations." Such statements, however, should not be read as a denial of the deep intercourse between art and religion. For the writer in the *Christian Index*, poetry may be unable to render the heartfelt emotion experienced during prayer, but poetry can capture the feeling of gratitude one feels after prayer. As for the author in the *Eclectic Review*, who initially sounded rather Johnsonian, versifying Scripture does indeed degrade it, but "human compositions are necessarily exalted by the felicitous introduction of sacred illusions."[97] Christianity may improve art, though art may not improve on Christianity.

Other writers cautioned against the "natural" tendency of human beings to love beauty rather than the God of Beauty. "Men are prone to idolatry," argued the *Christian Index*, "and image worship is idolatry. The more perfect and beautiful the picture as a work of art the more danger in that direction."[98] Hawley warned that "It is easier to reverence and adore what is seen than what is unseen; and all idolatry has its beginnings in a recognition and worship of secondary causes and visible causes, rather than of the unseen First Cause."[99] Some writers also maintained, following the Puritans, that art has no place in the sanctuary. The *Biblical Repertory and Princeton Review* doubted the congruity of Protestantism and cathedrals:

> We may imagine that our faith, in its higher spirituality, is above all visible symbolism except what we have in church and sacraments—we may fancy that we are capable of using indifferently all, any, or no art, and that we are far beyond the poetic period in these respects—but, notwithstanding all this, when we consider the native tendencies of our minds to form an idol, and the insidious sway which every religious symbolism has acquired over the hearts of its subjects, we cannot but tremble at the idea of the Protestant world generally making experiment with genuine cathedral art.

This article, in fact, resuscitated the Puritan distinction between religious and civil images. Calling for the ejection of "whatever goes by the name of rich, gorgeous, [or] elegant ... [from] our churches," the author nevertheless allowed that such things may be appropriate for "civil style."[100] It is worth noting, however, that while the author took advantage of the freedom granted by this distinction in the civil space, even within this space Puritan simplicity was no longer the norm.

Although evangelicals remained sensitive to the possibilities of idolatry, they were on the whole less anxious than their predecessors about art's tendencies in this direction. That is, they seemed far more interested in arguing the problem away. What about the Second Commandment? asked the Presbyterian *Christian*

---

[97] "Sacred Poetry," *ER* 1 (May 1837), 445, 446. See also "Religious Plays," *BM* 73 (May 1881), 208.
[98] "Pictures," 12.
[99] Hawley, "Christianity and Art," 419.
[100] "Church Architecture," 640, 648. Rosman, *Evangelicals and Culture*, 148, 152-53 also notes this paradox.

Advocate in 1823. "This command we have heard seriously urged against the whole of the engraver's art." But one must remember that the first portion of the command "is coupled with the additional injunction, 'thou shalt not bow down to them nor worship them;' and that it was to prevent this abuse, that the whole prohibition was given." Furthermore, "May it not be safely affirmed, that it is *impossible* not to form in our *minds*, the images of interesting visible objects when absent?" An exhaustive application of this prohibition, the author suggested, would preclude not only the art of engraving but the action of the mind itself.[101]

At the same time, as Morgan has described, American Protestant visual culture experienced an important shift after the 1860s. Instructional books for Sunday school classrooms, "picture cards" awarded to Sunday school students, and illustrated "lives of Christ" increasingly featured reproductions of religious fine art. American Protestants, primarily liberals but also some conservatives, were well on their way to a "devotional" use of visual art once reserved for Catholics. British Protestants, as Graham Howes notes, likewise welcomed "religious art" in ever greater numbers.[102] J.S. White reflected this trend. He conceded that all Protestants must reject the worship of images, "But it would be utterly irrational and unjust to condemn all religious art as bad and pernicious in its influence because of such vulgarities and inanities."[103] Evangelicals were relying once again on the use-misuse argument. It was not images per se that were problematic but the worship of these images. What differentiated nineteenth-century evangelicals from their forbears was their optimistic belief that one *could* in fact live in a state of perfect tension between undervaluing and overvaluing art; i.e., one could appreciate images, even religious ones, without slipping into misusing them. What for the Puritans had been a matter of near certainty was to nineteenth-century evangelicals only one possibility among many.

By the 1880s, some evangelicals were also calling for greater attention to aesthetics inside the sanctuary. Hawley, for instance, remained wary of idolatry and issued the usual condemnations of Romanism. Yet the question was no longer whether art should play a role in Protestant worship but rather what kind of devotional art Protestants should patronize: "When, therefore, there is such a blending and use of art as to aid to intelligent, pure, and acceptable worship, whether it be painting, statuary, architecture, or music, it is well to cultivate and use it."[104] By 1902, the *Primitive Methodist Quarterly Review* was close to suggesting that the aesthetic was essential for true worship: "A visible symbol reminding one of a far off love is a sacred tie which cannot easily be broken. The soul is assisted by sense.... Harmoniousness of design and taste assist reverent worship." "True

---

[101] B., "Influence of the Fine Arts," 113.
[102] Morgan, *Protestants and Pictures*, 292ff.; Howes, *Art of the Sacred*, 32ff.
[103] White, "Religion and Art," 130, 131.
[104] Hawley, "Christianity and Art," 419.

reverence," the writer continued, "is the offspring of a correct imagination."[105] These speculations came dangerously close to inverting the religio-aesthetic hierarchy mid-Victorian evangelicals had strived to maintain. To be sure, many were still uncomfortable with such statements, but the religio-aesthetic topography had changed. Anxieties about art's idolatrous potential had been relegated to the corner of the map.

The Religio-Aesthetic Balance II: Christianity as Aesthetic Condition

While many evangelicals agreed that religion imposes certain restrictions on art, they also proclaimed enthusiastically that Christianity was a prerequisite for genuine artistic production and valuation. To begin with, Christianity had profound implications for aesthetic perception. Only Christians, some argued, can fully appreciate the aesthetic—an idea that recalls Edwards's theory of primary and secondary beauty. This is because taste, like other faculties, is corrupted by sin. Sin, in fact, helps to explain the perennial difficulty of fixing a universal "standard of taste." "Were man in the primitive state of innocence, wisdom, and purity, in which he was first created," suggested the *Christian Advocate and Journal* in 1844, "probably there would be no difficulty in the case; for then his judgment would at once apprehend the propriety or impropriety, the suitability or the unfitness of things, and his pure and chaste habits of ratiocination and action would reject whatever was revolting to the most exalted standard of purity and propriety."[106] J.M.P. Otts articulated a similar viewpoint in 1866: "Taste is fallen, vitiated, darkened by sin. The ideal beauty was defaced and obscured by the fall.... The finer traces of the beautiful are with difficulty found in the shattered image; hence the great diversity in the details of the application of the fundamental principle of taste."[107] In taking recourse to the doctrine of depravity to account for deviations in aesthetic perception, these theorists were not only challenging romanticism's positive view of human nature but also offering a quintessentially evangelical solution to a longstanding debate. Hume, Kant, and others who had earlier wrestled with this problem had recognized the importance of "aesthetic attitude" to the apprehension of beautiful objects, but theological considerations had played little part in their analyses. For some evangelicals, depravity offered a plausible explanation for the lack of consensus that often arose among viewers when contemplating the same object.

Since sin was the root of the problem, only Christianity could cleanse "the doors of perception." In an 1812 review of Archibald Alison's *Essays on the Nature and Principles of Taste*, one writer noted Alison's conventional premise

---

[105] J.F., "Primitive Methodism and Art," *PMQR* 24 (Apr. 1902), 237, 239.

[106] J.T.D., "On Taste," *CAJ* 19 (11 Sep. 1844), 17.

[107] J.M.P. Otts, "The Beautiful," *SPR* 17 (July 1866), 51. See also "Moral Aesthetics," 44; Leconte, "On the Nature," 319-20; and John M. Titzel, "Beauty and Art," *RQR* 3 (1891), 396-97.

that "the cultivation of taste is calculated to promote religious sentiment"—a position reinforced by Alison's associationist psychology of beauty. That the appreciation of a sunset, for instance, might prompt one to praise the Creator was a tradition as old as the Psalms. The reviewer, however, suggested that the religio-aesthetic chronology be reversed: "[W]e endeavour to establish a far less dubious, and therefore more important, doctrine which is, the *necessity of religion for the highest enjoyments of taste.*"[108] Christianity guides and empowers aesthetic perception. The sort of aesthetic experience described by Alison is possible only for those whose perception has already been refined by grace. No poet, observed the *Christian Spectator* in 1827, could surpass Wordsworth in his descriptions of "the facts of natural Theology," but he fell short of the "illimitable tract of eternity" because he overlooked the fact that grace must precede perception: "It has long been a maxim with very respectable naturalists and poets that the contemplation of nature leads the mind intuitively to God. But why not reverse the process? Why not let the full light from eternity *first* pour upon the mind—before it fastens upon the wonders of the material creation?"[109] Twenty-five years later, the *Biblical Repertory and Princeton Review* implied that if one admits God's grace into the picture, only then are the claims of Wordsworth's "Tintern Abbey" valid: "It is only when natural objects are bathed in the light of the Sun of Righteousness that the beholder can attain 'A sense sublime / Of something far more deeply interfused....' Nature has been looked on with other eyes by the sons of God, than by the common children of this world."[110] "[R]eligion furnishes the conditions favorable to the full development of man's aesthetic nature," wrote another critic in 1865, and because of this, "He views the clover-field as the work of a divine Artist, and that Artist [as] his dearest friend."[111] Religion thus enables aesthetic perception, which in turn enlivens religious experience.

While such arguments addressed the mode of aesthetic perception, others suggested that Christianity expands the available field of perception by unlocking the supersensible, thus extending art's reach. In 1833, the *Quarterly Christian Spectator* rejected the view that religion stifles the poetic imagination. The effect of Christianity "is not to cramp or paralyze man's intellectual powers, but to quicken and invigorate them. We may go still farther. It has given more than it has taken away: it has not circumscribed, but enlarged the field of poetic invention." The influence of Christianity on poetry, the writer continued, "carries the

---

[108] "Alison's Theory of Taste," *CO* 11 (Feb. 1812), 102.
[109] A.S.E., "Remarks upon Wordsworth's Poetry," *CS* 1 (May 1827), 246.
[110] "Moral Aesthetics," 43.
[111] "Esthetic Culture," 386. See also "Reflections of the Christian in Viewing the Works of Nature," *ABM* 8 (Nov. 1828), 345; S.F.S., "Piety Essential to the Full Development of the Mental Powers," *ABM* 14 (Aug. 1834): 1-10; "The Poetical Element of the Bible," *SPR* 8 (July 1854), 103; and J. Wesley Horne, "The Book of Nature," *CA* 47 (27 Jan. 1872): 201.

poet beyond where the eye of sense can penetrate...."[112] Compared to the panoramic view that Christianity affords art, non-Christian art seems dull and circumscribed. "Indeed, so far from repealing the privileges or displacing the associations of the mind," wrote one "Episcopos" in 1881, "Christianity presents new themes for its contemplation, and new opportunities for its exercise." Once Christianity asserts its rightful "influence upon imagination," it "hold[s] out pictures of heaven" and "throw[s] over the future the halo of its own magnificence...."[113] Only Christians can appreciate the full range of artistic subjects.

Similar statements concerning the empowering effects of Christianity on aesthetic perception continued in some quarters throughout the century. As noted in the last chapter, however, the Edwardsean idea of a regenerate aesthetic vision gradually gave way to a "spiritualized" romantic imagination, which possessed the power of "deep" insight irrespective of traditional grace. Whereas a number of evangelicals before the 1870s qualified Wordsworth's claim to "see into the life of things" by bringing explicitly Christian theological considerations to bear, a less modified version of Wordsworthian romanticism eventually prevailed among some evangelicals during the last third of the nineteenth century.

For a time, however, the notion of Christianity's liberating effects on aesthetic perception coincided with a similar notion regarding artistic production. Critics sometimes posited, for example, that artists who had not experienced a "saving faith" were doomed, when dealing with sacred subjects, to produce art objects that lacked spiritual and aesthetic authenticity. Anyone can compose secular music, contended Thomas Hastings in 1844, "But in relation to religious subjects the case is far otherwise. Vital religion, though a precious reality to every one who embraces it, is not well understood by those who have never learned its nature by personal experience." For Hastings, mere notional apprehension was insufficient and indeed may lead to actual aesthetic blunders: "we hazzard nothing in saying, that the men whose lives are devoted to the secular drama are not the individuals who, in the oratorio, the sacred concert, the choir, or the organ loft, will enter, even with dramatic propriety, into the sweetness and tender solemnity of religious themes." If secular artists could represent sacred subjects apart from genuine personal faith, "if expressive tones, with corresponding sentimentalities, are so easily obtained from the irreligious, ... why, let us at once invite the *prima donnas* into the choir, and all will soon be right."[114] As Hastings's argument suggests, evangelical discussions of the effects of Christianity on *poiesis* were linked once again to the romantic conception of art as self-expression. Art is an outpouring of the inner self, but only Christianity can penetrate

---

[112] "Influence of the Christian Religion on Poetry," 204, 205.
[113] Episcopos, "The Relations of Christianity to the Human Mind," *BM* 73 (Apr. 1881), 170, 171-72. See also "Christianity: Its Influence on Modern Poetry," *CAJ* 37 (20 Mar. 1862), 91.
[114] Thomas Hastings, "Sacred Music: Source of the Prevailing Abuses in Cultivation, and the only Practical Remedy," *ABRCR* 11 (Apr. 1844), 433, 435, 436. See also Smetham, "Modern Sacred Art," 60.

the deepest recesses of the soul and rightly order one's affections. In fact, it is the subjective character of art that makes it most alive to Christianity's shaping power. Writing in 1852, one critic suggested how orthodox Christianity could improve upon Wordsworth's conception of the proper object of the poet:

> The soul of man, as Wordsworth has told us, is the "haunt and main region" of the poet's study and the poet's song. But the soul of man has depths which had never been sounded, sensibilities which had never been awakened, mysteries which had never been brought to light, and paths which the eye of man hand not pondered, until those depths were explored, those sensibilities stirred, those mysteries revealed, and those paths pointed out, by a supernatural revelation from God.[115]

The *Christian Advocate and Journal* even hinted that it was Christianity that had engendered the romantic lyricism with which nineteenth-century poetry had become almost entirely identified. "As to Christianity, its influence … in modern poetry has been immense…." It had "giv[en] value to the individual, and ma[de] his personal conviction a precious thing before God."[116] The implication was that a poem like *The Prelude*, with its assumption that an individual's unique perspective may translate into universal appeal, would have been impossible apart from Christianity. The lyric voice, it seems, owed its existence to Christianity.

The impact of Christianity on art was not limited to religious psychology, however. Critics also saw Christianity operating at the socio-cultural level. Over the course of the nineteenth century, art increasingly became part of a Protestant ideology that saw Christianity, morality, and "civilization" collaborating in mutually sustaining ways. A foundational assumption within this ideology held that Christianity helps to construct the kind of culture in which genuine art can prosper. Writing in 1873, Yale's president, Noah Porter, noted how a nation's literature is inextricably bound to its religion:

> It follows that if a people or an age is capable of literature, this literature must hold intimate relations to the religious faith and life of the people or the age…. A religion which is founded in the nature of man and is adapted to his wants, which commends itself to his conscience and transforms and purifies the springs of his action, cannot but act for good on both the matter and form of literature.[117]

Or as the *Methodist Review* put it in 1894: "As soon as Christianity became a creative, regenerative, and formative power in society new literatures, new laws, new sciences, and a new art began to appear and to develop toward perfection."[118] Typically, it was Protestant Christianity which these critics envisioned as fomenting cultural and aesthetic progress. As Smetham contended, "One would

---

[115] "National Literature, the Exponent of National Character," *BRPR* 24 (Apr. 1852), 224-25. See also Bennett, "Catholicism and Protestantism," 86.
[116] "Christianity: Its Influence on Modern Poetry," 91.
[117] Noah Porter, "Modern Literature and Christianity," *CA* (30 Oct. 1873), 346.
[118] Bristol, "Reciprocity of Art and Religion," 704.

think that the more pure the form of religion, the more complete would be the development of the entire range of human faculties. In science, in poetry, in general learning, Protestantism has justified this supposition." Smetham regretted that visual art had lagged behind these other advancements, but his faith in Protestant Christianity gave him hope that visual art, too, would eventually come into its own.[119] By century's end, some critics could occasionally imagine Christianity's cultural influence in even broader terms. In 1895, William G. Beardmore broke ranks and permitted Catholic history a place in Christian art's march of progress: "For more than six hundred years Christendom has been the foster-parent of the noblest and most enduring forms of art."[120] Many evangelicals, however, cleaved to the whiggish view that Protestantism alone could advance civilization.

This understanding of Christianity as an engine of progress was an extension of the Puritan and postmillennial emphasis on the transformation of culture. Postmillennialism, a popular eschatology among evangelicals until the mid-nineteenth century, fit well with Victorian myths of progress since it expected the last age to be ushered in both by the spread of the Gospel and the gradual reformation of society. As George Marsden has observed, evangelicals "saw signs of the approach of the millennial age not only in the success of revivals and missions, but also in general cultural progress." Indeed, "evangelicals generally regarded almost any sort of progress as evidence of the advance of the kingdom."[121] Art was therefore swept up in this tide of Christian cultural optimism. Protestant culture, moreover, would give rise to an art effectively surpassing all that had gone before. An author in the *Presbyterian Quarterly Review* reflected on the superiority of the art produced by Christian civilization to that of the Greeks. Recalling the moment he stood before Thorwaldsen's Christ in Copenhagen, the writer observed: "We felt, as we stood in its presence, that Christianity had demonstrated her artistic supremacy, and that the Greek, so great in the power of transcribing sensible objects, in setting forth form and sensuous beauty, nay, in the ideal of the Divine,—must, after all, bow to the loftier spirituality which our religion gives to art." The Greek artist had "worshipped form"; had he, however, known "the true God ... his [art would have] been glorified by a larger, purer conception."[122] On its face, this seems another incarnation of the eighteenth-century debate over the relative artistic merits of the Ancients and Moderns. Religion, however, rather than artistic considerations alone was the deciding factor. Christianity had provided western culture with a new form of the ideal resulting in an art of which the Greeks, despite their pagan splendor, or perhaps because of it, could

---

[119] Smetham, "Modern Sacred Art," 53.
[120] William G. Beardmore, "Wesleyan Artists, Past and Present," *WMM* 118 (Aug. 1895), 583.
[121] George Marsden, *Fundamentalism and American Culture* (Oxford: Oxford University Press, 2006), 49, 50. See also Bebbington, *Evangelicalism*, 62.
[122] "Symbols of Thought," *PQR* 10 (Apr. 1862), 630, 631.

not have dreamed. Without Christianity, evangelicals argued, art would flounder; with it, art would reach unprecedented heights.

Some Signs of Fatigue

Although many critics continued to see art as both limited and empowered by Christianity until the end of the century, beginning in the 1870s there were signs that this religio-aesthetic ideal was breaking down, at least in practice. On the one hand, a growing number of liberals had begun to identify Christianity almost exclusively with moral and cultural progress. While evangelicals had long understood cultural advancement as a function of Christian influence, they had seen Christianity and culture as distinct. Now this distinction had begun to evaporate. The postmillennial emphasis on cultural progress remained, but it was increasingly emptied of its eschatological content.[123] On the other hand, some conservatives were beginning to express doubts about whether Christianity really was an agent of aesthetic empowerment, as many wanted to believe. These critics no longer accepted with naïve optimism the possibility of a religious-aesthetic-cultural synthesis.

Signs of this conservative fatigue may be seen in an article by the Rev. K. Colman published in 1871. Colman agreed that, in theory, Christianity ought to create a culture conducive to good art: "Christianity is the great teacher, and again the great civilizer. There cannot fail to be a close relation between general civilization and all its parts. Christianity is civilization's foundation, fine art its cornice and turrets, and there can be no uncertain connection between the two." Still, he asked, "Is not the influence of Christianity upon fine art quite generally overestimated?" For starters, "The religion of the Bible is preeminently utilitarian," by which Colman meant that Christians should focus on the practical business of saving souls and doing good. True, "Utility may recognize the importance of supplying a God-given craving after the beautiful, but it has thus far found more pressing human needs." Furthermore, the doctrines of Christianity, with their "transcendent grandeur," satisfy in some measure our "longing for beauty." We thus have little need for art to gratify our aesthetic desires. Colman next turned to the problem of inverse proportion, or the view that those nations most revered for artistic achievement are those that embrace Christianity most superficially. France and Italy, he believed, excelled in art, but "Is the Christianity of these nations deeper than the skin of a political name?" After cataloguing the difficulties plaguing the thesis that Christian cultures enable the arts to thrive, Colman inquired whether history provides any evidence to support this idea. He admitted that Christianity had had some positive effect on music, poetry, and perhaps painting, but he denied that modern poetry and painting had eclipsed the

---

[123] On these changes, see Robert T. Handy, *A Christian America: Protestant Hopes and Historical Realities* (New York: Oxford University Press, 1984) and Marsden, *Fundamentalism*, 50-51.

Ancients. As for sculpture, he declared that "Christian sculpture has never *approached* the ancient."[124]

Ultimately, Colman arrived at a conclusion remarkable for its ambivalence: "While by developing civilization Christianity indirectly gives powerful aid to fine art, it has not greatly inspired it, has not stimulated it to the highest development known to history." Colman's hesitation reveals a first significant crack in the evangelical religio-aesthetic synthesis. Missing here is any faith in *inevitability*. He remained convinced that good art will not flourish without Christianity—"The fine arts and barbarism have only the relation of antagonism, while the Christian sun daguerreotypes fine art on the impressible human soul"—but he could offer no guarantee that art will flourish with Christianity.[125] Oddly, though, it appears Colman had not yet relinquished his optimism completely. Just as strangely ambiguous in this regard is Colman's final paragraph:

> The religion of the cross has not so purified the masses that they can *revel* in beauty without sinking in voluptuousness. Rich ornament in chancel or garb, in music or sermon, still attracts the worshiper from the Creator to the creature, from things heavenly to things earthly. The work is progressing; men are becoming holier; soon the energies now nobly spent in converting a world will make stepping-stones of perfected art, on which a pure worshiping spirit will ascend to the throne of God. Then such grand structures as have never yet gladdened the earth, all adorned with brush and chisel, will invite men heavenward; then music, making the past tame, worthless; then oratory which shall cause Whitefield and Simpson, Beecher and Spurgeon, Cicero and Demosthenes, to be forgotten, shall entrance the multitudes, and lift them to the very gates of the New Jerusalem.[126]

Colman had, in effect, relocated his optimism, along with the religious-aesthetic-cultural synthesis, to the distant future—perhaps even to eschatological time. Western culture, it turned out, was not nearly as far along the path of progress as many believed. Although Colman made no attempt to clarify his eschatology, and although this passage may still be read in a postmillennial sense, much of his logic resembles the sort of reasoning about culture associated with premillennialism and ultimately fundamentalism. It was during the 1870s and 1880s, in fact, when many evangelicals began turning to premillennialism—a development that would become a critical factor in the rise of fundamentalism.[127] For Colman,

---

[124] K. Colman, "Christianity and the Fine Arts," *CA* 46 (1 Jan. 1871), 170.

[125] Porter acknowledged a similar dynamic: "It does not necessarily follow that a very religious people or a religious era will necessarily produce a splendid literature" ("Modern Literature and Christianity," 346).

[126] Colman, "Christianity and the Fine Arts," 170

[127] See Marsden, *Fundamentalism*, 48-55; Bebbington, *Evangelicalism*, 81-83, 85-86, 192; Bebbington, "Evangelicalism in Modern Britain and America: A Comparison," *Amazing Grace: Evangelicalism in Australia, Britain, Canada, and the United States*, ed. George A. Rawlyk and Mark A. Noll (Montreal: McGill-Queen's University Press, 1994),

many of the old Puritan fears about the "voluptuousness" of art had resurfaced. Likewise, a new sobriety governed Colman's reflections, for though he had in one sense extended his religio-aesthetic timetable, he had in another sense shortened it. The end was fast approaching, and "There are more urgent demands for Christian activity than the culture of art."[128] In a world awash in the disorienting effects of urbanization and industrialization, a breezy faith in postmillennial progress seemed less compelling, and for some conservatives, a sustained investment in "the culture of art" was growing less clamant.[129]

Colman's article, with its tensions and uncertainties, illustrates the early stages of a transition in evangelical thinking. Although he had not altogether jettisoned the notion that Christianity furnishes a source of cultural and aesthetic renewal, he had begun the process of disjoining what many evangelicals had worked hard to suture. Christianity had ceased to be a mighty agent of aesthetic empowerment and was reduced instead to little more than a minimal condition. Colman's position was still something of an anomaly in 1871, but one can detect the makings of a religio-aesthetic divide. By the early twentieth century, liberal Protestants were less interested in the proscriptions that orthodoxy might impose on art. Art had become another manifestation of the evolution of divine consciousness in human history. For their part, fundamentalists were no longer interested in Christianity as a source of cultural and aesthetic rejuvenation; indeed, they showed little interest in considering art's relationship to Christianity in theoretical terms at all. The Victorian evangelical effort to synthesize orthodox Christianity and romantic aesthetics had begun to totter.

196-97; and Mark A. Noll, *The Scandal of the Evangelical Mind* (Grand Rapids: Eerdmans, 1994), 121-22.

[128] Colman, "Christianity and the Fine Arts," 170.

[129] On industrialization, urbanization, and the rise of fundamentalism, see James Davison Hunter, *American Evangelicalism: Conservative Religion and the Quandary of Modernity* (New Brunswick: Rutgers University Press, 1983), 34 and George M. Marsden, *Understanding Fundamentalism and Evangelicalism* (Grand Rapids: Eerdmans, 1991), 13-17.

CHAPTER 4

Aesthetic Ministrations: Art, Morality, and the Christian Nation

In 1835, Parliament selected fifteen members to form a special committee "to consider what measures ought to be adopted with regard to the native inhabitants of countries where British settlements are made ... in order to secure to them the due observance of justice, and the protection of their rights; to promote the spread of civilization among them, and to lead to the peaceful and voluntary reception of the Christian religion."[1] A brief account of the committee's proceedings later appeared in the American *Baptist Missionary Magazine*. This account focused on the testimony of Secretary Beecher of the Wesleyan Missionary Society. At issue in Beecher's testimony was a recurring question that had generated much debate among Protestants in both England and the United States. Should colonization efforts direct their energies principally to the spread of "civilization" or the spread of Protestant Christianity? Must an indigenous population first be Christianized that it might subsequently be civilized, or was it the reverse?[2]

In answering this question, Beecher was unequivocal:

> My attention has long been directed to this subject, and the firm conviction of my mind that Christianity must precede civilization, is the result of the inquiries and observations which I have made. So far has my experience been from proving that civilization is necessary to prepare barbarous nations for the reception of the gospel, that is has led me to the conclusion that the only effectual way to civilize them is first to evangelize them. I regard Christianity as the parent of civilization, and am persuaded that true civilization cannot be produced without it....

The problem, according to Beecher, was that not even the doughty achievements of British culture could convince "savages" to abandon their "superstitions" and the natural freedoms of a life unburdened by the trappings of English customs: "Civilized life is too tame, too insipid, to charm the roving barbarian, and his superstitions are generally found opposed to any change in his accustomed course of life." Yet if Beecher's statement sounds like a startling admission of cultural impotence, his confidence in the moral and intellectual superiority of

---

[1] "Testimony to the Success of Missions," *BMM* 19 (Dec. 1839), 291.
[2] On this debate, see Robert T. Handy, *A Christian America: Protestant Hopes and Historical Realities* (New York: Oxford University Press, 1984).

British civilization remained undiminished. Once "the higher motives of the gospel" were brought "to bear upon [the native] mind," what Beecher called "*true civilization*" would "invariably" follow. When the motive power of Protestant Christianity was applied from within, then the inhabitants of foreign lands would, so the logic went, spontaneously acknowledge the benefits of a culture that had itself emerged organically from its Christian soil. To further substantiate this conclusion, Beecher proceeded to read a letter to the committee which he had received from another missionary, John Evans. In this letter, Evans described how a band of drunken, polygamist, misogynist, and idolatrous Canadian Indians, when once converted to Christianity, had immediately begun to live by the values of white Protestant culture. Among the wealth of evidence Evans cited, he observed how "Tables, chairs, bedsteads, bed and window-hangings, and other necessaries, together with their regular family worship established in every house, morning and evening, proclaim, in language too forcible to be misunderstood, 'Christianity and civilization go hand in hand.'"[3]

During the same year in which Parliament convened its special committee, a young Methodist across the Atlantic delivered an address before the Boston Wesleyan Lyceum on "The Moral Influence of the Fine Arts." Edward Otheman, who had begun his studies at the Wesleyan Academy in Massachusetts under the direction of Wilbur Fisk, attended Brown University, from which he graduated in 1831 after delivering an oration on "Consecrated Talent." Returning to Massachusetts, Otheman took a position as Secretary of the Society for the Promotion of Common and Liberal Education, helping to found the Wesleyan Lyceum in 1833.[4] Now, two years later, he stood before a Lyceum audience, urging an increased attention to the fine arts in what he apparently intended as his own contribution to worldwide Christian progress. In this lecture, later published in the *Methodist Magazine and Quarterly Review*, Otheman sought to demonstrate that the arts, "as a class of human pursuits, and a source of human enjoyment," ought "to be either extensively or partially patronized and cultivated." Significantly, he aimed to justify this thesis by showing that the "*native* tendency" of the fine arts "is favorable to morality," both individual and social. Otheman noted carefully that he did not believe the arts were "any thing more than aids to morality," but he did "contend that, other things being equal, where they are cultivated in a proper manner there will be a more elevated, refined, elegant state of society...." As he later argued, "The fine arts always accompany civilization, and seem to be one of its essential, but, certainly, one of its universal elements, both in ancient

---

[3] "Testimony," 291, 292, 293, 294-95. On the place of aesthetics in British imperialism, see Elizabeth A. Bohls, "Standards of Taste, Discourses of 'Race,' and the Aesthetic Education of a Monster: Critique of Empire in *Frankenstein*," *Eighteenth-Century Life* 18 (Nov. 1994): 23-36.

[4] On Otheman, see K., "Brown University," *ABM* 11 (Oct. 1831), 316; "Editorial Comment," *ZH* 63 (17 Mar. 1886), 84; C. Adams, "Edward Otheman," *ZH* 63 (28 Apr. 1886), 134; and *Historical Catalogue of Brown University* (Providence: Brown University, 1914), 126.

and modern times."[5] If Secretary Beecher had glimpsed the intrinsic connections among Christianity, morality, and civilization, Secretary Otheman ostensibly glimpsed similar connections among civilization, morality, and art.

The interesting conceptual overlaps in Beecher and Otheman's texts throw into relief the constituent elements—Christianity, morality, and civilization—of what I have referred to as the Protestant ideology, which pervaded nineteenth-century evangelical thought.[6] Of course, the idea that a healthy civilization depended upon a broad-scale subscription to Protestantism was hardly novel. Victorian evangelicals had inherited this notion from the Puritans. What was novel was the enhanced role ascribed to art. As noted in chapter 3, many evangelicals had come to see art as both a beneficiary and a tangible manifestation of a Christianity-inspired process of cultural evolution.

Yet the notion that a developed art world is a natural expression of Protestant culture represents but one facet of the complex relationship critics perceived among Christianity, civilization, and art. As many argued, if a superior faith produced a superior civilization which in turn produced a superior art, it was also true that this art, once produced, could help secure the foundations of Christian civilization and contribute to its development. Critics understood this contribution mainly in terms of art's connection to another pillar of the Protestant ideological edifice—morality. As Morgan has noted, during the "third and fourth decades of the nineteenth century ... American artists, critics, and clergy came to regard the arts as fundamental to promoting national identity and assisting religion in fostering public manners and morals."[7] This idea was prominent in Britain as well. Art, many held, possessed a special capacity to shape the moral constitution of individuals—it exerted, in Otheman's characteristic nineteenth-century parlance, "moral influence"—and since morality, as the appropriate expression of Christian faith, established the grounds upon which social stability depended, art itself gradually assumed the role of guardian of and minister to Protestant civilization. As the *Eclectic Review* proclaimed, "The true vocation of the poet unquestionably is to animate the human race in its progress from barbarism towards virtue and greatness."[8] The fate of Anglo-American civilization was tied as never before to the fate of art.

While such high claims for art would not have occurred to most Puritans, it is tempting to read, as some late Victorians did, the evangelical insistence that art cater to morality and society as evidence of a protracted Puritan moralism. The Puritans had stressed the interconnectedness of Christianity, morality, and culture, and they had granted that arts like poetry possess some instructional value. But in fact what drove nineteenth-century evangelical discussions of art's socio-

---

[5] Edward Otheman, "The Moral Influence of the Fine Arts," *MMQR* 17 (July 1835), 318, 319, 330. Subsequent citations appear parenthetically in the text.
[6] See Handy, *Christian America*.
[7] David Morgan, *Protestants and Pictures: Religion, Visual Culture, and the Age of American Mass Production* (New York: Oxford University Press, 1999), 291.
[8] "Recent Poetry," *ER* 18 (Dec. 1845), 665.

moral influence was not a conception of the didactic possibilities of art but rather, as Morgan observes, the affective power of the arts to shape individual and national "character."[9] Although this theory was well adapted to the period's political needs, it also exposed the shifting fault lines within the Protestant ideology. Traditionally, writers had distinguished Christianity proper from both the morality and civilization it was said to foster. Claims for the relative autonomy of art's moral influence, however, suggest a softening of these longstanding distinctions as over the course of the century religion gradually became equated with morality and the progress of Christianity, once the "parent of civilization," was ignored in favor of the progress of civilization alone. Already by the 1840s, evangelical critics, following romantic poet-prophets, had begun to describe art in terms of "mission" and "ministry."[10] The liberal Gospel of Art was coming of age.

"Occult Pathos": Art and the Tradition of Anti-Didactic Moralism

Evangelical critics returned frequently to art's potential for shaping the moral character of individuals and societies. A statement in the *Christian Spectator* may substitute for numerous similar proclamations throughout the century. "A book of poetry," the author observed in 1827, "should furnish substantial nourishment. It ought to enlighten us in our duty, and stimulate us to walk firmly in the path of virtue. Harmonious versification and true taste may please us, but permanent benefit is the legitimate aim of poetry."[11] That critics would espouse a moral-instrumental view of art is not especially surprising. Few others could outstrip evangelicals in matters of conscience. Whether their goal was to root out slavery, "popery," or hard drink, evangelicals worked feverishly to cultivate personal purity, encourage good conduct, and strengthen the social fabric. Moreover, as noted in chapter 2, arguing for the positive moral effects of art proved useful in persuading more puritanically-minded readers that art ought, in Otheman's words, "to be either extensively or partially patronized." If one could show not only that art posed no threat to morality but also that it was *conducive* to morality, then one could secure for art a permanent place at the table.

For all their insistence on the salutary moral effects of art, however, evangelicals spent a remarkable amount of time attacking the "didactic." In 1814, the *Eclectic Review* was already questioning the merits of didactic (or "didascalic," as the author under review had it) poetry, suggesting that the term "involves [an] apparent ... contradiction (there being an obvious opposition between the demonstrations of reason applied to the reason, and the dreams of the imagination

---

[9] See Morgan, *Protestants and Pictures*, 268-92 on the transition among American Protestants from a "didactic" form of "visual piety" to a "devotional" one. While my narrative parallels Morgan's, I emphasize the Enlightenment roots of this transition.
[10] See, for example, "English Schools of Art," *ER* 23 (Jan. 1848), 76 and P. Wells, "Poetry: Its Social Uses and Religious Influences," *CAJ* 26 (8 Feb. 1849), 24.
[11] A.S.E., "Remarks upon Wordsworth's Poetry," *CS* 1 (May 1827), 244.

addressed to the imagination)...."[12] In his *Lectures*, James Montgomery criticized didactic poetry for its failure to equal prose as a mode of instruction and for its cramped style: "It is the misfortune of didactic poetry, that for the purposes of teaching, it has not advantage over prose; and, in fact, from the difficulty of adapting the elegances of verse to commonplace details, it often falls lamentably short of common sense, in unnatural attempts to convey the simplest meanings in bloated verbiage." In short, "in a didactic poem, the finest passages are those which are *not* didactic."[13] The *Eclectic Review* echoed Montgomery's sentiments in 1848 when it questioned "whether art advances itself or the world much, by ... stepping forth as a professed *schoolmistress*. The little good she is by these means enabled to effect, can be much more forcibly and adequately accomplished, and with infinitely less trouble in other more legitimate channels."[14] The *Mercersburg Review* acknowledged the good intentions of didactic verse—verse "so often recommended by those who have the interests of religion and morality at heart"—but denied that such productions qualify as genuine poetry: "Didactic poetry as such, that is poetry whose professed object is to teach or instruct ... is not pure poetry, or at least not in its higher form."[15] Henry Van Dyke, Jr. summed up what had become a critical commonplace when in 1883 he candidly declared: "Didacticism in art is false and impotent."[16]

Frequently, however, critiques of didacticism were issued alongside statements defending the power (and responsibility) of art to raise the moral consciousness of individuals and society. Thus Montgomery, though he decried didacticism, contended without any apparent sense of contradiction that moral "profit" is essential to poetry: "Nothing can endure, even in this 'naughty world,' but virtue. To profit mankind a poet *must* please them; but *unless* he profits them, he will not please them long."[17] C.T. Winchester, writing in 1882, agreed that "Poetry ... is not often didactic: the highest poetry never is." But like Montgomery, Winchester denied that art and morality can be separated, as in fact Oscar Wilde, to whom Winchester was responding, believed: "Th[e] doctrine, that there may be a morality good for society but irrelevant in art, is as pernicious as it is false. It is indeed, equally fatal to art and to morals."[18] For many evangelicals, therefore, the issue was not whether art is an instrument of moral suasion but rather how art functions as such. Art, they believed, must exert moral influence without also falling into didacticism.

---

[12] "Busby's *Lucretius*," *ER* 11 (Mar. 1814), 279. See also Orbilius, "To the Editor of the *Christian Spectator*," *CS* 4 (1 Feb. 1822), 80.

[13] James Montgomery, *Lectures on General Literature, Poetry, &c.* (New York: Harper, 1844), 157, 159.

[14] "English Schools of Art," 76.

[15] T.A., "What Is Poetry?" *MerR* 11 (July 1859), 393.

[16] Henry J. Van Dyke, Jr., "Art and Ethics: In Some of Their Relations," *PR* (Jan.-Jun. 1883), 99.

[17] Montgomery, *Lectures*, 190.

[18] C.T. Winchester, "Good Poetry and Good Morals," *CA* 57 (9 Mar. 1882), 147.

In discounting didacticism while upholding art as a moralizing force, evangelical theorists were participating in a well-established tradition of thought concerning the manner in which art facilitates the ethical interests of individuals and society. Broadly, this tradition of anti-didactic moralism held that art strengthens morality not by way of a cognitive address to the intellect but through its ability to stretch one affectively. In appealing to the intellect, didacticism relies upon abstract concepts, which, in the empiricist tradition of Locke, were thought to lack the intensity of concrete sensations. Genuine art, however, moves the emotions through the senses and thus "exercises" one's moral nature rather than instructs it. "High efforts of painting or sculpture, like those of poetry," observed the *Eclectic Review* in 1848, "are full of purpose and significance to those whose perceptions are fine enough to detect such. But, those of the two former departments of universal art more especially; they are *suggestive*, not didactic, in their influence; their teaching rather to be *felt*, than *expressed*."[19] Art, that is, operates morally via what Smetham called an "occult pathos." Though he used this term in reference to the entire range of art's affective powers, it captures nicely the nature of art's specifically moral effect as evangelicals conceived it.[20]

Among other nineteenth-century critics, Smetham's "occult pathos" was referred to more simply as moral "influence." In her classic study *The Feminization of American Culture*, Ann Douglas notes the prominent place that theories of literature's moral influence enjoyed among American women and northeastern clergymen between 1820 and 1875. Bound together by the fact that they "lacked power of any crudely tangible kind ... they were careful not to lay claim to it. Instead they wished to exert 'influence,' which they eulogized as a religious force." For Douglas, this mounting emphasis on influence resulted from "clerical" and "feminine disestablishment," developments that forced both groups to compete anew in the marketplace of ideas by turning to the emerging "mass medium" of popular literature.[21] Yet while disestablishment supplied the socio-political conditions in which theories of influence could thrive, it did not create such theories, nor were they the sole province of liberal clergymen and progressive women. As Morgan notes, influence was a concept embraced widely by nineteenth-century American Protestants.[22] The notion that art exerts a moral

---

[19] "English Schools of Art," 76.
[20] James Smetham, "Modern Sacred Art in England," *LQR* 18 (Apr. 1862), 65. Interestingly, Smetham speaks of paintings in terms of "preaching," which was what anti-didactic moralists would have denied. Nevertheless, the phrase is suggestive, so I have adopted it here. Philosophers continue to debate art's moral agency. See, for example, Noël Carrol, "Art and the Moral Realm," *The Blackwell Guide to Aesthetics*, ed. Peter Kivy (Malden, MA: Blackwell, 2004): 126-51 and Lester H. Hunt, "Sentiment and Sympathy," *Journal of Aesthetics and Art Criticism* 62 (Autumn 2004): 339-54.
[21] Ann Douglas, *The Feminization of American Culture* (New York: Anchor Press-Doubleday, 1988). The quotation appears on pp. 8-9. See also Apostolos-Cappadona, *Spirit*, 7-8.
[22] Morgan, *Protestants and Pictures*, 19-24, esp. 22-23. There were, in fact, various theories of influence in circulation during the nineteenth century. Hodge and Bushnell, for

force was entertained by conservatives as well as by Unitarians and other proto-liberals. Furthermore, this idea was not simply an American phenomenon. It was as prevalent in Britain, where different political variables obtained, as in post-disestablishment America.

The theory was in fact a product of Enlightenment mental philosophy and aesthetics. It had entered the evangelical bloodstream through the transfusion of Scottish thought and its later romantic appropriations (e.g., in Wordsworth). It is true, as Morgan has argued, that Horace Bushnell's ideas of "unconscious influence" and "nurture," which he articulated in the 1840s, aided American Protestants' movement towards "the appreciation and use of fine art in religious character formation."[23] But the idea of the affective moral influence of art dates back to eighteenth-century theories with which educated evangelicals were conversant. The rudiments of this view were already present in the aesthetic reflections of both Edwards and Wesley. In addition, the impact of Bushnell's theory of nurture in Britain was limited until the early 1860s, when a reprint of *Christian Nurture* appeared.[24] Like their American counterparts, however, British evangelicals had begun long before to see the arts as agents of socio-moral development, not in didactic terms but in terms of affective influence. Already in 1836, the *Wesleyan-Methodist Magazine* had published an excerpt from Bernard and Lucy Barton's *The Reliquary*, in which Bernard argued that poetry, as the language of feeling, contains "much that tends to soften and humanize, and not less to elevate and spiritualize, our imperfect and fallen nature, much to check and counteract

---

example, championed different theories of "nurture". See Charles Hodge, Review of *Discourses on Christian Nurture*, by Horace Bushnell, *Dr. Tyler's Letter to Dr. Bushnell on Christian Nurture*, and *An Argument for "Discourses on Christian Nurture," addressed to the Publishing Committee of the Massachusetts Sabbath School Society*, by Horace Bushnell, BRPR 19 (Oct. 1847): 502-39 and James Hastings Nichols, *Romanticism in American Theology: Nevin and Schaff at Mercersburg* (Chicago: University of Chicago Press, 1961), 239-44. See also Newell Dwight Hillis, *The Investment of Influence: A Study of Social Sympathy and Service*, 24th ed. (Chicago: Fleming H. Revell, 1897).

[23] Morgan, *Protestants and Pictures*, 270-75; the quotation appears on p. 270. See also Horace Bushnell, *Christian Nurture* (New Haven: Yale University Press, 1916) and "Unconscious Influence," *Sermons for the New Life* (New York: Charles Scribner, 1858): 186-205.

[24] Bushnell delivered his address on the "Influence of Example" (later "Unconscious Influence") in London in 1846, but the impact seems to have been minimal among British evangelicals. An 1861 article in the *ER* mentions the British reprint of *Christian Nurture*. See "A Church for Children," *ER* 5 (June 1861), 607 n. In 1862, the *LQR* observed that "Dr. Bushnell has, within a year or two, come to be extensively known and much admired in this country" (Rev. of *Nature and the Supernatural, as Together Constituting the One System of God*, by Horace Bushnell, *LQR* 18 [Apr. 1862], 100).

the deadening influence of a worldly spirit...."[25] Consequently, I want to emphasize here how evangelicals inherited this idea from eighteenth-century aesthetics.[26]

The proximate source for the theory of anti-didactic moralism was of course romantic poets and critics. Wordsworth, Hazlitt, Hunt, and DeQuincey all subscribed to some version of this tradition,[27] as did Shelley, whose expression of this idea in his *Defense of Poetry* (drafted in 1821 but not published until 1840) may serve as a representative example: "The great instrument of moral good is the imagination; and poetry administers to the effect by acting upon the cause.... Poetry strengthens that faculty which is the organ of the moral nature of man, in the same manner as exercise strengthens a limb." When poets abandon their high calling to act "upon the cause" and instead focus on producing a particular moral effect—when, in other words, poets assume "a moral aim" by turning to didacticism—"the effect of their poetry is diminished in exact proportion to the degree in which they compel us to advert to this purpose."[28] For Shelley, there is an inverse relationship between the didactic and moral: the more didactic a poem, the less morally efficacious it is.

Romantics like Shelley, however, were extending a line of argument developed by Enlightenment thinkers, one of the more important of which was Lord Kames. In his *Elements of Criticism*, Kames had laid out a detailed affective theory of art's moral influence, arguing "that no occupation attaches a man more to his duty, than that of cultivating a taste in the fine arts."[29] While not all eighteenth-century theories shared Kames's idiosyncrasies, his text did offer a relatively precise formulation of art's role as a moral agent. His attempt at a comprehensive account of the principles underlying the science of criticism also made the *Elements* a popular choice in college classrooms, especially in the United States, where it remained part of the curriculum at some smaller institutions until the Civil War. When, for example, evangelical Wheaton College opened its doors

---

[25] Bernard Barton, "An Appeal for Poetry and Poets," *WMM* 15 (Aug. 1836), 589.

[26] Elements of this theory go back even further. Sidney, for instance, noted poetry's ability to "move" one to action (*Apology for Poetry*, The Longman Anthology of British Literature, Volume 1B, The Early Modern Period, ed. Clare Carroll and Andrew Hadfield [New York: Longman, 2010], 1010-1014).

[27] See M.H. Abrams, *The Mirror and the Lamp: Romantic Theory and Critical Tradition* (London: Oxford University Press, 1953), 326-35 on Wordsworth, DeQuincey, and Shelley. See also William Hazlitt, "Introductory—On Poetry in General," vol. 2 of *The Selected Writings of William Hazlitt*, ed. Duncan Wu (London: Pickering and Chatto, 1998), 177 n. and Leigh Hunt, "An Answer to the Question, 'What Is Poetry?,'" *Later Literary Essays*, ed. Charles Mahoney (London: Pickering and Chatto, 2003), 5.

[28] Percy Bysshe Shelley, *A Defence of Poetry*, Shelley's Prose and Poetry, ed. Donald H. Reiman and Sharon B. Powers (New York: Norton, 1977), 488. See also Shelley's Preface to *Prometheus Unbound*, Shelley's Poetry and Prose, 135.

[29] Henry Home, Lord Kames, *Elements of Criticism*, ed. Peter Jones (Indianapolis: Liberty Fund, 2005), 1:17. Subsequent citations appear parenthetically in the text.

in 1860, Kames was assigned reading for male undergraduates.[30] Some thirty-one editions of the *Elements* were published in America between 1796 and 1883, while the library at Andover Seminary held five copies alone.[31] Thus Kames's arguments had a widespread and in many cases direct impact on evangelical understandings of art's moral influence.

Kames's theory is rooted in the sentimentalist ethical tradition of Shaftesbury and Hutcheson, which postulated that the springs of moral action reside in the emotional constitution of human beings. "It is a law in our nature," he observes, "that we never act but by the impulse of desire; which in other words is saying, that passion, by the desire included in it, is what determines the will" (1:131; cf. 1:37). Kames makes a technical distinction between passion and emotion, the latter being an "internal motion or agitation of the mind" that "passeth away without desire" (1:37). Passions are those feelings which, accompanied by desire, motivate an individual to act. In keeping with his empiricist philosophy of mind, Kames also holds that objects apprehended either visually or aurally can raise within us both passions and emotions. Since the arts appeal predominantly to the eye and ear, a connection exists between an appreciation for the arts and the moral action of the will. "The principles of the fine arts," argues Kames, "appear in this view to open a direct avenue to the heart of man" (1:32). This logic provides the basis for his more extended speculations on the moral power of art.

Kames suggests two ways in which art, or a taste for art, works on the feelings, thereby contributing to moral formation. First, he posits that refined taste serves "to moderate the selfish affections: by sweetening and harmonizing the temper, it is a strong antidote to the turbulence of passion and violence of pursuit: it procures to a man so much mental enjoyment, that in order to be occupied, he is not tempted to deliver up his youth to hunting, gaming, drinking; nor his middle age to ambition; nor his old age to avarice" (1:16). This argument reflects the old notion, one the Puritans appreciated, that healthy amusement occupies one's mind, thus preventing more illicit behaviors. Because of their unique position between the purely intellectual and the purely sensuous, "The pleasures of the eye and ear ... are perfectly well qualified ... to revive the spirits when sunk by sensual gratification" (1:12). But according to Kames art also assists one in combating selfishness by cultivating an appreciation for the "agreeable" in others:

> Pride and envy, two disgustful passions, find in the constitution no enemy more formidable than a delicate and discerning taste: the man upon whom nature and culture have bestowed this blessing, delight in the virtuous dispositions and actions of others: he loves to cherish them, and to publish them to the world: faults and

---

[30] *Wheaton College Bulletin, 1860-61*, 13. Kames was dropped from the curriculum in 1866-67 (*Wheaton College Bulletin, 1866-67*, 16).

[31] William Charvat, *The Origins of American Critical Thought 1810-1835* (Philadelphia: University of Pennsylvania Press, 1936), 30. See also Terence Martin, *The Instructed Vision: Scottish Common Sense Philosophy and the Origins of American Fiction* (New York: Krause, 1969), 10-11.

failings, it is true, are to him no less obvious; but these he avoids, or removes out of sight, because they give him pain. (1:16)

Behind this argument lies the Hutchesonian premise that humans possess an innate capacity for spontaneously valuing both the moral and aesthetic, and that a facility in one type of apprehension improves one's facility in the other. The arts allow a person to experience agreeable feelings firsthand; once one has learned to appreciate such feelings, one will be less apt to relish disagreeable ones. Hence the arts regulate and harmonize the mind. This tempered state of mind is advantageous in that it leads naturally to greater social interaction. Even gardening, for instance, may advance social benevolence: "The gaiety and harmony of mind it produceth, inclining the spectator to communicate his satisfaction to others, and to make them happy as he is himself, tend naturally to establish in him a habit of humanity and benevolence" (2:698-99). Aesthetic pleasure acts as a propaedeutic to positive moral action.

Art's moral influence, however, goes beyond its capacity to keep bad passions at bay by replacing them with good ones; art also helps to develop what Kames terms *"the sympathetic emotion of virtue"* (1:50). This concept holds a unique place in the affective economy of *Elements*. Indeed, it is difficult to see how one could hold to a theory of art's moral influence without such a theory. According to Kames, it is virtually impossible to determine whether the sympathetic emotion of virtue is technically an emotion or a passion. He hesitates to call it an emotion "because it involves desire," but he is equally reluctant to designate it a passion since it "has no object" (1:48). It is, in short, a feeling that gives rise to an objectless desire. This formulation provides a rather ingenious solution to a problem facing any moral-instrumental conception of art that is at the same time anti-didactic, namely, how it is that beholding a representation can lead to practical action by the percipient. What permits one to transmute an admiration for, say, a virtuous act represented in a painting into concrete acts of goodness in real-world contexts?

Kames's answer is the sympathetic emotion of virtue. When, for instance, a spectator observes another person acting virtuously, two feelings arise: first, the spectator experiences esteem for the noble individual who performed the virtuous act; secondly, the spectator experiences the sympathetic emotion of virtue. "We approve every virtuous action, and bestow our affection on the author," argues Kames, "but if virtuous actions produced no other effect upon us, good example would not have great influence." Positive ethical examples, whether in art or life, would have little consequence if they only prompted gratitude for the example itself. However, "the sympathetic emotion under consideration bestows upon good example the utmost influence, by prompting us to imitate what we admire" (1:49). Hence the sympathetic emotion of virtue involves an intrinsic desire to reproduce in different contexts those actions one perceives as ethically valuable. For Kames, moreover, the very objectless-ness of this feeling permits an amazing flexibility of application. One turns from a virtuous representation charged with an intensified sense of sympathetic emotion that drives one to locate a fit object for the further bestowal of benevolence. Under the influence of this emotion, the spectator "longs for proper objects upon which to exert this emotion," and, Kames insists, "This singular emotion will readily find an object to exert itself upon" (1:49, 51). Most importantly, however, he contends that the sympathetic emotion of virtue is itself an exercise of virtue, the repeated experience of which leads to moral habits. This emotion

> never exists without producing some effect; because virtuous emotions of that sort, *are in some degree an exercise of virtue*; they are a mental exercise at least, if they appear not externally. And every exercise of virtue, internal and external, leads to habit; for a disposition or propensity of the mind, like a limb of the body, becomes stronger by exercise. Proper means, at the same time, being ever at hand to raise this sympathetic emotion, its frequent reiteration may, in a good measure, supply the want of a more complete exercise. Thus, by proper discipline, every person may acquire a settled habit of virtue.... (1:51; italics mine)

Even when the sympathetic emotion of virtue does not lead directly to action, the sensation itself qualifies as an internal act of virtue. As a result, the more habitual this experience becomes through constant repetition, the more virtuous one becomes.

Kames's theory of art's moral influence was not the only one in circulation during the eighteenth and nineteenth centuries. Like Kames's, though, most stressed the moral role of sympathy and imagination, as well as art's ability to strengthen these powers.[32] It was from these kinds of theories and their romantic offshoots that Victorian evangelical discussions of morality and art took their cue. The genealogy of this line of thought was highlighted in 1847 by the *Methodist Quarterly Review*, which cited both Hazlitt and Wordsworth for support:

> It is not the mere ability to recapitulate numerous beauties that give rank to the poet; it is not a solitary enthusiasm which enrages his own bosom that measures his genius; but, superadded to all this, the power of expression, whereby he warms the fancy and arouses the faculties of the reader. Not mere fluency of expression, but the "power of moving and infusing the warmth of his own rapt mind into that of his reader;" (*Hazlitt;*) the ability to conjure up in the minds of men "passions, which are, indeed, far from being the same as those produced by real events, but which yet do more strongly resemble those passions, than anything which, from the motions of their own minds merely, other men are accustomed to find in themselves;"

---

[32] See, for example, Edmund Burke, *A Philosophical Enquiry into the Origins of Our Ideas of the Sublime and Beautiful, A Philosophical Enquiry into the Sublime and Beautiful and Other Pre-Revolutionary Writings*, ed. David Womersley (London: Penguin, 1998), 198 and Alexander Gerard, *An Essay on Taste. To Which Is Now Added Part Fourth, of the Standard of Taste; with Observations Concerning the Imitative Nature of Poetry* (Edinburgh, 1780), 160. On sympathy, see James Engell, *The Creative Imagination: Enlightenment to Romanticism* (San Jose: toExcel, 1999), 143-60.

(*Wordsworth*;) the faculty of awakening, by his descriptions of nature or of man, sensations nearly similar to those produced by the real object.[33]

For many evangelicals, art was not primarily a vehicle of instruction, though it may involve this; rather, art conditioned morality by targeting the source of action—the feelings. Good art need not and should not preach, for it practiced a subtler alchemy. In fact, the distinction between the respective duties of preacher and poet appeared in the *Christian Spectator* as early as 1825. In the second of three articles on "Lyric Poetry," a genre including "psalmody," the author noted the distinct spheres over which sermons and poetry held sway: "The cultivation of that understanding and belief is exclusively the business of the preacher; after his duties are performed, it is within the province of psalmody to excite and animate the feelings and emotions which such doctrines are calculated to produce. Hence, a mere *allusion* to them is sufficient to answer the purpose of musical expression."[34] In this case, the emotional power of poetry, which the writer elsewhere described as "calculated to move and purify our feelings and affections,"[35] had not yet been wholly severed from doctrine, for the excitement of psalmody still depended on the prior work of the preacher; but the necessity for religious poetry to deliver sound doctrinal statements had clearly diminished. A "mere allusion" to such doctrine was enough, and while the author did "not say that instruction is entirely foreign to the object of psalmody," neither did he "hesitate to say that it does not constitute its chief design."[36]

One of the more comprehensive evangelical articulations of anti-didactic moralism was Otheman's lecture on "The Moral Influence of the Fine Arts." Otheman would likely have encountered Kames's *Elements* in the course of his studies at Brown,[37] and in fact his argument shows a decidedly Kamesian bent. His lecture's central purpose was to justify patronage of the arts on the basis of their powerful moral influence. Far from advocating art as an instructional tool, however, Otheman grounds his case on the Kamesian premise that art exercises people's emotions:

> That department of the mind over which the fine arts peculiarly and immediately preside, is an important one, and is, in fact, that over which morality and religion exercise their greatest control. It is the sensitive part of our nature—the passions and the emotions. And here we see the grand reason why their moral influence should be seriously considered, because they touch the springs of action.... (320)

---

[33] D., Review of *Poems*, by William W. Lord, *MQR* 7 (July 1847), 369.
[34] "Lyric Poetry," *CS* 7 (1 Aug. 1825), 411.
[35] "Lyric Poetry," *CS* 7 (1 July 1825), 358.
[36] "Lyric Poetry," 411. See also "The Study of Hymnology," *BM* 84 (May 1892), 230-31.
[37] Otheman attended Brown during a transitional period when Kames was jettisoned. Yet even if Otheman did not read Kames as part of the curriculum, he undoubtedly interacted with those familiar with the *Elements*. See Walter C. Bronson, *The History of Brown University 1764-1914* (Providence: Brown University, 1914), 204-17.

Otheman's dependence on Kames is evident in both the logic and language of this passage. Like Kames, Otheman suggests that art bears a natural affinity to morality and religion since all three deal with feeling. He also lifts the phrase "the sensitive part of our nature" directly from the introduction to the *Elements* (1:18), while the implicit distinction between passions and emotions evinces a further indebtedness to Kames. And although Otheman does not credit Kames explicitly, it is the Kamesian proposition that art addresses the human emotions that leads him to declare that art "is certainly a proper subject for the scrutiny and guardianship of the Christian and the philanthropist" (321).

Specifically, Otheman differentiates two kinds of moral influence wielded by art—what he calls "original, native or inherent, and relative or derived" (321). Otheman's terminology parallels another common division found in Kames, Hutcheson, Hume, Smith, and others between "intrinsic" and "relative" beauty. According to these writers, an object possesses intrinsic beauty by virtue of its formal properties. Relative beauty, by contrast, is a function of an object's relationship to some end. Although Otheman speaks of inherent and relative moral influence rather than the intrinsic and relative beauty of conventional eighteenth-century discourse, the traditional distinction continues to underwrite his arguments. Original and relative influence, he notes, generally operate within the same art object, although "the latter influence must be, or may be made, far greater than the former, since into the latter can be thrown all the incentives to vice or virtue, all the elements of moral purity or corruption" (322). Despite the typically superior power of relative influence, however, Otheman devotes much of his lecture to demonstrating the "native influence [of art] on individual and social morality" (323). His aim, therefore, is to establish the moral import of purely *aesthetic* experience. To this end, he advances several arguments, three of which are worth noting here.

First, Otheman contends that art's main object "is consistent with, and promotive of morality. This object is, in general, to please; in particular, to please by exciting the emotions of beauty and sublimity" (323). The primary purpose of art is pleasure, and Otheman suggests that this pleasure not only conduces to happiness but also that pleasure itself is "a purpose not unworthy of, nor neglected by the Deity" (323). Following Kames, Otheman also sees aesthetic pleasure as preparing the way for morality and religion: "The mind, under the benignant influence of the charms of nature, is either softened or elevated, and is thus better prepared to attend to the lessons of religion, and, indeed, to be affected by the moral reflections which come from every point of the universe. And the same effect do the beauties of the fine arts produce on those who contemplate and admire them" (323-24). In moderating the affections, aesthetic pleasure generates a mental state that enhances one's capacity for attending to truth and goodness. What's more, beauty and sublimity have been designed by God to contribute to moral improvement by virtue of their peculiar effects on the mind. As Otheman declares, "The moral effect of these emotions is always good." Drawing upon Kames (and other eighteenth-century writers), who had noted "that many emotions have some resemblance to their causes" (1:129), Otheman argues that mental states reflect external objects of perception. Beautiful objects cause "an expansion and complacence of mind," while sublime objects lead to "mental elevation and vigor." In either case, these mental agitations "are very far removed from the low and grovelling dispositions of vice. Indeed, a vicious man cannot have a full impression of the pure beauties of nature or of art." As with Kames (as well as Wordsworth), beauty and sublimity "insinuate themselves ... in an agreeable, undefinable manner, into [one's] heart, and insensibly mould [one's] character." Momentarily at least, art enables one to transcend "sensual gratification" in favor of purer pleasures (324).

Expanding on his first, Otheman's second point offers a lengthier meditation on "the susceptibility of the human mind to imbibe the spirit of the scenes and circumstances by which it is employed and interested" (324). Otheman's psychology, in fact, is so empiricist that it verges on determinism. He does leave room for the creative prerogative of the imagination, but on the whole,

> Most men are what they are more from the ideas which they receive from the world around them, than from those which they originate. Indeed, by far the greater number of our first ideas are suggested by surrounding persons and objects; and, excepting the faculties, by which we receive, combine, and employ these ideas, and which, in some instances, create a world of their own, we grow up mere copies or imitations of what has already been.

Since the arts are characterized by singular vividness and intensity, it is only natural to assume that they would have a profound effect on "character and deportment": "How then is it possible for us to be unaffected by the fine arts, whenever seen, which appeal so powerfully and triumphantly to our taste and sentiments?" (325). What follows from this model of mind is a doctrine of sympathetic identification, in which the passions represented in art are recreated in the minds of the beholder. "When art is thus successful," writes Otheman, "we seem, sometimes, by beholding to become the beings which it represents. We feel the inspiration which they are made to feel, the same emotions and passions agitate our breast ... till we are as wise as the wisest, good as the best" (326). Art capacitates one to experience vicariously what virtue feels like, allowing one to become more virtuous in the process.

Central to this process, Otheman argues, is the imagination, which "has the widest and strongest control over men in general." The imagination "is one of the chief instruments of the happiness or misery of man" (326). In these exalted claims for the imagination, Otheman shows his accord with the romantics, and indeed his conception of the imagination is akin to Wordsworth's. For Otheman, the imagination is a faculty of both creation and perception, or as he puts it, of "genius" and "taste." Its main value is its ability to receive and store perceptual stimuli and to re-present these to the mind once the originals have faded: "Now the employment of either genius or taste in the fine arts rouses and stimulates the imagination, so that, even after this enjoyment, it is apt to form combinations of thought and sentiment similar to those on which it has been exercised through the senses" (326-27). It is through the imagination, therefore, that "the mind receive[s] a lasting impression—a fadeless hue, from those qualities which are presented to its perception. These ideas of the imagination have a powerful influence on all the character, and give their peculiar expression to the conduct" (327). Like Wordsworth's "beauteous forms" that have had "no slight or trivial influence / On that best portion of a good man's life, / His little, nameless, unremembered, acts / Of kindness and of love,"[38] Otheman insists that "The forming of mental images of rare and exquisite natural or moral grace ... always produces a good effect upon the character and manners" (327). Many Puritans may have questioned such a theory; art and imagination, however, were assuming a prominent place in evangelical theories of moral action.

Otheman's third argument for art's original moral influence concerns its purported ability to heighten one's sensitivity to the actual world. "The exercise or cultivation," he writes, "which the study and examination of works of art give to the sensitive part of our nature, refines and improves our sensibilities, and thus renders us more easily and deeply affected by the scenes of real life." Underwriting this transferability of feeling from aesthetic engagement to "real life" is a general conception, also evident in Kames, of the fungibility of the mental powers. Otheman states this principle openly: "the cultivation of any power of the mind on a given subject prepares that power to be used more easily on every other subject; so, by a proper employment of our taste or sensibility in the fine arts, it becomes more readily excited in the common affairs of life" (327). Art helps to calibrate a person's emotional receptivity; once calibrated, one will naturally repel (i.e., feel) the immoral as distasteful. As Otheman observes, "persons of refined taste and genius abhor every thing vulgar and mean" (328).

Otheman's lecture, though notable for its scope and precision, was hardly unique in its orientation. Evangelicals increasingly followed suit in arguing for art's ethical significance using the language of anti-didactic moralism. As Drummond observed in his *Letter to Thomas Phillips*, "an increased feeling for the fine arts can really contribute to elevate the minds and characters of man...."[39] In 1849, P. Wells urged that poetry might be "the means of effecting much real and practical good" precisely because "The mass of men decide, and act, from the impulse of the heart, rather than from the convictions of the head."[40] The *Christian Observer* similarly pointed out that "There is, in fact, a *humanising* power in all true poetry.... As the nourisher of all human and sacred sympathies, the poet becomes a teacher of morality by being an inspirer of *right feeling*."[41] Such

---

[38] William Wordsworth, "Lines Composed a Few Miles above Tintern Abbey, on Revisiting the Banks of the Wye during a Tour. July 13, 1798," *William Wordsworth: Selected Poems*, ed. John O. Hayden (London: Penguin), ll. 22, 32-35.

[39] Henry Drummond, *Letter to Thomas Phillips, Esq., R.A., on the Connexion between the Fine Arts and Religion, and the Means of Their Revival* (London: Fraser, 1840), 44.

[40] Wells, "Poetry," 24.

[41] "Poetry and Its Uses," *CO* 66 (1866), 118.

rhetoric could sometimes reach an astonishing pitch. No doubt one of the more bombastic claims on behalf of the moral power of poetry came from S.D. Burchard, who accorded poetry the honor of having launched many a revolution throughout history: "Our moral sensibilities are so arranged and attuned that true poetry will find its way to the heart and leave its impress there. Hence its influence, during all time, over the moral feelings and habits of men. Some of the grandest revolutions and changes that have signalized the world's history have been effected through the instrumentality of poetry."[42] This kind of claim, bold though it was, was not without precedent. Dugald Stewart had speculated that "in … earlier periods of society, the rude compositions of the bard and the minstrel may have been instrumental in humanizing the minds of savage warriors, and accelerating the growth of cultivated manners."[43] Whether stirring humankind to greatness or pacifying brutes, art boasted a power that made society possible.

Anti-didactic moralism also informed evangelical discussions of nature. Reflecting on "The Advantages of a Taste for the Beauties of Nature," Dr. Percival observed how "By a sweet contagion, the soul catches the harmony which it contemplates.... In this state we become susceptible of virtuous impressions from every surrounding object; [and] an equal and extensive benevolence is called forth into exertion." Evangelicals, especially when nature was the aesthetic object of choice, tended to move through nature to the Creator, just as the Puritans had. A "taste for natural beauty ... elevates [us] to the love and admiration of that Being who is the author of all that is fair, sublime, and good in the creation."[44] In calling attention to the personal character of God, writers like Percival also resisted the pantheistic tendencies that lay behind radical romantic conceptions of nature.[45] Still, the moral encounter with nature was more affective than rational: natural beauty "not only refines and humanizes, but dignifies and exalts the affections."[46] The appreciation of natural beauty was not simply an occasion for meditating upon the superlative merits of heavenly beauty, nor was it, at least for Percival, a chance to read objects Edwards-like as "images of divine things". One's confrontation with beauty was a moment of transport in which one *felt* God and experienced moral empowerment.[47]

---

[42] S.D. Burchard, "Moral Uses of Poetry," *CAJ* 22 (18 Aug. 1847), 132.
[43] Dugald Stewart, *Elements of the Philosophy of the Human Mind, Vol. 1, to Which Is Prefixed, Introduction and Part First of the Outlines of Moral Philosophy. With Many New and Important Additions*, ed. Sir William Hamilton (Westmead: Gregg, 1971), 469.
[44] Dr. Percival, "The Advantages of a Taste for the Beauties of Nature," *CAJ* 8 (11 Oct. 1833), 28.
[45] Cf. the discussion of Transcendentalist and Christian Romantic conceptions of nature in Diane Apostolos-Cappadona, *The Spirit and the Vision: The Influence of Christian Romanticism on the Development of 19th-Century American Art* (Atlanta: Scholars, 1995), 58-59.
[46] Dr. Percival, "The Advantages," 28.
[47] See also "Æsthetic Influence of Nature," *CR* 83 (1 Jan. 1854): 1-34, esp. 5-6.

The widespread acceptance of anti-didactic moralism, drawn from the romantics and from Enlightenment writers like Kames, highlights the ethical and aesthetic distance that evangelical cultural elites had traveled in less than a century. Many critics, following the eighteenth-century sentimentalist tradition, embraced an ethico-aesthetic theory that included both a more positive view of human nature (for his part, Kames stated plainly that "no man hath a propensity to vice as such" [1:51]) and a model of moral progress dependent upon a naturalistic "influence" emanating from aesthetic experience. For Edwards, the exercise of true virtue and the perception of primary beauty—as well as whatever moral improvement was derivable from secondary beauty—were possible only for those whom the Holy Spirit had regenerated; for theorists like Otheman, by contrast, virtue was in part an ordinary product of aesthetic exposure and education.[48] Especially instructive here are John Foster's astute reflections on the aesthetic experience of nature:

> It would be a matter of very great interest to determine, under what conditions this influence of nature, where it does actually operate on the taste and imagination, shall also be salutary in a *moral* respect. It has been a favourite doctrine with many men of sensibility and genius, that these captivations of nature are absolutely and almost necessarily conducive to the moral rectitude of the mind; that they unconditionally tend to purify, to harmonize, and to exalt, the principles and affections. If the maintainers of this opinion, so kind to our nature, had not examined the human mind enough to know, from its very constitution, that in some modes and degrees of its depravity, it not only may fail to be corrected by the perception of these charms of nature, but may receive their influence so that it shall augment the depravity—it is strange that their faith was not shaken by the notorious fact, that many fine geniuses of the very class most alive to beauty and sublimity of nature, poets and painters, have been among the most profligate of men....[49]

Foster pinpointed exactly the potential theological difficulty with anti-didactic moralism. Proponents of this theory had been overly "kind" in their estimation of human nature.

What makes Otheman's particular case so revealing, however, is that such principles co-existed, albeit tenuously, with an otherwise solid theological conservatism.[50] Otheman, it seems, was not unaware that the anti-didactic moralism he ardently preached conceivably stood at odds, at least in its unqualified form,

---

[48] A possible exception was Henry N. Day, who approximated Edwardsean language in discussing the moral influence of the aesthetic (although he also cited Kames on another matter). See "Taste and Morals:—The Necessity of Aesthetic Culture to the Highest Moral Excellence," *ABRCR* 3 (July 1847), 538-39. Elsewhere, Day comes close to describing the Atonement in the aesthetic manner of liberals (542-43).

[49] John Foster, "Philosophy of Nature," *Biographical, Literary, and Philosophical Essays: Contributed to the* Eclectic Review (New York: D. Appleton, 1844), 310.

[50] The extant sources suggest that Otheman, who died in 1886, avoided the gathering forces of liberalism. See "An Interesting Scene," *ZH* 50 (10 July 1873), 1.

with the traditional doctrine of depravity. In fact, his efforts to introduce conventional theological concerns into his basically Kamesian paradigm constitute some of the more illuminating, because ultimately ineffectual, moments in his lecture. At one point, for example, Otheman refers suggestively to two types of genius, indicating a lingering consciousness of the Puritan distinction between regenerate and unregenerate: "Subjects and emotions are ... the instruments which both depraved and consecrated genius employs to effect its purposes" (322). This passing distinction, however, remains undeveloped. Later, he explicitly raises the problem of the Fall in formulating his principle of sympathetic identification. Our ability "to become the beings which [art] represents" points to a "desire of improving our condition, ... that undefinable longing after something great and glorious, which, though perverted by the fall, still clings to our nature" (326). Again, though, Otheman fails to explore the consequences of this doctrine, and in fact his emphasis lies on that part of human nature which, he argues, remains untouched by the Fall. Perhaps his fullest effort to give due weight to the doctrine of depravity arises during his treatment of the imagination. Otheman allows that "Under the influence of a depraved heart, this faculty is apt to be disordered in its aims and operations." Yet even here he is quick to explain the problem away: "but God has wisely so ordained that it can be, and *ordinarily* is gratified with the exhibition of those qualities which are harmless, if they are not as holy, and contain as much earthly, if not as much heavenly purity, as the sublimer attributes of religion" (326; italics mine). Otheman's Methodism may help to explain his more positive view of human nature, but even conservative Arminians acknowledged depravity's extensive effects. Ultimately, then, he was either unwilling or unable to pursue the deeper tensions between his ethico-aesthetics and his theology.

There were evangelical writers who refused to accept casually the sentimentalist premises underlying anti-didactic moralism; nor were they content simply to remain in Otheman's state of unresolved tension. These writers called attention to the potential incompatibility of an ethico-aesthetic system founded on the inherent goodness of human nature and a Christian system that took depravity seriously, locating moral action not in "sensibility" alone but in God's laws and the enabling power of grace. "Young persons," noted the *Christian Advocate and Journal* in 1836, "are too apt to think that sensibility of heart is in itself a meritorious trait of moral character. This I consider a serious misconception. In itself it is possessed of neither a virtuous nor reprehensible quality."[51] In 1857, the *Mercersburg Review* blasted Dickens and Thackeray for belonging to that school of sentimental novelists whose "good [characters] are good on no principle of goodness recognized by Christianity, or even in any sound ethical system" and whose "bad [characters] are bad with an equal absence of all reason for being

---

[51] "Sensibility," *CAJ* 10 (15 July 1836), 188. This author questions the moral status of sensibility; however, he also leaves room for sensibility guided by Christianity and reason (see p. 188). He does not so much reject anti-didactic moralism as modify it.

such, except the fancy of the writer." The problem was that these novelists' character depictions were the products not of a clearheaded theological appraisal of reality, nor even a carefully reasoned ethical theory, but rather of feeling alone:

> Ethical systems recognize a difference of culture and education. The Scriptures make a difference of faith, of discipleship, and, above all, of *grace*. Men may dislike the word and the idea. A difference of grace! they cannot bear the sound or the thought of it. But surely it is more rational than no ground of difference at all. With this school there is no such rational, to say nothing of any Scriptural ground. In fact, there is no *reason* in it; it is all *feeling*; *good feeling* on the one side, and *bad feeling* on the other. This difference, too, of goodness and badness, as thus presented, is simply another matter of feeling....

Neither did such novelists have any place for original sin, "for all writers of this school, with hardly an exception, reject it as a most atrocious and man-libelling tenet."[52] Still others echoed the Edwardsean supposition that nature alone lacks the power of moral purification. To reap its rewards requires a preceding act of grace. "O, why is it," asked J. Wesley Horne in 1872, "that so many of the sons of God—for whom all these things were made, that they might 'ascend through nature up to nature's God,' their own heavenly Father and friend—see not, know not, commune not with these handiworks of His, though glowing all around them? Is it because 'of the darkness that is in them?'" The only remedy, Horne counseled, was to "go to the good Physician, that he 'may anoint their eyes with eye-salve that they may see....'"[53]

Critiques of this sort, however, did little to undermine evangelicals' general enthusiasm for anti-didactic moralism. By the century's close, this theory would assume a prominent role not only in liberal Protestant aesthetics but also liberal theology through the influence of figures like Bushnell and Henry Ward Beecher. It was already evident, for example, in Beecher's conception of the rapturous gaze in which union with aesthetic objects yields a blessed though unconscious moral harvest:

> The first merit of pictures is the effect which they can produce upon the mind;—and the first step of a sensible man should be to receive involuntary effects from them. Pleasure and inspiration first, analysis afterward. The more perfectly one can abandon himself, the more true he can be to his real feelings and impressions, the wiser he is.... In these higher moods of feeling there is intuitional moral instruction, to the analysis of which the intellect comes afterward with slow steps. Therefore, I said to the pictures, "I am here; I am yours; do what you will with me; I am here to

---

[52] T.L., "The Anatomy of Sentimentalism," *MerR* 9 (Jan. 1857) 35, 35-36. See also "Periodical Literature," *CAmb* 3 (Feb. 1865), 67.

[53] J. Wesley Horne, "The Book of Nature," *CA* 47 (27 Jan. 1872), 201. See also "Moral Aesthetics; or, the Goodness of God in the Ornaments of the Universe," *BRPR* 24 (Jan. 1852), 43, 44, 50.

be intoxicated...." They took me at my word, and such another revel—such an ethereal intoxication, drunk from the cup of heavenly beauty, I shall not have again, until I drink that new wine of the Kingdom of Heaven![54]

Such romantic reverie, of course, was fast becoming the stock-and-trade of emergent liberals, yet behind such reverie and the ethico-aesthetic theory on which it was based stood, oddly enough, the likes of Otheman, a conservative Methodist. And alongside Beecher stood a body of evangelical romantic critics who, though they may have disagreed with Beecher's theology, would surely have affirmed his claims for the "intuitional moral instruction" afforded by art.

"Occult Pathos" Gone Wrong: Negative Influence, Sentimentality, and the Novel

The notion that art operates morally via an "occult pathos" dominated evangelical aesthetics for much of the nineteenth century. This theory, however, was not without dangers, and it thus engendered a counter-discourse among some critics who, following in the footsteps of More's Preface, expressed concerns about the negative effects of art precisely because they had already internalized the principle that art has direct access to the emotional well-springs of human behavior. The basic dilemma was that if one accepts the hypothesis that art exerts an influence on the feelings in the interests of morality, then what is to stop it from exerting its influence in the interests of *im*morality? Writing on "Music and Poetry" for the *London Quarterly Review*, H. Buxton Forman observed that "music, poetry, and the rest of the fine arts" possess "the power of importuning us with more or less definite influences for good." The influence of music in particular is "vague, subtle, and indirect," and "It is thus a tremendous humanising agent in its possibilities." Yet it is the very "fact that it can be abused as frightfully as other humanising agents can" which "adds importance to this function."[55] Music's power to humanize is also, paradoxically, its power to dehumanize. The possible extent of this dehumanization was depicted graphically by the *Christian Advocate* in 1882: "The impure thoughts and images infused into the moral being by ... unhallowed poetry, like certain poisons taken into the blood, may remain there for life...." The only antidote to this pernicious "Influence of Demoralizing Art and Literature" was a "continual resort to Divine grace."[56] To some extent, this recognition of the dual potential of art for good and evil was yet another incarnation of the paradox that prompted Plato to deny poets a place in the Republic: if poets weren't so powerful, they wouldn't need banishing. Puritan fears regarding the overactive imagination reflected a similar paradox. Yet what appears to be little more than a manifestation of puritanical anxieties looks different

---

[54] Henry Ward Beecher, *Star Papers; or, Experiences of Art and Nature* (New York: J.C. Derby, 1855), 63-64.
[55] H. Buxton Forman, "Music and Poetry: Their Origin and Functions," *LQR* 39 (1872), 24-25.
[56] "Influence of Demoralizing Art and Literature," *CA* 57 (15 June 1882), 7.

when one recognizes in such a complaint a categorical acceptance of both contemporary aesthetics and the mental philosophy on which it was based. The well-known evangelical reluctance, for example, to sanction the novel could lay claim in part to a respectable Enlightenment pedigree.

In fact, it is in evangelical discussions of the novel that the dark side of anti-didactic moralism is most evident. Critics did at times include other art forms in their discussions of negative influence, but more often than not the "fine arts" (a category to which the novel struggled to gain access[57]) were imagined in positive terms, whereas the novel was seen as a moral and aesthetic aberration. "Novels," as one writer phrased it in 1890, "are the weeds in Literature's garden."[58] As Terence Martin has pointed out, it was the novel *as a genre* that often attracted the criticism of evangelicals and non-evangelicals alike. Common arguments against the genre ranged from doubts about the metaphysical status of fiction (an argument with Scottish philosophical precedents that also reached back to Puritanism's epistemological realism) to doubts about whether novel-reading was consistent with the time constraints of those charged with evangelizing the earth (another argument with Puritan roots).[59] However, a brief examination of another critique may illustrate how evangelical fears regarding immoral influence were the natural corollary of a faith in art's occult pathos.

A major problem with the novel, critics alleged, was its tendency to generate emotional excess, which led to both a diminished desire for moral action in the real world and an increased desire for emotional stimulation. These ideas came to be encapsulated in the term "sentimentality," or what the *Biblical Repertory and Princeton Review* called "the Gospel of Sentimentalism."[60] The novel's ability to stimulate emotion could, if left unchecked, lead to over-stimulation, fol-

---

[57] See, for example, R.C. Schiedt, "Is the Modern Novel a Work of Art?" *RQR* 3 (July 1891): 370-88.

[58] John F. Hume, "Literary Dissipation," *BQR* 12 (July 1890), 300.

[59] See Martin, *Instructed Vision*. On evangelical attitudes towards fiction, see John O. Waller, "The *Methodist Quarterly Review* and Fiction, 1818-1900," *Bulletin of the New York Public Library* 71 (1967): 573-90; Elisabeth Jay, *The Religion of the Heart: Anglican Evangelicalism and the Nineteenth-Century Novel* (Oxford: Clarendon, 1979); David M. Reynolds, *Faith in Fiction: The Emergence of Religious Literature in America* (Cambridge: Harvard University Press, 1981); Doreen M. Rosman, *Evangelicals and Culture* (London: Croom Helm, 1984), 184-93; Jan Blodgett, *Protestant Evangelical Culture and Contemporary Society* (Westport: Greenwood, 1997), 11-32; and Lynn S. Neal, *Romancing God: Evangelical Women and Inspirational Fiction* (Chapel Hill: University of North Carolina Press, 2006), 15-41. Some evangelical discussions of the novel that articulate typical criticisms even as they reflect a growing openness to the genre are "The Novel and Novel-Reading," *BRPR* 41 (Apr. 1869): 202-34; the four-part series by J.P. Barnett: "Novels and Novel Reading: A Familiar Address to the Young," *BM* 74 (Aug., Sep., Oct., Nov. 1882): 358-66, 415-19, 452-59, and 498-503; and "Novel Reading," *CI* 63 (30 July 1885): 3.

[60] "The Novel and Novel-Reading," 231.

lowed by desensitization and apathy for actual suffering. Put simply, sentimentality was the relishing of feeling for its own sake. This logic surfaced in the arguments of one "Miranda" in 1828:

> Houses of distress, poverty, sickness, and death diversify the scenery of the moral world, calculated to touch the finer feelings of our natures, and cause the tear of sympathy to fill the eye. All these circumstances come within our daily observation; yet they are overlooked by those who feed their imaginations with fictitious woe, and cherish that luxury of grief which blunts the keenest sensibilities of the heart, and raises an insuperable barrier to moral excellences. Theatrical and novel characters shed an abundance of tears, yet they seldom fall upon the couch of distress to soothe the agonies of a heart riven from earth by affliction, or mingle with those which drop from the eye of the widow and the orphan, to mitigate their woes.[61]

The *Record* made a similar case, with considerably greater vitriol, in 1862. Describing the "slave of imaginative literature," the author lamented that "The toil that yields him no profit will continue to absorb his energies; and the mind, wearied with its shallow pursuits, and sickened with its own folly, will yet be cursed with a keener appetite for the garbage it feeds upon."[62] The argument that novels deaden the moral sensibility by repeated over-stimulation was still being cited by the *Christian Index* in 1882. In this case, the writer did express reservations about the argument's merits, explaining that it seemed "rather theoretical,"[63] but his need to address it suggests the endurance of this view among the novel's evangelical detractors.

Critics identified various means by which desensitization and moral dullness could occur. They sometimes posited, for example, that an indulgence in fictitious suffering weakened, through recurring exposure, human beings' intrinsic discomfort with the distresses of others. In other instances, the problem lay in fiction's propensity to idealize suffering and its refusal to depict the harshness of reality. The natural effect of this romanticized outlook was a maladjusted taste, which because of its acquired hyper-sensitivity turned from the horrors of genuine suffering in favor of the stylizations of literature. Whatever their exact details, these anti-sentimentalist/anti-fictional arguments, while not inconsistent with earlier Puritan concerns about the wayward imagination, were the immediate offspring of eighteenth and early-nineteenth-century moral philosophy. Stewart, the great codifier of common sense realism, had after all explained with much rigor the psychological principles that rendered the novel a deadly weapon, determining that "an habitual attention to exhibitions of fictitious distress, is in every view calculated to check our moral improvement."[64] Ironically, the novel was initially

---

[61] Miranda, "Novel Reading," *CAJ* 11 (23 May 1828), 149.
[62] [Untitled], *Rec* (17 Mar. 1862), 2.
[63] H., "Novel Reading," *CI* 60 (5 Oct. 1882), 2
[64] Stewart, *Elements*, 465. Charvat also notes the early-nineteenth-century American critical opposition to sentimentalism and "egotism" (*Origins*, 23-6).

a victim of the very psychology that had served to invest other art forms with a transformative moral power.

Evangelical anti-sentimentalist discourse was thus in many ways a protest against the perceived abuses of the reigning psycho-aesthetic system. Because, as Kames had contended, the arts "open a direct avenue to the heart of man" (1:32), this avenue required strict surveillance. This protest, however, also left the basic principles of this system intact. This stance is evident, for example, in one writer's efforts to differentiate ordinary "sensibility" from the more menacing "super-sensibility": "there is, perhaps, some danger lest we should substitute effeminacy of manners and sickly sentimentality for plain integrity and genuine sensibility. Our excessive fondness for novels and works of romance betrays vitiated feelings, as well as vitiated taste." Such vitiated feelings could be classified as a form of "super-sensibility," and novels were especially to blame for its cultivation, not least in unsuspecting youth. Still, this same critic supported fostering what he termed "genuine sensibility," for "Such sensibility is the key-stone of all our social affections, the very cement of society, the well-spring of beneficence, and the true genius of poetry, painting, sculpture, and all the graces of the fine arts."[65] "Sentimentality" was morally dangerous not only because it could lead individuals astray but also because it threatened to disrupt the prevailing ethico-aesthetic paradigm. "[M]ost books of fiction," argued the *Christian Index* in 1885, "appeal almost exclusively to the emotional nature—to the feelings and passions—and these, in their turn, react upon the body, mind and morals, inducing courses of action which entail disease and ruin."[66] Sentimentality was, in effect, occult pathos gone berserk.

The specters of immoral influence and sentimentalism, therefore, were the inevitable byproducts of an ethico-aesthetic theory that so closely linked morality to feeling and saw art as a special means of tapping into such feeling. Of course, anti-sentimentalism was a multilayered, often politically charged discourse. As scholars have long recognized, anti-sentimentalist discourse was frequently gendered, equating sentimentalism with the feminine or "effeminate."[67] The writer quoted above who associated sentimentality with an *"effeminacy* of manners" was hardly atypical in this regard. Critics likewise came to identify sentimentality with the "low" or "popular." Fiction, the primary offender, was contrasted unfavorably with the superior art of poetry, and even evangelicals sometimes rejected fiction on the basis of aesthetic considerations rather than, or in addition

---

[65] "Sensibility and Super-Sensibility," *CAJ* 19 (26 Feb. 1845), 116. This distinction also parallels an older one between taste and sensibility. See Dugald Stewart, "Essay Third: On the Faculty of Taste," *Philosophical Essays. With Many New and Important Additions*, ed. Sir William Hamilton (Westmead: Gregg, 1971), 340.

[66] "Novel Reading," 3.

[67] See Douglas, *Feminization*.

to, moral ones.[68] Such realities, however, merely underscore that both anti-didactic moralism and the anti-sentimentalism it spawned were predominantly the discourses of an educated elite. The same holds true for much of the anti-novel rhetoric propagated by evangelical critics, which has sometimes been viewed as evidence of evangelicalism's puritanical, anti-aesthetic, or anti-intellectual bias. In reality, the evangelical campaigns against sentimentalism and the novel suggest quite the opposite—namely, the existence of a privileged class of intellectuals committed to the Anglo-American institution of high art and the maintenance of a specific type of Protestant society.[69]

Thanks to anti-didactic moralism, mental faculties such as the taste and imagination were for many evangelicals rife with tensions. Utilized properly, these faculties could literally determine the fate of a nation. Taste, as one writer put it, "is susceptible of very high culture,—much higher than any of our external senses, and it exerts a strong and very direct influence on the rest of our being.... If our taste could thus be elevated, how elevated would become our entire nature; mind, heart, and soul would all turn from the things of the earth to dwell on purer and higher things."[70] Such religio-moral rectitude was a key to healthy Christian cultures. Utilized improperly, these faculties could prove disastrous, individually and socially. Sentimental fiction was not just a personal vice; it threatened to subvert the very structure of society. "What in time," asked one critic who found himself deeply troubled by the novel's popularity, "must be the effect upon the national character of so much pollution passing into the minds and souls, the hearts and consciences of our people, and filling them with false impressions and false sentiments?" In response, he offered a characteristically evangelical solution to his nightmarish vision of social collapse at the feet of the novel. He called for the establishment of Novel Societies, which, like the Temperance Society, would stem the negative effects of rampant, fiction-induced intoxication. Given the psychological premises behind Victorian critiques of the novel, this suggestion was not nearly as far-fetched as it may seem to modern readers. As this critic put it, "The novel is to the mind what strong drink is to the body"—a warning as applicable to the body politic as to individual readers.[71]

---

[68] See, for example, "The Novel and Novel-Reading," 204-06, 221-22 and Barnett, "Novels and Novel Reading," 501.

[69] Cf. Neal's discussion of the "evangelical aesthetic" of twenty-first-century America, which she describes in terms of four emphases: "mediocrity, predictability, utility, and sentimentality" (*Romancing God*, 190). This aesthetic, however, represents one strain of the evangelical tradition. Even as nineteenth-century evangelical novelists were embracing the sentimental fiction, many critics were strongly opposing sentimentalism.

[70] H., "Novel Reading," 2

[71] Hume, "Literary Dissipation," 304, 310-11, 307.

"A mighty engine ... for the elevation of the nation":
Art's Service to Christian Society

Nineteenth-century evangelical thinking about art was profoundly implicated in the discourses of British and American nationalism, as well as the broader discourse of "civilization". Surveying the "Prospects of British Art" in 1845, one optimistic writer noted how art "is now for the first time becoming a thing for the people; not an object of worth to a fortunate few, but a mighty engine, if it shall yet be carried out in all its capabilities, for the elevation of the nation." Whereas the arts had once been the province of wealthy aristocrats, they were at last available for the benefit of the masses—an observation confirmed by the growing number of museums, galleries, and mass-produced prints throughout the century. This democratization of the arts, the writer believed, carried with it a new obligation, for if anything could inspire the British artist to reach beyond the "noblest efforts of bygone times," it was "surely the consciousness that he is painting—not for a patron, but for a people—not as a mere higher-class decorator, adorning the mansions of the wealthy, but rather as a priest, ministering to the national mind."[72] Once art ceases to be a "plaything" of the privileged and becomes an object for the "people," its social importance expands dramatically. Accordingly, art's solemn mission was to advance the interests of the nation; its ultimate objective was the securement of a stable society.

The argument for art's contribution to national betterment, however, must be understood within the context of evangelical conceptions of the nation itself. For evangelicals, and indeed for many non-evangelicals, the "nation" was far more than a political, ethnic, or geographical construct. Nation was also an inherently spiritual and moral category, for Britain and the United States, Victorians believed, were *Christian* nations. As numerous scholars have shown, Protestantism formed a key component in the national identities of both countries throughout the nineteenth century.[73] To be English or American was to be Protestant. This idea had been handed down from the Puritans, and it survived even after developments in the 1820s and 1830s (e.g., Catholic Emancipation in Britain in 1829 or disestablishment in America) had begun to erode its political and legal supports. As the *Biblical Repertory and Princeton Review* could still declare in 1852,

---

[72] "Prospects of British Art," *BrQR* 2 (Nov. 1845), 467, 478.
[73] See Handy, *Christian America*; Linda Colley, *Britons: Forging the Nation, 1707-1837* (New Haven: Yale University Press, 1992); Tony Claydon and Ian McBride, eds., *Protestantism and National Identity: Britain and Ireland, c. 1650-c. 1850* (Cambridge: Cambridge University Press, 1998); J.C.D. Clark, "Protestantism, Nationalism, and National Identity, 1660-1832," *Historical Journal* 43 (2000): 249-76; Sarah Barber, "Antithesis: How to Create a Nation," *History, Nationhood and the Question of Britain*, ed. Helen Brocklehurst and Robert Phillips (Houndmills: Palgrave Macmillan, 2004): 171-83; Sabina Mihelj, "'Faith in nation comes in different guises': Modernist Versions of Religious Nationalism," *Nation and Nationalism* 13 (2007): 265-84; and Stephanie Kermes, *Creating an American Identity: New England, 1789-1825* (Houndmills: Palgrave Macmillan, 2008), esp. 169-95.

"The most important element of national, as of individual character, is Christianity."[74] Protestantism, of course, was but one thread in the complex fabrics of these respective nationalisms, for as Tony Claydon and Ian McBride have cautioned, "Protestantism ... always interacted with beliefs about the constitution, race, language, and relations between local and European culture."[75] Moreover, important differences between Britain and America remained. Contrasting opinions about the value of religious establishment, for example, not only implied divergent conceptions of how best to safeguard the Protestant character of the two nations but also led to slightly different notions of exactly what that character was.[76] Nevertheless, Anglo-American Protestants shared the conviction that they lived in Christian nations, and they understood this concept in similar ways.

The concept of the Christian nation embodied fundamental assumptions about the role of both Protestantism and morality in national life. As noted in chapter 3, evangelicals saw Protestantism not only as the authentic revelation of God's plan for personal salvation through Christ but also as a powerful initiator of cultural development. "[T]he progress of Christianity," wrote Otheman in 1833, "is identified with the progress of political enjoyment and prosperity...."[77] Christianity provided the necessary conditions for material, social, and intellectual progress. "There are two pillars on which a nation's strength and security rest," declared John Baker in 1856: "1. *The possession and maintenance of the true religion.* 2. *The diffusion of that religion.*"[78] At the same time, many believed that the continued relationship between Christianity and culture depended upon the work of a specially appointed intermediary: morality. As Robert Handy has observed, throughout the nineteenth century there "was virtually universal and consistent emphasis among Protestants" that morality was "the all-important link between religion and civilization."[79] Morality, the fruit of genuine Christian faith, was seen as the crux of social stability, without which nations would inevitably crumble. "Do you believe that any State, community, or nation can be powerful, tranquil, and permanently happy, if their morals are extensively depraved? Would not the most alarming depravation of morals result from a general disbelief in the Christian religion?" asked Jesse Appleton, the Congregationalist president of Bowdoin College, in an 1814 election sermon on the "True Sources

---

[74] "National Literature, the Exponent of National Character," *BRPR* 24 (Apr. 1852), 217.
[75] Tony Claydon and Ian McBride, "The Trials of the Chosen Peoples: Recent Interpretations of Protestantism and National Identity in Britain and Ireland," *Protestantism and National Identity*, 9. See also Steven Pincus, "'To protect English liberties': The English Nationalist Revolution of 1688-1689," *Protestantism and National Identity*, 93.
[76] See John Wolffe, "A Transatlantic Perspective: Protestantism and National Identities in Mid-Nineteenth-Century Britain and the United States," *Protestantism and National Identity*, 304.
[77] [Edward Otheman], "Consecrated Talent," *ABM* 13 (Oct. 1833), 6.
[78] Rev. John Baker, "Causes of the Decline and Fall of Nations," *WMM* 2 (Dec. 1856), 1082.
[79] Handy, *Christian America*, 32. See also Kermes, *Creating an American Identity*, 195.

of National Prosperity". For evangelicals like Appleton, Christianity was to serve as the "guardian of morals," and morality was to serve in turn as the guardian of society.[80]

In a basic sense, the idea that morality aids national interests was understood simply in terms of the minimal ethical conditions requisite for the smooth functioning of human communities. One cannot expect to conduct business or live at peace where dishonesty and selfishness are the norm. In another sense, however, evangelicals believed that national stability was *spiritually* contingent upon a strict adherence to Judeo-Christian ethical principles. Like the Puritans, evangelicals viewed modern nations as existing in a convenant relationship with God modeled on Old Testament Israel.[81] If a nation does not respect God's laws, it will face God's judgment. As George Cubitt stated it in 1831: "The favour and blessing of God can only be secured by national righteousness; while their forfeiture is the appointed penalty of obstinate national transgression."[82] More than fifty years later, H.C. Westwood could still attribute the national successes of Britain and America to Protestantism and morality: "These nations have reached their present important place in civilization and in virtue because they have fostered the religion of Jesus Christ, whose transcendent moral power is daily shown in the national life and government."[83] The maintenance of faith and morals was thus a matter of national security, not to mention national prosperity and progress.

In this context, the theory of art's moral influence must have seemed a welcome ally to many evangelicals, not least because it offered a means of moral improvement that purportedly circumvented the difficulties of political agitation and intellectual debate. Art's power was non-sectarian and non-partisan. Indeed, the real endgame of the occult pathos theory was not the improvement of individual morals (important though this was) but of collective ones. This national impulse had in fact been present early on, occupying a prominent place, for instance, in Kames's *Elements*. "The Fine Arts," he argued in his preface "To the King," "have ever been encouraged by wise Princes, not singly for private amusement, but for their beneficial influence in society… (1:3). Nineteenth-century evangelicals readily echoed Kames's sentiments. Already in 1812, Samuel Stanhope Smith, president of the College of New Jersey and a strong supporter

---

[80] Qtd. in Handy, *Christian America*, 32. For a relatively late expression of this idea, see Frank E. Sickels, "Tent Evangelist—A Review," *NYE* 72 (17 Oct. 1901), 5.

[81] Though often associated with (American) Puritanism, this idea had existed in Britain since the fourteenth century. See Clark, "Protestantism," 270.

[82] George Cubitt, "National Prosperity Dependent on the Divine Blessing: A Sermon," *WMM* 10 (Aug. 1831), 525. See also Peter Peckard, "National Crimes the Cause of National Punishments: A Discourse, Delivered in the Cathedral Church of Peterborough, on the Fast-Day, February 25th, 1795," *WMM* 7 (Aug. 1861), 687-95.

[83] H.C. Westwood, "Art as a Moral Reformer," *CA* 60 (9 July 1885), 438. Westwood actually casts doubt on art's capacity for moral influence, although he remains committed to the interconnectedness of Protestantism, morality, and civilization.

of Scottish philosophy, had encouraged the cultivation of art for national reasons: "As the studies and pursuits of men have an influence on that character of soul which is transfused on the countenance by the habits of life, it is not unimportant to observe that the national physiognomy of any people may be greatly improved by the cultivation of the arts...."[84] By the 1840s, this idea had taken firm hold of the evangelical imagination. As Henry N. Day declared, "The æsthetic element of our nature, that element which finds its employment and its gratification in the forms of things, as distinguished from their essences, is working in society now, with a force and prevalence that are giving character to the age, and are moulding the destiny of coming generations." Whether this aesthetic element would ultimately be a force for good or evil would depend on the concerted efforts of "the wise and good," but Day could not deny that the fate of the nation paralleled that of aesthetics.[85] In 1880, the *British Quarterly Review* urged that "there must be some attempt to carry artistic beauty ... into our homes, and knead its impressions into our daily life": "By communing with the loftier types of excellence, nations as well as individuals are stimulated to constant efforts in the paths of social as well as moral regeneration."[86] Renewal might come about one person at a time, but national improvement remained the final objective.

When singling out national vices that art was specially suited to combat, evangelicals sounded much like their non-evangelical contemporaries. Materialism, utilitarianism, commercialism, sensuality, and worldliness—ideas Arnold associated with "Philistinism"—topped the list. Day, for example, catalogued what he called the "grosser tendencies and characteristics" of the age: "... the prevalent disposition to subordinate the inward and spiritual to the outward and sensual; the enduring and changeless, to the immediate and transient; fixed rational principles living deep in the soul, to superficial impulsive and therefore vapid, spiritless feeling; [and] a subordination of spirit to sense...."[87] Critics commonly depicted art as locked in a life-and-death struggle with these social vices for the hearts of the people. On the one hand, such tendencies heralded the swift decline of the nation and even art itself. Drummond lamented what he saw as the English habit of judging all things by the standard of wealth, leading him to conclude that "For the most part the English in these days seem totally incapable of estimating or of understanding the highest branches of the fine arts."[88] In 1854, the *Christian Advocate and Journal* employed Ruskin as a mouthpiece for the condemnation of America's utilitarian spirit. In a passage from volume two of his *Modern Painters* (reprinted in the *Advocate*), Ruskin had described how "people speak,

---

[84] Samuel Stanhope Smith, *The Lectures, Corrected and Improved, which Have Been Delivered for a Series of Years, in the College of New Jersey; On the Subjects of Moral and Political Philosophy* (New York: Whiting and Watson, 1812), 1:202-203. See also pp. 207ff.
[85] Day, "Taste and Morals," 524.
[86] "Practical Aesthetics," *BrQR* 71 (Jan. 1880), 49, 55.
[87] Day, "Taste and Morals," 527.
[88] Drummond, *Letter to Thomas Phillips*, 29.

in this working age ... as if houses, and lands, and food, and raiment, were alone useful, and as if sight, and thought, and admiration, were all profitless; so that men insolently call themselves utilitarians, who would turn if they had their way, themselves and their race into vegetables...."[89] Taking stock of Tennyson's poetry in 1889, Eugene Parsons similarly noted that "The period to which Tennyson belongs is not an age calculated to foster in a high degree poetic greatness." The poet's accomplishments were thus all the more remarkable in an era given over to commercial, technological, and material interests.[90]

On the other hand, critics also viewed art as an antidote to these woes. The nineteenth century may have been too commercial for Parsons, but he could still find comfort in the "growing appreciation for the beautiful in our age."[91] Art offered possibilities for social renewal precisely because of its appeal to the emotional, intellectual, and moral (or what was increasingly described by the catch-all "spiritual") dimensions of existence over and against the crudely material. "It is a great thing in the nineteenth century," wrote Adeline E.H. Slicer in 1876, "to be able to love a picture—to be so unworldly as to speak of a work of art with tears in the eyes. In this practical age to bow reverently to a *sentiment* is part of the old world culture."[92] Slicer's general criticism of "this practical age" could sometimes find more pointed expression in critics' concerns over the perceived character flaws of individual nations, as when George Lansing Taylor, writing early in the Gilded Age, suggested that Americans "are one of the most thoroughly realistic and materialistic peoples of all history." Americans must understand, however, "that civilization is not wholly material and mechanical." What they needed most was a vibrant art culture: "There is nothing which the intellectual life of America so needs, and begins to feel its need of, as an aesthetic inspiration. Nothing else of human origin can so smooth out the hard lines of our national character, and refine our national thought."[93] Yet despite these occasional expressions of aesthetic and national exceptionalism, the belief that art delivers an effective counterpoint to national vices spanned the Atlantic.[94] The Protestant ideology had discovered a new partner in the arts.

---

[89] John Ruskin, "The Useful and the Beautiful," *CAJ* 29 (22 June 1854), 97.

[90] Eugene Parsons, "Tennyson's Art and Genius," *BQR* 11 (Jan. 1889), 43.

[91] Parsons, "Tennyson's Art," 46.

[92] Adeline E.H. Slicer, "The Art Student Abroad—Second Paper," *CA* 51 (12 Oct. 1876), 321.

[93] George Lansing Taylor, "Fine Art: Its Nature, Necessity, and Offices," *MQR* 34 (1874), 241.

[94] On the unique cultural environments and/or art worlds of America and Britain, see "Montgomery's *Lectures on Poetry*," *ER* 10 (July 1833), 2; "The Evils of an Unsanctified Literature," *BRPR* 15 (Jan. 1843), 68ff.; D., Review of *Poems*, 358-64; "Domestic Literature," *SPR* 1 (July 1851), 1-3; "American Art," *CAJ* 38 (23 July 1863), 235; F.K. Levan, "National Literature," *MerR* (Oct. 1867), 578; Forman, "Music and Poetry, 15; "How the Fine Arts of Europe are Being Perfected in the New World," *CA* 48 (17 Apr. 1873), 127; and H.M. Du Bose, "Authority in Art and Religion," *MR*[S] 42 (1895), 213.

Evangelicals were thus active participants in the development of modern conceptions of "art" and "culture" as a response to the demands of industrialized life.[95] As an emotional and intellectual pursuit, art provided a curative to the afflictions of a Utilitarian Age. As one writer stated in an essay on "The Ministry of Art": "Any influence, whether in art or life, that leads men away from the merely material, from the mere facts of existence, should be commended."[96] It is important not to overlook the sweeping nature of this claim. The threat of materialism loomed so large that *any* non-material influence would suffice to counter its ills. Christianity had long denounced materialism and sensuality, in principle if not always in practice, but after the 1820s and 1830s evangelicals increasingly regarded art as another influence capable of routing such evils. Although the Puritans had entertained the notion that the intellectual pursuit of an art like poetry could assist one in keeping fleshly desires at bay, art had often represented the worldly, sensual, and material. The romantics, however, had succeeded in shifting the balance of the material and intellectual in art. Art expressed the infinite in the finite, the eternal in the temporal, and as such it had become the solution to the very problems represented by its former self. In fact, the evangelical acceptance of the paradox that the pitfalls of sensuality and materialism can be transcended by sensuous and material art forms is a crucial development in the history of evangelical aesthetics. "[W]e are to bear in mind," wrote Day,

> that the moral influence of æsthetic culture reaches men in their own sphere of sense. Imprisoned, as he is, in the flesh, it visits him in his prison, and with a gentle hand unrivets his fetters. It takes the wise in their own craftiness, and with the weapons of sense destroys the dominion of sense. The elevation and purification of men, instrumentally through their aesthetic culture, is thus a process fitted to their condition; adapted to reach the soul without awakening its prejudices or its apprehensions; inviting and attracting in its outward character, and drawing under its influence, and effecting its work before the subject is hardly aware of its design.

Day was still theologically conservative enough to temper his faith in aesthetic culture with the insistence that "the only effectual cure" for a "depraved heart" is "the gospel,"[97] but the incarnational and salvific language in this passage indicates that the evangelical romantic spiritualization of art was well underway. It was in part the desire to drive out materialism, sensuality, and commercialism that led to the gradual fusion of art and religion among many liberals.[98]

For evangelicals, art's influence acted as a "mighty engine ... for the elevation of the nation." But art, these same critics believed, was also a product of that

---

[95] See Raymond Williams, *Culture and Society, 1780-1950* (Harmondsworth: Penguin Books, 1971) and Lawrence W. Levine, *Highbrow/Lowbrow: The Emergence of Cultural Hierarchy in America* (Cambridge: Harvard University Press, 1988).
[96] D. Dorchester, "The Ministry of Art," *MR* 60 (Nov. 1900), 884.
[97] Day, "Taste and Morals," 543-44, 533.
[98] See, for example, Joseph LeConte, "On the Nature and Uses of Art," *SPR* 15 (Jan. 1863), 322.

society. It was, as the *Eclectic Review* explained in 1855, both "the means of mental advancement" and "the measure," both "the agent of civilization" and its "product."[99] Art objects, suggested Taylor, "are ... expressions of the state of life and grade of development enjoyed by their creators. Hence comes *the power of fine art as an expression and record of civilization*.... The art-life of a people records and perpetuates their most secret thoughts, their sublimest aspirations."[100] As Taylor's diction reveals, this idea was simply romantic expressivism extrapolated to the national level—an extrapolation made possible by the added assumption that nations behave fundamentally like individuals. Nations, like people, possess unique characters. "To pass from the proposition that the writings of an individual indicate his individual character, to the position that the literature of a nation is the exponent of the nation's character," explained the *Biblical Repertory and Princeton Review*, "is only to pass from a lower and more limited generalization to one higher and larger.... The literature of a nation is the purest expression of the nation's life."[101]

The claim that art and literature express national life has roots in both Enlightenment and romantic thought, but it was A.W. Pugin, William Morris, and above all John Ruskin who helped to popularize this idea among Victorians.[102] In general, this proposition could be interpreted to mean that, as the handiwork of a specific people group residing in a given region and climate, speaking a particular language, and governing itself by distinctive laws, art somehow embodies the unique identity formed by these conditions: "The literature of a particular period is the reflex of the agencies at work. It is the general *resultant* of the forces, operating on the nation's mind at the time."[103] As Ruskin argued, however, art also epitomizes the *moral* disposition of a nation: "The art of any country *is the exponent of its social and political virtues*. The art, or general productive and formative energy, of any country, is an exact exponent of its ethical life. You can have noble art only from noble persons, associated under laws fitted to their time and circumstances."[104] Evangelicals were familiar with Ruskin's theories, and these critics often spoke in markedly Ruskinian terms when considering art's relationship to the nation. Yet Ruskin's theories were as much the symptom of a larger intellectual trend as a cause. This idea had already appeared (albeit with reference to the rather loose category of "literature") in the pages of some evangelical periodicals in the 1820s. "The literary character of a people is their character as rational and reflective beings," suggested the *Christian Spectator* in

---

[99] "Art: Its Aspirations and Prospects," *ER* 9 (Feb. 1855), 144.
[100] Taylor, "Fine Art: Its Nature," 233; italics in original.
[101] "National Literature," 205, 206.
[102] See Williams, *Culture and Society*, 137-61.
[103] "National Literature," 209.
[104] John Ruskin, *Lectures on Art and Aratra Pentelici, with Lectures and Notes on Greek Art and Mythology*, ed. E.T. Cook and Alexander Wedderburn (London: George Allen, 1905), 74.

1825.[105] The *Christian Observer* echoed this sentiment four years later: "the character of a nation will always be found strictly analogous to the character of its popular floating literature...."[106] Art and literature were the natural outgrowths of a nation's, not simply an individual artist's, moral ethos.

A major consequence of this idea was that art could serve, theoretically, as a reliable index to a nation's moral well-being. "The advance of civilization is marked by the improvement of taste ...," observed the *Baptist Quarterly* in 1881. "As mind improves, the love of the beautiful increases."[107] By extension, a decline in love for the beautiful would suggest a civilization in disrepair. "There is no surer index of the moral health of any society," contended C.T. Winchester the following year, "than the imaginative literature it craves and produces."[108] J.S. White, drawing on Ruskin, likewise concluded that "art is the principal key to the history of nations, to their prevailing characteristics, to their sentiments and beliefs, to their mental and moral conditions generally."[109] One will "find their art forever indicating their mental and moral, and even their social and political, tendencies as clearly and positively as do their science, their laws, and their letters."[110] Consequently, a nation's art furnished a measuring-stick for the state of a nation's morality and its progress generally: "The character of the national literature ...," the *Biblical Repertory and Princeton Review* charged, "must of necessity vary, at the different periods of the nation's progress or decline.... Thus the actual progress of a people may be inferred from the species of literature which it has produced, as well as from the success with which it has been cultivated."[111] A thriving art world suggested a vigorous moral life, which in turn suggested the continuation of God's blessing on the nation; a diseased art, on the other hand, betokened a Christian nation in decline.

Evangelicals thus envisioned a kind of repeating religious-moral-aesthetic circuit at work during the healthy periods of a nation when people were firmly committed to both Protestantism and Judeo-Christian morality. A society suffused with faith and morality would beget art that expressed the Protestant character of its people. In return, this art would invigorate the morality of the people, thereby helping to reinforce the social stability of the Christian nation. "The art of every country," asserted the *Eclectic Review* in 1848, "in all its developments, in painting as in poetry, should be the expression of national character, should take its form from the soil whence it springs, should reflect and develop the feelings of

---

[105] L.L., "On the Proper Influence of Christianity over Literature," *CS* 7 (1 Apr. 1825), 186.
[106] "The Obligations of Genius," *CO* 29 (Aug. 1829), 488.
[107] William Carey Crane, "Commerce and Literature," *BR* 3 (Apr. 1881), 176.
[108] Winchester, "Good Poetry and Good Morals," 147.
[109] J.S. White, "Religion and Art," *PMQRCAmb* n.s. 9 (Jan. 1887), 129.
[110] F.M. Bristol, "Reciprocity of Art and Religion," *MR* 54 (1894), 697-98.
[111] "National Literature," 209.

its own time, in order to lead and advance them."[112] F.K. Levan, discussing "National Literature" in 1867, saw this "apparent paradox" clearly in the history of Greek literature and civilization: "Though an apparent paradox it is notwithstanding true, that as Hellenic civilization produced the literature we have been sketching, so this literature produced Hellenic civilization." Yet this paradox was no less true for modern nations like Germany, Britain, and the United States—nations "united ... in closer bonds" than were ancient nations by "[t]he spread of civilization and Christianity." The literature of modern nations, Germany and Britain especially, had "not only kept pace with their growth, but ha[d] also been a main cause of it."[113] It is true, argued Noah Porter in 1873, that "The character and influence of a literature" depend in part on "the community whose opinions and culture it reflects." It is also true, however, that "great writers do much more than reflect an age. They reach upon it and mold it by their individual influence and energy, as they instruct and elevate it, or delude or debase it."[114] Art, evangelicals believed, was both produced by and a producer of the morality and mind of the Christian nation.

For many evangelicals, then, art was a conservative social force. By exercising the moral feelings and sympathies of individual members of society, it helped maintain social intercourse and harmony. This stability signified divine favor and the hope of future blessings. Furthermore, since art expressed national character, its development and the development of an accompanying aesthetic discourse helped shape and perpetuate this identity. In another sense, however, art also acted as a progressive force in that it symbolized the triumph of Anglo-American civilization. Before the 1860s, critics tended to view this progress in postmillennial terms; but even after the 1860s the narrative of postmillennial progress persisted among some conservatives and, in an increasingly secularized sense, among most liberals.[115] Art was therefore conservative and progressive at the same time, for paradoxically the idea of progress was often rooted in a type of conservatism. True progress depended on a basic social stability. Yet the occult pathos theory also relied on an ethical system potentially at odds with traditional doctrine. Although for much of the century ethico-aesthetic sympathy worked in tandem with the Puritan concept of the covenant nation, it also offered the possibility of re-establishing the bonds of society on secular grounds.

Defending the Moral Influence Theory amid Growing Doubts

Evangelical support for the theory of art's moral influence and its role in the health of Christian nations continued in some quarters into the early twentieth century. Beginning in the late 1870s and early 1880s, however, the Protestant ideology faced new challenges that threatened to sever the bonds of art, morality,

---

[112] "English Schools of Art," 72-73.
[113] Levan, "National Literature," 571, 575, 577.
[114] Noah Porter, "Modern Literature and Christianity," *CA* (30 Oct. 1873), 346.
[115] See Morgan, *Protestants and Pictures*, 10.

and society. The first of these was the rise of aestheticism, which became fashionable in the 1880s thanks to persuasive devotees like Walter Pater, James Abbott McNeill Whistler, and Oscar Wilde. The dictum "art for art's sake" claimed for the aesthetic a radical autonomy—"An ethical sympathy in an artist is an unpardonable mannerism of style," mused Wilde in his famous preface to *The Picture of Dorian Gray* (1891)[116]—and in doing so it targeted the very heart of the Protestant ideology that had presided over evangelicals' rising aesthetic interests. Not surprisingly, both conservatives and the growing number of liberals at century's end reacted negatively to aestheticism. A second challenge came from within evangelicalism itself. This challenge was the dawning awareness among some that despite more than a century's worth of theoretical support for art's role as a moral reformer, neither art nor society appeared to have much to show for it. Some critics began asking for tangible evidence of art's socio-moral influence and increasingly found it wanting. Together, these two challenges, though radically different in origin and aim, called into question art's status as an instrument of improvement. Those evangelicals who held to their convictions concerning the moral benefits of aesthetic appreciation struggled to shore up the theory that had prevailed for much of the nineteenth century, but whether due to the alleged purity of art or to rising anxieties about its performance on behalf of morality, art was progressively in danger of becoming, as Wilde liked to say, "quite useless."[117]

Aestheticism was a bit like the rebellious child of the late-Victorian art world, for it was in many ways the offspring of the critical establishment it meant to subvert. Pressing concepts from the Enlightenment and romantic aesthetic traditions (e.g., Kant's disinterestedness, Shelley's poet who "sings to cheer [his] own solitude"[118]) to their extremes, aestheticism preached the ideal of "pure art" and the absolute freedom of artists. Evangelical critics had themselves inadvertently assisted in laying the groundwork for the popular aestheticism of the 1880s and 1890s. Their willingness, for example, to join Edgar Allan Poe in upbraiding what he called "the heresy of *The Didactic*" paved the way for the aestheticist notion of art's amorality.[119] In addition, evangelical support for the anti-commercialist potential of art, which had initially invested art with its prophetic moral power, ironically contributed to the eventual withdrawal of art from any meaningful contact with the ordinary, workaday world. At least one evangelical critic seemed to grasp this odd twist of fate:

---

[116] Oscar Wilde, Preface, *The Picture of Dorian Gray*, *Oscar Wilde: Collected Works* (New York: Barnes & Noble, 2006), 3.
[117] Wilde, Preface, 4.
[118] See Immanuel Kant, *Critique of Judgment* (Indianapolis: Hackett, 1987), 44-53 (1.1.1-5); Shelley, *Defense*, 486.
[119] Edgar Allan Poe, "The Poetic Principle," *Essays English and American*, ed. Charles W. Eliot (New York: P.F. Collier, 1968), 375.

> We hear a great deal in these days about "art for art's sake".... Doubtless the phrase was first used as a protest against the degradation of art from the position of the beautiful mistress of genius to that of the slave of greed; but in the latter half of the nineteenth century "art for art's sake" is used as a protest against the pure motive [i.e., morality] without which art is not art, but only the ghastly simulacrum of a living thing from which the vital principle has fled.[120]

For this critic, aestheticism was not so much a wrong impulse as an impulse which, in the course of aesthetic history, had gone wrong. He held firmly to the romantic conviction that art transcends base materialism, and insofar as the idea of a pure art may act as a corrective to more mercenary conceptions (e.g., those associated with the sort of "kitsch" turned out solely for profit), it may have originally served a useful purpose. But this passage underscores the irony of late-nineteenth-century evangelical repudiations of aestheticism: evangelicals were battling a monster they had helped to create.

For the most part, evangelicals' complicity in the rise of aestheticism was indirect—an unintended consequence of their investment in romantic aesthetics. Even so, aestheticist sentiments, or something like them, were not altogether alien even to the pages of evangelical periodicals. As early as 1845, an author reviewing Leigh Hunt's *Imagination and Fancy* found himself grappling with the logic of decadence popularized later in the century. In particular, he wrestled with two related questions concerning the link between art and morality that were to become talking-points for fin-de-siècle aesthetes. The first question, which can itself be subdivided into two parts, was how, if at all, an artist's personal morality relates to the creative process and how this process relates in turn to an artist's obligations to society. This question arose necessarily as a corollary to Hunt's expressivist definition of poetry as "'the utterance of a passion,'" to which the reviewer heartily subscribed. According to Hunt, *passio* may be defined as "'suffering in a good sense,'" or the "'ardent subjection of oneself to emotion.'" From this it follows that for poets to express genuine emotion in their poetry, they must first experience things deeply. The difficulty, of course, is that there exist a great many morally dubious experiences. In a series of rhetorical questions, the reviewer wryly parodied the decadent reasoning that sought to rationalize illicit pursuits in the interests of almighty art:

> How far is the poet entitled to claim exemption from the ordinary rules of citizenship and decorum? If a man frequents profligate society, and you take him to task for doing so, and he answers, 'O, I am a poet, and I wish to understand this particular phase of human nature,' ought you to answer, 'That quite alters the case, sir; I did not know you were a poet?' If a man in your presence takes up his hat, and is for going out into a forest during a thunderstorm at night, telling you that he is a poet

---

[120] Spes, "Art and Morals," *WMM* 119 (May 1896), 338.

wishing to embrace the opportunity of understanding a thunderstorm, are you to sit still, and let the idiot go?

The reviewer did not deny that personal experience could provide a powerful incentive to poetry: "It is questionable if passages written from poetical intuition [i.e., from imagining situations not rooted in direct experience] can ever affect the heart so deeply as those written from personal experience."[121] Clearly, though, "experience" was no license for immoral or anti-social behavior on the part of artists.

Yet this critic's answer to the first question concerning art's relationship to morality renders his answer to a second question all the more interesting. This second question was whether art has any obligation to act as a moral instrument within society. Later aesthetes like Wilde thought not, and somewhat surprisingly, this reviewer agreed. Unlike "most authors," whose business it is "to produce the maximum of good effect upon society" (a responsibility demanding engagement with the day's controversies), artists are beholden to an ideal that transcends the vicissitudes of the moment. "Art does not vary, like opinion," claimed the reviewer, "nor can a poem ever be superseded, like a system of philosophy. Hence the poet ought to take delight in perfecting his productions for their own sake, without condescending to think of them as instruments for producing social effect."[122] Art's value lies in itself and to imagine otherwise would require artists to descend from their exalted state to mingle with the masses. Although this critic refused to suspend the moral code for individual artists, he quite willingly allowed that art has no immediate obligation to serve the ethical interests of society.[123]

Such aestheticist, or quasi-aestheticist, positions, however, constituted a minority tradition within evangelical aesthetics. The typical reaction to late-Victorian aestheticism was horror and disdain, and evangelicals were quick to sound the alarm. Already in 1878, J.C. Shairp observed that "The great poet, we are sometimes nowadays told, must be free from all moral prepossessions," a position he subsequently countered at some length.[124] By 1883, W.J. Dawson was reminding readers "how often of late years we have heard high critical authorities insisting that art must be loved for art's sake, and that our common notions of morality are wholly opposed to art."[125] Other critics turned to more vivid language to describe the fast-growing phenomenon, employing the rhetoric of mental pathology or contagion to characterize aestheticism's spread. "The word 'aestheticism' is one of the most prominent words of the hour," wrote T.W. Hunt in 1882. "The American nation, practical as it is, is for the time partially *bewitched*,

---

[121] "Leigh Hunt's *Imagination and Fancy*," *BrQR* 1 (May 1845), 571, 572, 575.
[122] "Leigh Hunt's *Imagination and Fancy*," 579.
[123] For a later example of praise for an aestheticist position, see "English Sacred Song," *BM* 82 (Jan. 1890), 10.
[124] J.C. Shairp, "The Aim of Poetry," *PR* (July-Dec. 1878), 467.
[125] W.J. Dawson, "Religious Doubt in Modern Poetry," *WMM* (Aug. 1883), 607.

and the *craze* must have its natural course."[126] Edwin Mims noted in the mid-90s how trendy, and thus how dangerous, *l'art pour l'art* had become: "The expression, 'Art for art's sake,' has become a proverbial one in our day...." If this doctrine confined itself to "the circles of dilettante artists who gather in the various Bohemian resorts, the evil might not be so far-reaching; but through magazines and books and papers the idea has spread...."[127] Evangelicals were united in their conviction that the aestheticism which had rapidly infected Anglo-American culture was in dire need of purging.

Critics attacked the notion of art's autonomy on several fronts. One line of argument, taking its cues from anti-fiction discourse, denounced aestheticism as a form of "sentimentalism." What for Hunt epitomized "the school of Wilde" was a total "absence of the intellectual element." The sentimentalism of Wilde's school was a perversion of certain tendencies within the romantic tradition which, if properly controlled, were good in their place, but if uncontrolled led simply to nonsense. Thus romanticism had stressed the "emotive element" in the creative process, but what Hunt wanted was a renewed attention to intellect and truth:

> It is true that the poetic art has to do largely with the imagination and the feelings, but these are the media only through which the thought of the poet expresses itself; and tho [sic] pleasure is said to be its final end, it is that kind of pleasure which arises from the reception of the truth in attractive forms. In all genuine poetry, as in the more substantial form of prose, truth is the subject matter, the love of the truth is the inspiring principle, and its expression to the world for the worthiest ends its final purpose.[128]

Hunt was by no means proposing a didactic conception of art in which "intellect" and "truth" are synonymous with propositional content and art is judged by its ability to deliver this content successfully; nor was he rejecting the whole of the romantic tradition. He was, as other sections of his article reveal, a dedicated idealist whose aesthetic heroes were Plato and Cousin. Too great an emphasis on the emotive aspect of poetry, however, leads to the idea of poetry's near-total irrelevance except as an occasion for raw pleasure. Mims articulated this same logic in his own critique of aestheticism: "It may be said that the popular conception of poetry [i.e., the aestheticist conception] is that it is characterized by a 'poetic prettiness,' nicety of phrase, jingle, sentimentality—a pretty good thing 'to while away the tedium of a railway journey or to amuse a period of rest or convalescence'; it is 'mere byplay.'"[129] Just as some evangelicals condemned the

---

[126] Theodore W. Hunt, "Modern Aestheticism," *PR* 9 (1882), 148; italics mine.

[127] Edwin Mims, "Poetry and the Spiritual Life," *MR*[S] 44 (1896-7), 389, 389-90. See also Winchester, "Good Poetry and Good Morals," 147; Van Dyke, Jr., "Art and Ethics," 91-110; and White, "Religion and Art," 32.

[128] Hunt, "Modern Aestheticism," 154.

[129] Mims, "Poetry and the Spiritual Life," 390.

novel for the inaction to which it supposedly gave way, so critics of aestheticism rejected it for its lack of practical application.

As Hunt's article suggests, however, sentimentalism also signaled psychological excess: it was an indulgence of the emotional side of the human personality to the exclusion of others. Aestheticism seemed bent on making a virtue of the kind of psychic one-dimensionality that the time-tested whole-person argument had earlier helped evangelicals overcome. It is not surprising, therefore, to find Shairp recommending the psychological wholeness of Shakespeare as a counteractant to the splintering effects of aestheticism: "Shakespeare ... being a *whole natural man,* 'the moral, imaginative, and intellectual parts of him did not lie separate,' but move at once and all together. Being wholly unembarrassed with aesthetic theories, 'his poetical impulse and his moral feelings were one.'"[130] Ironically, the argument which had once enabled evangelicals to reexamine the moral exclusivity of the Puritans, thus making room for a loftier vision of art, was now forced to defend morality against the aesthetic exclusivity of Wilde and his followers.

Ultimately, though, the risk of fragmentation extended beyond individual psyches; the bigger problem with aestheticism was the menace it posed to social stability. In tugging at one thread of the Protestant ideology—the link between art and morality—aestheticism threatened to unravel the entire social fabric. "[H]ere is the point at which the great danger of modern æstheticism lies," wrote Hunt. "Pitiable as is its want of mental stamina, this is incidental in comparison with the untold harm that may accrue to the rising authors of a nation and to the people at large."[131] The *Christian Advocate* concurred: "Aestheticism is part of the great wave of sentimentality which has swept over the country of late years; and not whether a thing is best, most useful, most profitable to the race at large, but whether it is prettiest to look at according to the present taste, is the central canon of the aesthete's religion."[132] For Mims, too, the great poets throughout history had always had "the self-consciousness of prophets, and to them their mission was apostolic": "When we read the truly great poets we feel that poetry is no longer a mere plaything, it is not a self-indulgence; it is a challenge to man's higher spirit; it is the expression of life, and it speaks to life. Poetry has no excuse for being unless it does contribute to the life of man."[133] J. Hunt Cooke combined his condemnation of aestheticist claims and his concern for society's future with a reassertion of art's power as an agent of both positive and negative moral influence: "Considering the great and subtle influences of art, the assertion to artists that it has nothing to do with morality ought to be severely reprehended. The painter of an impure picture may influence an untold number of our young people

---

[130] Shairp, "The Aim of Poetry," 468.
[131] Hunt, "Modern Aestheticism," 158.
[132] "The True Notion of the Picturesque," *CA* 58 (15 Nov. 1883), 726.
[133] Mims, "Poetry and the Spiritual Life," 390, 391.

for evil. The painter of a wholly good picture opens a fountain of blessing, perhaps for generations to come. We need to have Art baptized into Christianity."[134] In praising the essential uselessness of art, Wilde the provocateur knew quite well what he was attacking, just as members of the evangelical critical establishment knew quite well that they were under attack.

From the late eighteenth century, evangelicals had fought to justify art largely on the basis of its socio-moral relevance, just as they had struggled against the puritanical elements within their tradition. Many thus reacted fiercely to an aestheticism that imperiled the delicate balance they had worked to achieve. This reaction, moreover, bridged the conservative-liberal divide that had begun to open up among late-Victorian evangelicals. Liberals were as outspoken in defense of art's connection to morality as conservatives—perhaps more so. Liberal Protestants had increasingly begun to see religion in terms of morality and culture-building rather than traditional doctrine. With these developments came the gradual abandonment of the historic understanding of the supernatural, further contributing to an increased emphasis on this-worldly affairs.[135] Morality and "civilization" became the centerpieces of the liberal agenda, and liberals were not about to surrender the moral assistance that a long aesthetic tradition had convinced them art could provide. One of the stiffest critiques of aestheticism, in fact, came from Washington Gladden, the father of the Social Gospel. Describing the conflict that inevitably arises between art and morality in advanced civilizations, Gladden concluded:

> All men can then perceive that these two are rival kingdoms, and that each makes exclusive claims; that no man can make the one supreme without rejecting the supremacy of the other. To be a Christian disciple, it is not necessary that one should abjure the pleasures of a refined taste, but it is necessary that he should make these pleasures subordinate and tributary to the service of God and men. The love of beauty is not denied to the Christian, but the love of righteousness and of humanity is with him the master passion.

Such a statement would have resonated with evangelicals of all kinds, conservatives as well as liberals (not to mention a broad swath of the Victorian population). Yet Gladden's "Christianity" began and ended with a hearty dose of liberal morality, as his article made clear:

> It is true that the supremacy of the ethical has not always been well understood by the professors of Christianity; its ritual and dogmatic elements have sometimes been unduly exalted, but the fact is there in the documents, and it has not been possible for the most perverse interpretation wholly to conceal it. At the end of nineteen

---

[134] J. Hunt Cooke, "London Letter," *W* 76 (22 Aug. 1895), 8.
[135] See George Marsden, *Fundamentalism and American Culture* (Oxford: Oxford University Press, 2006), 24, 85; Handy, *Christian America*, 95-100; Joseph Haroutunian, *Piety Versus Moralism: The Passing of the New England Theology* (New York: Henry Holt, 1932).

Christian centuries we find this truth generally recognized among Christians, that the end of religion is right character; that no philosophy of Christianity will stand that does not make character the supreme thing.[136]

If character is "the supreme thing," then liberals like Gladden could not afford to allow aestheticism to trample it down.

Evangelicals, of course, were not lone warriors in their campaign against the fashionable aestheticism of the fin de siècle. Diverse figures from Tennyson and Ruskin to Gilbert and Sullivan condemned what was rightly perceived as an assault on Victorian norms. Mainstream Victorians, evangelical and otherwise, sensed the danger in Wilde's new-fangled apologia for art. Thus the evangelical denunciation of aestheticism participated in what may be seen as the Victorian critical establishment's last concerted effort to defend its vision of art's social obligations. By the same token, the evangelical backlash against the notion of pure art confirms not only evangelicals' status as card-carrying members of this establishment but also its role as longtime servant to the Protestant ideology. This ideology would never wholly die out in certain circles, but aestheticism's increasing vogue in the late nineteenth century bore witness to the fact that this ideology was beginning to exhaust itself.

Another sign of this exhaustion came from a small band of critics who began asking tough questions about art's real-world performance as a source of moral influence. Interestingly, this fresh approach to the conventional wisdom also emerged in the 1880s. "What is the true way to determine the influence of art upon morals?" asked Dr. Buckley in 1885. Buckley, who had traveled through Europe searching for an answer, looked to Germany as a test case: "In Germany, music, painting, sculpture, architecture, the ornamentation of parks and gardens, and the drama, reach an unsurpassed modern development, and there moral and social conditions must throw light upon the relation of art to morals." Unfortunately, however, "It is here that perplexing questions spring up." According to Buckley, late-nineteenth-century Germany was enslaved to sensuality. He cited the prevalent public display of the "Nude in Art," which he linked to all sorts of debauchery, including "unchastity" leading to a high percentage of out-of-wedlock births, the poor treatment of women, and a general "licentiousness." In Germany, "Art and amusements are, practically, substitutes for religion to a large extent"—so much so that any preacher who speaks out against this is like "the voice of one crying in the wilderness." In the end, Buckley disavowed art's capacity to exert a meaningful moral influence in society:

> The conclusions compelled by these facts are that art cannot be relied on as a moral force. It does not instruct the conscience nor strengthen its foundations. It educates, refines, it may raise a people from barbarism, but it cannot be depended on to prevent or diminish immorality. The extremes of refinement and coarseness may exist

---

[136] Washington Gladden, "Christianity and Aestheticism," *AR* 1 (Jan. 1884), 23, 14.

in the same person or the same nation. When the mind is drawn toward the contemplation of art it is elevated; but when it is turned toward the gratification of passion it may and will yield unless the conscience, instructed and sanctioned by religion, restrains it.

Although Buckley granted that art may exercise some positive influence in particular cases (taste may raise one above the "barbaric"), his article represented a flat reappraisal of nearly a half-century of evangelical thinking about the morality of art. Art was virtually stripped of its paradoxical power to transcend sensuality, and it became instead a major source of this sensuality. Concomitantly, the pervasive art-worship he perceived all around him served only to "weaken the springs of morality."[137]

For better or worse, art was for some evangelicals no longer a dependable ally in the quest to nourish morality and through this to ensure the security and progress of Christian nations. This change coincided with a period of growing detachment from socio-political concerns among conservative evangelicals—a development that eventually led to what has been called the "Great Reversal" of the early twentieth century, in which fundamentalists abandoned social concerns almost completely.[138] Others would continue to promote the socio-moral "mission" of art, but these others were increasingly to be found within the liberal wing of evangelicalism.[139] Between the 1820s and the 1880s, however, the theory of art's moral influence was the province of a wide range of evangelicals, all of whom would have earnestly endorsed the aesthetic creed of W.J. Dawson: "The world asks that its poets shall be prophets; that its singers shall be believers; that their inspiration shall be drawn from above, else it were better that their gift died with them, and their song were never sung."[140]

---

[137] Dr. Buckley, "Art and Morals in Art Centers," *CA* 60 (12 Mar. 1885), 166-67. See also Westwood, "Art as a Moral Reformer," 438-39 and T. Harwood Pattison, "The Relation of Art to Religion," *BQR* 8 (1886), 324-26.

[138] Marsden, *Fundamentalism*, 85; David Bebbington, *Evangelicalism in Modern Britain: A History from the 1730s to the 1980s* (Grand Rapids: Baker, 1992), 214-17.

[139] See Morgan's discussion of "Religious Art and the Formation of Character," esp. 305-26.

[140] Dawson, "Religious Doubt," 609.

CHAPTER 5

Art, Aesthetics, and the Fundamentalist-Modernist Controversy

By the end of the nineteenth century, evangelicalism, which had shaped the religio-cultural landscape of the Anglo-American world since the eighteenth century, found itself on shaky ground.[1] To the casual observer, evangelicalism no doubt looked much as it always had. Evangelicals continued to extol the virtues of the "Christian nation," and their missionary efforts both at home and abroad continued unabated. Between 1860 and 1900, Protestant churches in the United States actually witnessed a threefold increase in membership. Behind this gilded façade, however, many struggled to make sense of social and intellectual challenges that had been chipping away at the foundations of the evangelical edifice since the 1860s. Darwinian evolution and German Higher Criticism had combined to cast doubt on the reliability of Scripture; rapid urbanization had led to the erosion of rural social networks that had long supported traditional religious values; and a general process of secularization had begun to transform universities that had once maintained close ties to orthodox Protestantism.[2] As the twentieth century approached, evangelicals faced sharp disagreement about the most

---

[1] On fundamentalism and modernism, see the following, on which my own account is based: Sydney E. Ahlstrom, *A Religious History of the American People* (New Haven: Yale University Press, 1972), 763-824; David Bebbington, *Evangelicalism in Modern Britain: A History from the 1730s to the 1980s* (Grand Rapids: Baker, 1992), 181-228; James Davison Hunter, *American Evangelicalism: Conservative Religion and the Quandary of Modernity* (New Brunswick: Rutgers University Press, 1983), 23-48; George Marsden, *Fundamentalism and American Culture* (Oxford: Oxford University Press, 2006) and *Understanding Fundamentalism and Evangelicalism* (Grand Rapids: Eerdmans, 1991); Ferenc M. Szasz, *The Divided Mind of Protestant America, 1880-1930* (Tuscaloosa: University of Alabama Press, 1982); Mark A. Noll, *A History of Christianity in the United States and Canada* (Grand Rapids: Eerdmans, 1992), 363-89 and *The Scandal of the Evangelical Mind* (Grand Rapids: Eerdmans, 1994), 109-45. See also Ernest R. Sandeen, *The Roots of Fundamentalism: British and American Millenarianism* (Grand Rapids: Baker, 1978), although this work has largely been surpassed by Marsden and others. It is important to recall that there existed not only various strands within the liberal/modernist and conservative/fundamentalist movements but also a "moderate" center within evangelicalism as a whole (see Bebbington, *Evangelicalism*, 220-23).

[2] Marsden, *Understanding Fundamentalism*, 13-17.

effective means of addressing these challenges. For some, the appropriate strategy was to defend traditional values, even if this meant separating from "mainstream" culture;[3] for others, the most reasonable response to modernity was not rejection but accommodation. What became known as the "fundamentalist-modernist controversy" resulted in a radical intellectual, social, and theological reconfiguration of Anglo-American evangelicalism.

Of course, the dispute between fundamentalists and modernists was not distributed evenly across evangelicalism. As David Bebbington has observed, fundamentalism was more pronounced among American evangelicals than British, who often responded differently to perceived threats like Darwinism.[4] In America, moreover, the controversy affected denominations disproportionately. Its effects were strongest among Northern Baptists and Presbyterians, while it had less impact on Northern Methodists and lesser still on the majority of Congregationalists, many of whom had embraced liberalism well before the turn of the century. In the American South, long a conservative stronghold, many denominations sympathized with the fundamentalist position.[5] Modernism, meanwhile, appealed primarily to elite northern intellectuals, and its influence in the early twentieth century was confined largely to universities, while fundamentalism, with its more populist orientation, made notable inroads among local congregations.[6] Despite such differences, however, the controversy impacted a wide cross-section of evangelicals. As James Davison Hunter writes, "By 1919, it was clear even to the man on the street that a bifurcation had emerged within American Protestantism."[7] Even in Britain, where evangelicals sometimes expressed confusion over the struggles of their American counterparts, the confrontation between conservatives and liberals was real enough. Noting the rise of fundamentalism in America, one Scottish writer conceded in 1924 that while "fundamentalism" was not a word widely used in Britain, "the thing which the uncomely word describes is not unfamiliar to us here."[8]

Although they came to anathematize one another, fundamentalists and modernists were in fact cut from the same evangelical cloth. Both parties believed they were preserving the truths of Christianity in the face of new difficulties. Each group, however, emphasized different aspects of the nineteenth-century evangelical tradition. Fundamentalism, which Marsden has defined as "militantly anti-modernist Protestant evangelicalism,"[9] brought together elements of revivalism, common sense realism, Judeo-Christian morality, and biblical liter-

---

[3] Fundamentalism also involved some accommodations to modern life. See Noll, *History of Christianity*, 381 and Bebbington, *Evangelicalism*, 183-84.
[4] Bebbington, *Evangelicalism*, 207, 221-23.
[5] Szasz, *Divided Mind*, 467-77.
[6] Noll, *History of Christianity*, 374.
[7] Hunter, *American Evangelicalism*, 32.
[8] Qtd. in Bebbington, *Evangelicalism*, 182.
[9] Marsden, *Fundamentalism*, 4.

alism. Added to these elements were two other late-nineteenth-century theological developments: dispensational premillennialism and holiness teachings. Both of these developments fostered in their respective ways an otherworldly perspective that encouraged a retreat from the cultural engagement that had distinguished nineteenth-century evangelicalism. While fundamentalists did not abandon all concern for social welfare, they accentuated the individual, supernatural, and ahistorical. Modernists, on the other hand, perpetuated the social consciousness of Victorian evangelicalism. What modernists emphasized, following early liberalizers like Bushnell, was the immanence of God in the progress of human culture. The most effective response to the crises of modernity was not to rehash what they saw as tired and powerless dogmas but to translate Christianity's essentials into a contemporary idiom. Mocking what he saw as the shortcomings of fundamentalist solutions to social woes, Shailer Mathews, a prominent liberal and dean of the University of Chicago Divinity School, wrote in *The Faith of Modernism* (1924): "The world needs new control of nature and society and is told that the Bible is verbally inerrant. It needs a means of composing class strife, and is told to believe in the substitutionary atonement.... It needs faith in the divine presence in human affairs and is told it must accept the virgin birth of Jesus Christ."[10] For modernists, Christianity's potential resided mainly in its ethical contribution to social transformation, and indeed modernists were instrumental in advancing the Social Gospel around the turn of the century—a movement which fundamentalists, for their part, prided themselves on rejecting. Ultimately, the fundamentalist-modernist controversy marked the collapse of the cooperative spirit that had typified nineteenth-century evangelicalism. Modernists accused fundamentalists of sticking their heads in the sand, while fundamentalists accused modernists of distorting the faith beyond all recognition. The rift that developed had serious implications for how evangelicals approached a range of cultural and intellectual activities, including science, politics, and art.[11]

This final chapter examines the relationship between the evangelical aesthetic tradition and the fundamentalist-modernist controversy. Historians have often discussed the effects of this controversy on different aspects of evangelical thought, including science, politics, and culture in general, but the impact of this debate on aesthetics has received far less attention.[12] The struggle between liberals and conservatives proved a significant turning-point for evangelical thinking about art, as for evangelical thought overall. It signaled a breakdown of the evangelical romantic consensus and its relationship to the Protestant ideology that had predominated since the 1830s. No longer did a broad coalition of evangelicals agree on the value of art, either for its own sake or its service to Protestant culture,

---

[10] Qtd. in Noll, *History of Christianity*, 375-76.
[11] See Noll, *Scandal*, 149-208. Noll mentions the arts but does not treat them in detail.
[12] An exception here is Roger Lundin, "Offspring of an Odd Union: Evangelical Attitudes toward the Arts," *Evangelicalism and Modern America*, ed. George Marsden (Grand Rapids: Eerdmans, 1984): 135-49. See also the end of this chapter.

nor could they agree on the importance of thinking philosophically about aesthetics. The interest in aesthetic theory that had been a hallmark of nineteenth-century evangelicalism became in some quarters a thing of the past. A religio-aesthetic chasm opened up between fundamentalists and modernists that spelled the end of the evangelical *pax aesthetica*.

Liberals, Evangelical Romanticism, and the Protestant Ideology

From one perspective, liberals were more obviously the torchbearers of the Protestant ideology and the aesthetic tradition of evangelical romanticism. Art and culture remained an important part of their agenda. Speaking on "Gospel and Culture" in 1912, J.R. Darbyshire bemoaned the fact that evangelicals were still far too preoccupied with preaching a "traditional" gospel to the detriment of cultural pursuits: "We must be for ever so presenting the Gospel to the unlearned in terms of a traditional phraseology if we are to be recognized as Evangelical, that we have not time to feed the thoughtful, inspire the ambitious, and shew the glory of consecrating the secular." Accordingly, Darbyshire called for greater attention to arts and letters.[13] Liberals continued to emphasize key themes in nineteenth-century evangelical aesthetics, including art's essential connection to religion, its capacity for moral influence, and its role in Protestant civilization. Indeed, the aesthetics of liberal Protestantism represented the final triumph of the romanticizing trend in evangelical thinking about art. Whereas mid-nineteenth-century evangelical aesthetics had been characterized by attempts to negotiate between the principles of romantic criticism and the claims of orthodox Christianity, liberal aesthetics escaped this tension by adjusting traditional doctrine. In fact, liberalism was itself an outgrowth of the romantic impulse in Anglo-American Protestantism. Drawing inspiration from thinkers like Hegel, Schleiermacher, Coleridge, and Bushnell, liberalism stressed the presence of God in all things, the union of subject and object, and the "consubstantiality" of the natural and supernatural.[14] "God" was no longer the personal deity of orthodoxy but the force or spirit at work in the universe and human culture. The essence of religion resided in "religious experience" or fidelity to an ethical ideal like sacrificial love rather than scriptural revelation or historic doctrines. People, moreover, could encounter the "divine" or aspire to a high moral standard on their own. Supernatural regeneration by the Holy Spirit was no longer a prerequisite for holy living or authentic spiritual experience. Within this theological and philosophical context, liberals could embrace the full spiritual and socio-moral potential of art as defined by the romantic tradition.

One crucial feature of liberal thought was the close relationship many perceived between aesthetic and religious experience, which were often seen as

---

[13] Qtd. in Bebbington, *Evangelicalism*, 199-200.
[14] See Ahlstrom, *Religious History*, 780-81. Ahlstrom writes, "the natural and the supernatural were consubstantial," citing Bushnell (780), although Bushnell had borrowed the word from Coleridge.

nearly identical. This notion had evolved over the course of the nineteenth century and had faced strong resistance (before the 1880s) from critics who favored a subordinationist model of religion and art. Now, however, the seeds sown by early innovators like Bushnell and H.W. Beecher had matured, and many liberals accepted the fusion of the aesthetic and religious as a matter of course.

It is helpful to distinguish two basic ways this fusion manifested itself among liberal thinkers. The first was the spiritualization of art, in which aesthetic appreciation was held to be a form of religious experience and/or art was seen as a contact point with the divine. "Something like a Religion of Culture," writes James Turner, "flourished [near the end of the nineteenth century] on both sides of the Atlantic, without much regard to traditional religious beliefs. Art museums and concert halls became, in the then-current phrase, temples of culture." As Turner notes, progressive evangelicals like Beecher and Bushnell had contributed to the rise of this Religion of Culture, as had revivalism's emphasis on "feeling".[15] But evangelicals had also assisted this development in more specific ways. Some critics' fascination with aesthetic idealism, to take one example, had furnished an important antecedent to the spiritualization of art. The second way was the aestheticization of religion. This aestheticization assumed a number of forms from the Christ-as-Artist cult popular around the turn of the century to revised understandings of biblical inspiration. J.A. Chapman illustrated this trend when he compared biblical to aesthetic inspiration, construing it as "that which yields insight into beauty, truth, goodness, and God." The effects of the Bible differed little, if at all, from those of music or poetry.[16] Its most important embodiment, however, concerned the nature of religion itself. Religion was believed to be essentially "aesthetic." Religious doctrines, for instance, were best understood not as propositional formulae that appeal to the intellect but as suggestive poetic utterances that target the emotions and intuition. Behind this view stood a long line of writers, most notably Coleridge and Bushnell. These two varieties of religio-aesthetic fusion, though distinct, were closely related, and early-twentieth-century liberals endorsed both.

When it came to the spiritualization of art, liberals sometimes took precautions to avoid the impression that they were espousing the "worship" of art itself, although numerous turn-of-the-century liberals did counsel an enhanced attention to the aesthetic within worship.[17] Time-honored Puritan-evangelical concerns about the idolatry of art wielded enough residual force to prevent such art-

---

[15] James Turner, *Without God, Without Creed: The Origins of Unbelief in America* (Baltimore: Johns Hopkins University Press, 1985), 252, 253. The quotation occurs on p. 252.

[16] Qtd. in Bebbington, *Evangelicalism*, 183. The idea of Christ-as-Artist or Christ-as-Poet appears, for instance, in Oscar Wilde, *De Profundis, Oscar Wilde: Collected Works* (New York: Barnes & Noble, 2006), 1085 and Edward B. Pollard, "Aesthetic and Imaginative Elements in the Words of Jesus," *BW* 30 (Nov. 1907): 339-45. For a response to Wilde's aestheticization of Christ, see "A Romantic Christ," *MR* (Sep. 1907): 788-801.

[17] See David Morgan, *Protestants and Pictures: Religion, Visual Culture, and the Age of American Mass Production* (New York: Oxford University Press, 1999), 315-16 and

worship, at least in theory. For this reason, some also stopped short of the Arnoldian position that art can act as a substitute for religion. Most liberals did not petition for a Church of Art to replace institutional Protestantism; rather, they reiterated, following mid-nineteenth-century evangelical idealists, that art is a reflection of the divine mind, a manifestation of the "ideal." In *The Evolution of Christianity* (1892), Lyman Abbot, Beecher's influential successor at the Plymouth Church in Brooklyn, described art, and in fact all human activity, as an expression of both the "divine artist" and the universal human search for the "Infinite":

> The cry of the human being from the earliest age—the cry of Job, "Oh that I knew where I might find him!"—is still the cry of humanity. All history is the search after God. All science, whether the scientist knows it or not, is the thinking of the thoughts of God after him, the trying to find him. All art is the search after the ideal art as it exists in some true, divine artist.... All men have at the hearts of them more or less of this hunger and desire to know the Infinite and the Eternal.[18]

For Abbot, art was a record of humanity's religious consciousness and hence a reflection of Infinite Consciousness itself. Viewed against the backdrop of evangelical aesthetic history, the suggestion that art discloses a divine plenitude marks a reversal of the Puritan position. The problem of presence that the Puritans had bequeathed to Protestant aesthetics had essentially vanished. The cost of resolving the problem, however, was the Puritan conception of the radical transcendence of God.

Perhaps even more central to liberal thought than the spiritualization of art was the aestheticization of religion. As described in chapter 3, the aestheticization of religion originated partly as a defense against the onslaughts of modern science. Whereas many fundamentalists opted to defend Christianity by meeting science on its own ground, many liberals turned to inherited aesthetic concepts in an attempt to place religion safely beyond science's grasp. Because art and science offer distinct approaches to the world, art possesses a natural immunity to scientific analysis. Moreover, since religious experience is akin to aesthetic experience (both are grounded in feeling), it too is impervious to scientific attacks. In 1913, Walter Sargent, Professor of Fine and Industrial Art at the University of Chicago, advanced a slightly different but complementary version of this argument. Whereas science "regards as knowledge only those matters which have been conclusively demonstrated by an impartial analysis of all the available facts," religion relies on "an immediate sympathetic response between the individual and his surroundings." Sargent was keenly aware that the intuitive claims

---

Bebbington, *Evangelicalism*, 203. For a liberal warning against too-elevated conceptions of "culture," see Gerald Birney Smith, Review of *The Field of Ethics*, by George Herbert Palmer and *Culture and Restraint*, by Hugh Black, *BW* 20 (July 1902): 70-72.

[18] Lyman Abbot, *The Evolution of Christianity* (Boston: Houghton, Mifflin, 1900), 237. See also "Lesson of a Picture," *O* 48 (16 Dec. 1893): 1116-17.

of religion lack easy verification according to scientific standards. If, however, one could point to another example "where ranges of experience apparently closed to scientific approach had been opened up by immediate emotional response," then such an example "would help to authenticate the kind of experience which religion claims." This other range of experience is art: "The fine arts also tend to quicken a highly complex type of emotional life and thus to refine those powers of sympathetic response which alone are capable of knowing God...."[19] For Sargent, the phenomenology of aesthetic experience lent credence to religious experience.

In fairness, many liberals did not intend to reduce religion entirely to the subjective, although conservatives often accused them of doing so. On the contrary, they believed they were making epistemological claims about *how* one encounters the divine (e.g., through feeling)—claims that assumed the externality of the divine object. Liberals, therefore, could be quite sensitive to the dangers of subjectivism, much as some mid-nineteenth-century aesthetic idealists had been. This sensitivity is evident in an article entitled "Yes, But Religion Is an Art!" written by the liberal Baptist minister Harry Emerson Fosdick in 1931. Fosdick opened with a rehearsal of themes that had been mainstays of evangelical aesthetics since the nineteenth century. He lamented the aesthetic vacuity of the Protestant tradition, warned against addressing this lack by flying to Rome, and called for greater attention to art and beauty. Fosdick's principal concern, however, was the faith-killing effect of modern science, and his solution, predictably, was to recognize religion as an "art." "No folly of religion ...," he claimed, "could be more ruinous than the endeavor to jam itself within the categories and vocabulary of contemporary science. What religion most wants to say must be put into artistic vehicles." Fosdick acknowledged this view's susceptibility to the critique that "religion is altogether subjective, that no objective cosmic reality corresponds with our similes ...," but he replied that there exist other kinds of "truth" than the scientific: "it seems clear that a scientific description never tells the whole truth about anything." Science does not exhaust reality. One must also cultivate religio-aesthetic truth, or an objective truth subjectively apprehended.[20] Still, epistemological claims of this kind remained inseparable from theological claims about the nature of God's self-revelation and thus God himself. Theologically, the independent existence of a metaphysical entity is but a minimal condition for faith; the precise character of this entity matters as well. So although Fosdick and other liberals wished to avoid a thoroughgoing solipsism, many were far from maintaining a traditional conception of the personhood of God.[21]

---

[19] Walter Sargent, "One Contribution which Art Makes to Religion," *BW* 41 (June 1913), 359, 362, 363, 365.
[20] Harry Emerson Fosdick, "Yes, But Religion Is an Art!," *HMM* 162 (Jan. 1931) ,131, 132, 133.
[21] Some liberals went even further. R.J. Campbell of London's City Temple claimed in *The New Theology* (1907) that the human and divine are "fundamentally and essentially

Turn-of-the-century liberals also insisted on the essential connection between art and morality that had featured prominently in nineteenth-century evangelical aesthetics. Many Victorians had increasingly come to understand religion in moral rather than doctrinal terms, and liberalism represented a culmination of this evolution. Anti-didactic moralism had played a role in this evolution as well by reinforcing the sense that moral cultivation was a function not of a supernatural process of sanctification but of natural psychological, aesthetic, and ethical laws. The great weight liberals placed on morality and social progress led, not surprisingly, to the perpetuation of such theories. In his *Protestants & Pictures*, Morgan provides a detailed account of early-twentieth-century American liberal Protestantism's emphasis on "character formation" and art's role in this process. As Morgan explains, liberals clung to a belief in social and national progress, the keys to which were "character" cultivation and "self-realization." Relying on earlier Bushnellian ideas of nurture in addition to then-current psychological and pedagogical theories that "stressed the developmental structure of character formation and the emergence of personal identity," liberals argued for the importance of strong moral character as a way to ensure social progress. This emphasis on character formation also led to a series of educational reforms that altered the established system of religious education. Above all, there was a "shift ... from teaching the Bible to forming 'religious persons'." With this shift came an increased attention to art. Whereas older Sunday school curricula had utilized visual imagery primarily as a means of illustration, liberals encouraged art appreciation as a means of developing "religious persons." The introduction of new visual reproduction technologies (e.g., the halftone) in the later nineteenth century facilitated such policies by providing increased public exposure to the arts.[22]

Yet while liberals availed themselves of new technologies and theories, and lobbied for a heightened attention to art in sanctuaries and classrooms, they were in fact playing variations on themes inherited from nineteenth-century evangelical aesthetics. In suggesting that art hones moral character and does so not didactically but affectively, they were extending the tradition of anti-didactic moralism. Writing "On the Religious Significance of Poetry" in 1909, Marietta Neff employed terminology that countless Victorian evangelicals would have recognized:

> But if the function of poetry be after all the religious function of stirring high passion, of making the heart sensitive to the finer issues of life, of speaking to the listening soul with voices that are not heard on earth forever save in dreams—if these appeals constitute the function of poetry, then indeed its essence must be not a ponderous didacticism, but even so frail and fleeting a thing as beauty like the poignant fairness of moonlight waters, or of silvery pools under the sun of early

---

one" (qtd. in Bebbington, *Evangelicalism*, 198).
[22] Morgan, *Protestants and Pictures*, 305-37, esp. 305-11, 315, 324. The quotations occur on p. 315. Cf. Ahlstrom, *Religious History*, 781.

winter, or of blue lakes at peace with the blue sky; even, moreover, beauty as vast and terrible as the surge and thunder of multitudinous seas.[23]

If Neff's understanding of the non-didactic function of poetry differed at all from its nineteenth-century predecessors, it did so by virtue of the fact that it was underwritten by a comprehensive ontological diagnosis of the final impenetrability of reality. "The fundamental objection to didacticism in literature," noted Neff, "is not ... any subjective criterion of taste, but the simplest of logical principles—that life is larger than anything one can say about it, experience more complex than any formula...." Thus, "Things that are generally accepted are generally wrong; truths that can be reduced to a proposition have lost their vitality." Such ideas were common enough in the romantic philosophical tradition, and many Victorian evangelicals would have supported on some level the notion of extra-propositional truths. Yet they would also have shied away from this kind of statement as an exhaustive account of reality. Twentieth-century liberals like Neff, however, were pressing the legacy of anti-didactic moralism to its extreme.

Furthermore, the liberal ideal of character formation and art's role in this process echoed aspects of the whole-person argument that had been instrumental in encouraging sustained reflection on the aesthetic among evangelicals. Writing in *Outlook*, Harvard's President Emeritus, Charles W. Eliot, pointed in 1911 to the importance of the beautiful in children's holistic development:

> The sense of the beautiful or the lovely is ... something which should be developed and cultivated throughout all education. Through all school life the utmost pains should be taken to stimulate in every child love of the beautiful, to keep the sentiment pure and noble, and to give the child through its gratification genuine joy and a satisfaction which will increase as the child's whole nature develops, and will mount as life goes on. This sentiment is an important element in the spirit of man. Fed through the bodily senses, it is essentially an ethereal and religious delight.[24]

When liberal Protestants addressed the moral potential of aesthetic appreciation, the context, as here, was often educational. Noting the growing public attendance at art galleries on Sundays, the *Biblical World* suggested in 1913 that "pastors and Sunday-school teachers would do well to make a study, not only of the picture galleries in great cities, but of the numerous prints which may represent these to those who are remote from them." The *Biblical World* did express a wish that "more could be done to make more effective in the inspiration of definite religious thought ... this Sunday afternoon ministry of art to the public," but it commended the educational value of this "ministry" nonetheless. "Art has yet to make its strongest appeal in religious education.... It is our own fault if we do

---

[23] Marietta Neff, "On the Religious Significance of Poetry," *The Christian Century Reader: Representative Articles, Editorials, and Poems Selected from More than Fifty Years of* The Christian Century, ed. Harold E. Fey and Margaret Frakes (New York: Association Press, 1962), 383-84.

[24] Charles W. Eliot, "The Religious Ideal in Education," *O* 99 (21 Oct. 1911), 413-14.

not make use of it."[25] This rhetoric of art as "ministry" had been common among evangelicals since the 1840s.

Liberals remained committed to art's role within a broad Protestant ideology that linked religion, morality, and cultural progress. They acted as spokespeople for an Arnoldian model of culture, which they saw as a key to social stability and as a manifestation of the developing Kingdom of God. Granted, some resisted Arnold's complete dismantling of the hierarchical relationship of Christianity and culture that had prevailed (in theory) among nineteenth-century evangelicals,[26] but culture had clearly become the focal point for many Anglo-American liberals. This ensured an ongoing interest in art and aesthetics. Art continued to be seen as an index to the cultural progress that was itself an embodiment of the divine. As Josiah Strong argued in 1893, artistic development (among other things) "helps to prepare the way for the full coming of the Kingdom": "When men generally have risen to a consciousness of God, the discoveries of science, legislation, business, manufactures, agriculture, art—all human activities will enter into the harmony of the divine plans for perfecting the race, not because they are *overruled* by infinite wisdom, but because men consciously and intelligently co-labor with God to this glorious end."[27] This esteem for art and aesthetics endured, however, at the expense of orthodoxy.

Conservatives and the Return of Ambivalence

In contrast to liberals, conservative evangelicals in the early decades of the twentieth century present a more complex picture. In one sense, fundamentalism marked a return to the ambivalence that had characterized the Puritan aesthetic tradition. Many conservatives withdrew from active participation in the early-twentieth-century critical establishment. The chief symptom of this withdrawal was the general abandonment of critical reflection on the arts that had been a perennial feature of many nineteenth-century denominational periodicals. As Roger Lundin concluded after an extensive survey of American fundamentalist publications, "Fundamentalists of the first half of [the twentieth century] wrote almost no essays of significance on the arts."[28] Yet even as fundamentalists pulled away from the Anglo-American "institution of high art" that Victorian

---

[25] "Religious Education: The Educational Value of Religious Art," *BW* 41 (Feb. 1913), 134. For other discussions of art, morality, and education, see Emma T. Wilkinson, "Morality versus Materialism in Our Schools," *O* 50 (18 Aug. 1894): 258-60 and Clyde Weber Votaw, "Moral Training in the Public Schools," *BW* 34 (Nov. 1909): 295-306.

[26] For Arnold, religion was an expression of culture rather than its prime mover. See *Culture and Anarchy*, ed. J. Dover Wilson (Cambridge: Cambridge University Press, 1963), 48.

[27] Josiah Strong, *The New Era; or, The Coming Kingdom* (New York: Baker & Taylor, 1893), 250-51, 249-50.

[28] Lundin, "Offspring," 144.

evangelicals had helped to foster, they maintained some of the aesthetic principles of their predecessors. Both liberals and conservatives, therefore, may be seen as heirs to the evangelical romantic tradition.

To some extent, the exodus of conservatives from the twentieth-century critical establishment may be attributed to many of the same factors that induced them to turn their backs on other sorts of cultural and intellectual pursuits. One such factor was the rapid growth of premillennialism near the end of the nineteenth century, which displaced the postmillennialism that had earlier held sway. Premillennialism triggered among fundamentalists a heightened sense of social disillusionment. The master narrative of postmillennialism had been one of inexorable cultural progress; premillennialism, by contrast, predicted inexorable cultural decline. Society was speeding towards its God-appointed doom, and the only appropriate response was to step up evangelistic efforts in order to rescue as many souls as possible. Art, whatever its intrinsic merits, could in this context amount to little more than a distraction. Late-nineteenth-century evangelical doubts about the social potential of art already reflected this growing pessimism. Society was fast becoming a lost cause, and the only hope was individual salvation. What was needed was the Gospel of Christ, not the Gospel of Art.

Aesthetic theorizing also fell victim to what may be seen as the critical narrowness of fundamentalism. To some degree, aesthetics was merely another casualty of the shift in vision that occurred as fundamentalists focused their attention on what they viewed as more pressing issues. Preeminent among these was Darwin's theory of evolution, which fundamentalists interpreted as a direct challenge to Christian orthodoxy. Other fundamentalist priorities included defending biblical inerrancy and preserving a traditional, supernatural understanding of Christian doctrines such as the Incarnation and Atonement.[29] In concentrating their efforts almost exclusively on such concerns, fundamentalists in effect resurrected the logic of the exigency argument. Nineteenth-century evangelicals had employed this rationale to honor Puritan piety while campaigning for their own departure from the Puritan aesthetic tradition. Implicit in the argument, however, had always been the dispensability of art; now, fundamentalists put this logic into practice, suspending their interest in aesthetics to tend to the more urgent business of shielding the faith against an encroaching liberalism. By extension, many fundamentalists also surrendered the ideal of wholeness that had characterized and helped to legitimize the aesthetic thought of Victorian evangelicals. Suppressed was any widespread concern for the standard of balance that had informed earlier conceptions of the human person and had stressed the momentousness of the aesthetic in attaining this standard. Ironically, fundamentalists and aesthetes could agree on one point: art and religion need not associate with one another.

---

[29] See R.A. Torrey, A.C. Dixon et al., eds., *The Fundamentals: A Testimony to the Truth* (Grand Rapids: Baker, 2003).

The changing scope of many conservative periodicals during the early twentieth century exemplified this narrowing of vision. Although evangelicals had always sponsored periodicals devoted solely to religious matters, many had developed formats during the nineteenth century that encouraged reflection on an assortment of cultural issues. Victorian evangelicals envisioned a thoroughly Christian civilization, and periodicals that intelligently surveyed an expansive cultural terrain played a key part in promulgating this vision. By contrast, the content of many fundamentalist periodicals was given over almost entirely to articles dealing with evolutionary theory, biblical criticism, and the interpretation of prophecy. The contrast with liberals here is instructive. Not only did many liberal periodicals continue to publish articles on art and aesthetics, but liberal writers also remained actively engaged with the broader culture. (It is significant, for example, that a liberal like Fosdick was at home among readers of *Harper's*.) Furthermore, conservative voices were progressively marginalized even within periodicals that had once served as forums for conservative thought. The *Methodist Review*, which published writers that entertained identifiably conservative viewpoints on theological issues into the 1910s, thereafter inclined steadily towards modernism until its eventual dissolution in 1931 (although it published moderate writers as well). One of its final issues contained an article by none other than Shailer Mathews.[30] As conservatives gradually acquired the status of "cognitive minority," to use Hunter's phrase,[31] they lost the ability and sometimes the will to speak authoritatively about cultural topics to a modern society with which they were increasingly at odds.

Closely related to this narrowing of interests was what some scholars have described as fundamentalism's anti-intellectualism, which may also have contributed generally to a decline in philosophical aesthetics among conservatives. Anti-intellectualism, of course, is a knotty term since it always pivots on one's ideological commitments regarding what counts as "intellectual." Many fundamentalists, for instance, believed they were merely practicing intellectual honesty by pointing to what they regarded as the flaws in evolutionary theory or the interpretive missteps of the Higher Criticism. As Marsden has argued, fundamentalists often attempted to combat evolutionary theory not on the grounds of an

---

[30] See Shailer Mathews, "Business as the Maker of Morals," *MR* 47 (May 1931): 407-17. For articles that attempt to balance the claims of conservatives and liberals, see James H. Snowden, "Modernism in the Bible," *MR* 44 (July 1928): 487-99; "An Aggressive Christianity," *MR* 44 (Jan. 1928): 131-32; and "Fundamentalism and Modernism," *MR* 42 (May 1927): 483-85. On conservative reactions in the *MR* to liberal biblical criticism during the 1890s, see Robert E. Chiles, *Theological Transition in American Methodism, 1790-1935* (Lanham: University Press of America, 1983), 69-71. Other periodicals that followed the general liberalizing trend were the *Princeton Review* (formerly the *BRPR*) and *Christian Advocate*.

[31] Hunter, *American Evangelicalism*, 34ff.; however, cf. Marsden's claim that fundamentalists possessed a "strikingly paradoxical tendency to identify sometimes with the 'establishment' and sometimes with the 'outsiders'" (*Fundamentalism*, 6).

uncritical acceptance of Genesis but on the grounds of the Baconian common sense tradition of scientific inquiry to which fundamentalists remained attached. Evolution, many believed, was simply bad science, just as modern biblical criticism was simply bad hermeneutics. Still, if one understands anti-intellectualism as self-conscious opposition to the perspectives of a predominantly liberal intelligentsia or to the influential worldviews emanating from largely secularized universities, then many fundamentalists were unquestionably anti-intellectual. According to Marsden, fundamentalists found humor in the "suggestion that the ancestors of Ph.D.'s were monkeys and baboons," and for an added laugh they would sometimes list the initials associated with advanced degrees as "D.D., Ph.D., L.L.D., Litt.D., A.S.S." To the theories issuing from universities concerning the origins of the earth or the Bible, fundamentalists opposed the canons of common sense reasoning, which stressed the ability of ordinary individuals to apprehend the facts.[32] Their loyalty to the epistemological claims of common sense realism consequently drove fundamentalists in an increasingly populist direction, while their repeated skirmishes with modernist academics further intensified their anti-intellectual stance. This growing polarization may have added, at least obliquely, to the diminution of interest among fundamentalists in aesthetics as a formal philosophical discourse.

Yet while these factors indirectly hastened fundamentalist withdrawal from the critical establishment, there were other developments that bore a closer relationship to the late-nineteenth and early-twentieth-century art world that also raised suspicions about the relative value of art and aesthetics. The most important of these was the fusion of aesthetic and religious experience that had followed in romanticism's wake. Liberal Protestants, as noted above, increasingly welcomed this union of art and religion, as did other late-Victorian and modernist thinkers who claimed little or no allegiance to Christianity.[33] To conservatives, however, both the spiritualization of art and the aestheticization of religion seemed repulsive, for they threatened to substitute a bastardized form of Christianity for the orthodoxy of old. Conservative critics had of course labored against these developments since the mid-nineteenth century, but with little success. By the early twentieth century, traditionalists had had enough.

A pair of articles published in the *Methodist Review* highlights the mounting frustration of conservatives with the spiritualization of art among elite thinkers. Writing in 1908, Peter Thompson betrayed exasperation with those Beecheresque preachers who replaced the Gospel with appeals to a congregation's taste:

> Ministers of other communions, not less devoted than we are, may think their commission is to reach the human heart through the medium of an ornate ritual, and by

---

[32] Marsden, *Fundamentalism*, 212-21. The quotations appear on p. 212.
[33] See, for example, Brendan Cole, "Jean Delville's *La Mission de l'Art*: Hegelian Echoes in Fin-de-siècle Idealism," *Religion and the Arts* 11 (2007): 330-72.

developing the holiest and best in humanity through aesthetic forms of worship; we feel that our high calling is to preach the Word; that our first business is to declare the unsearchable riches of Christ. Our fundamental conception of a minister's work is that of preaching.[34]

Similarly, a 1917 article on "Substitutes for Christianity" described the new "religious" spirit sweeping across Europe and America. While this general disposition towards the religious was useful in counteracting "aggressive naturalism" and materialism, it was not to be confused with Christianity proper: "To be 'for religion,'" the author observed, "is not always to be for Christ. Even Antichrist is not anti-religion." Among the many so-called religious replacements for Christianity was "the aesthetic substitute for religion": "This idea is that the satisfaction and ennobling of life is to be sought not in the worship of a postulate Deity, but by means of the beautiful in nature and art." Such substitutes, however, "radically pervert biblical and historical Christianity."[35] In cautioning against the dangers of substituting aesthetic experience for religion, conservatives were sounding a familiar Protestant alarm over the idolatrous potential of art—an alarm that had become much less clamorous throughout the nineteenth century but had never fully ceased. What looked to early-twentieth-century conservatives like the growing "worship of art," however, prompted a renewed sense of urgency.

Conservatives reacted even more virulently, however, to the aestheticization of Christianity, for this aestheticization posed an immediate challenge to orthodox understandings of Christian doctrine. For liberals in the tradition of Bushnell, theology was best understood as a form of "poetic" language. A doctrine like the Atonement was not to be valued as an objective description of God's redemption of humanity from the bondage of sin but rather aesthetically as a moral exemplar. This view of the Atonement had come to be known, in a poignant example of how theology, morality, and aesthetics had commingled during the nineteenth century, as the "moral-influence theory." This theory was directly criticized in the third installment of *The Fundamentals* (1910-15). Summarizing the moral-influence theory, Franklin Johnson wrote: "the sole mission of Christ was to reveal the love of God in a way so moving as to melt the heart and induce men to forsake sin." The problem with this theory, he argued, is that it "makes the death of Christ predominantly scenic, spectacular, an effort to display the love of God rather than an offering to God in its nature necessary for the salvation of man." Johnson's visual metaphors underscore the aesthetic dimension of the liberal position. The principal power of the Atonement derived from its status as a species of the sublime or beautiful, and in fact such a conception was little more than Otheman's Kamesian theory applied to the Crucifixion. As long as the idea of

---

[34] Peter Thompson, "The Minister in His Study," *MR* (Sep. 1908), 771. For an earlier British example of this sentiment, see Thomas G. Selby, "Irreligious Civilizations," *WMM* 120 (May 1897), 327.
[35] "Substitutes for Christianity," *MR* 33 (Nov. 1917), 969, 970, 972.

ethico-aesthetic influence remained confined to aesthetics proper, it presented comparatively minor difficulties for evangelical orthodoxy; once this theory seeped into the discipline of theology, however, it endangered everything which, according to fundamentalists, made Christianity uniquely what it is. Johnson did not deny that the Crucifixion is worthy of imitation—that it does possess a moral-aesthetic dimension—nor did he begrudge the aesthetic per se. Indeed, with no little irony he suggested that the moral-influence theory of the Atonement is deficient not only on theological grounds but also aesthetic and moral ones: "The man who dies to rescue one whom he loves from death is remembered with tears of reverence and gratitude; the man who puts himself to death to show that he loves is remembered with horror."[36] Even on its own terms, the moral-influence theory, Johnson implied, qualifies as bad theater. Nevertheless, too great an emphasis on the Atonement's aesthetic aspects threatens to obscure its status as a real substitutionary transaction between the Father and Son.

Although Johnson avoided indiscriminately assailing the aesthetic, the concept, it seems, did not escape conservative opposition to the aestheticization of religion unscathed. What fundamentalists wanted was to recoup the cognitive, objective content of Christianity, a content arguably on the run since the late eighteenth century. The style and substance of fundamentalist arguments were themselves nothing new. (Johnson's criticism of the moral-influence theory sounded remarkably like Hodge's criticism of Bushnell.) Yet a perhaps unintended consequence of the attempt to fortify traditional doctrine against modernist reinterpretations was that the word "aesthetic" itself became tarnished. In some contexts, "aesthetic" began to acquire pejorative connotations. Something of this growing negativity towards the term may be glimpsed in P.T. Forsyth's reaction to a progressive creed adopted by the Bowdoin College Class of 1903. Forsyth, once a rising star among liberal Congregationalists in England, had gradually embraced a traditional understanding of Christianity. He now took aim at those liberals who had "nothing to say of sin, faith, or repentance; nothing of salvation, redemption, or reconciliation." What people need most, insisted Forsyth, is the forgiveness of sin, a power that rests solely "in the revelation which forgives. It resides in the gospel, in the act of deliverance, in the person of the Redeemer." Liberals, by contrast, made too much of the "character" of Christ at the expense of his "*person*": "It is not the character of Christ that is the revelation of God; that is too aesthetic a position for the final and requisite religion.... Christ came not as a spectacle, ethical or spiritual, but as an agent and a power."[37] Clearly, aesthetic had become shorthand for heterodox. To conservatives, the Cross was more than a "spectacle," and they sometimes expressed consternation

---

[36] Franklin Johnson, "The Atonement," *Fundamentals* 3:65, 71, 70.
[37] P.T. Forsyth, "The Need for a Positive Gospel," *LQR* 11 (Jan. 1904), 65, 82. On Forsyth, see M. Husbands, "Forsyth, Peter Taylor," *Biographical Dictionary of Evangelicals*, ed. Timothy Larsen, David Bebbington, and Mark A. Noll (Downers Grove: Intervarsity, 2003), 232-36.

that liberals, instead of claiming for themselves the true redemptive power of the Cross, seemed content merely to gaze at it as they would a fine painting.

Although the aesthetic appears to have suffered among some conservatives due to its alleged misapplication by liberals, one must not overstress this point. Modernists, too, were capable of using "aesthetic" negatively when it suited their agendas. Describing the inability of an age enthralled by "commercialism" to comprehend Jesus' ethic of love as manifested on the Cross, Mathews inquired: "For how is it possible for an age that honors the victories of force to appreciate, in anything more than an æsthetic way, the victories of the cross?"[38] For fundamentalists, it was liberals who misguidedly approached the Cross in aesthetic terms; for Mathews, it was the robber barons and captains of industry. In both instances, however, "aesthetic" signified the opposite of some reality associated with the Cross—for conservatives an act of atonement, for liberals a moral example deserving imitation. Meanwhile, even for many fundamentalists the problem was not so much with the aesthetic taken on its own terms as with the aesthetic imported carelessly into the domain of theology. There was, it seems, a correct application of the aesthetic to the theological. Forsyth, after criticizing a "too aesthetic" interpretation of Christ's character (the qualifying adverb is not irrelevant here), proceeded, like Johnson, to draw upon an aesthetic analogy, the effect of which was to incriminate liberals once again for being inept aestheticians as well as inept theologians: "A gospel is not a novel but a drama; it is not an exhibition of divine character or psychology, but the achievement of an act final for human destiny, central for human history, relevant to all thought, and exhaustive for God's heart and will."[39] What fundamentalists were implicitly attempting to do was to safeguard the subordinationist model of religion and art that many nineteenth-century writers had proposed. They did not disallow that Christianity has an aesthetic dimension; they merely protested the notion that Christianity can be *reduced* to this dimension. Still, the constant need to deflect interpretations that relished the Cross for its "poetry" seems to have taken a toll on conservative attitudes towards the aesthetic.

This toll may also have resulted from conservatives' growing discomfort with the unapologetically social focus of liberal Protestantism at the expense of doctrine. Whereas nineteenth-century evangelicals had understood social activism as the normal outworking of a converted heart, the Social Gospel Movement stressed the primacy of moral action apart from a strict adherence to traditional doctrinal formulae. Social rather than salvific transformation became central.[40] This absorption in the here-and-now rekindled conservative anxieties about the dangers of earthly-mindedness (anxieties already acute among premillennialists). "The adversary the Church has most to fear," asserted the *Watchman* in 1896, "is worldliness." Worldliness was defined as anything that draws one's attention

---

[38] Shailer Mathews, *The Gospel and the Modern Man* (New York: Macmillan, 1912), 302.
[39] Forsyth, "The Need for a Positive Gospel," 82.
[40] Marsden, *Fundamentalism*, 92.

away from the truths of Christianity: "We do not use the term 'worldliness' in any cant sense. We mean by it a complacent satisfaction in the pursuit of physical comfort and pleasure, a disposition that bounds the horizon of the spirit by the narrow arc of what appeals to the physical, the intellectual or aesthetic faculties." The aesthetic, which had been viewed by nineteenth-century evangelicals as a potential cure for the commercialism and materialism of modern industrialized societies, was once more becoming an ally of worldliness rather than its sworn foe. This reversal stemmed in part from the adamant refusal by conservatives to entertain broad and often ambiguous conceptions of the spiritual as referring to all things non-material. If "spiritual" includes intellect, mind, or feeling, then it is expansive enough to encompass the aesthetic; once it is limited to traditional Christian understandings of the supernatural, however, the spiritual stands opposed to the mundane categories of "the physical, intellectual or aesthetic." Most revealing, however, was the *Watchman*'s linking of this worldliness to those liberals who prioritized the social over the spiritual: "The purely philanthropic, humanitarian directions in which so many of our churches are spending their most strenuous efforts are a witness to the truth of our observations." Attending to salvation need not entail the neglect of the body, but "The [liberal] zeal for ameliorating untoward conditions of life far outruns the desire for winning men to a life of fellowship with God."[41] In guarding orthodox understandings of the spiritual against liberalism's putatively disproportionate concern for this world, some conservatives may have been impelled to dwell anew on the hazardous materiality of art and its power to distract Christians from their true calling.

In addition to threats to orthodoxy posed by the aesthetic, certain features of the turn-of-the-century art world also helped to drive fundamentalists away from high aesthetic culture. The evidence suggests that many conservatives were coming to view the art world of the late nineteenth and early twentieth centuries as a citadel of immorality. Wherever they looked, they discovered signs of moral degradation. The influence of aestheticism continued to swell in spite (or because) of Wilde's criminal trial and imprisonment in 1895. Not surprisingly, evangelical periodicals were still publishing condemnations of aestheticism into the first decade of the twentieth century, and Wilde remained the poster-child for the moral bankruptcy to which artists, as a class, seemed prone. Excoriating aestheticism, however, had become a kind of rearguard action, and it was yet another sign that the modern world was beginning to pass conservatives by. Progressive artists, moreover, increasingly explored subjects that rebelled against the strict codes of Victorian morality to which conservatives conformed. Critics, to cite one outstanding example, had been complaining since the 1870s about the growing number of nudes in galleries and museums throughout the United States and Europe. As the *Baptist Magazine* expressed it in 1890:

---

[41] "The Foe of the Church," *W* 77 (31 Dec. 1896), 7.

The talk about "the exigencies of art" is sheer nonsense, and it is time we remembered the exigencies of religion and morality. "Reverent gaze" there may be: "to the pure all things are pure"; but who that knows human nature can look without apprehension on the matter-of-course way in which it is taken for granted in artistic circles that these exhibitions of "the nude" are the highest form of art, and must be secured at all costs? To us they are indicative of a corrupt taste, and of a degradation which cannot be too strenuously resisted.[42]

"Reverent gaze" was another (interestingly religious) term for the supposed disinterestedness of aesthetic contemplation. Many conservatives, however, had little room for such theoretical constructs where nudes were concerned, for the one "that knows human nature" knows the difficulty, if not the sheer impossibility, of a depraved human being beholding the nakedness of another with anything approximating a pure, asexual gaze.[43] Disciples of Hegel, symbolists, and other early-twentieth-century experimentalists may have celebrated nudes as the highest expression of the human form and spirit,[44] but traditionalists had a difficult time seeing this as anything other than a deviant sexuality run amok.

As the turn-of-the-century art world did its best to cast off the last vestiges of its Victorian sensibilities, conservatives, who retained these sensibilities, perceived the behavior and attitudes of artists as immoral, eccentric, and pretentious. Modernist artists may have approached their art with great seriousness, but such earnestness only helped to bring out the underlying populism of some fundamentalists. Fundamentalists were not above the use of sarcasm when it came to modern science's suggestion that Ph.D.'s were the descendants of apes, and the same held true when it came to the ease with which the modern art world seemed prepared to flout common decency, whether the goal was high art or its subversion. Just how irksome the art world and its values had become to some fundamentalists may be detected in a rather humorous account of a band of nude female revelers who descended upon the small town of Rock Island, Illinois one fateful night in 1919. The account, which appeared in the American fundamentalist periodical the *Searchlight*, is worth quoting at length:

> The good people of Rock Island are not especially "sot" against dancing, but they have not yet arrived at that plane of aesthetic culture which tolerates the gamboling

---

[42] "Mr. Browning's 'Asolando,'" *BM* 82 (Apr. 1890), 176. See also "Nude Exhibitions in Art," *CA* 53 (29 Aug. 1878), 550; Henry J. Van Dyke, Jr., "Art and Ethics: In Some of Their Relations," *PR* (Jan.-Jun. 1883), 105; and [Untitled], *NYE* 58 (3 Mar. 1887): 2.

[43] Contemporary evangelical attitudes towards nudes differ dramatically from those of earlier generations. Many art departments at evangelical colleges, for example, ask students to conduct studies of nude models. Doing so, however, often requires careful justification. See the thoughtful reflections of my colleague Bruce Herman, "Policy on the Use of Nude Models in Art," Gordon College, <http://www.gordon.edu/fs_download/pages/ArtPolicy_NudeModels.pdf>.

[44] See Cole, "Jean Delville's *La Mission*," 354-62.

of woodland nymphs, clad only in scintillating moonbeams, amid the town's glades and dells.

Recently, a number of young women here became inoculated with the craze for classic terpsichore distinguished from other forms of dancing chiefly by an absence of clothing and conventionalities.

All might have gone well had the young women confined their Grecian revels in a house, with the shades down, but this they would not do because they felt it did not coincide with the principles of true art. Full expression of self they decided required that they go a-gamboling in Rock Island's great out-of-doors.

Hence it was that a dignified deacon of one of the town's leading churches had his sensibilities shocked severely last night when on chancing to look from his window, he observed three September Morns flitting about from bush to bush in what was afterward described as "Dancing to the Pipes of Pan." He promptly sent for a constable....

"Forty days in jail," was the sentence of an unsympathetic judge this morning. "We will have no shimmy shaking in Rock Island."[45]

The humor, of course, derives not so much from the event itself (a petty piece of juvenile stupidity), but rather from the reporter's ironic narration. Through a series of metaphors and allusions, he links the dancing girls to the art culture of ancient Greece, casting them in the role of pagan sensualists. As much as the actions of the girls themselves, however, the target of the writer's mockery is the kind of "aesthetic culture" and the "principles of true art" that would presume to authorize such behavior. The account is, in effect, a reductio ad absurdum. If the highest value of modern aesthetic culture is the "full expression of self," then one may reasonably expect, so the writer hints, that such bacchanalian displays—such "shimmy shaking"—may soon be the norm in small towns everywhere. The implicit contrast between small-town rural America and high Hellenic culture is in fact part of the point.

To be sure, the supposed moral laxity of the modern art world was not a uniquely conservative dilemma. Liberals also frowned upon any so-called "principles of true art" that sought to rationalize unlawful behavior in the name of aesthetic inspiration. "I warn you," wrote Beecher in his *Addresses to Young Men*, "with yet more solemn emphasis, against EVIL BOOKS and EVIL PICTURES."[46] A reviewer in *Outlook* put the matter in more positive terms: "Art ... can justify itself only so far as it promotes wholesome thought and conduct."[47] Unlike many conservatives, however, liberals also retained a more positive con-

---

[45] "Nude Dancers Shock Deacon; Jail for Girls," *S* 2 (4 Sep. 1919), 4.
[46] H.W. Beecher, *Addresses to Young Men* (Philadelphia: Henry Altemus, 1895), 214.
[47] Review of *The Essentials of Æsthetics in Music, Poetry, Sculpture, and Architecture*, by George Lansing Raymond, *O* 85 (16 Mar. 1907), 621.

ception of art's socio-moral possibilities, as well as greater sympathy with cultural elites, which together may have militated against an overly narrow view of the art world as a bastion of immorality and idiosyncrasy.

In contrast to liberals, many conservatives abandoned the critical thinking about aesthetics that had been an important feature of nineteenth-century evangelicalism. Feeling increasingly alienated by the turn-of-the-century art world and embattled by the claims of both modern scientists and liberal Christians, conservatives gradually lost the will to spend whatever cultural and philosophical capital they possessed on behalf of art. Such capital, they felt, was better spent securing Protestant orthodoxy against the scientific threats of Darwinism and the Higher Criticism. Significantly, it may have been fundamentalism's affinity for Baconian science that helped to bring about the sort of critical shortsightedness that led to the exclusion of aesthetics. Science, many conservatives believed, deals with facts, and therefore bad science could be overcome with better science. Art, by contrast, as the nineteenth century had repeatedly stressed, was by nature subjective. *De gustibus non est disputandum*. Many fundamentalists may thus have chosen to concentrate their energies on an area of controversy purportedly governed by the rules of scientific proof, thereby offering reasonable prospects for success. The result was that in relation to aesthetics many fundamentalists looked more like the Puritans than their immediate predecessors.

Yet this conservative flight from aesthetics is only half the story. No subculture can be completely *a*-aesthetic in practice, nor can it wholly avoid reflection on the arts (even if this involves little more than thinking about why art is not worth thinking about). This relative withdrawal by conservatives from the modern critical establishment should not, therefore, be misconstrued as evidence of an unqualified bias against art or the aesthetic. As already observed, Johnson's and Forsyth's cases against a "too aesthetic" interpretation of Christ's Atonement were themselves grounded in part on aesthetic premises. There existed, moreover, some notable exceptions to the generalization that conservative thinkers failed to endorse the arts.

One such thinker was Abraham Kuyper, the Dutch theologian, prime minister, and father of Neo-Calvinism, who delivered the Stone Lectures at Princeton Theological Seminary in 1898. A thoroughgoing Calvinist, Kuyper had no interest in a fundamentalist-style retreat from culture, and he argued persuasively for a version of the transformational model of Christ and culture that had long been a hallmark of the Reformed tradition. He devoted his penultimate lecture to the topic of "Calvinism and Art," in which he confronted the thorny problem of Calvinism's seemingly poor track record in relation to art and defended art's intrinsic value. Kuyper began his address by acknowledging the "almost fanatical worship of art" in the present age, a tendency he found inconsistent with true Christianity.[48] The abuse of art, however, should not prevent Christians from patronizing it fully. Kuyper then turned his attention to the question of why, historically, Calvinism had not "develop[ed] *an art-style of its own*" (145). Drawing upon the developmentalism of Hegel and Karl Robert Eduard von Hartmann, Kuyper contended that for most of human history art and religion had been closely intertwined. Art, in fact, had "derived her richest motives from religion." According to Kuyper, however, this "alliance of religion and art represents a *lower* stage of religious, and in general of human development...." (146). As religion approached its full maturity (which Kuyper associated with Calvinism), art and religion gradually developed along distinct lines. Such was Kuyper's explanation for why Calvinism did not develop an "art-style" of its own. This explanation clearly pitted him against those in the late nineteenth century who were calling for an increased aesthetic dimension in worship. His appropriation of Hegel and von Hartmann was in reality a clever way to revive the Puritan distinction between religious and civil space, and the lawful and unlawful uses of art. Calvinism worships God in spirit and truth, not in material form. Yet even if art could not lawfully aid worship, this did not mean it lacked all religious significance, as Kuyper proceeded to show. Asking *"what interpretation of the nature of art flows from [Calvinism's] principle"* (152), Kuyper concluded, just as some earlier evangelicals had, that "art has the mystical task of reminding us in its productions of the beautiful that was lost and of anticipating its perfect coming luster" (155). Art, that is, looks back to Paradise and forward to Heaven. Beauty is also a gift of God, and it is our "privilege" as human beings both to appreciate and create it (156-57). In simultaneously restricting art and advancing high arguments on its behalf, Kuyper was laying claim to a version of the subordinationist model that had typified the evangelical aesthetics of the preceding decades. In addition, Kuyper offered one other way in which Calvinism had aided art, namely, in furthering its advancement throughout history. Echoing the whig interpretations put forth by critics like C.W. Bennett, Kuyper argued that Calvinism "has put an end to the unjustified tutelage of the church over all human life, art included" (160). By freeing art from the shackles of the (Catholic) Church, Calvinism had won for art a space of its own.

Aside from its erudition, perhaps the most noteworthy feature of Kuyper's lecture is its near-total lack of originality. Even the foregoing précis reveals just how much his aesthetics owed to the broad intellectual currents of the nineteenth century. Almost all of his arguments had been anticipated by earlier evangelical critics. Like these critics, for Kuyper "art is no fringe that is attached to the garment, and no amusement that is added to life, but a most serious power in our present existence..." (151). Art is certainly liable to abuse, but this should not obscure its noble, God-given calling. In regard to aesthetics at least, Kuyper was

---

[48] Abraham Kuyper, "Calvinism and Art," *Lectures on Calvinism* (New York: Cosimo, 2007), 142. Subsequent references appear parenthetically in the text.

one of the last great representatives of a Victorian evangelical intellectual culture that had located art in the context of a holistic Protestant ideology and had expounded this ideology in systematic ways. Kuyper's thought would later serve as an important roadmap for neo-evangelicals in search of a way out of what Mark Noll has called the "intellectual disaster of fundamentalism."[49] If subsequent generations of evangelicals did not always adopt the precise details of his theory of art, they often looked to Kuyper for an alternative to the aesthetic vacuum left by fundamentalism.

Another conservative thinker who continued to champion art was J. Gresham Machen, a Presbyterian whose *Christianity and Liberalism* (1923) became a central document in the history of American fundamentalism. Frequently caricatured by friends and foes alike, Machen was a complex figure who resists easy classification. Although he took the lead in articulating a rationale for fundamentalist separatism and rescuing Reformed Christianity from what he saw as modernist dilutions, Machen strongly opposed other aspects of fundamentalism. As Marsden explains, "He did not like being called a fundamentalist, he was an intellectual, he was ill-at-ease with the emotionalism and oversimplifications of revival meetings ... and he declined to join the antievolution crusade."[50] In contrast to liberals who made Christianity synonymous with the advancement of civilization and fundamentalists who spurned mainstream culture, Machen fought to uphold the Reformed understanding of culture upon which nineteenth-century evangelical aesthetics had been built. Addressing students at Princeton Seminary in 1912, Machen affirmed a hierarchical view of "Christianity and Culture," which must include cultivation of the arts:

> Are then Christianity and culture in a conflict that is to be settled only by the destruction of one or the other of the contending forces? A third solution, fortunately, is possible—namely, consecration. Instead of destroying the arts and sciences or being indifferent to them, let us cultivate them with all the enthusiasm of the veriest humanist, but at the same time consecrate them to the service of our God. Instead of stifling the pleasures afforded by the acquisition of knowledge or by the appreciation of what is beautiful, let us accept these pleasures as the gifts of a heavenly Father. Instead of obliterating the distinction between the kingdom and the world, or on the other hand withdrawing from the world into a sort of modernized intellectual monasticism, let us go forth joyfully, enthusiastically to make the world subject to God.[51]

Both Machen's conception of Christianity's relationship to culture and his willingness to see "the appreciation of what is beautiful" as part of this conception

---

[49] Noll, *Scandal*, 109.
[50] Marsden, *Understanding Fundamentalism*, 182. On Machen, see Marsden's final chapter.
[51] J. Gresham Machen, "Christianity and Culture," *Selected Shorter Writings*, ed. D.G. Hart (Phillipsburg: P&R, 2004), 402.

reveal him, like Kuyper, to be a faithful recipient of the nineteenth-century evangelical aesthetic tradition. For Machen, too, "high art" was not something to be scorned but something to be admired and guarded. Unlike some fundamentalists, he eschewed populist sensibilities. He was an intellectual who spoke boldly on behalf of culture even as he spoke, somewhat reluctantly, on behalf of fundamentalism.

Kuyper's and Machen's reasoned support for art and culture, however, were fast becoming atypical.[52] Many conservatives no longer shared their, and nineteenth-century evangelicalism's, faith in the possibility of a rapport between Christianity and culture, and art and aesthetics were left by the wayside. Even so, fundamentalists rarely berated art as such, despite their sometimes disparaging references to the aesthetic; and although philosophical reflection on art declined relative to Victorian evangelicals, many of the aesthetic suppositions of evangelical romanticism remained intact. Critical theorizing may largely have disappeared, but foundational convictions regarding art did not.

One can, for example, catch romantic expressivist assumptions at work in a discussion of John Henry Newman's hymn "Lead Kindly Light," published, oddly enough, in a conservative American periodical, the *Bible Student and Teacher*, in 1908. At the time, the *Bible Student and Teacher* was a periodical in transition. Affiliated with the Bible League of North America and edited by Presbyterian academics, it quickly expanded to include dispensationalists and non-Presbyterian evangelicals. In 1913, it was renamed the *Bible Champion* and accordingly adopted a more populist outlook.[53] Despite its transitional status, this periodical provides a glimpse of at least one branch of conservative thought during the early twentieth century. The article in question was occasioned by "a series of articles" recently appearing in the *Sunday School Times*. This series, the author alleged, had committed serious errors of interpretation in relation to Newman's hymn, and he issued a stern warning against even the most well-intentioned eisegesis. The article began, however, with a revealing attempt to formulate the essence of hymns as aesthetic objects:

> A hymn may or may not be poetry, judged by the strict canons of the poetic art. But, to serve its purpose and justify its creation a hymn must have an indefinable something that throbs the heart, thrills the imagination, touches the longings, uplifts the soul. Simplicity, nay even a certain *naïveté*, in an attempt to express deep religious feelings; a reaching out and after God; a trustfulness in Him and His love; and an assured and buoyant belief in the immortality of the soul,—these are some of the essential expressings of hymns, keyed in their appropriate notes of joy or of

---

[52] One does, however, meet with other conservative attempts to reconcile Christianity and culture, if not always between Christianity and art specifically. See, for example, W.M. Lisle, "Christianity and Culture: Their Divorce and Reconciliation," *BST* 5 (Sep. 1906): 169-82.

[53] See Marsden, *Fundamentalism*, 118.

sadness or of semi-tones. How great an influence can a simple hymn exert! It becomes a *multum in parvo* volume of emotion and aspiration, resignation or self-sacrifice. It is a world-long ejaculatory epitome of a lifetime's experience.[54]

Clearly, romantic notions of art as an expression of emotion, as well as art's capacity to exert an empowering influence via the feelings, were alive and well among at least some conservatives early in the century.

Another article published two years later suggests that not all conservative evangelicals had yet relinquished the ideal of psychic wholeness either, nor the conviction that the aesthetic plays an indispensable part in achieving it. In "The Beauty of Heaven," Horace C. Stanton described with great fervor the "aesthetic sense" and the intrinsic longing for beauty all humans possess: "Beauty is a thing which the heart naturally craves. As much as there is a mathematical faculty which desires accuracy in calculation and a moral instinct which appreciates the right, there is also an æsthetic sense which desires beauty." This Platonic-triad-turned-faculty-psychology scheme had been a recurring theme since the eighteenth century, and it is therefore no surprise that both Plato and Edmund Burke, among others, receive mention. To ignore any one of these cardinal values—truth, goodness, or beauty—is to fall short of being fully human; it is to lack culture in the Arnoldian sense. "Any person who has not this love for beauty," wrote Stanton, "is regarded by us as deficient in an important element of mental culture. But, if he possess this instinct in a high degree, we concede that he has at least a certain type of cultivation." As the title of the article makes clear, Stanton's primary concern was with the perfect "beauties of Heaven" that "shall never be exhausted," and to this end he focused more on the otherworldly than the worldly—an approach that perhaps fit well with the disenchantment many conservatives had come to feel towards modernity. Yet Stanton did not ignore worldly beauty entirely. For him, as for Anne Bradstreet nearly three centuries earlier, the beauties of heaven did not efface the beauties of earth but rather gave them meaning as a foretaste of those to come. True, the beauty of heaven "goes vastly beyond our fondest imaginations," but Stanton also portrayed this heavenly beauty as a fulfillment of one's desire for earthly beauty. In fact, to prepare for the beauties of heaven one ought to cultivate the beauties of earth:

> There are many ambitions of this world, that may be realized, or may not.... But we need never fail to reach the abode of beauty by and by, and to find satisfaction there. How inspiring the thought, that, when these lower struggles and conflicts are overpast, we shall enter such an abode as that which awaits us! Those whose environment on earth has most lacked for beauty, and those who have revelled in it most, may enjoy dreams unrestrained about the beauty that is to come. And if, in the city where the ransomed dwell, there is such beauty, what a stimulus it should be to us to cultivate beauty in manners, in speech, in spirit, and in everything that

---

[54] D. Havelock Fisher, "'Reading Into' a Hymn: On a Recent Criticism of 'Lead Kindly Light,' *BST* 9 (Nov. 1908), 279.

pertains to our life! What a failing in our duty, if we do not cultivate all beauty now![55]

Not unlike Keats, who compared the Imagination to "Adam's dream" and speculated that "we shall enjoy ourselves here after by having what we called happiness on Earth repeated in a finer tone,"[56] Stanton saw the beauty of heaven as a culmination of the beauty of earth. Furthermore, Stanton's argument for the present vitality of the aesthetic (rather than simply its eventual eschatological completion) and his fidelity to the ideal of the cultured individual point to the enduring influence of the nineteenth-century evangelical aesthetic tradition.

Another idea that some fundamentalists carried over was the notion that art registers the moral health of civilization. Now, however, when conservatives gazed into their aesthetic crystal balls, they often saw ruin instead of splendor and progress. In 1919, the *Searchlight* quoted approvingly a Catholic bishop who had glimpsed in America's art culture the seeds of national destruction: "'We are living in a decadent age, our music, literature and poetry, theaters and art all bear the stigma of degeneracy. The world is rushing back to paganism, divorcing itself from Christ more each day.'" As if to impress upon readers the gravity of this verdict, the writer added: "When a Roman Catholic Bishop condemns public amusements, it is time the rest of the folks were sitting up and taking notice."[57] Machen, writing in 1931, also read modern art as evidence of the "appalling spiritual decline which has come over the world within the last fifty years": "High poetry, for the most part, is silent; art is either imitative or bizarre. There is advance in material things, but in the higher ranges of the human mind an amazing sterility has fallen on the world."[58] It was this very principle that fueled in part conservative criticisms of the modern art world described above. If fundamentalists had perceived the moral and spiritual corruption of the art world simply as an indication of the devolution of art itself, this devolution, though regrettable, may have seemed manageable. They viewed this corruption, however, as symptomatic of a much broader decline. The state of the nation's art became yet another confirmation of the coming apocalypse, though ironically it was the aesthetic theory of the nineteenth century that in some measure enabled conservatives to draw this conclusion.

Perhaps the greatest legacy of the nineteenth-century evangelical aesthetic tradition, which surfaces in Machen's reference to "high poetry," was the concept

---

[55] Horace C. Stanton, "The Beauty of Heaven," *BST* 12 (May 1910), 375, 377, 376, 381, 380.
[56] John Keats, Letter to Benjamin Bailey, 22 November 1817, *Complete Poems and Selected Letters of John Keats* (New York: The Modern Library, 2001), 489.
[57] "Modern Dancing Is Stamped as 'Brutally Indecent' by Rt. Rev. A.J. Drossaerts, Bishop of San Antonio," *S* 2 (25 Sep. 1919), 1.
[58] J. Gresham Machen, "Christianity and Liberty," *Selected Shorter Writings*, 357. See also *Christianity and Liberalism* (Grand Rapids: Eerdmans, 2009), 8.

of "high art." As noted earlier, fundamentalists sometimes expressed their displeasure with the twentieth-century art world in decidedly populist terms, which could sound very much like a blanket condemnation of the whole notion of high art. But in some cases the ideal of high art itself drove conservative critiques of late-nineteenth and early-twentieth-century art culture. Some conservatives chided progressive art not only for its moral turpitude but also for falling short of what they regarded as the highest aesthetic standards. One early example of this attitude may be seen in evangelical censures of those artistic movements near the turn of the century (e.g., the Expressionists or the literary naturalists) that seemed bent on tracking down the "real" in all of its shocking ugliness. Robert Waters, lambasting the "so-called Realists" in 1888 for being a "contagious disease," described them as follows:

> Not a taste for the good and the pure; not an eye for the beautiful, the noble, and the sublime; but a nose for the foul, the hateful, and the mean—that is their characteristic. Prowling around among degraded men and still more degraded women, the residuum of humanity, they rake up a mass of maggoty, foul, and putrid matter, stir it up with a spice of sugar and salt, dub it with a fair name, and send it out to the world as a work of art![59]

This passage is itself a fine specimen of the grotesque. The key point, however, is that Waters directs his indignation at both the moral and the aesthetic. Not only the conscience ought to be offended by the "prowling" naturalists who offer up images of a "degraded" humanity for ordinary, middle-class consumption but also the aesthetic sense. The naturalists' "mass of maggoty, foul, and putrid matter" qualifies by Waters's standards as nothing but pseudo-art. Merely giving one's creation "a fair name" does not automatically make it "a work of art." The repudiation of such movements, not to mention later "extremist movements" such as the Dadaists, was hardly restricted to evangelicals. The growth of these movements, some of which set out to supplant the very notion of high art, marked the dissolution of the Romantic-Victorian concept of the "ideal" (both of beauty and morality), and they therefore met with widespread resistance.[60] But this point only highlights the fact that evangelical reactions to the artistic innovations of the early twentieth century cannot be chalked up to mere prudishness. On the contrary, this reaction resulted from a keen sense of aesthetic dissatisfaction and the growing awareness that so-called high art was not quite high enough.

That this sort of aesthetic critique persisted among some conservatives finds confirmation in yet another of Machen's essays, "The Responsibility of the Church in Our New Age," published in 1933. Machen argued that while the "new age" mistakenly believed that whatever it "favors is always really new," there were in fact "old things which ought to remain." Among these were "the literary and artistic achievements of past generations":

---

[59] Robert Waters, "Genius in Action: The Realists," *CA* (18 Oct. 1888), 687.
[60] See E.H. Gombrich, *The Story of Art* (London: Phaidon, 2006), 437, 467.

Those are things which the new age ought to retain, at least until the new age can produce something to put in their place, and that it has signally failed to do. I am well aware that when I say to the new age that Homer is still worth reading, or that the Cathedral of Amiens is superior to any of the achievements of the *art nouveau*, I am making assertions which it would be difficult for me to prove. There is no disputing about tastes. Yet, after all, until the artistic impulse is eradicated more thoroughly from human life than has so far been done even by the best efforts of the metallic civilization of our day, we cannot get rid of the categories of good and bad or high and low in the field of art. But when we pay attention to those categories, it becomes evident at once that we are living today in a drab and decadent age, and that a really new impulse will probably come, as it has come so many times before, only through a rediscovery of the glories of the past.[61]

The concept of high art, which Victorian evangelicals had helped to foster, remained an important criterion for evaluating modern art. (This was true even though conservatives themselves rarely produced anything that to most observers would qualify as high art.) One reason for this may have to do with the social function of the concept understood in Machen's sense. Insofar as it looks to the past to demonstrate its own supposedly trans-historical character, high art is an inherently conservative category. It points to the existence of an axiological absolute, however difficult it may prove to substantiate this absolute in reality. Thus "high art" serves as a means of passing judgment on the progressive.

Of course, fundamentalism also bore the marks of the nineteenth-century sentimentalist tradition—a tradition often contrasted to both the high and avant-garde. Warner Sallman's well-known paintings of Christ, a plethora of religious novels, and countless poems and hymns all testify to the impact of sentimentalism on early-twentieth-century evangelicalism. Even so, the sentimentalist bent of many evangelical artifacts only confirms in yet another way the romantic lineage of fundamentalist thinking about the arts, for sentimentalism was itself an outgrowth of romanticism,[62] although it was a development that many nineteenth-century critics, evangelical and otherwise, had tried to stifle. Sentimentalism, however, with its ties to the popular and lowbrow, was only one offshoot of the romantic tradition. While this tradition led on the one hand to the sentimental and low, it led on the other to the serious and high. And just as a large body of late-nineteenth and early-twentieth-century critics inherited this latter half of the

---

[61] J. Gresham Machen, "The Responsibility of the Church in Our New Age," *Selected Shorter Writings*, 365.

[62] In addition to revivalism in general, the immediate theological contribution to fundamentalist sentimentalism was the holiness movement. Bebbington notes the connection between romanticism, American Transcendentalism, and the holiness movement, and he describes how Keswick spirituality was often condemned for being "all gush and no sinew" (*Evangelicalism*, 167).

romantic tradition, so too did some fundamentalists.[63] Recognizing the continuing influence of this latter half of the romantic tradition also offers a seamless explanation for the preponderance of "high romantic" views of art that Lundin has noticed among many contemporary, post-fundamentalist evangelicals. In his discussion of this phenomenon, Lundin describes the late-nineteenth-century shift in evangelical attitudes towards culture, but he ultimately stops short of offering a thoroughgoing historical account of modern evangelicalism's attraction to romantic aesthetics. His explanation for the romantic character of much present-day evangelical thinking about art turns largely on ahistorical (though certainly correct) commonalities between fundamentalism and romanticism. There was, for instance, a "distinctly Protestant tone" to "a great deal of romanticism." Likewise, both romantics and fundamentalists held similar "perceptions of culture," viewing "themselves as the rightful proprietors of a world from which they had been displaced." Thus Lundin concludes that "In retrospect, it seems quite logical that when we as evangelical students of culture began to emerge from the dusky passageways of fundamentalism, our eyes would be dazzled by the enchanting romantic tradition.... [R]omantic theory has offered an appealing sight to those of us whose aesthetic lenses have been ground ... in the shop of American fundamentalism."[64] If this chapter's analysis is correct, however, then it points to a direct descent from the romantic evangelical aesthetics of the nineteenth century to the romantically-inclined aesthetics of contemporary evangelicalism. Although fundamentalists forsook the aesthetic theorizing promoted by nineteenth-century evangelicals in order to defend an endangered Gospel, they also carried over some of the less obviously threatening romantic assumptions about art propagated by their predecessors.

---

[63] An article in the *BST*, for instance, rehearses the classic arguments against the novel, including that novel-reading leads to a "mawkish sentimentalism." See "Wise Words to Novel-Readers," *BST* 8 (May 1908): 358-60.

[64] Lundin, "Offspring," 142, 144.

CONCLUSION

Theology, Aesthetics, and Liberalization

Although this book forms a crucial chapter in the history of evangelical aesthetics, it does not tell the whole story. The fundamentalist-modernist controversy did not impose a moratorium on evangelical thinking about art. On the contrary, since the advent of neo-evangelicalism in the mid-twentieth century, something like a renaissance has taken place. Not only are evangelicals meditating on the philosophy of art in a way that has not been done since the nineteenth century but they are also *creating* art to a prodigious extent. Even those who have maintained ties to fundamentalism have welcomed the arts with fresh enthusiasm. Thus another complex chapter in the history of evangelical aesthetics remains to be written. In the course of this chapter, one would encounter a fresh cast of characters from C.S. Lewis and Clyde S. Kilby to Francis Schaeffer and Nicholas Wolterstorff. One would likewise discover an expanding network of institutions devoted to the arts, from periodicals like *Image, Books & Culture*, and *Christianity and Literature* to the many museums and art galleries scattered across evangelical college campuses throughout the United States. (Perhaps the gallery most in need of explanation from an historical perspective is the Museum and Gallery at Bob Jones University!) In addition, new trends would have to be considered, including a noticeable thawing of relations between evangelicals and Catholics, the institutionalization of art programs at many Christian colleges, and theological movements such as the Emergent Church and the recent revitalization of Calvinism, to name but a few. Yet even without this chapter, one may begin to draw some useful lessons from the history of evangelical aesthetics before the mid-twentieth century. It remains, therefore, to say a brief word about the shape of the preceding narrative and its potential implications for contemporary evangelical thinking about the arts.

This study has depicted the transition in evangelical aesthetics from the eighteenth to the mid-twentieth century as a joint movement towards romanticism on the one hand and away from Puritanism on the other. There is a third trend, however, which has served as a continuous subtext throughout the foregoing narrative: *liberalization*. Liberalization, as I use it here, describes the gradual departure of a given faith community from a body of doctrines embraced (at least outwardly if not always inwardly) by the majority of earlier members of this community. In theological terms, it represents a transition from orthodoxy to heterodoxy. At times, as in the case of some liberal Protestants, this movement towards heterodoxy may actually entail anti-doctrinalism, or the abdication of doctrine qua doctrine. In other cases, revised doctrines replace traditional ones once held as universal. If one accepts this basic definition, it quickly becomes apparent that the changes in evangelical aesthetic discourse outlined in this study occurred against the backdrop of a steady process of theological drift among Anglo-American evangelicals. That the nineteenth century experienced a theological sea-change is of course nothing to write home about, but it is worth pausing for a moment to consider in more detail the relationship between this process of liberalization and the development of an aesthetic discourse by evangelicals.

To begin with, one might ask to what extent nineteenth-century evangelical aesthetic discourse may have contributed to liberalization. Did aesthetics somehow advance the sort of doctrinal drift characteristic of the history of Victorian theology? The answer, I think, is that aesthetics did not *cause* this drift. No single factor, including aesthetics, drove the theological and cultural transition to modernism. But nineteenth-century evangelical aesthetic discourse can be understood as yet another locus of dispute, an influential space in which heterodox ideas could be broadcast and played out. Widespread notions of art's ordinary moral influence, for example, slowly chipped away at theological notions of depravity and the need for supernatural intervention by the Holy Spirit. Conversion, some came to feel, was simply too unreliable as a social stabilizer, and although critics frequently acknowledged that not everyone's taste could achieve the same level of refinement, the idea that aesthetic appreciation fosters morality placed a solution to the problem of social cohesion within reach. Taste, after all, could always be "cultivated" through education. To take another example, the aesthetics of the eighteenth and nineteenth centuries had helped to drive a wedge between reason and feeling. When traditional religious claims fell under scientific scrutiny in the middle of the nineteenth century, an ostensible solution to the dilemma was therefore ready and waiting. Aesthetic theory provided needed ammunition in the conflict between religious faith and modern science.

Yet while nineteenth-century evangelical thinking about art may have acted as an accomplice to theological drift, it was also symptomatic of this drift. That is, broad theological changes gave shape to evangelical aesthetics, and evangelical aesthetics in turn helped to reinforce these changes. As this study has repeatedly suggested, the orientation of nineteenth-century evangelical aesthetic discourse was made possible in part by the declining authority, both cultural and theological, of the Reformed tradition. The Puritans also bequeathed to their evangelical descendants some key elements—most notably a positive view of culture—without which Victorian evangelical aesthetics could not have thrived. But the basically romantic character of evangelical aesthetics was enabled by a turn away from the theology of the Puritans, which had stressed the total depravity of humankind, the radical transcendence (but also the personhood) of God, the impossibility of communing with God apart from grace through Christ, the importance of carefully formulated doctrine, and the reliability of a theological language that corresponded adequately with the transcendent reality it sought to describe. The ideas that governed the evangelical aesthetics of the nineteenth century—ideas of art's natural moral influence, of human art objects as an expression of the divine mind, of the transcendental potential of the imagination, of the new authority ascribed to the subjective mediation of the world—could never have passed muster with the Puritans. Certain emphases carried over from Puritan theology continued to influence evangelical thinking about the arts throughout the nineteenth century—many evangelicals, for example, held to a traditional view of God's personhood and transcendence, as well as a subordinationist conception of Christianity and art—but on the whole evangelical aesthetics was built on the ruins of Puritan orthodoxy.

For those within the liberal tradition of evangelicalism or for other neutral observers, this narrative may not raise any special difficulties; for theologically conservative evangelicals, however, this narrative presents a much grimmer picture. Chapter 3 touched on what I referred to as the problem of inverse proportion, which some evangelical critics believed had been at work throughout the history of Christianity and had arisen anew during the fin de siècle. T. Harwood Pattison stated this problem succinctly in 1887: "As Christianity became artistic, it became corrupt."[1] Looking back over the shape of the preceding narrative, it strikes me that in many ways it confirms Pattison's anxieties. As evangelical interest in aesthetics grew, evangelicals, like much of the rest of western culture, were undergoing a process of liberalization and even secularization.[2] This liberalization and secularization did not always affect all evangelicals in the same way everywhere, just as not all evangelicals were equally interested in aesthetics. A general correlation, however, appears to have existed between the forces of liberalization and an increased attention to art.

The question, then, is whether the problem of inverse proportion ought to be accepted, reluctantly perhaps, as some kind of law: *As evangelical Christianity becomes artistic, it becomes corrupt.* If so, then the lesson of this study for contemporary evangelical artists and theorists is to pack up their bags and go home. Earnest Christians committed to living lives of obedience to Christ will pursue the arts at their peril. The obvious alternative is to interpret the problem of inverse proportion as merely an unfortunate dimension of evangelical aesthetic history before the twentieth century. For my own part, I lean (with cautious optimism) towards the latter. Yet if the problem is historical rather than universal, then the challenge for theologically conservative evangelicals is to draw what lessons they can from the past in order to avoid repeating the mistakes of their predecessors. Exactly where, from an orthodox vantage-point, did nineteenth-century evangelicals go wrong? What, if anything, could have prevented the aesthetic

---

[1] T. Harwood Pattison, "The Relation of Art to Religion," *BQR* 8 (1886), 327.
[2] See Graham Howes, *The Art of the Sacred: An Introduction to the Aesthetics of Art and Belief* (London: I.B. Tauris, 2007), 33ff. for some sociological speculations on the "apparently inverse relationship between [the increase in] religious art and [the decrease in] religious belief" in nineteenth-century Britain.

collapse among conservative evangelicals described in this book? And how, moving forward, might evangelical artists and philosophers avoid a similar fate? Unfortunately, answers to these questions are beyond the scope of this book. It is my sincere hope, however, that this study may provide a useful historical framework within which evangelicals can continue to wrestle with these important issues.

Bibliography

Primary Sources

Abbot, Lyman. *The Evolution of Christianity*. 1892. Boston, MA: Houghton, Mifflin and Company, 1900.

Adams, C. "Edward Otheman." *Zion's Herald* 63 (28 Apr. 1886): 134.

"Administrative Economy of the Fine Arts." *Eclectic Review* 10 (Sep. 1841): 241-53.

"Æsthetic Influence of Nature." *Christian Review* 83 (1 Jan. 1854): 1-34.

"Æsthetics." *Christian Review* 26 (Oct. 1861): 585-91.

"Aesthetics." *Presbyterian Quarterly Review* 10 (Apr. 1861): 26-37.

"An Aggressive Christianity." *Methodist Review* 44 (Jan. 1928): 131-32.

"Alison's Theory of Taste." *Christian Observer* 11 (Feb. 1812): 91-105.

"American Art." *Christian Advocate and Journal* 38 (23 July 1863): 235.

Arnold, Matthew. "Author's Preface, 1853." *The Works of Matthew Arnold*. Intro. Martin Corner. Wordsworth Poetry Library. Ware, England: Wordsworth Editions, 1995. 1-16.

—. *Culture and Anarchy*. Ed. J. Dover Wilson. Cambridge: Cambridge University Press, 1963.

—. "The Study of Poetry." *Essays English and American*. Ed. Charles W. Eliot. The Harvard Classics. New York: P.F. Collier & Son, 1938. 65-90.

"Art and Religion." *Christian Advocate and Journal* 37 (8 May 1862): 147.

"Art and Religion." *The Record*, n.s. 10 (22 May 1891): 499.

"Art Education: The Place Art Should Take in a Christian Education." *Christian Review* 25 (Oct. 1860): 618-31.

"Art: Its Aspirations and Prospects." *Eclectic Review* 9 (Feb. 1855): 129-44.

A.S.E. "Remarks upon Wordsworth's Poetry." *Christian Spectator* 1 (May 1827): 244-47.

B. "Influence of the Fine Arts." *Christian Advocate* 1 (Mar. 1823): 113-16.

Baker, John. "Causes of the Decline and Fall of Nations." *Wesleyan-Methodist Magazine* 2 (Dec. 1856): 1078-85.

Barnett, H[enrietta] O. "Passionless Reformers." *Fortnightly Review* 32 (1882): 226-33. Rpt. In *Aesthetics and Religion in Nineteenth-Century Britain*. Vol. 6. Ed. Gavin Budge. Bristol, England: Thoemmes, 2003.

—. "Pictures for the People." *Cornhill Magazine* 47 (1883): 344-52. Rpt. In *Aesthetics and Religion in Nineteenth-Century Britain*. Vol. 6. Ed. Gavin Budge. Bristol, England: Thoemmes, 2003.

Barton, Bernard. "An Appeal for Poetry and Poets." *Wesleyan-Methodist Magazine* 15 (Aug. 1836): 588-92.

— and Lucy Barton. *The Reliquary: by Bernard and Lucy Barton. With a Prefatory Appeal for Poetry and Poets*. London: John W. Parker, 1836.

Baxter, Richard. *The Catechising of Families*. 1707. *Digital Library of Classic Protestant Texts*. 13 Aug. 2012.

Beardmore, William G. "Wesleyan Artists, Past and Present." *Wesleyan-Methodist Magazine* 118 (Aug. 1895): 583-90.

"The Beauties of Music." *Christian Advocate and Journal and Zion's Herald* 5 (5 Aug. 1831): 197.

"The Beautiful." *Christian Advocate and Journal* 36 (12 Sep. 1861): 294.

Beecher, Henry Ward. *Addresses to Young Men*. Philadelphia, PA: Henry Altemus, 1895.

—. *Star Papers; or, Experiences of Art and Nature*. New York: J.C. Derby, 1855.

Bennett, C.W. "Catholicism and Protestantism as Patrons of Christian Art." *Methodist Quarterly Review* 29 (1877): 79-100.

Blake, William. "To the Reverend John Trusler." 23 Aug. 1799. Letter. *Blake's Poetry and Designs*. Ed. Mary Lynn Johnson and John E. Grant. New York: W.W. Norton & Company, 1979. 448-49.

Bowen, W.H. "Æsthetical Culture." *Freewill Baptist Quarterly* 3 (Oct. 1860): 414-425.

Bradstreet, Anne. "Contemplations." *The Works of Anne Bradstreet*. Vol. 2. Ed. Jeannine Hensely. Cambridge, MA: The Belknap Press of Harvard University Press, 1967.

Bristol, F.M. "Reciprocity of Art and Religion." *Methodist Review* 54 (Sep. 1894): 697-712.

Buckley, Dr. "Art and Morals in Art Centers." *Christian Advocate* 60 (12 Mar. 1885): 166-67.

Burchard, S.D. "Moral Uses of Poetry." *Christian Advocate and Journal* 22 (18 Aug. 1847): 132.

Burke, Edmund. *A Philosophical Enquiry into the Origin of Our Ideas of the Sublime and Beautiful. A Philosophical Enquiry into the Sublime and Beautiful and Other Pre-Revolutionary Writings*. Ed. David Womersley. London: Penguin Books, 1998. 49-199.

"Busby's *Lucretius*." *Eclectic Review* 11 (Mar. 1814): 279-91.

Bushnell, Horace. *Christian Nurture*. 1847. New Haven, CT: Yale University Press, 1916.

—. *God in Christ: Three Discourses, Delivered at New Haven, Cambridge, and Andover, with a Preliminary Dissertation on Language*. 3rd ed. 1849. Hartford, CT: Wm. James Hamersley, 1867.

—. *Horace Bushnell: Selected Writings on Language, Religion, and American Culture*. Ed. David L. Smith. AAR Studies in Religion 33. Chico, CA: Scholars Press, 1984.

—. "Unconscious Influence." *Sermons for the New Life* (New York: Charles Scribner, 1858): 186-205. Rpt. of "Influence of Example," *American National Preacher* 20 (Aug. 1846): 169-79.

Calvin, John. *Institutes of the Christian Religion*. Trans. Henry Beveridge. 1845. Peabody, MA: Hendrickson Publishers, 2008.

Cereticus. "On Sacred Poetry." *Christian Observer* 16 (Oct. 1817): 644-50.

"Church Architecture." *Biblical Repertory and Princeton Review* 27 (Oct. 1855): 625-49.

"A Church for Children." *Eclectic Review* 6 (June 1861): 607-612.

"Christianity: Its Influence on Modern Poetry." *Christian Advocate and Journal* 37 (20 Mar. 1862): 91.

"Christian Lyric Poetry." *Primitive Methodist Quarterly Review and Christian Ambassador* n.s. 1 (Jan. 1879): 129-38.

"Coleridge and Southey." *Christian Review* 15 (July 1850): 321-53.

Coleridge, Samuel Taylor. *Aids to Reflection*. Ed. John Beer. Princeton, NJ: Princeton University Press, 1993. Vol. 9 of *The Collected Works of Samuel Taylor Coleridge*. Bollingen Series 75. 16 vols. 1971-2001.

—. "On Poesy or Art." *Lectures 1808-1819 On Literature II*. Ed. R.A. Foakes. Princeton, NJ: Princeton University Press, 1987. 213-25. Vol. 5 of *The Collected Works of Samuel Taylor Coleridge*. Bollingen Series 75. 16 vols. 1971-2001.

—. "On Poesy or Art." *Notes and Lectures upon Shakespeare and Some of the Old Poets and Dramatists with Other Literary Remains*. Ed. H.N. Coleridge. New York: Harper & Brothers, 1853. 328-36. Vol. 4 of *The Complete Works of Samuel Taylor Coleridge*. Ed. W.G.T. Shedd. 7 vols. 1853.

—. "To John Ryland." 3 Nov. 1807. Letter. *Collected Letters of Samuel Taylor Coleridge*. Vol. 3. Ed. Earl Leslie Griggs. Oxford: Clarendon Press, 1959. 35.

Colman, K. "Christianity and the Fine Arts." *Christian Advocate* 46 (1 Jan. 1871): 170.

"Comparative Literary Rank of Nations." *London Quarterly Review* 11 (Jan. 1859): 377-95.

Cooke, J. Hunt. "London Letter." *Watchman* 76 (22 Aug. 1895): 7-8.

Crane, William Carey. "Commerce and Literature." *Baptist Review* 3 (Apr. 1881): 171-84.

Cubitt, George. "National Prosperity Dependent on the Divine Blessing: A Sermon." *Wesleyan-Methodist Magazine* 10 (July 1831): 459-71.

—. "National Prosperity Dependent on the Divine Blessing: A Sermon." *Wesleyan-Methodist Magazine* 10 (Aug. 1831): 525-36.

"Culture." *Christian Advocate and Journal* 37 (30 Jan. 1862): 36.

D. Review of *Poems*, by William W. Lord. *Methodist Quarterly Review* 7 (July 1847): 357-78.

Dawson, W.J. "Religious Doubt in Modern Poetry." *Wesleyan-Methodist Magazine* 7 (Aug. 1883): 604-609.

Day, Henry N. "The Nature of Beauty." *American Presbyterian and Theological Review* 6 (July 1867): 391-419.

—. "Taste and Morals: – The Necessity of Aesthetic Culture to the Highest Moral Excellence." *American Biblical Repository and Classical Review* 3 (July 1847): 524-46.

Dennis, John. *The Grounds of Criticism in Poetry, Contain'd in Some New Discoveries Never Made Before, Requisite for the Writing and Judging of Poems Surely* (London: 1704). *Eighteenth Century Collections Online*. 12 Aug. 2012.

"Domestic Literature." *Southern Presbyterian Review* 1 (July 1851): 1-12.

Dorchester, D. "The Ministry of Art." *Methodist Review* 60 (Nov. 1900): 879-87.

Drummond, Henry. *Letter to Thomas Phillips, Esq., R.A., on the Connexion between the Fine Arts and Religion, and the Means of Their Revival*. London: Fraser, 1840.

Du Bose, H.M. "Authority in Art and Religion." *Methodist Review* [south] 42 (1895-96): 202-16.

Dyer, Sidney. "Literary Criticism." *Baptist Quarterly* 1 (July 1867): 310-24.

East, James T. "The Ministry of Beauty." *Wesleyan-Methodist Magazine* 123 (July 1900): 502-505.

The Editor [J.P. Barnett]. "Novels and Novel Reading: A Familiar Address to the Young." *Baptist Magazine* 74 (Aug. 1882): 358-66.

—. "Novels and Novel Reading: A Familiar Address to the Young." *Baptist Magazine* 74 (Sep. 1882): 415-19.

—. "Novels and Novel Reading: A Familiar Address to the Young." *Baptist Magazine* 74 (Oct. 1882): 452-59.

—. "Novels and Novel Reading: A Familiar Address to the Young." *Baptist Magazine* 74 (Nov. 1882): 498-503.

"Editorial Comment." *Zion's Herald* 63 (17 Mar. 1886): 84.

Edwards, Jonathan. "Experiencing God." *Theological Aesthetics: A Reader*. Ed. Gesa Elsbeth Thiessen. Grand Rapids, MI: William B. Eerdmans, 2004. 172-74.

—. *The "Miscellanies" (Entry nos. a-z, aa-zz, 1-500)*. Ed. Thomas A. Schafer. New Haven, CT: Yale University Press, 1994. Vol. 13 of *Works*.

—. *The Nature of True Virtue*. *Ethical Writings*. Ed. Paul Ramsay. New Haven, CT: Yale University Press, 1989. 537-627. Vol. 8 of *Works*.

—. *A Treatise Concerning Religious Affections*. Ed. John E. Smith. New Haven, CT: Yale University Press, 1959. Vol. 2 of *Works*.

—. *Typological Writings*. Ed. Wallace E. Anderson and Mason I. Lowance, Jr. with David H. Watters. New Haven, CT: Yale University Press, 1993. Vol. 11 of *Works*.

—. *The Works of Jonathan Edwards*. 26 vols. to date. New Haven, CT: Yale University Press, 1957-.

Eliot, Charles W. "The Religious Ideal in Education." *Outlook* 99 (21 Oct. 1911): 411-14.

Emerson, Ralph Waldo. "Nature." *Nature, Addresses and Lectures*. Centenary ed. Boston, MA: Houghton, Mifflin and Company, 1904. 1-77. Vol. 1 of *The Complete Works of Ralph Waldo Emerson*. 12 vols. 1903-1904.

—. "Poetry and Imagination." *Letters and Social Aims*. Centenary ed. Boston, MA: Houghton, Mifflin and Company, 1904. 1-75. Vol. 8 of *The Complete Works of Ralph Waldo Emerson*. 12 vols. 1903-1904.

Emmett, John T. "Religious Art." *British Quarterly Review* 62 (Oct. 1875): 297-335.

"The Empire of Poetry, by Fontenelle." *Christian Index* 5 (22 Oct. 1831): 264-65.

"English Sacred Song." *Baptist Magazine* 82 (Jan. 1890): 9-15.

"English Schools of Art." *Eclectic Review* 23 (Jan. 1848): 68-83.

An Episcopalian. Letter to the Editor of the *Christian Index*. *Christian Index* 6 (12 May 1832): 300.

Episcopos. "The Relations of Christianity to the Human Mind." *Baptist Magazine* 73 (Apr. 1881): 167-74.

"Esthetic Culture." *Christian Advocate and Journal* 40 (7 Dec. 1865): 386.

"Esthetics in Religion." *Christian Advocate* 42 (13 June 1867): 188.

"The Evils of an Unsanctified Literature." *Biblical Repertory and Princeton Review* 15 (Jan. 1843): 65-77.

Excubitor. "On the Influence of the Literature of Fiction." *Christian Observer* 16 (July 1817): 425-29.

"Fergusson on True Principles in Art." *Eclectic Review* 25 (Apr. 1845): 420-37.
Finlayson, T.C. "The Practical Uses of the Imagination." *Congregationalist* 7 (1878): 385-400.
Fisher, D. Havelock. "'Reading Into' a Hymn: On a Recent Criticism of 'Lead Kindly Light.'" *Bible Student and Teacher* 9 (Nov. 1908): 279-82.
"The Foe of the Church." *Watchman* 77 (31 Dec. 1896): 7.
Forman, H. Buxton. "Music and Poetry: Their Origin and Functions." *London Quarterly Review* 39 (Oct. 1872): 1-41.
Forsyth, P.T. "The Need for a Positive Gospel." *London Quarterly Review* 11 (Jan. 1904): 64-99.
Fosdick, Harry Emerson. "Yes, But Religion Is an Art!" *Harper's Monthly Magazine* 162 (Jan. 1931): 129-41.
Foster, John. "Dyer's Poetics." *Eclectic Review* 11 (Apr. 1814): 366-80.
—. "Philosophy of Nature." *Biographical, Literary, and Philosophical Essays: Contributed to the* Eclectic Review. New York: D. Appleton & Company, 1844. 303-16. Rpt. of Review of *The Philosophy of Nature; or, the Influence of Scenery in the Mind and Heart. Eclectic Review* 11 (May 1814): 457-70.
"Fundamentalism and Modernism." *Methodist Review* 42 (May 1927): 483-85.
Gerard, Alexander. *An Essay on Taste. To Which Is Now Added Part Fourth, of the Standard of Taste; with Observations Concerning the Imitative Nature of Poetry.* 3rd ed. (Edinburgh, 1780). *Eighteenth Century Collections Online.* 13 Aug. 2012.
Gladden, Washington. "Christianity and Aestheticism." *The Andover Review; a Religious and Theological Monthly* 1 (Jan. 1884): 13-24.
"Glimpses of Old English Life: Puritan and Actor." *Baptist Magazine* 72 (Aug. 1880): 337-43.
Gosse, Edmund. *Father and Son: A Study of Two Temperaments.* Ed. Peter Abbs. 1907. London: Penguin Books, 1989.
"Guide Books to the Crystal Palace." *London Quarterly Review* 3 (Oct. 1854): 232-79.
H. "Novel Reading." *Christian Index* 60 (5 Oct. 1882): 2.
Hall, Robert. "Poetry and Philosophy." *Christian Advocate and Journal and Zion's Herald* 6 (22 June 1832): 169.
Harris, Samuel. *The Kingdom of Christ on Earth: Twelve Lectures Delivered before the Theological Seminary, Andover.* Andover, MA: Warren F. Draper, 1874.
Hastings, Thomas. "Sacred Music: Source of the Prevailing Abuses in Cultivation, and the only Practical Remedy." *American Biblical Repository and Classical Review* 11 (Apr. 1844): 425-40.
Hawley, B. "Christianity and Art." *Christian Advocate* 55 (1 July 1880): 419-20.
Hazlitt, William. "Introductory – On Poetry in General." *The Selected Writings of William Hazlitt.* Vol. 2. Ed. Duncan Wu. London: Pickering & Chatto, 1998. 165-80.
Hegel, Georg Wilhelm Friedrich. *The Philosophy of Fine Art.* Vol. 1. Trans. F.P.B. Osmaston. London: G. Bell and Sons, 1920.
Higbee, E.E. "The Relation of Christianity to Art." *Mercersburg Review* 21 (July 1874): 341-73.

Hillis, Newell Dwight. *The Investment of Influence: A Study of Social Sympathy and Service*. 24th ed. Chicago, IL: Fleming H. Revell Company, 1897.

Historical Catalogue of Brown University. Providence, RI: Brown University, 1914.

Hodge, Charles. Review of *Discourses on Christian Nurture*, by Horace Bushnell, *Dr. Tyler's Letter to Dr. Bushnell on Christian Nurture*, and *An Argument for "Discourses on Christian Nurture," Addressed to the Publishing Committee of the Massachusetts Sabbath School Society*, by Horace Bushnell. *Biblical Repertory and Princeton Review* 19 (Oct. 1847): 502-39.

—. Review of *God in Christ; Three Discourses delivered at New Haven, Cambridge, and Andover; with a Preliminary Dissertation on Language*, by Horace Bushnell. *Biblical Repertory and Princeton Review* 21 (Apr. 1849): 259-98.

Horne, J. Wesley. "The Book of Nature." *Christian Advocate* 47 (27 Jan. 1872): 201.

"How the Fine Arts of Europe Are Being Perfected in the New World." *Christian Advocate* 48 (17 Apr. 1873): 127.

Hume, John F. "Literary Dissipation." *Baptist Quarterly Review* 12 (July 1890): 300-11.

Hunt, Leigh. "An Answer to the Question, 'What Is Poetry?'" *Later Literary Essays*. Ed. Charles Mahoney. London: Pickering and Chatto, 2003. 5-41. Vol. 4 of *The Selected Writings of Leigh Hunt*. 6 vols. 2003.

Hunt, Theodore W. "Modern Aestheticism." *Princeton Review* 9 (Jan.-June 1882): 148-63.

Hutcheson, Frances. *An Inquiry into the Original of Our Ideas of Beauty and Virtue*. Ed. Wolfgang Leidhold. Rev. ed. Natural Law and Enlightenment Classics. Indianapolis, IN: Liberty Fund, 2008.

"The Imagination in Sin." *Wesleyan-Methodist Magazine* 123 (Dec. 1900): 901-905.

"Influence of Demoralizing Art and Literature." *Christian Advocate* 57 (15 June 1882): 7.

"Influence of the Christian Religion on Poetry." *Quarterly Christian Spectator* 5 (June 1833): 196-208.

Irving, Edward. "Idolatry." *The Collected Writings of Edward Irving*. Vol. 4. Ed. G. Carlyle. London: Alexander Strahan, 1865. 3-16.

J.D.T. "Wordsworth's Conception of Nature." *Primitive Methodist Quarterly Review and Christian Ambassador* n.s. 6 (July 1884): 462-76.

J.F. "Primitive Methodism and Art." *Primitive Methodist Quarterly Review* 24 (Apr. 1902): 233-40.

J.M.W. "Pictures." *Christian Index* 61 (26 Apr. 1883): 6.

Johnson, Franklin. "The Atonement." Torrey, Dixon et al. 3:64-77.

Johnson, Samuel. *Lives of the Poets*. Literary Club ed. Vol. 8 of *The Works of Samuel Johnson*. Troy, NY: Pafraets Press, 1903. 16 vols.

J.T.D. "On Taste." *Christian Advocate and Journal* 19 (11 Sep. 1844): 17.

K. "Brown University." *American Baptist Magazine* 11 (Oct. 1831): 316-18.

Kames, Lord (Henry Home). *Elements of Criticism*. Ed. Peter Jones. 2 vols. Natural Law and Enlightenment Classics. Indianapolis, IN: Liberty Fund, 2005.

"Kant, and Kantism." *Methodist Quarterly Review* 5 (Jan. 1845): 43-54.

Kant, Immanuel. *Critique of Judgment*. Trans. Werner S. Pluhar. Indianapolis, IN: Hackett Publishing Company, 1987.

Keats, John. "To Benjamin Bailey." 22 Nov. 1817. Letter. *Complete Poems and Selected Letters of John Keats*. New York: The Modern Library, 2001. 489-91.

Knight, William A. "A Contribution towards a Theory of Poetry." *British Quarterly Review* 57 (Jan. 1873): 178-89.

Kuhns, L. Oscar. "The Ancient and Modern Feeling for Nature." *Methodist Review* 13 (Nov. 1897): 920-24.

Kuyper, Abraham. "Calvinism and Art." *Lectures on Calvinism*. 1931. New York: Cosimo Classics, 2007. 142-70.

LeConte, Joseph. "On the Nature and Uses of Art," *Southern Presbyterian Review* 15 (Jan. 1863): 311-48.

—. "On the Nature and Uses of Art," *Southern Presbyterian Review* 15 (Apr. 1863): 515-48.

Leigh, Edward. *A Treatise of Religion & Learning*. 1656. *Digital Library of Classic Protestant Texts*. 13 Aug. 2012.

"Leigh Hunt's *Imagination and Fancy*." *British Quarterly Review* 1 (May 1845): 563-81.

"Lesson of a Picture." *Outlook* 48 (16 Dec. 1893): 1116-17.

Levan, F.K. "National Literature." *Mercersburg Review* 14 (Oct. 1867): 564-78.

Leyburn, Dr. "Esthetics." *Christian Advocate and Journal* 36 (25 Apr. 1861): 6.

Lisle, W.M. "Christianity and Culture: Their Divorce and Reconciliation." *Bible Student and Teacher* 5 (Sep. 1906): 169-82.

L.L. "On the Proper Influence of Christianity over Literature." *Christian Spectator* 7 (1 Apr. 1825): 185-88.

Locke, John. *An Essay Concerning Human Understanding*. Ed. John W. Yolton. London: J.M. Dent, 2001.

"Lyric Poetry." *Christian Spectator* 7 (1 July 1825): 356-59.

—. *Christian Spectator* 7 (1 Aug. 1825): 408-11.

MacDonald, George. "Imagination." *Christian Ambassador* 7 (Feb. 1869): 77-87.

—. "The Imagination: Its Function and Its Culture." *British Quarterly Review* 46 (July 1867): 45-70.

Machen, J. Gresham. "Christianity and Culture." *Selected Shorter Writings*. Ed. D.G. Hart. Phillipsburg, NJ: P&R Publishing, 2004. 399-410.

—. *Christianity and Liberalism*. New ed. 1923. Grand Rapids, MI: William B. Eerdmans Publishing Company, 2009.

—. "Christianity and Liberty." *Selected Shorter Writings*. Ed. D.G. Hart. Phillipsburg, NJ: P&R Publishing, 2004. 355-63.

—. "The Responsibility of the Church in Our New Age." *Selected Shorter Writings*. Ed. D.G. Hart. Phillipsburg, NJ: P&R Publishing, 2004. 364-76.

Macmaster, J. Milner. "Il Penseroso and L'Allegro." *Baptist Magazine* 71 (Apr. 1879): 168-73.

Mather, Cotton. "Of Poetry and Style." *The Puritans: A Sourcebook of Their Writings*. Ed. Perry Miller. Vol. 2. Rev. ed. New York: Harper Torchbooks, 1963. 684-89.

Mathews, Shailer. "Business as the Maker of Morals." *Methodist Review* 47 (May 1931):

407-17.

—. *The Gospel and Modern Man.* 1910. New York: Macmillan, 1912.

M.C.H. "On Sacred Poetry." *Wesleyan-Methodist Magazine* 10 (Sep. 1831): 604-12.

—. "On Sacred Poetry." *Wesleyan-Methodist Magazine* 10 (Oct. 1831): 676-83.

—. "On Sacred Poetry." *Methodist Magazine and Quarterly Review* 14 (Jan. 1832): 72-96.

M'Nicholl, Thomas. "Modern Poetry: Its Genius and Tendencies." *London Quarterly Review* 2 (Mar. 1854): 238-57.

"Men of Taste." *Christian Advocate and Journal* 29 (23 Mar. 1854): 48.

"The Methodist Quarterly." *Zion's Herald* 51 (30 Apr. 1874): 139A.

Mill, John Stuart. "The Spirit of the Age." *Mill's Essays on Literature & Society.* Ed. J.B. Schneewind. 1831. New York: Collier Books-Macmillan, 1965. 28-78.

—. "What Is Poetry?" *Mill's Essays on Literature & Society.* Ed. J.B. Schneewind. 1833. New York: Collier Books-Macmillan, 1965. 102-17.

Miller, Henry J. "The Teutonization of English Literature." *Primitive Methodist Quarterly Review* n.s. 7 (Jan. 1885): 132-41.

Mims, Edwin. "Poetry and the Spiritual Life." *Methodist Review* [south] 44 (1896-97): 387-403.

"The Minister and Fiction-Reading." *Methodist Review* 16 (Sep. 1900): 715-24.

Miranda. "Novel Reading." *Christian Advocate and Journal* 11 (23 May 1828): 149.

"Modern Dancing Is Stamped as 'Brutally Indecent' by Rt. Rev. A.J. Drossaerts, Bishop of San Antonio." *Searchlight* 2 (25 Sep. 1919): 1.

Montgomery, James. Introductory Essay. *The Christian Poet; or, Selections in Verse, on Sacred Subjects.* Ed. Montgomery. Glasgow: William Collins, 1828. v-xxxiii.

—. Introductory Essay. *The Christian Psalmist; or, Hymns, Selected and Original.* Ed. Montgomery. Glasgow: Chalmers and Collins, 1825. v-xxxiii.

—. *Lectures on General Literature, Poetry, & c.* New York: Harper & Brothers, 1844.

"Montgomery's *Lectures on Poetry.*" *Eclectic Review* 10 (July 1833): 1-22.

"Moral Aesthetics; or the Goodness of God in the Ornaments of the Universe." *Biblical Repertory and Princeton Review* 24 (Jan. 1852): 38-52.

More, Hannah. "Preface to the Tragedies." *Works* 1: 502-10.

—. *Strictures on the Modern System of Female Education. Works* 1: 311-417.

—. *The Works of Hannah More.* 2 vols. 1st Amer. ed. New York: Harper & Brothers Publishers, 1852.

"Mr. Browning's 'Asolando.'" *Baptist Magazine* 82 (Apr. 1890): 175-78.

"Music: Its Uses, Secular and Sacred." *Christian Ambassador* 4 (Feb. 1866): 17-27.

"National Literature, the Exponent of National Character." *Biblical Repertory and Princeton Review* 24 (Apr. 1852): 201-25.

"Nature Guiding Up to God." *Christian Index* 7 (29 Sep. 1832): 204-205.

"The Necessity of a Religious Literature." *American Baptist Magazine* 15 (Jan. 1835): 5-9.

Neff, Marietta. "On the Religious Significance of Poetry." The Christian Century *Reader: Representative Articles, Editorials, and Poems Selected from More than Fifty Years of*

The Christian Century. Ed. Harold E. Fey and Margaret Frakes. 1909. New York: Association Press, 1962. 383-84.

"The Novel and Novel-Reading." *Biblical Repertory and Princeton Review* 41 (Apr. 1869): 202-34.

"Novel Reading." *Christian Index* 63 (30 July 1885): 3.

"Nude Dancers Shock Deacon; Jail for Girls." *Searchlight* 2 (4 Sep. 1919): 4.

"Nude Exhibitions in Art." *Christian Advocate* 53 (29 Aug. 1878): 550.

"The Obligations of Genius." *Christian Observer* 29 (Aug. 1829): 485-90.

"Occasional Pieces of Poetry." *Christian Spectator* 7 (1 June 1825): 324-27.

"On the Influence of the Literature of Fiction." *Christian Observer* 16 (June 1817): 370-74.

"On the Moral and Religious Improvement that May Be Derived from Natural Beauty and Sublimity." *Christian Spectator* 6 (1 Nov. 1824): 561-62.

Orbilius. "To the Editor of the *Christian Spectator*." *Christian Spectator* 4 (1 Feb. 1822): 78-82.

Otheman, Edward. "Consecrated Talent." *American Baptist Magazine* 13 (Oct. 1833): 1-13.

—. "An Interesting Scene." *Zion's Herald* 50 (10 July 1873): 1.

—. "The Moral Influence of the Fine Arts," *Methodist Magazine and Quarterly Review* 17 (July 1835): 318-32.

—. [Untitled]. *Christian Advocate and Journal* 8 (22 Nov. 1833): 49.

Otts, J.M.P. "The Beautiful." *Southern Presbyterian Review* 17 (July 1866): 31-52.

Owen, John. *The Glory of Christ*. Excerpted in *Theological Aesthetics: A Reader*. Ed. Gesa Elsbeth Thiessen. Grand Rapids, MI: William B. Eerdmans, 2004. 167-70.

Park, Edwards Amasa. "The Theology of the Intellect and That of the Feelings." *American Philosophical Addresses, 1700-1900*. Ed. Joseph L. Blair. College Studies in American Culture 17. New York: Columbia University Press, 1946. 627-58.

Parsons, Eugene. "Tennyson's Art and Genius." *Baptist Quarterly Review* 11 (Jan. 1889): 29-47.

Pattison, T. Harwood. "The Relation of Art to Religion." *Baptist Quarterly Review* 8 (July 1886): 324-37.

Peckard, Peter. "National Crimes the Cause of National Punishments: A Discourse, Delivered in the Cathedral Church of Peterborough, on the Fast-Day, February 25th, 1795." *Wesleyan-Methodist Magazine* 7 (Aug. 1861): 687-95.

Percival, Dr. "The Advantages of a Taste for the Beauties of Nature." *Christian Advocate and Journal* 8 (11 Oct. 1833): 28.

"Periodical Literature." *Christian Ambassador: A Quarterly Review, and Journal of Theological Literature* 3 (Feb. 1865): 57-66.

Perkins, William. *A Golden Chain*. 1616. Digital Library of Classic Protestant Texts. 13 Aug. 2012.

—. *A Reformed Catholic*. 1616. Digital Library of Classic Protestant Texts. 13 Aug. 2012.

—. *A Treatise of Man's Imaginations*. 1617. Digital Library of Classic Protestant Texts. 13 August 2012.

—. *A Warning Against Idolatry*. 1616. Digital Library of Classic Protestant Texts. 13 Aug.

2012.

"The Pictorial Edition of Shakespeare, Parts I to XXXI." *Eclectic Review* 9 (May 1841): 541-63.

"Pictures." *Christian Index* 60 (22 June 1882): 12.

Poe, Edgar Allan. "The Poetic Principle." *Essays English and American*. Ed. Charles W. Eliot. The Harvard Classics. New York: P.F. Collier & Son Corporation, 1968. 371-92.

"The Poems of Lewis Morris." *Baptist Magazine* 82 (Sep. 1890): 408-15.

"The Poetical Element of the Bible." *Southern Presbyterian Review* 8 (July 1854): 91-112.

"Poetry and Civilization." *British Quarterly Review* 4 (Aug. 1846): 350-78.

"Poetry and Its Uses." *Christian Observer* 66 (Feb. 1866): 111-24.

"The Poetry of Puritanism." *Baptist Magazine* 49 (Feb. 1857): 101.

Pollard, Edward B. "Aesthetic and Imaginative Elements in the Words of Jesus." *Biblical World* 30 (Nov. 1907): 339-45.

Porter, Noah. "Modern Literature and Christianity." *Christian Advocate* (30 Oct. 1873): 346.

"Practical Aesthetics." *British Quarterly Review* 71 (Jan. 1880): 82-107.

"The Preacher and the Poet." *Methodist Review* 19 (Mar. 1903): 211-20.

"Prospects of British Art." *British Quarterly Review* 2 (Nov. 1845): 466-90.

R., "Popish Paintings." *Edinburgh Christian Instructor* 28 (July 1829): 492-98.

Ramsay, Julian. "Percy Bysshe Shelley." *Primitive Methodist Quarterly Review* n.s. 11 (Oct. 1889): 577-94.

"Recent Poetry." *Eclectic Review* 18 (Dec. 1845): 662-78.

"Reflections of the Christian in Viewing the Works of Nature." *American Baptist Magazine* 8 (Nov. 1828): 345-47.

Reid, Thomas. *Thomas Reid's Lectures on the Fine Arts*. Transcribed by Peter Kivy. International Archives of the History of Ideas, Series Minor 7. The Hague: Martinus Nijhoff, 1973.

Reily, W.M. "The Artist; the Seer and Minister of Beauty." *Reformed Quarterly Review* (July 1881): 378-429.

"The Relation of Roman Catholicism and Protestantism to the Fine Arts." *Eclectic Review* 3 (Jan. 1858): 1-21.

"Religion of the Imagination." *Christian Advocate and Journal and Zion's Herald* 4 (16 Oct. 1829): 28.

"Religious Education: The Educational Value of Religious Art." *Biblical World* 41 (Feb. 1913): 133-34.

"Religious Plays." *Baptist Magazine* 73 (May 1881): 205-209.

"Religious Poets and Poetry." *Christian Review* 14 (May 1849): 271-85.

"Rev. George Lansing Taylor, D.D." *Alumni Record of Wesleyan University, Middletown, Conn.* 3rd ed. 1881-3. Hartford, CT: Press of The Case, Lockwood & Brainard Company, 1883. 642-44

Review of *Nature and the Supernatural, as Together Constituting the One System of God*, by Horace Bushnell. *London Quarterly Review* 18 (Apr. 1862): 100-23.

Review of *Philosophical Essays*, by Dugald Stewart. *Christian Observer* 11 (Oct. 1812): 654-75.

Review of *Robert Burns; as a Poet, and as Man*, by Samuel Tyler. *Biblical Repertory and Princeton Review* 21 (Apr. 1849): 251-58.

Review of *The Elements of Intellectual Philosophy*, by Francis Wayland; *A System of Intellectual Philosophy*, by Asa Mahan; and *Empirical Psychology; or, the Human Mind as Given in Consciousness*, by Laurens P. Hickok. *Biblical Repertory and Princeton Review* 27 (Jan. 1855): 69-102.

Review of *The Essentials of Æsthetics in Music, Poetry, Sculpture, and Architecture*, by George Lansing Raymond. *Outlook* 85 (16 Mar. 1907): 621-22.

Review of *The Historical Development of Speculative Philosophy, from Kant to Hegel*, from the German of Dr. H.M. Chalybäus, by Rev. Alfred Edersheim. *London Quarterly Review* 2 (Mar. 1854): 285-87.

Review of *The Widow of the City of Nain and Other Poems*, by an Undergraduate of the University of Cambridge. *Christian Observer* 18 (Feb. 1819): 114-20.

Rigg, J.H. Review of *The Gay Science*, by E.S. Dallas. *London Quarterly Review* 28 (Apr. 1867): 140-66.

Rogers, G. "The Advantages of Cultivating the Love of Nature." *The Sword and the Trowel; A Record of Combat with Sin and of Labour for the Lord* (Sep. 1876): 391-402.

Rogers, James. "The Science and Poetry of Art." *London Quarterly Review* 4 (July 1855): 403-25.

"A Romantic Christ." *Methodist Review* 22 (Sep. 1907): 788-801.

Ruskin, John. *Lectures on Art and Aratra Pentelici, with Lectures and Notes on Greek Art and Mythology*. Ed. E.T. Cook and Alexander Wedderburn. Library ed. London: George Allen, 1905. Vol. 20 of *The Works of John Ruskin*. 39 vols. 1903-1912.

—. *Modern Painters*. Vol. 2. Ed. E.T. Cook and Alexander Wedderburn. Library ed. London: George Allen, 1903. Vol. 4 of *The Works of John Ruskin*. 39 vols. 1903-1912.

—. "The Useful and the Beautiful." *Christian Advocate and Journal* 29 (22 June 1854): 97.

"Sacred Poetry." *Eclectic Review* 1 (May 1837): 441-63.

"Samuel Taylor Coleridge." *Freewill Baptist Quarterly* 3 (Oct. 1855): 361-89.

Sargent, Walter. "One Contribution which Art Makes to Religion." *Biblical World* 41 (June 1913): 359-65.

Schiedt, R.C. "Is the Modern Novel a Work of Art?" *Reformed Quarterly Review* 3 (July 1891): 370-88.

Selby, Thomas G. "Irreligious Civilizations." *Wesleyan-Methodist Magazine* 120 (May 1897): 323-31.

"Sensibility." *Christian Advocate and Journal* 10 (15 July 1836): 188.

"Sensibility and Super-Sensibility." *Christian Advocate and Journal* 19 (26 Feb. 1845): 116.

S.F.S. "Piety Essential to the Full Development of the Mental Powers." *American Baptist Magazine* 14 (Aug. 1834): 1-10.

Shaftesbury, Third Earl of (Anthony Ashley Cooper). *Characteristics of Men, Manners,*

Opinions, Times, Etc. Ed. John M. Robertson. 2 vols. 1711. Gloucester, MA: Peter Smith, 1963.

Shairp, J.C. "The Aim of Poetry." *Princeton Review* (July-Dec. 1878): 449-70.

Shedd, William G.T. "The Fundamental Properties of Style." *American Presbyterian and Theological Review* (Oct. 1864): 561-85.

Shelley, Percy Bysshe. *A Defence of Poetry. Shelley's Prose and Poetry.* Ed. Donald H. Reiman and Sharon B. Powers. New York: W.W. Norton & Co., 1977. 480-508.

—. Preface to *Prometheus Unbound: A Lyrical Drama in Four Acts. Shelley's Prose and Poetry* 132-36.

Sickels, Frank E. "Tent Evangelist – A Review." *New York Evangelist* 72 (17 Oct. 1901): 5-8.

Sidney, Philip. *The Apology for Poetry. The Longman Anthology of British Literature, Volume 1B, The Early Modern Period.* 4th ed. Ed. Clare Carroll and Andrew Hadfield. New York: Longman, 2010. 999-1032.

Slicer, Adeline E.H. "The Art Student Abroad – Second Paper." *Christian Advocate* 51 (12 Oct. 1876): 321.

Smetham, James. "Modern Sacred Art in England." *London Quarterly Review* 18 (Apr. 1862): 51-79.

Smith, Gerald Birney. Review of *The Field of Ethics*, by George Herbert Palmer and *Culture and Restraint*, by Hugh Black. *Biblical World* 20 (July 1902): 70-72.

Smith, Samuel Stanhope. *The Lectures, Corrected and Improved, which Have Been Delivered for a Series of Years, in the College of New Jersey; On the Subjects of Moral and Political Philosophy.* Vol. 1. New York: Whiting and Watson, 1812.

Smyth, Thomas. "The War of the South Vindicated." *Southern Presbyterian Review* 15 (Apr. 1863): 479-514.

Snowden, James H. "Modernism in the Bible." *Methodist Review* 44 (July 1928): 487-99.

Spes. "Art and Morals." *Wesleyan-Methodist Magazine* 119 (May 1896): 338-39.

Spurgeon, Charles. "The Power of Nonconformity." *The Sword and the Trowel; A Record of Combat with Sin and of Labour for the Lord* (July 1876): 304-307.

Stanton, Horace C. "The Beauty of Heaven." *Bible Student and Teacher* 12 (May 1910): 375-81.

Stewart, Dugald. *Elements of the Philosophy of the Human Mind, Vol. 1, to Which Is Prefixed, Introduction and Part First of the Outlines of Moral Philosophy. With Many New and Important Additions.* Ed. Sir William Hamilton. 1854. Westmead, England: Gregg International Publishers, 1971.

—. "Essay Third: On the Faculty of Taste." *Philosophical Essays. With Many New and Important Additions.* Ed. Sir William Hamilton. 1855. Westmead, England: Gregg International Publishers, 1971.

Stowe, Harriet Beecher. *The Minister's Wooing.* 1859. Hartford, CT: Harriet Beecher Stowe Center-Rutgers University Press, 1998.

Strong, Josiah. *The New Era; or, The Coming Kingdom.* New York: The Baker & Taylor Company, 1893.

—. *Our Country: Its Possible Future and Its Present Crisis.* Rev. ed. New York: The Baker & Taylor Co. for the Home Missionary Society, 1891.

"The Study of Hymnology." *Baptist Magazine* 84 (May 1892): 226-32.
"Substitutes for Christianity." *Methodist Review* 33 (Nov. 1917): 969-74.
"Symbols of Thought." *Presbyterian Quarterly Review* 10 (Apr. 1862): 623-53.
T.A. "What Is Poetry?" *Mercersburg Review* 11 (July 1859): 382-403.
Taylor, George Lansing. "Fine Art a Record of Civilization." *Wesleyan-Methodist Magazine* 20 (Aug. 1874): 703-709.
—. "Fine Art: Its Nature, Necessity, and Offices." *Methodist Quarterly Review* 34 (Apr. 1874): 231-46.
—. "Syracuse University—Inauguration of the College of the Fine Arts." *Christian Advocate* 48 (2 Oct. 1873): 317.
"Taylor, George Lansing." *Appleton's Cyclopedia of American Biography*. Vol. 6. Ed. James Grant Wilson and John Fiske. New York: D. Appleton and Company, 1889. 44.
Taylor, Henry. Preface. *Philip van Artevelde; A Dramatic Romance, in Two Parts*. Boston, MA: James Munroe & Company, 1835. v-xxii.
Taylor, W.F. "Christ in Art." *Baptist Quarterly Review* 8 (1886): 462-77.
"Testimony to the Success of Missions." *Baptist Missionary Magazine* 19 (Dec. 1839): 291-97.
Thompson, Peter. "The Minister in His Study." *Methodist Review* 23 (Sep. 1908): 771-79.
"Thoughts on Church Music." *Presbyterian Magazine* 4 (July 1854): 303-08.
Titzel, John M. "Beauty and Art." *Reformed Quarterly Review* 3 (July 1891): 389-405.
T.L. "The Anatomy of Sentimentalism." *Mercersburg Review* 9 (Jan. 1857): 28-46.
Torrey, R.A., A.C. Dixon et al., eds. *The Fundamentals: A Testimony to the Truth*. 4 vols. 1917. Grand Rapids, MI: Baker Books, 2003.
Traver, Allen. "Thinking; Thought; Literature." *Reformed Quarterly Review* 28 (Jan. 1881): 178-97.
"The True Notion of the Picturesque." *Christian Advocate* 58 (15 Nov. 1883): 726.
Turner, Daniel. *Devotional Poetry Vindicated, in Some Occasional Remarks on the Late Dr. Samuel Johnson's Animadversions Upon That Subject in His Life of Waller, To Which Is Added a Short Essay on Genius*. Oxford: Printed for the Author, 1785. *Eighteenth Century Collections Online*. 26 June 2012.
"Unsymmetrical Lives." *Primitive Methodist Quarterly Review and Christian Ambassador* n.s. 3 (1881): 519-26.
[Untitled]. *New York Evangelist* 58 (3 Mar. 1887): 2.
[Untitled]. *Record* (17 Mar. 1862): 2.
Upham, Thomas C. *Mental Philosophy; Embracing the Three Departments of the Intellect, Sensibilities, and Will*. 2 vols. New York: Harper & Brothers, 1869.
Van Dyke, Henry J., Jr. "Art and Ethics: In Some of Their Relations." *Princeton Review* (Jan.-June 1883): 91-110.
Votaw, Clyde Weber. "Moral Training in the Public Schools." *Biblical World* 34 (Nov. 1909): 295-306.
Waters, Robert. "Genius in Action: The Realists." *Christian Advocate* 63 (18 Oct. 1888): 687-88.
Wayland, Francis. "The Abuse of the Imagination." *Christian Advocate and Journal* 10

(13 Apr. 1836): 133-34.

Welling, James C. "The True Sources of Literary Inspiration." *Biblical Repertory and Princeton Review* 43 (Jan. 1871): 102-20.

Wells, P. "Poetry: Its Social Uses and Religious Influences." *Christian Advocate and Journal* 26 (8 Feb. 1849): 24.

Wesley, John. "On Conscience." Sermon CV. *Second Series of Sermons, Third Series of Sermons, Fourth Series of Sermons, Fifth Series of Sermons*. 186-94. Vol. 7 of *Works* 7.

—. "Preface to *A Pocket Hymn Book, for the Use of Christians of All Denominations.*" *Grammars, Musical Works, Letters, and Indexes*. 343-45. Vol. 14 of *Works* 14.

—. "Preface to Extracts from the Works of the Puritans." *Grammars, Musical Works, Letters, and Indexes*. 228-30. Vol. 14 of *Works*.

—. *A Roman Catechism, Faithfully Drawn Out of the Allowed Writings of the Church of Rome, with a Reply Thereto. Letters, Essays, Dialogs, and Addresses*. 107-12. Vol. 10 of *Works*.

—. "Thoughts on Genius." *Letters*. 477-79. Vol. 13 of *Works*.

—. "Thoughts on the Character and Writings of Mr. Prior." *Letters*. 418-25. Vol. 13 of *Works*.

—. "Thoughts on the Power of Music." *Letters*. 470-73. Vol. 13 of *Works*.

—. "Thoughts upon Taste." *Letters*. 465-70. Vol. 13 of *Works*.

—. "To the Same" [Mr. Walter Churchey, of Brecon]. 6 Dec. 1788. Letter CCCCXCVII. *Letters*. 437. Vol. 12 of *Works*.

—. *The Works of John Wesley*. 3rd ed. 14 vols. 1872. Grand Rapids, MI: Baker Books, 2007.

Westwood, H.C. "Art as a Moral Reformer." *Christian Advocate* 60 (9 July 1885): 438-39.

"What Is Poetry?" *Christian Advocate and Journal* 26 (30 Oct. 1851): 173.

[Wheatley, Phillis]. "On Imagination." *Arminian Magazine* 7 (Dec. 1784): 672-73.

Wheaton College Bulletin. Buswell Memorial Library, Wheaton College, Wheaton, IL.

White, J.S. "Religion and Art." *Primitive Methodist Quarterly Review and Christian Ambassador* n.s. 9 (Jan. 1887): 127-33.

Wilberforce, William. *A Practical View of Christianity*. Ed. Kevin Charles Belmonte. Peabody, MA: Hendrickson Publishers, 1996. Rpt. of *A Practical View of the Prevailing Religious Conceptions of Professed Christians in the Higher and Middle Classes in This Country Contrasted with Real Christianity*. 1797.

Wilde, Oscar. Preface. *The Picture of Dorian Gray*. *Oscar Wilde: Collected Works*. New York: Barnes & Noble, 2006. 1-4.

—. *De Profundis*. *Oscar Wilde: Collected Works*. New York: Barnes & Noble, 2006. 1033-1120.

Wilkinson, Emma T. "Morality versus Materialism in Our Schools." *Outlook* 50 (18 Aug. 1894): 258-60.

Winchester, C.T. "Good Poetry and Good Morals." *Christian Advocate* 57 (9 Mar. 1882): 147.

"Wise Words to Novel-Readers." *Bible Student and Teacher* 8 (May 1908): 358-60.

"Wordsworth Considered as a Religious Poet." *Christian Review* 16 (July 1851): 434-60.

Wordsworth, William. *The Excursion*. Ed. Sally Bushell, James A. Butler, Michael C. Jaye, with David Garcia. Cornell Wordsworth. Ithaca, NY: Cornell University Press, 2007.

—. "Lines Composed a Few Miles above Tintern Abbey, on Revisiting the Banks of the Wye during a Tour. July 13, 1798." *William Wordsworth: Selected Poems*. Ed. John O. Hayden. London: Penguin Books, 1994. 66-70.

—. "Preface to *Lyrical Ballads*." *Wordsworth's Literary Criticism*. Ed. Nowell C. Smith. New preface and intro. Howard Mills. 1905. Bristol: Bristol Classical Press, 1980. 11-41.

—. *The Prelude*. 1850. *The Prelude: 1799, 1805, 1850*. Ed. Jonathan Wordsworth, M.H. Abrams, and Stephen Gill. New York: W.W. Norton & Co., 1979.

"The Works of the Rev. Richard Watson: with Memoirs of His Life and Writings." *London Quarterly Review* 2 (Mar. 1854): 185-237.

Wright, J.W. "The Aesthetic in Religion." *Methodist Review* 9 (Jan. 1893): 90-96.

W.R.J. "Characteristics of Wordsworth's Poetry." *Wesleyan-Methodist Magazine* 15 (Apr. 1869): 319-27.

Secondary Sources

Abrams, M.H. *The Mirror and the Lamp: Romantic Theory and the Critical Tradition*. London: Oxford University Press, 1953.

Ahlstrom, Sydney E. *A Religious History of the American People*. New Haven, CT: Yale University Press, 1972.

—. "The Scottish Philosophy and American Theology." *Church History* 24 (1955): 257-72.

Allan, David. *Virtue, Learning and the Scottish Enlightenment: Ideas of Scholarship in Early Modern History*. Edinburgh: Edinburgh University Press, 1993.

Altholz, Josef L. *The Religious Press in Britain, 1760-1900*. Contributions to the Study of Religion 22. New York: Greenwood Press, 1989.

Altick, Richard D. *The English Common Reader: A Social History of the Mass Reading Public, 1800-1900*. 2nd ed. Columbus, OH: Ohio State University Press, 1998.

—. *Victorian People and Ideas: A Companion for the Modern Reader of Victorian Literature*. New York: W.W. Norton, 1973.

Anderson, Wallace E. "Editor's Introduction." *Scientific and Philosophical Writings*. Ed. Wallace E. Anderson. New Haven, CT: Yale University Press, 1980. 1-143. Vol. 6 of *Works*.

Apostolos-Cappadona, Diane. *The Spirit and the Vision: The Influence of Christian Romanticism on the Development of 19th-Century American Art*. American Academy of Religion Academy Series 84. Atlanta, GA: Scholars Press, 1995.

Ashfield, Andrew and Peter de Bolla, eds. *The Sublime: A Reader in Eighteenth-Century Aesthetic Theory*. Cambridge: Cambridge University Press, 1998.

Barber, Sarah. "Antithesis: How to Create a Nation." *History, Nationhood and the Ques-*

tion of Britain. Ed. Helen Brocklehurst and Robert Phillips. Houndmills, England: Palgrave Macmillan, 2004. 171-83.

Barth, J. Robert, S.J. *Coleridge and Christian Doctrine*. Rev. ed. 1969. New York: Fordham University Press, 1987.

—. *Romanticism and Transcendence: Wordsworth, Coleridge, and the Religious Imagination*. Columbia, MO: University of Missouri Press, 2003.

—. *The Symbolic Imagination: Coleridge and the Romantic Tradition*. 2nd ed. New York: Fordham University Press, 2001.

Barzun, Jacques. *The Use and Abuse of Art*. The A.W. Mellon Lectures in the Fine Arts. Bollingen Series 35. Princeton, NJ: Princeton University Press, 1974.

Bate, Walter Jackson. *From Classic to Romantic: Premises of Taste in Eighteenth Century England*. New York: Harper Torchbooks, 1946.

Beardsley, Monroe C. *Aesthetics from Classical Greece to the Present: A Short History*. 1966. Tuscaloosa, AL: University of Alabama Press, 1975.

Bebbington, David W. *Evangelicalism in Modern Britain: A History from the 1730s to the 1980s*. 1989. Grand Rapids, MI: Baker Book House, 1992.

—. "Evangelicalism in Modern Britain and America: A Comparison." *Amazing Grace: Evangelicalism in Australia, Britain, Canada, and the United States*. Ed. George A. Rawlyk and Mark A. Noll. Montreal: McGill-Queen's University Press, 1994. 183-212.

Beckson, Karl. *The Religion of Art: A Modernist Theme in British Literature 1885-1925*. AMS Studies in Cultural History 8. New York: AMS Press, 2006.

Blodgett, Jan. *Protestant Evangelical Culture and Contemporary Society*. Contributions to the Study of Religion 51. Westport, CT: Greenwood Press, 1997.

Bohls, Elizabeth A. "Standards of Taste, Discourses of 'Race,' and the Aesthetic Education of a Monster: Critique of Empire in *Frankenstein*." *Eighteenth-Century Life* 18 (1994): 23-36.

Bozeman, Theodore Dwight. *Protestants in an Age of Science: The Baconian Ideal and Antebellum American Religious Thought*. Chapel Hill, NC: University of North Carolina Press, 1977.

Bradley, Ian. *The Call to Seriousness: The Evangelical Impact on the Victorians*. London: Jonathan Cape, 1976.

Brake, Laurel. "Literary Criticism and the Victorian Periodicals." *Yearbook of English Studies* 16 (1986): 92-116.

Bronson, Walter C. *The History of Brown University 1764-1914*. Providence, RI: Brown University, 1914.

Buckley, Jerome Hamilton. *The Victorian Temper: A Study in Literary Culture*. New York: Vintage Books, 1951.

Budge, Gavin, ed. *Romantic Empiricism: Poetics and the Philosophy of Common Sense, 1780-1830*. Lewisburg, PA: Bucknell University Press, 2007.

Butterfield, Herbert. *The Whig Interpretation of History*. New York: W.W. Norton, 1965.

Carrol, Noël. "Art and the Moral Realm." *Blackwell Guide to Aesthetics*. Ed. Peter Kivy. Malden, MA: Blackwell Publishing, 2004: 126-51.

Carwardine, Richard. *Transatlantic Revivalism: Popular Evangelicalism in Britain and*

America, 1790-1865. Westport, CT: Greenwood Press, 1978.
Charvat, William. *The Origins of American Critical Thought 1810-1835*. Philadelphia, PA: University of Pennsylvania Press, 1936.
Cherry, Conrad. *Nature and Religious Imagination: From Edwards to Bushnell*. Philadelphia, PA: Fortress Press, 1980.
Chiles, Robert E. *Theological Transition in American Methodism, 1790-1935*. Lanham, MD: University Press of America, 1983.
Chitnis, Anand C. *The Scottish Enlightenment and Early Victorian Society*. London: Croom Helm, 1986.
Clark, J.C.D. "Protestantism, Nationalism, and National Identity, 1660-1832." *Historical Journal* 43 (2000): 249-76.
Claydon, Tony and Ian McBride, eds. *Protestantism and National Identity: Britain and Ireland, c. 1650-c. 1850*. Cambridge: Cambridge University Press, 1998.
—. "The Trials of the Chosen Peoples: Recent Interpretations of Protestantism and National Identity in Britain and Ireland." *Protestantism* 3-29.
Cole, Brendan. "Jean Delville's *La Mission de l'Art*: Hegelian Echoes in Fin-de-siècle Idealism." *Religion and the Arts* 11 (2007): 330-72.
Colley, Linda. *Britons: Forging the Nation, 1707-1837*. New Haven, CT: Yale University Press, 1992.
Conforti, Joseph A. *Jonathan Edwards, Religious Tradition, and American Culture*. Chapel Hill, NC: University of North Carolina Press, 1995.
Davies, Horton. *Worship and Theology in England: From Watts and Wesley to Maurice, 1690-1850*. Princeton, NJ: Princeton University Press, 1961.
Dayton, Donald W. and Robert K. Johnston, eds. *The Variety of American Evangelicalism*. Knoxville, TN: University of Tennessee/Knoxville; Downer's Grove, IL: Intervarsity Press, 1991.
Dickie, George. *The Century of Taste: The Philosophical Odyssey of Taste in the Eighteenth Century*. New York: Oxford University Press, 1996.
Dillenberger, John. *The Visual Arts and Christianity in America: From the Colonial Period to the Present*. New ed. New York: Crossroad, 1989.
Douglas, Ann. *The Feminization of American Culture*. 1977. New York: Anchor Press-Doubleday, 1988.
Dunlap, Barbara J. "The London Quarterly and Holborn Review." *British Literary Magazines: The Victorian and Edwardian Age, 1837-1913*. Ed. Alvin Sullivan. Historical Guides to the World's Periodicals and Newspapers. Westport, CT: Greenwood Press, 1984. 203-209.
Dyrness, William A. *Reformed Theology and Visual Culture: The Protestant Imagination from Calvin to Edwards*. Cambridge: Cambridge University Press, 2004.
Elliott-Binns, L.E. *The Early Evangelicals: A Religious and Social Study*. London: Lutterworth Press, 1953.
Engell, James. *The Creative Imagination: Enlightenment to Romanticism*. 1981. San Jose, CA: toExcel, 1999.
Erdt, Terrence. *Jonathan Edwards: Art and the Sense of the Heart*. Amherst, MA: University of Massachusetts Press, 1980.

Fackler, P. Mark and Charles H. Lippy. Preface. *Popular Religious Magazines of the United States*. Ed. Fackler and Lippy. Historical Guides to the World's Periodicals and Newspapers. Westport, CT: Greenwood Press, 1995. vii-ix.

—. Introduction. *Popular Religious Magazines of the United States*. Ed. Fackler and Lippy. Historical Guides to the World's Periodicals and Newspapers. Westport, CT: Greenwood Press, 1995. xi-xvii.

Fiering, Norman. *Jonathan Edwards's Moral Thought and Its British Context*. Chapel Hill, NC: University of North Carolina Press, 1981.

Foster, Charles I. *An Errand of Mercy: The Evangelical United Front, 1790-1837*. Chapel Hill, NC: University of North Carolina Press, 1960.

Foster, Stephen. *The Long Argument: English Puritanism and the Shaping of New England Culture, 1570-1700*. Chapel Hill, NC: University of North Carolina Press, 1991.

Fraser, Hilary. *Beauty and Belief: Aesthetics and Religion in Victorian England*. Cambridge: Cambridge University Press, 1986.

Garland, Martha McMackin. *Cambridge Before Darwin: The Ideal of a Liberal Education, 1800-1860*. Cambridge: Cambridge University Press, 1980.

Gauvreau, Michael. "The Empire of Evangelicalism: Varieties of Common Sense in Scotland, Canada, and the United States." *Evangelicalism: Comparative Studies of Popular Protestantism in North America, the British Isles, and Beyond, 1700-1990*. Ed. Mark A. Noll, David W. Bebbington, and George A. Rawlyk.

Gill, Frederick C. *The Romantic Movement and Methodism: A Study of English Romanticism and the Evangelical Revival*. 1937. London: The Epworth Press, 1954.

Gombrich, E.H. *The Story of Art*. Pocket ed. London: Phaidon Press, 2006.

Gordis, Lisa M. *Opening Scripture: Bible Reading and Interpretive Authority in Puritan New England*. Chicago, IL: University of Chicago Press, 2003.

Grabo, Norman S. "Running the Gauntlet: Seventeenth-Century Literary Criticism." *ELH* 67 (2000): 697-715.

Grave, S.A. *The Scottish Philosophy of Common Sense*. Oxford: Clarendon Press, 1960.

Guyer, Paul. "The Origin of Modern Aesthetics: 1711-35." *The Blackwell Guide to Aesthetics*. Ed. Peter Kivy. Malden, MA: Blackwell Publishing, 2004. 15-44.

Hammermeister, Kai. *The German Aesthetic Tradition*. Cambridge: Cambridge University Press, 2002.

Handy, Robert T. *A Christian America: Protestant Hopes and Historical Realities*. 2nd rev. ed. New York: Oxford University Press, 1984.

Haroutunian, Joseph. *Piety Versus Moralism: The Passing of the New England Theology*. New York: Henry Holt and Company, 1932.

Harris, Neil. *The Artist in American Society: The Formative Years 1790-1860*. Chicago, IL: University of Chicago Press, 1982.

Hatch, Nathan O. *The Democratization of American Christianity*. New Haven, CT: Yale University Press, 1989.

Heimert, Alan. *Religion and the American Mind: From the Great Awakening to the Revolution*. Cambridge, MA: Harvard University Press, 1966.

Herman, Bruce. "Policy on the Use of Nude Models in Art." Gordon College, Wenham, MA. 6 Aug. 2012. http://www.gordon.edu/fs_download/pages/

ArtPolicy_NudeModels.pdf.

Hipple, Walter John, Jr. *The Beautiful, the Sublime, & the Picturesque in Eighteenth-Century British Aesthetic Theory*. Carbondale, IL: Southern Illinois University Press, 1957.

Houghton, Walter E. *The Victorian Frame of Mind 1830-1870*. New Haven, CT: Yale University Press for Wellesley College, 1957.

—— et al., eds. *The Wellesley Index to Victorian Periodicals, 1824-1900*. Vol. 4. Toronto: University of Toronto Press, 1987.

Howe, Daniel Walker. *The Political Culture of the American Whigs*. Chicago, IL: University of Chicago Press, 1984.

Howes, Graham. *The Art of the Sacred: An Introduction to the Aesthetics of Art and Belief*. London: I.B. Tauris, 2007.

Hunt, Lester H. "Sentiment and Sympathy." *Journal of Aesthetics and Art Criticism* 62 (2004): 339-54.

Hunter, James Davison. *American Evangelicalism: Conservative Religion and the Quandary of Modernity*. New Brunswick, NJ: Rutgers University Press, 1983.

Husbands, M. "Forsyth, Peter Taylor." Larsen, Bebbington, and Noll 232-36.

Introduction. *The Longman Anthology of British Literature, Volume 2B, The Victorian Age*. 4th ed. Ed. Heather Henderson and William Sharpe. Boston: Longman, 2010. 1049-1073.

Jay, Elisabeth. *The Religion of the Heart: Anglican Evangelicalism and the Nineteenth-Century Novel*. Oxford: Clarendon Press, 1979.

Jones, W.R. "Lollards and Images: The Defense of Religious Art in Later Medieval England." *Journal of the History of Ideas* 34 (1973): 27-50.

Jump, J.D. "Matthew Arnold and the *Spectator*." *Review of English Studies* 25 (1949): 61-64.

Kermes, Stephanie. *Creating an American Identity: New England, 1789-1825*. Houndmills, England: Palgrave Macmillan, 2008.

Kilby, Clyde S. "The Aesthetic Poverty of Evangelicalism." Excerpted in *The Christian Imagination*. Ed. Leland Ryken. Rev. ed. Colorado Springs, CO: Shaw Books-WaterBrook Press, 2002. 277-78.

Krapohl, Robert H. "Christian Advocate." *Popular Religious Magazines of the United States*. Ed. P. Mark Fackler and Charles H. Lippy. Westport, CT: Greenwood Press, 1995. 101-109.

Kristeller, Paul Oskar. "The Modern System of the Arts: A Study in the History of Aesthetics (I)." *Journal of the History of Ideas* 12 (1951): 496-527. Rpt. in *Essays on the History of Aesthetics*. Ed. Peter Kivy. Rochester, NY: University of Rochester Press, 1992. 3-34.

—. "The Modern System of the Arts: A Study in the History of Aesthetics (II)." *Journal of the History of Ideas* 13 (1952): 17-46. Rpt. in *Essays on the History of Aesthetics*. Ed. Peter Kivy. Rochester, NY: University of Rochester Press, 1992. 35-64.

Kuklick, Bruce. *Churchmen and Philosophers: From Jonathan Edwards to John Dewey*. New Haven, CT: Yale University Press, 1985.

LaPorte, Charles. *Victorian Poets and the Changing Bible.* Victorian Literature and Culture Series. Charlottesville, VA: University of Virginia Press, 2011.

Larsen, Timothy. *Contested Christianity: The Political and Social Contexts of Victorian Theology.* Waco, TX: Baylor University Press, 2004.

—. Introduction. Larsen, Bebbington, and Noll 1-2.

—, David Bebbington, and Mark A. Noll, eds. *Biographical Dictionary of Evangelicals.* Downers Grove, IL: Intervarsity Press, 2003.

Latané, David E., Jr. "Literary Criticism." *A Companion to Victorian Literature & Culture.* Ed. Herbert F. Tucker. Malden, MA: Blackwell Publishers, 1999. 388-404.

Lee, Sang Hyun. "Mental Activity and the Perception of Beauty in Jonathan Edwards." *Harvard Theological Review* 69 (1976): 369-96.

Levine, Lawrence W. *Highbrow/Lowbrow: The Emergence of Cultural Hierarchy in America.* Cambridge, MA: Harvard University Press, 1988.

Lewis, Donald M., ed. *Dictionary of Evangelical Biography, 1730-1860.* 2 vols. 1995. Peabody, MA: Hendrickson Publishers, 2004.

Lippy, Charles H. Preface. *Religious Periodicals of the United States: Academic and Scholarly Journals.* Ed. Lippy. Historical Guides to the World's Periodicals and Newspapers. New York: Greenwood Press, 1986. vii-ix.

Lundin, Roger. "Offspring of an Odd Union: Evangelical Attitudes towards the Fine Arts." *Evangelicalism in Modern America.* Ed. George Marsden. Grand Rapids, MI: William B. Eerdmans, 1984. 135-49.

Lyerly, Cynthia Lynn. *Methodism and the Southern Mind, 1770-1810.* New York: Oxford University Press, 1998.

Mallet, Charles Edward. *Modern Oxford.* 1927. New York: Barnes & Noble, 1968. Vol. 3 of *A History of the University of Oxford.* 3 vols. 1927.

Marini, Stephen. "From Classical to Modern: Hymnody and the Development of American Evangelicalism, 1737-1970." *Singing the Lord's Song in a Strange Land: Hymnody in the History of North American Protestantism.* Ed. Edith L. Blumhofer and Mark A. Noll. Tuscaloosa, AL: University of Alabama Press, 2004. 1-38.

Marsden, George. *The Evangelical Mind and the New School Presbyterian Experience: A Case Study of Thought and Theology in Nineteenth-Century America.* New Haven, CT: Yale University Press, 1970.

—. *Fundamentalism and American Culture.* New ed. Oxford: Oxford University Press, 2006.

—. *Jonathan Edwards: A Life.* New Haven, CT: Yale University Press, 2003.

—. *The Soul of the American University: From Protestant Establishment to Established Nonbelief.* New York: Oxford University Press, 1994.

—. *Understanding Fundamentalism and Evangelicalism.* Grand Rapids, MI: William B. Eerdmans Publishing Company, 1991.

Martin, Terence. *The Instructed Vision: Scottish Common Sense Philosophy and the Origins of American Fiction.* 1961. New York: Kraus Reprint, 1969.

McCoy, Michael R. "The Methodist Review." *Religious Periodicals of the United States: Academic and Scholarly Journals.* Ed. Charles H. Lippy. Historical Guides to the World's Periodicals and Newspapers. New York: Greenwood Press, 1986. 353-57.

McGiffert, Michael. "God's Controversy with Jacobean England." *American Historical Review* 88 (1983): 1151-74.

Mihelj, Sabina. "'Faith in nation comes in different guises': Modernist Versions of Religious Nationalism." *Nation and Nationalism* 13 (2007): 265-84.

Miller, Perry. "Literary Theory." *The Puritans: A Sourcebook of Their Writings*. Ed. Perry Miller. Vol. 2. Rev. ed. New York: Harper Torchbooks, 1963. 665-69.

—. *The New England Mind: The Seventeenth Century*. Cambridge, MA: The Belknap Press of Harvard University Press, 1982.

—. "Poetry." *The Puritans: A Sourcebook of Their Writings*. Ed. Perry Miller. Vol. 2. Rev. ed. New York: Harper Torchbooks, 1963. 545-52.

Morgan, David. *Protestants & Pictures: Religion, Visual Culture, and the Age of American Mass Production*. New York: Oxford University Press, 1999.

—. *Visual Piety: A History and Theory of Popular Religious Images*. Berkeley, CA: University of California Press, 1998.

Morgan, Marjorie. *National Identities and Travel in Victorian Britain*. Houndmills, England: Palgrave, 2001.

Nahm, Milton C. "The Theological Background of the Theory of the Artist as Creator." *Journal of the History of Ideas* 8 (1947): 363-72. Rpt. in *Essays on the History of Aesthetics*. Ed. Peter Kivy. Rochester, NY: University of Rochester Press, 1992. 75-84.

Neal, Lynn S. *Romancing God: Evangelical Women and Inspirational Fiction*. Chapel Hill, NC: University of North Carolina Press, 2006.

Neville, Graham. *Coleridge and Liberal Religious Thought: Romanticism, Science and Theological Tradition*. International Library of Historical Studies 63. London: I.B. Tauris, 2010.

Nichols, James Hastings. *Romanticism in American Theology: Nevin and Schaff at Mercersburg*. Chicago, IL: University of Chicago Press, 1961.

Niebuhr, H. Richard. *Christ and Culture*. Exp. ed. San Francisco, CA: Harper SanFrancisco, 2001.

Noll, Mark A. *America's God: From Jonathan Edwards to Abraham Lincoln*. Oxford: Oxford University Press, 2002.

—. *Between Faith and Criticism: Evangelicals, Scholarship, and the Bible in America*. San Francisco, CA: Harper & Row, 1986.

—. "Common Sense Traditions and American Evangelical Thought." *American Quarterly* 37 (1985): 216-38.

—. *A History of Christianity in the United States and Canada*. Grand Rapids, MI: William B. Eerdmans, 1992.

—. *The Scandal of the Evangelical Mind*. Grand Rapids, MI: William B. Eerdmans Publishing Company, 1992.

Noll, Mark A. and Cassandra Niemczyk. "Evangelicals and the Self-Consciously Reformed." Dayton and Johnston 204-21.

Otto, Rudolph. *The Idea of the Holy: An Inquiry into the Non-Rational Factor in the Idea of the Divine and Its Relation to the Rational*. Trans. John W. Harvey. London: Oxford University Press, 1950.

Pincus, Steven. "'To protect English liberties': The English Nationalist Revolution of 1688-1689." Claydon and McBride, *Protestantism* 75-104.

Reynolds, David M. *Faith in Fiction: The Emergence of Religious Literature in America*. Cambridge, MA: Harvard University Press, 1981.

Rosman, Doreen. *Evangelicals and Culture*. London: Croom Helm, 1984.

Rudolph, Frederick. *Curriculum: A History of the American Undergraduate Course of Study Since 1636*. San Francisco, CA: Jossey-Bass Publishers, 1977.

Ryken, Leland. *Worldly Saints: The Puritans as They Really Were*. Grand Rapids, MI: Academie Books, 1986.

—, ed. *The Christian Imagination*. Rev. ed. Colorado Springs, CO: Shaw Books-WaterBrook Press, 2002.

Ryken, Philip Graham. *Art for God's Sake: A Call to Recover the Arts*. Phillipsburg, NJ: P&R Publishing, 2006.

Sandeen, Ernest R. *The Roots of Fundamentalism: British and American Millenarianism*. New ed. Grand Rapids, MI: Baker Book House, 1978.

Schaeffer, Francis. *Art and the Bible: Two Essays*. Downers Grove, IL: Intervarsity Press, 1974.

Schaeffer, Franky. *Addicted to Mediocrity: Contemporary Christians and the Arts*. Wheaton, IL: Crossway Books, 1981.

Shattock, Joanne and Michael Wolff, eds. *The Victorian Periodical Press: Samplings and Soundings*. Leicester, England: Leicester University Press, 1982.

Sizer, Sandra S. *Gospel Hymns and Social Religion: The Rhetoric of Nineteenth-Century Revivalism*. Philadelphia, PA: Temple University Press, 1978.

Smith, Jonathan. *Fact & Feeling: Baconian Science and the Nineteenth-Century Literary Imagination*. Madison, WI: University of Wisconsin Press, 1994.

Smith, Ryan K. *Gothic Arches, Latin Crosses: Anti-Catholicism and American Church Designs in the Nineteenth Century*. Chapel Hill, NC: University of North Carolina Press, 2006.

Stanford, Ann. *Anne Bradstreet: The Worldly Puritan: An Introduction to Her Poetry*. New York: Burt Franklin & Co., 1974.

Stephens, Lester D. *Joseph LeConte: Gentle Prophet of Evolution*. Southern Biography Series. Baton Rouge, LA: Louisiana State University Press, 1982.

Szasz, Ferenc M. *The Divided Mind of Protestant America, 1880-1930*. Tuscaloosa, AL: University of Alabama Press, 1982.

Taylor, Charles. *A Secular Age*. Cambridge, MA: The Belknap Press of Harvard University Press, 2007.

—. *Sources of the Self: The Making of the Modern Identity*. Cambridge, MA: Harvard University Press, 1989.

Tennyson, G.B. *Victorian Devotional Poetry: The Tractarian Mode*. Cambridge, MA: Harvard University Press, 1981.

Townsend, Dabney. *An Introduction to Aesthetics*. Introducing Philosophy 5. Malden, MA: Blackwell Publishers, 1997.

Trier, Daniel J., Mark Husbands, and Roger Lundin, eds. *The Beauty of God: Theology and the Arts*. Downers Grove, IL: IVP Academic, 2007.

Turner, James. *Without God, Without Creed: The Origins of Unbelief in America*. Baltimore, MD: The Johns Hopkins University Press, 1985.

Tuveson, Ernest Lee. *The Imagination as a Means of Grace: Locke and the Aesthetics of Romanticism*. Berkeley, CA: University of California Press, 1960.

Waller, John O. "The *Methodist Quarterly Review* and Fiction, 1818-1900." *Bulletin of the New York Public Library* 71 (1967): 573-90.

Weber, Max. *From Max Weber: Essays in Sociology*. Trans. and ed. H.H. Gerth and C. Wright Mills. New York: Oxford University Press, 1946.

Williams, Raymond. *Culture and Society 1780-1950*. Harmondsworth, England: Penguin, 1971.

Wolffe, John. "A Transatlantic Perspective: Protestantism and National Identities in Mid-Nineteenth-Century Britain and the United States." Claydon and McBride, *Protestantism* 291-309.

Wolterstorff, Nicholas. "Art and the Aesthetic: The Religious Dimension." *The Blackwell Guide to Aesthetics*. Ed. Peter Kivy. Malden, MA: Blackwell Publishing, 2004. 325-39.

—. *Art in Action: Toward a Christian Aesthetic*. Grand Rapids, MI: William B. Eerdmans, 1980

Index

Abbot, Lyman, 184
Abrams, M.H., 5, 60, 67, 71
Absolute, the, 67, 76, 82, 116
Addison, Joseph, 47, 49, 70
aesthetic experience: and religious experience, conflation of, 11, 100, 115-120, 123-124, 126, 141, 167, 182-185, 191-194. *See also* art
aestheticism, 48, 120, 171-177, 195
aesthetics, philosophical: breakdown of evangelical, 181-198; emergence of evangelical, 6, 33-57, 100; evangelical, relationship to Puritan aesthetics, 9, 19, 24-26, 31-32, 33, 38, 56, 90, 91, 100-102, 104, 106, 111, 113, 123, 126, 128, 129, 134, 137, 140, 146, 152, 153, 157, 175, 198, 199, 208-209; and liberalization, 8, 84, 97, 116, 156-157, 170, 188, 193, 194, 207-210; tone of evangelical, 97-98.
Ahlstrom, Sydney, 68
Akenside, Mark, 53
Alison, Archibald, 35, 56, 130-131
American Tract Society, 45
amusement. *See* art
Andover Theological Seminary, 69, 108, 146
anti-Catholicism, 3, 9, 20-21, 26, 33, 108, 110-111, 123, 126, 129, 185
anti-didactic moralism: and the Christian nation, 10, 140, 161, 162-167, 170 (*see also* Protestant ideology); evangelical criticisms of, 154, 155-156, 171, 177-178; evangelical embrace of, 93, 140-155, 156-157, 186-187; and negative influence, 157-161; and regeneration, 49, 154, 186, 208. *See also* art

anti-Puritanism, 5, 8-9, 37, 57, 64, 84, 91, 103, 108-110, 111, 113, 114, 155, 176, 189, 207, 208-209
Appleton, Jesse, 163-164
Aristotle, 65
Arminianism, 48, 109, 155
Arnold, Matthew, 8, 14, 87, 100-101, 103, 109, 113, 116, 122, 165, 184, 188, 202
art: as amusement, 32, 38, 54-55, 59, 64, 90, 92-93, 97, 146; anxieties regarding, 49-53, 90, 119, 137, 189, 195; and the appeal to emotion, 50-52, 93; changing evangelical attitudes towards, 55-56, 59-60, 64, 90, 91-92; defining, 58-59; as expression of emotion (*see* expressivism); and idolatry, 104, 105, 115, 126-130, 183, 192 (*see also* imagery, visual); increased exposure to, 99-100; and instruction, 91-92, 93 (*see also* anti-didactic moralism); as mediator between spiritual and material, 63-64, 70, 72, 74, 75, 146; as product of the *zeitgeist*, 85-86; and Protestant history, 104-111; purposes of, 89-97; relationship to religion, 54-55, 76, 97, 99-137 (*see also* aesthetic experience); —, and artistic creation, 132-133; —, and problem of inverse relationship, 104, 135; —, subordinationist view of, 103, 112-115, 125, 130, 135-137, 183, 194, 199, 209; and representations of God, 126-127; and salvation, 115, 120-126; and science, 51, 90, 93-94, 95, 96-97, 117-118, 184, 185, 198; uniqueness of, 93, 96; and utilitarianism, 90, 91, 96, 165, 166. *See also* pleasure, aesthetic
art for art's sake. *See* aestheticism

Index

Augustine, 39, 112
autonomy: of the artist, 84

Bacon, Francis, 51
Baker, John, 163
balance, psychological. *See* mental philosophy
Bangs, Nathan, 14
Barnett, H.O., 116-117, 122
Barth, J. Robert, 71n. 54, 72
Barton, Bernard, 144
Barton, Lucy, 144
Baumgarten, Alexander, 35
Baxter, Richard, 21
Beardmore, William G., 134
Beattie, James, 33
beauty, 34, 71, 83, 95, 128, 199: hierarchy of, 43, 80, 125, 202-203; intrinsic vs. relative, 150; Puritan views of, 30-31, 43, 202; as revelation of God, 125-126; vs. utility, 91. *See also* Edwards, Jonathan
Bebbington, David, 180
Beecher, Henry Ward, 156-157, 183, 184, 197
Beecher, Secretary (of Wesleyan Missionary Society), 138-139, 140
Bell, Clive, 117
Bellamy, Joseph, 45
Bennett, C.W., 105, 110, 111, 199
Berkeley, George, 77
Bible League of North America, 201
Blair, Hugh, 35, 55
Blake, William, 63, 64
Bob Jones University, 207
Boileau-Despréaux, Nicolas, 54
Boston Wesleyan Lyceum, 139
Bowdoin College, 163, 193
Bowen, W.H., 95, 114, 126
Brake, Laurel, 11n. 22
Bradstreet, Anne, 30, 31, 202
Brown University, 139, 149
Bucer, Martin, 25
Buckley, Dr., 177-178

Burchard, S.D., 153
Burke, Edmund, 35, 202
Bushnell, Horace, 116, 119, 120-121, 143n. 22, 144, 144n. 24, 156, 181, 182, 183, 186, 192, 193
Byron, Lord, George Gordon, 87, 88, 89, 107

Calvinism 28, 45, 106, 109-110, 198-199
Calvin, John, 20, 21, 23, 24, 26, 30, 105, 106
Cambridge Platonists, 43
Cambridge University, 36
Campbell, R.J., 185n. 21
Carlyle, Thomas, 82, 83
Catholic Emancipation, 162
Chapman, J.A., 183
Christian-Platonic tradition, 30, 43, 51, 112
Civil War: American, 1, 145; English, 27
Clapham Sect, 56
Claydon, Tony, 163
Coleridge, H.N., 73n. 57
Coleridge, Samuel Taylor, 7, 60, 63, 68, 69, 70-75, 81-82, 84, 124, 182, 183. *See also* consubstantiality; idealism; imagination; imitation
Collier, Jeremy, 51
Colman, K., 135-137
common sense realism. *See* Scottish philosophy
consubstantiality, 71, 73, 74, 182
Cooke, J. Hunt, 175
Cotton, John, 22
Cousin, Victor, 76, 82, 174
creation, artistic (*poiesis*). *See* art, relationship to religion; expressivism
critical establishment, evangelical, 11-16, 46, 177: ecumenism of, 15-16; fundamentalist withdrawal from, 188-198; professionalization of, 11; transatlantic scope of, 14-15
Cromwell, Oliver, 26
Cubitt, George, 164

Dadaism, 204
Dallas, E.S., 58
Darbyshire, J.R., 182
Darwin, Charles, 90, 179, 180, 189, 198
Dawson, W.J., 122, 173, 178
Day, Henry N., 82, 92, 118, 120, 125, 154n. 48, 165, 167
Dennis, John, 78n. 71
DeQuincey, Thomas, 145
Dickens, Charles, 155
didacticism. *See* anti-didactic moralism
Dillenberger, John, 26, 30
disinterestedness, 41-42, 45, 171
Douglas, Ann, 143
Drummond, Henry, 94, 122, 123, 152, 165
Du Bose, H.M., 103
Dyer, Sidney, 59, 64
Dyrness, William A., 23, 24, 34

East, James T., 82, 83
Edwards, Edward, 122, 123
Edwards, Jonathan, 6, 55, 83, 84, 106, 107, 153: aesthetic legacy of, 44-45, 53; and beauty, 41-43, 44, 125, 130, 132; —, and moral role of, 43, 49, 144, 154, 156; *A Dissertation on the Nature of True Virtue*, 31, 38-45, 46; and Enlightenment philosophy, 39; and imagination, 29; and spiritual sense, 81; and taste, 47; *A Treatise Concerning Religious Affections*, 29, 45. *See also* perception, aesthetic
Edwards, Timothy, 30n. 35
Eliot, Charles W., 187
Emergent Church, 207
Emerson, Ralph Waldo, 68, 82, 83, 124
emotion. *See* anti-didactic moralism; art
Enlightenment. *See* Scottish philosophy; mental philosophy
Episcopos, 132
evangelical romanticism. *See* romanticism

evangelicalism: anti-aesthetic bias of, 3-5; defined, 2; and Puritan theological tradition, 19 (*see also* anti-Puritanism)
Evangelical Revival, 117
Evans, John, 139
evolution, theory of, 11, 179, 180, 189, 190-191, 198
exigency argument, 107-108, 109, 189
Expressionism, 204
expressivism: in Coleridge, 70; evangelical criticisms of, 84, 87; and evangelical aesthetics, 7, 54, 60-66, 73-74, 172, 201-202; and national culture, 168-170, 188, 203; and *poiesis*, 132-133

Fackler, P. Mark, 12
Fall, doctrine of the, 78, 155
Fergusson, James, 81
Fichte, Johann Gottlieb, 82
fiction. *See* novels.
Fiering, Norman, 40, 41, 43
fine arts, the (concept of), 6, 34, 91, 158
Fisk, Wilbur, 139
Fontenelle, Bernard Le Bovier de, 65
Forman, H. Buxton, 84, 157
Forsyth, P.T., 193, 194, 198
Fosdick, Harry Emerson, 185, 190
Foster, John, 91, 154
Fraser, Hilary, 99, 102
fundamentalism: aesthetic ambivalence of, 4, 10-11, 109, 137, 188-206, 207; and aestheticization of religion, 192-194; and anti-intellectualism, 190-191; contrasted to modernism, 179-182; eschatology of (*see* premillennialism); and the "Great Reversal," 178; and the modern art world, 11, 109, 191-198, 203, 204; and spiritualization of art, 191-192; and use of "aesthetic", 193-195

genius, 54, 75, 111, 155
Gerard, Alexander, 35, 46, 47, 48, 49
German Reformed Church, 2, 69, 100

Gilbert, W.S., 177
Gladden, Washington, 176-177
Gosse, Edmund, 79n. 75
Great Awakening, 38, 117
Great Reversal. *See* fundamentalism
Gregory II (pope), 23

Hall, Robert, 34
Handy, Robert, 163
Harris, Neil, 103, 112n. 35
Harris, Samuel, 108
Hartmann, Karl Robert Eduard von, 199
Harvard University, 15, 187
Hastings, Thomas, 132
Hawley, B., 122, 128, 129
Hazlitt, William, 62, 65, 145, 148
Hegel, Georg Wilhelm Friedrich, 36n. 60, 67, 68, 75, 82, 182, 196, 199
Heimert, Alan, 43n. 78
Henry VIII, 26
Herman, Bruce, 196n. 43
Higbee, E.E., 96, 114
high aesthetic culture: development of, 12-13; distinguished from low, 12, 160; within evangelicalism, 12, 14, 101-102, 109, 111, 161, 195
high art, 3, 13, 85, 91, 188, 196, 201, 204, 205
Higher Criticism, 11, 179, 190, 191, 198
Hilliard, Nicholas, 20
Hodge, Charles, 119, 120, 143n. 22, 193
Holbein, Hans, 20
Holiness Movement, 181, 205n. 62
Hopkins, Gerard Manley, 3
Hopkins, Samuel, 45, 106
Horace, 91, 93
Horne, J. Wesley, 156
Howes, Graham, 129
Hume, David, 35, 39, 49, 130, 150
Hunt, Leigh, 60, 145, 172
Hunt, Theodore W., 76, 173, 174, 175
Hunter, James Davison, 180, 190
Hutcheson, Frances, 35, 39-43, 45, 46, 47, 48, 146, 147, 150

iconoclasm, 99
ideal: art as, 66, 71, 72, 73, 74, 184, 204; —, and salvation, 124, 125; changing conceptions of the, 67-68; classical, and anti-romantic criticisms, 84-86, 88; empirical, 67; and eschatology, 77-78; transcendental, 67n. 42; vagueness of the term, 76
idealism: and Christian orthodoxy, 76-77; aesthetic, among evangelicals, 66-78, 84, 118, 174, 183, 184, 185; criticisms of, 71, 85-86, 88-89; German, 7, 45, 60, 67, 68, 76, 85, 88, 89, 113, 116; and Jonathan Edwards, 43, 45, 77
idolatry. *See* art; imagery, visual
imagery, visual: for civil use, 24-25, 100, 128; and idolatry, 21-22; lawful vs. unlawful, 23-24, 199; Puritan attitudes towards, 20-27, 102. *See also* presence, problem of.
imagination, 95, 96, 116, 148: Cartesian attitudes towards, 28; changing evangelical views of, 53-54, 64, 78-84, 132, 151-152; Coleridge's theory of, 74, 79, 81, 82, 83; Puritan conceptions of, 27-29, 64, 78, 152, 157, 159; and regeneration, 81, 83-84, 132, 155; and Scottish philosophy, 49, 79-80, 81
imitation: Coleridge's conception of, 66, 70-71, 74, 124; in evangelical theory, 65-66, 72, 73, 74, 124; neoclassical conceptions of, 61; in romantic theory, 65
influence, moral: and art (*see* anti-didactic moralism); theory of the Atonement, 192-193
invention: Puritan anxieties regarding, 22, 123; in eighteenth-century aesthetics, 86
inverse relationship, problem of (between art and religion). *See* art
Irving, Edward, 94, 118

Johnson, Franklin, 192-193, 194, 198
Johnson, Samuel, 54, 114n. 46, 128

Kames, Lord, Henry Home, 35, 37, 49, 145-150, 151, 154, 155, 160, 164, 192
Kant, Immanuel, 42, 67, 68, 116, 130, 171
Keats, John, 85, 203
Keble, John, 65
Kilby, Clyde S., 4, 207
Knight, William A., 75
Kuyper, Abraham, 198-200, 201

Latané, David E., Jr., 7
LeConte, Joseph, 65-66, 85, 108
Lee, Sang Hyun, 44
Leigh, Edward, 64
Levan, F.K., 170
Lewis, C.S., 207
liberalization: and aesthetics. *See* aesthetics, philosophical
liberalism (theological). *See* modernism
Lippy, Charles H., 12
Locke, John, 35, 39, 47, 51, 51n. 52, 64, 143
Lollards, 20
low (popular) art. *See* high aesthetic culture; high art
Lundin, Roger, 11, 188, 206
Luther, Martin, 20, 105

Macaulay, Thomas Babington, 90
MacDonald, George, 78
Machen, J. Gresham, 200-202, 203, 204-205
Macmaster, J. Milner, 107-108, 109
Marsh, James, 69
Marsden, George, 134, 180, 190, 191, 200
Martin, Terence, 49, 158
Martyn, Henry, 34, 44, 53, 114
Mather, Cotton, 30
Mathews, Shailer, 181, 190, 194
McBride, Ian, 163
M.C.H., 61-62

mental philosophy: and aesthetic conservatism, 49-53; and psychological balance, 37, 95-96; and evangelical aesthetics, 6, 34-37, 53, 94, 158; university courses in, 6, 36
Mercersburg theology. *See* German Reformed Church
Middle Ages, 104
Mill, John Stuart, 62, 85n. 94
Miller, Henry J., 88-89
Miller, Perry, 27
Milton, John, 30, 80, 106
mimesis. *See* imitation
Mims, Edwin, 102, 174, 175
Miranda, 159
misuse argument, 105, 109, 129
M'Nicholl, Thomas, 85-87, 88, 89
modernism (theological): and aestheticization of religion, 116, 119, 183, 184-185, 191; contrasted to fundamentalism, 179-182; and morality in art, 176, 178, 186-187, 197-198; and positive attitudes toward art, 10, 115, 137, 182; and spiritualization of art, 183-184, 191; and use of "aesthetic", 194
Montgomery, James, 61, 142
moral sense: relation to aesthetic sense, 39-41, 48, 147; school of philosophy, 39, 146, 154
More, Hannah, 49-53, 157
Morgan, David, 9, 42, 127, 129, 140, 141, 143, 144, 186
Morris, William, 168

nation (Christian): evangelical conceptions of. *See* anti-didactic moralism; expressivism; Protestant ideology
naturalism (literary), 204
Neal, Lynn S., 161n. 69
Neff, Marietta, 186-187
neo-calvinism, 198
neoclassicism, 33, 34, 61, 67, 68, 87. *See also* imitation
neo-evangelicalism, 4, 200, 207

Nevin, John Williamson, 2
Newman, John Henry, 201
Niebuhr, H. Richard, 31
Noll, Mark A., 56, 200
Notre Dame, University of, 15
novels: changing attitudes towards, 56; evangelical suspicion of, 34, 49, 83, 157-160, 175
nude (in art), 177, 195-196

occult pathos. *See* anti-didactic moralism
original sin, 39, 48, 156
Otheman, Edward, 139-140, 141, 149-155, 157, 163, 192
Otto, Rudolph, 117
Otts, J.M.P., 130
Owen, John, 31
Oxford University, 36

pantheism, 71, 72, 153
Park, Edwards Amasa, 116
Parsons, Eugene, 166
Pater, Walter, 171
Pattison, T. Harwood, 104, 110, 112, 114, 126, 209
Paul, Apostle, 104
perception, aesthetic: nature of, 94; and regeneration, 44, 55, 80, 125, 130-132. *See also* imagination
Percival, Dr., 153
periodicals, denominational: academic vs. popular, 12; changes in format, 13, 190; and evangelical aesthetic discourse, 11, 46, 55-56; publication schedules of, 12
Perkins, William, 20, 21, 22, 23, 24, 27
Plato, 52, 65, 76, 82, 90, 112, 125, 157, 174, 202
Platonism, 71n. 54, 75, 77, 81, 112, 125, 202
pleasure, aesthetic: as end of art, 91, 93; and morality, 147 (*see also* anti-didactic moralism); and Puritanism, 24, 49, 91

Plymouth Church (Brooklyn), 184
Poe, Edgar Allan, 171
Pope, Alexander, 33
Porter, Noah, 133, 136n. 125, 170
postmillennialism, 134, 135, 137, 170, 189
preaching: necessity of Gospel, 123; Puritan, 29, 102
premillennialism, 10, 136, 181, 189, 194
presence, problem of, 22-23, 25, 125-126, 184
Princeton Theological Seminary, 198, 200
Princeton University (College of New Jersey), 33, 62, 164
Protestant ideology: art's inclusion in, 10, 56, 111, 140, 141, 164-170, 182-188, 200; challenges to, 170-178, 181; and cultural conditions for art, 133-135; explained, 9, 162-164; Puritan contribution to, 162, 164
Pugin, A.W., 168
Puritan aesthetics: asymmetry of, 19-33, 188; and epistemological realism, 27-28, 64, 158; and lack of developed art culture, 32, 56, 109; and limits to art, 102, 112; moralistic tendencies of, 25-26, 140; and non-visual arts, 29-30; and poetry, 30, 167; and positive view of culture, 31, 134, 208; and socio-political factors, 26-27; utilitarian emphasis of, 32-33. *See also* aesthetics, philosophical; art; anti-Puritanism; beauty; imagery, visual; imagination; invention; pleasure, aesthetic; presence, problem of
Puritans: aestheticization of, 106-107, 109

Racine, Louis, 54
Ramsay, Julian, 77n. 68
Raphael, 67
realism, Dutch, 28, 73
Reformation, 3, 99, 103, 104, 105, 106, 109, 126: and liberation of art, 9, 110-111. *See also* Puritan aesthetics

regeneration. *See* anti-didactic moralism; imagination; perception, aesthetic
Regulative Principle, 22, 105, 123
Reid, Thomas, 35, 36n. 60, 48, 88
Reily, W.M., 76, 82, 93
religious experience. *See* aesthetic experience
religious tests, 36
revivalism, 117, 120, 180, 205n. 62
Reynolds, Joshua, 73-74
Rigg, J.H., 58, 81, 92
Rogers, G., 125
Rogers, James, 58, 59, 60, 72-73, 74
romanticism: evangelical criticisms of, 8, 84-89, 101, 115, 121, 130; influence on evangelical aesthetics, 6-8, 10, 11, 53-57, 60, 65, 78, 88, 92, 93, 97, 111, 113, 115, 125, 132, 137, 145, 151-152, 154, 157, 167, 172, 174, 182, 189, 201-206; and Protestant doctrine, 8, 103, 113, 121, 125, 149, 154-155, 156, 170, 184
Rosman, Doreen, 3, 55, 59, 67
Ruskin, John, 81, 82, 83, 165, 168, 169, 177

Sallman, Warner, 109, 205
salvation. *See* art
Sargent, Walter, 184-185
Schaeffer, Francis, 207
Schaff, Philip, 2
Schelling, Friedrich Wilhelm von, 36n. 60, 67, 70, 71, 73, 82, 92, 116
Schlegel, Friedrich von, 61, 75
Schleiermacher, Friedrich, 117, 182
science: and art (*see* art); Baconian, and evangelical commitment to, 65, 191, 198; and religion, 10, 116, 208
Scottish philosophy: and growth of aesthetics, 6, 35; influence on evangelicals, 35-36, 45, 46, 55, 65, 68, 79, 80, 144, 145, 154, 158, 159, 180, 191. *See also* imagination; mental philosophy
sensibility, 155, 160
sentimentalist ethics. *See* moral sense

sentimentality, 158-161, 174, 205
Shaftesbury, Third Earl of, Ashley Anthony Cooper, 39, 43, 146
Shairp, J.C., 173, 174
Shakespeare, William, 90, 102, 106, 174
Shedd, W.G.T., 69, 96
Shelley, Percy Bysshe, 62, 75, 77n. 68, 85, 86, 88, 96, 145, 171
Shepard, Thomas, 30
Sibbes, Richard, 28, 29
Sidney, Philip, 65n. 33, 145n. 26
Slicer, Adeline E.H., 166
Smetham, James, 97, 105, 112, 126, 133-134, 143
Smith, Adam, 150
Smith, Ryan K., 9, 111
Smith, Samuel Stanhope, 164
Social Gospel, 176, 181, 194
Society for the Promotion of Common and Liberal Education, 139
Spurgeon, Charles Haddon, 100, 125
Stanton, Horace C., 202-203
Stewart, Dugald, 35, 56, 79, 80, 81, 88, 153, 159
Stowe, Harriet Beecher, 106-107
Strong, Josiah, 188
Stubbes, Philip, 106
subjectivism, 63, 71-72, 74, 75, 85, 87-88, 185
sublime, 107, 150-151
subordinationist view (of art and religion). *See* art
Sullivan, Arthur, 177
Swift, Jonathan, 33
sympathy, 147-148, 151, 155
Syracuse University College of Fine Arts, 15-16

taste, aesthetic, 34, 35, 46, 47-49, 95, 96, 126, 130, 208. *See also* perception, aesthetic; Wesley, John
Taylor, Edward, 30
Taylor, George Lansing, 15, 95, 166, 168
Taylor, Henry, 87-88

Index 241

Taylor, W.F., 104-105, 106, 127
Tennyson, Lord, Alfred, 122, 166, 177
Tertullian, 99
Thackeray, William Makepeace, 155
theater: evangelical resistance to, 33-34; Puritan resistance to, 30, 50, 51. *See also* More, Hannah.
Thompson, Peter, 191-192
Tractarianism, 100, 112n. 39, 123
Transcendentalism, 68, 83, 205n. 62
Turner, Daniel, 54-55, 59, 61, 63, 93
Turner, James, 183
Tuveson, Ernest Lee, 84

University of Chicago, 181, 184
utilitarianism. *See* art
ut pictura poesis (poetry is like painting), 86

Van Dyke, Henry, Jr., 122, 142

Waters, Robert, 204
Welling, James C., 62
Wells, P., 152
Wesleyan Academy (Massachusetts), 139
Wesleyan Missionary Society, 138
Wesley, John, 6: and moral role of aesthetic pleasure, 49, 144; critique of Frances Hutcheson, 48; *Pocket Hymn Book*, 34; "Thoughts upon Taste," 46-49, 53, 54; and visual imagery, 33
Westwood, H.C., 164
Wheatley, Phillis, 53-54, 55
Wheaton College, 4, 145
whig version of history, 111, 134, 199
Whistler, James Abbot McNeill, 171
White, J.S., 120, 129, 169
whole-person argument, 95-96, 100, 109, 175, 187, 189, 202
Wigglesworth, Michael, 30
Wilberforce, William, 55
Wilde, Oscar, 142, 171, 173, 174, 175, 176, 177, 195
Winchester, C.T., 142, 169

Witherspoon, John, 33
Wolterstorff, Nicholas, 207
Wordsworth, William, 54, 60, 63, 79, 81, 82, 93, 121, 131, 132, 133, 144, 145, 148, 151, 152-153

Yale Report of 1828, 37, 95
Yale University, 37, 108
Young, Edward, 33

Zwingli, Huldrych, 105

www.ingramcontent.com/pod-product-compliance
Lightning Source LLC
Chambersburg PA
CBHW050439240426
43661CB00055B/2449